The A70 UFO

(Scotland's First 'Officially Reported' UFO Abduction)

By Malcolm Robinson

ISBN: 9798403696364

CONTENTS

This book is dedicated to my mother and father
in spirit.
Till we meet again.

DISCLAIMER

The author gratefully acknowledges the permission granted to reproduce the copyright material in this book. Every effort has been made to trace copyright holders and to obtain their permission for the use of copyright material. The author apologises for any errors or omissions in the book and would be grateful if notified of any corrections that should be incorporated in future reprints or editions of this book.

Other books by Malcolm Robinson

UFO Case Files of Scotland (Volume 1)

UFO Case Files of Scotland (Volume 2)

Paranormal Case Files of Great Britain (Volume 1)

Paranormal Case Files of Great Britain (Volume 2)

Paranormal Casc Files of Great Britain (Volume 3)

The Monsters of Loch Ness (The History and the
Mystery)

The Dechmont Woods UFO Incident (An ordinary
day, An Extraordinary Event)

The Sauchie Poltergeist (And other Scottish Ghostly
Tales)

Please Leave Us Alone (The true and terrifying story
of an Irish family and their desperate fight against the
'Hat Man' and supernatural forces)

(All by Publish Nation www.publishnation.co.uk)

Book Cover by Jason Gleaves – UFONLY

jasonufonly@outlook.com
www.facebook.com/ufonly
www.youtube.com/ufonly
www.twitter.com/@jasonufonly

Non Fiction / Body, Mind & Spirit /
Parapsychology / Unexplained Phenomena

GUEST FOREWORD

BY
Mary Rodwell

It is my pleasure to provide a foreword for this book '*The A70 UFO Incident*' by author, and Ufologist Malcolm Robinson. Malcolm is one of the most respected authors and investigators in the UK on both UFOlogical and Paranormal research. He has already authored an impressive number of books in his search to understand the nature of human Contact with Non-Human Intelligences (NHI) and unidentified ariel phenomenon (UAP) more popularly known as UFO's.

In this book Malcolm uses his extensive knowledge and experience as an investigator to detail the A70 Incident. It is thorough and comprehensive, not only because of the extremely detailed accounts of conscious recall from those involved, but what is later conveyed through hypnotic regression. This information echoes recognized patterns of Contact experiences. This information is extremely valuable not only for investigators of this intriguing phenomenon, but for those with Contact experience who seek to validate their own encounters. The information also highlights the complexity and compelling nature of this phenomenon which can have a deep and abiding impact on individuals who experience it. With the public disclosure of UAP's in our airspace by some governments recently, such as the release of information from the Pentagon, these accounts are gaining more public credibility. This is so important because I as a researcher, believe the numbers who are experiencing this phenomenon, are far greater than is generally realized. However due to many years with a 'truth embargo' on this subject, public ignorance is such, that many with experiences will never speak about it for fear of derision or for being judged as mentally ill. This is why such books are so important to show the veracity of the experience, the truth of this reality.

In the book Malcolm has stated that hypnotic regression has been used as a tool to gain more information on experiences that can be blocked from the conscious mind. The trance state can often unlock what is hidden. For those skeptical of this process I would like to make some points as to is use as a valuable tool. I am a trained Clinical hypnotherapist and have used this process with great success with literally hundreds of individuals. it has proved invaluable in eliciting recall of memories blocked by the conscious mind. It can offer a far more detailed understanding of what occurred to the individual. The subconscious mind unlike the conscious mind, which edits what's unacceptable, the subconscious records without prejudice, so can offer a more detailed account of what may have occurred during an experience on board space craft, and also communication with the Non-Human Intelligences they may encounter. These details are not always available to the conscious mind, and this may be due to trauma or because the conscious mind may struggle to accept the reality of what may have happened. It only requires the person to be sufficiently relaxed and has trust in the hypnotherapist. The subconscious can also reveal in greater detail much of what occurred depending on the focus of the questions.

In terms of hypnosis and its usefulness to elicit credible information, the late Dr John Mack, former professor of Psychiatry, Harvard University, used it and shared his findings in two seminal books on the phenomenon. *'Abduction Human Encounters with Aliens', and 'Passport to the Cosmos'.* Dr Mack stated that he believed information recalled through hypnosis had more veracity than even conscious recall. He qualified this statement by commenting that it is because the subconscious does not edit out what is unacceptable or confronting. I concur with his understanding, as it is what I have also discovered with my experience as a clinical hypnotherapist of twenty-five years in this field of research. Therefore, I believe such information gained through hypnosis should be taken very seriously. Certainly, this process can be very invaluable to those seeking answers and understanding. It can also offer new perspectives that may completely change a person's understanding on their encounter. It is tremendously healing to have their questions answered.

Apart from the fascinating information of personal Contact accounts in this book and impressive research, the statements from notable investigators in the field of Ufology which convey interesting personal and professional perspectives on this Intriguing enigma, It is notable that there is a real diversity of understanding and opinion. It is clear that every perspective depended on their own research and how they have chosen to understand and explore the phenomena. This diversity of perspectives also demonstrates how complex this phenomenon is. As a therapist my professional perspective stems from assisting and supporting the individual through their own personal journey to integrate what they experienced through their own resonance to truth. To find their own understanding of what this Contact means to them. This process has led to many individuals not only accepting their encounters but even embracing them as they shifted into a multi-dimensional understanding that made more sense.

Dr John Mack stated at the end of his second book.

"In the end the abduction phenomenon seems to me to be to be a part of a shift in consciousness that is a collapsing duality enabling us to see that we are connected beyond the earth at a cosmic level" (*page 280*) *Passport to the Cosmos*.

For many the Contact experience elicits deep questions about our species, our genetic and Cosmic origins, possible agendas and programs. The questions asked by the Experiencer (individual with Contact) Am I crazy? 'Why me? What does this all mean? Malcolm's research offers intriguing insights into some of these deep questions, as he supports and validates those with Contact experiences. His support and compelling research are important as so many individuals are fearful and uncertain after Contact, and fearful they may be mentally ill as they question what happened and what it may mean. Identifying the patterns of Contact can help to validate them and assist with understanding. We need more dedicated researchers like Malcolm to offer help and support, not only in the personal way but through their research.

As Principal of ACERN (Australian Close Encounter Resource Network) I have supported over 3,500 individuals globally. The most important part of the resource is helping the individual by hearing their story without judgment as they begin to connect the dots for themselves. Malcolm has been doing this through his research. To be heard non judgmentally is vital as it begins the healing and understanding to take place. The Dr Edgar Mitchell Foundation for Extraterrestrial Experience Research (FREE) surveyed 4,200 individuals and discovered 75% of Contact experiences were in out of body states, only 25% is physical. This fact alone creates a challenge to quantify and qualify this experience in three dimensional terms. Malcolm has done an extraordinary job through his book to help with understanding its physical reality and its complexity with the paranormal elements. To demonstrate how these two phenomena are often linked to complicate this research even more.

The book has accounts which will help those who are still questioning their experiences and seek validation. Accounts shared can help this process of acceptance and can be very healing. It is important to note that these experiences do not rely on belief in UAP's which is a misconception in public thinking. Garry Wood had no interest in UFO's until the incident, as is the case with many I have worked with. Malcolm admits that the A70 UFO incident was the catalyst for him personally to accept its reality. For myself it was the numbers of individuals coming forward with similar patterns of experiences. This story of classic UFO encounter, from sighting a craft to experiencing i.e. 'missing time' then dreams with Grey non-human beings with psychological trauma something very real occurred. The book is a valuable addition to the growing evidence of the reality of Contact and Encounters with non-human intelligences on our planet and in our airspace. The evidence we are not alone in the Universe and never have been.

The evidence is laid out very succinctly in this book. And it's because of dedicated researchers such as Malcolm that we can thank for adding to our knowledge and understanding of this compelling and intriguing phenomenon. An excellent and compelling read.

Mary Rodwell Principal and founder of ACERN, Clinical Hypnotherapist. Author of AWAKENING. *'How Extraterrestrial Contact Can Transform Your life'*. THE NEW HUMAN. *'Awakening to Our Cosmic Heritage'*.

PREAMBLE
(Why a 'stand alone book'?)

As an author, its very important to ensure that any UFO or Paranormal case that you work on gets to see the light of day within the public domain, and that's why I write my books. I keep saying that information is for the people, and not for filing cabinets. And whilst the following case you are about to read was featured in my first book, UFO Case Files of Scotland (Volume 1) available on Amazon, I always felt that in all honesty, it deserved to have its own place in a 'stand alone' book, and this is it. It has been revised and updated with new material, and contains material which was not featured in the original version of the incident. There is no denying that this one case did indeed merit its own book, as did another book of mine, 'The Dechmont Woods UFO Incident' which also was featured in my first book, stated above. Cases of the magnitude of the A70 Incident are few and far between, and I hope that my updated version of this case will show you, the reader, how enormous this case was. There is no denying that it has left a mark on both witnesses, but like me, they felt that this intrusion into their daily life must be told, and must add to the growing weight that is the UFO enigma. As with most of my incidents of a strange and bizarre nature, I have provided a number of possibilities which might account (or not!) for this case. When it comes to any bizarre UFO Incident, one must look to provide all alternative explanations, should they fit the criteria, and once more, I hope I have done that. As to what I believe happened to both men on that August night back in 1992, well, that will be coming up later. We all go through life and we learn various things. They say that life is an education, that each and every one of us takes on board lessons that either we learn from or ignore. Wisdom may come through searching and learning various facts and information. Life is the proverbial school, and we are conditioned by television and radio to buy certain brands of breakfast cereal because *"they"* say that *"their"* product is better than anyone else's. 'But what constitutes proof when it comes to claims of UFOs and UFO abduction'? Is it a good

UFO photograph? Or a good UFO video? People believe in a whole range of things for a whole range of different reasons. So what am I driving at? What I'm saying is, *"Why do people believe in UFOs"?* Now that is a big question of which no doubt some would argue has many connotations. As stated above, is it through photographs, video footage, or witness testimony? Do people believe in UFOs and UFO abductions simply through reading various books? Indeed, do people believe in things simply because other people do?

Millions of people believe in God and his son Jesus and yet they have never seen them. It's fair to say that more people across the world have seen UFOs than witnessed God or Jesus! That may be a controversial statement, but its true. Most, if not all serious UFO researchers the world over, will tell you that in their own personal UFO files, there are one or two which shine out above all others. Cases of which even the most hardened sceptics would find hard to disprove. It wasn't until 1993 that this actually happened to me, in which a case was presented to me, which took me off the proverbial sceptical fence, and placed me slap bang into the believers camp. Now this was no mean task, as I have always gone into every UFO case that I researched with a sceptical mind, awaiting the evidence to prove otherwise. And as the years have rolled by, that accumulative evidence has shown me that there 'are' things in the skies above this planet which are not of our own making. But the one case that *'did it for me'* was the A70 UFO Incident. This, as we will learn shortly, concerned the abduction of two Edinburgh gentlemen by (if we are led by the evidence!) 'beings' from 'elsewhere'! These gentlemen were not interested in matters relating to UFOs, but were more interested in going out with their wives and doing ordinary mundane things, just your ordinary men in the street basically. Becoming involved with this case as I inevitably did, changed my whole perception of UFOlogy. It changed my whole perception of life. It changed the way I viewed things, and even today, I am still very much touched by 'their' event.

The following account that you are about to read, may sound incredible, it may seem unreal, but by golly it happened alright, and it didn't just happen in their 'minds' as some sceptics would have you believe. Speaking with these individuals, and working with them ever so closely, It became very clear to me of their sincerity. They were not out to pull the wool over my eyes or the eyes of my fellow researchers, they wanted answers, and they wanted answers badly. So badly, that they were prepared to go to the end's of the Earth to find them. They found my society, Strange Phenomena Investigations (SPI), and what you are about to read, may seem incredible, but it is consistent with other world wide UFO abduction accounts. It is a fascinating if not disturbing account, of a night which is now firmly etched in both of their minds. As I stated above, I knew that I had to cover this incredible case in a 'stand alone' book. Not only is there updated information which was not featured in my previous book, but I also take a look at what possibly may lie behind the UFO Abduction phenomenon. Not only that, I also provide the thoughts of what some of my fellow world wide UFOlogists think about what's going on. There clearly is something going on across the skies of our planet, but what? I do hope that you, the reader of this book, will be concerned enough to make a leap of faith and realise that mankind is most certainly dealing with 'something' which demands the utmost of attention. What you are about to read was not something that both men wanted to intrude into their lives, but what transpired on that eventful night is now given over to you the reader to digest and realise, that the world in which you and I live in, is far more stranger than you can ever imagine, as you are about to find out.

CHAPTER ONE

THE A70 UFO INCIDENT

SCOTLAND'S FIRST 'REPORTED' UFO ABDUCTION

Date of Incident: 17th August 1992.
Location of Incident: On the A7O Road near Harperrig
Reservoir. Lothian District, Central Scotland.

*"I've never seen anything like it before, but I knew it was a
UFO. It was floating 20ft above the road. As we were going
underneath, a shimmering curtain fell, and we went into total
blackness. This long arm extended over my chest. It was like a
skeleton with flesh round it"*
Testimony of witness Garry Wood.

THE A70 ROAD. SOME FACTS.

We should remember that not only were Garry Wood and Colin
Wright the principle subjects of this incredible event, another
player was the actual A70 Road itself. So why, if at all! was
this road so special? What makes it stand out from all the other
roads in Scotland for an event of this nature to occur? Well, let
us now take a look at this stretch of road known as the A70, but
to locals and regular travellers, its better known as the 'Lang
Whang'. That font of knowledge Wikipedia, tells us that the
A70 runs for a total of 74.3 miles (119.6km) between
Scotland's capital City Edinburgh down to the town of Ayr. I
should point out that a great deal of the road is elevated over
desolate moorland to heights of over 1000 feet above sea level,
which some might say made it a perfect location for an incident
of this nature to occur. Due to the road's isolation (in part)
during winter time, the road is often closed by snow.
Apparently the famous Scottish poet Robert Burns made a stop
on the A70 road at the formerly thatched, 'Wee Bush Inn' in
Carnwath on his way to Edinburgh. Of course this makes
sense, as the road stretches from Burn's native home in Ayr to

1

Edinburgh. The road also has a grisly past, in that two famous murderers, William Burke and William Hare were responsible for 16 murders over a period of ten months in 1828. They used the road to bring their cadavers to the Edinburgh Medical College where they sold them to Robert Knox for dissection at his anatomy classes. According to the Collins 2012 Big Road Atlas, it states that the A70 is one of the five most dangerous roads in Scotland based on a number of serious and fatal accidents, most of which occur at some of the right angled bends in the road, and it was at one of those right angled bends in the road, that both Garry and Colin experienced something other than a crash as we will learn shortly. Apparently there is barley a half mile stretch of the A70 road between Balerno and Carnwath that hasn't witnessed a fatal accident over the past twenty years. So, for anyone travelling down this stretch of road, it goes without saying, please be careful.

So we now have looked at this 74.3 mile stretch of road. Let us now turn our attention over to the actual incident itself. So sit, back, pour yourself a drink, for you are about to enter a realm of which two men's lives were soon to be catapulted into something akin to the Twilight Zone.

THE A70 UFO INCIDENT

Before we discuss the A70 Incident itself, just a few facts on both of the witnesses, starting with Garry Wood. Garry at the time of the incident was 29 years of age and a loving father of three children, two boys and a girl. He has two sisters and one brother, and his daily job at that time was an ambulance service repair man. At the time of the sighting, Garry lived at an address in Edinburgh and has since moved to another address in Edinburgh. He had no prior interest in UFOs, and is an honest and good natured citizen. Colin Wright at the time of the incident was 27 years of age and worked as a painter and decorator. Like Garry, he had no interest in UFOs and concerned himself with normal mundane matters such as D.I.Y and sports.

2

It was a warm cool August night just after 11:3Opm, on the 17th of August 1992, when 29 year old Garry Wood and his friend 27 year old Colin Wright, left Scotland's Capital city of Edinburgh in Garry's car on what should have been a short half hour drive down the A7O road to drop off a satellite system to a friend's house in Tarbrax West Lothian.   As we have read above, the A7O, in part, is a very desolate stretch of road and is bordered by fields on either side with only the odd house dotted around the barren landscape. During the journey, both men were discussing the days events and what they intended to do for the following week.   In the background, could be heard music coming from Garry's C.D. system. Garry's G registration Vauxhall Astra was travelling at roughly 4O miles per hour and there were very little traffic on the road which should have made the 30 minute journey even quicker. The car had just past Harperrig Reservoir to the west of the Pentland Hills which brought them towards a blind bend in the road.   It was at this point that Colin, who was sitting in the passenger seat, shouted out to Garry, *"What on Earth is that",?* Garry immediately looked in the direction in which Colin was pointing, and was confronted with an unearthly sight.   For hovering around 2O feet above the surface of the road, was a strange looking shiny black three tiered disc shaped object which looked decidedly out of place. Both men knew straight away, that this wasn't a conventional aircraft or helicopter, this was something totally out of the ordinary and foreign to their perception of normal aircraft design.   At this point both men became very alarmed, more so as they were now heading towards the direction of this strange looking object.   Garry thought about his options, he could either perform a three point turn on the road and head back the way he came, or take a chance and put his foot down on the accelerator and drive quickly underneath this hovering object, whereby getting away from it as fast as possible. This he did, and he quickly slammed his foot down hard on the accelerator and screamed underneath the object. At the same time, with his elbow, he pushed down to lock the car door. Soon the car was heading quickly towards the object of which he further noticed that it took up the entire width of the road.

The object did not have any windows or exterior structure and appeared to be of a solid metallic substance of some sort.

A SILVER SHIMMERING CURTAIN OF MIST

Garry, who at the time worked as an Ambulance repair man, went on to inform me that as he was a trained mechanic who worked with a lot of metals, he found the structure and polished effect of this object, most unusual. At this point however, things began to get even more strange, for as the car was fast approaching this object, the object emitted some kind of silver shimmering mist, Garry likened this effect to one of those old television set's when it was tuned onto an offset channel, (it didn't give you a picture just a maze of hazy shimmering lines). This silver shimmering effect descended from beneath this object and touched the car, and as it did so, both men were enveloped in total and inky blackness, they couldn't even see themselves, they couldn't see the dash board of the car, it was a complete and utter black void.   Seconds later, (or what appeared to them to be seconds later), they regained their sight, there was a huge shudder from the car and they could now see the landscape around them. Colin recalls that at this point, that Garry was driving 'like a bloody mad man' in an effort to get away from this alarming scene. Fighting hard to control the car (as it was on the wrong side of the road,) Garry's car screamed away from the area and continued on to their destination of Tarbrax. As they arrived at Tarbrax, Colin reached down to unbuckle his seat belt and was startled to find that his seat belt was already unbuckled! Colin is very safety conscious in a car and always ensures that he secures his seat belt and found this most surprising. Both men were by now quite distressed, and Garry recalls after getting out of the car at their destination, of 'banging' on his friends door. He was surprised that no one was answering and thought that perhaps they weren't home, even although they had arranged to see them. Some minutes later however, Katrina, one of the occupants of the house, answered the door, whereupon she asked Garry where had he been? And did he know that he was an hour and a half late! Garry at this point was very confused, as he knew only too well, that this journey, (a journey that he had made many times before) should only have taken him around 30 to 35 minutes, how on Earth had it taken him an hour and a half! Garry and Colin quickly entered the home and began speaking about what they had both seen on the A70, they even asked for some pens and paper in order to draw what they had seen. Katrina (the lady of the house) remembers only too well that particular night, and in a phone call to the author recalled the fear and distress that both men were in. She further stated that in no way were Garry and Colin making this all up, she had known both men for a number of years and she knew them well enough to state that they were not in the habit of telling tall tales. Indeed, when Katrina was later interviewed for the television series, 'Strange But True'? Hosted by Michael Aspel, she had this to say, and I quote,

"Garry was hysterical, he knows that I have got four kids. There is no way that he is going to come to my door, pound on it, push me right out of the road, and enter the way he did. Something dramatically happened to him"

THE MEMORIES BEGIN TO SURFACE

After a period of time in Katrina's home, where they unloaded their incredible tale to both Katrina and her husband, they left to return to Edinburgh. Garry related to the author that he could remember very little about his journey home that night, but does recall that he took a different route! The following day, Garry found himself extremely tired, more tired than he had ever been for a long time. As the days progressed, Garry knew deep down that 'something else' had transpired that night. He was bothered by strange dreams, and his sleeping patterns had changed. He developed severe headaches, so much so, that he had to attend his local doctor who suggested that he should have a cat scan. This Garry did, but nothing unusual was found. Garry also had a spinal tap, of which again nothing abnormal was found. *"What could that object have been"?* he thought to himself. He knew that it wasn't conventional, and began to think that perhaps it was one of those strange Unidentified Flying Object's that people had reported throughout the world. Garry didn't want to accept this, as he thought that it was only crazy people that saw UFOs. The subject of UFOs were of no interest to him whatsoever, and he had only read what he had come across about them in various newspapers.

I should point out here, that the night that Garry saw this strange object and the following nights thereafter, he had strange dreams. Dreams that contained small grey creatures. Nightmarish dreams which he quickly awoke to covered in sweat. Colin was also not interested in UFOs, both men were more involved with their day to day work and enjoying family life. UFOs did not feature at all anywhere in their daily life. But still Garry harboured these intense feelings that 'something else' had happened that night. What could he do about it,? Who do you turn to about something like this? Eventually he decided that his best course of action would be to phone a number of UFO societies, one of which was BUFORA (The British UFO Research Association), sadly they didn't get back to him! So he then decided to go along to his local library and try and find some UFO books where he might be able to get some answers. This he did, and in checking, he came across the address and phone number of my society, Strange Phenomena Investigations, (SPI). I remember the night when Garry Wood called me, I listened intently as his strange tale unfolded and I knew straight away that something very strange indeed had occurred to both men. This for me was head and shoulders above the normal mundane close encounter experience.

I quickly arranged for Garry and Colin to visit my home in Tullibody, Clackmannanshire Central Scotland, (where I lived at that time) where I would have the chance to speak directly to both men and discuss with them at great length exactly what they saw. That day came, and the honesty and conviction coming from both men really had to be seen to be believed. I had never ever met such sincere and honest individuals as Garry Wood and Colin Wright. One could readily see the intense emotion and trauma that both of these men had suffered, (and to

6

some extent were still suffering). It was a grasping story, and one that sent shivers down my spine, and believe you me, I have heard and read a lot about such cases in my time. After both men had recounted their experiences, there was a silence in the room, a silence which was eventually broken by my comments that I 'believed' in them, that it was clear to me, that 'something else' had indeed happened that night, and that one of the ways that 'might' elicit possible further recall of that night's events, would be to put both men under hypnotic regression.

THE USE OF HYPNOSIS

I explained to both men about hypnosis, and also that it was not always the best tool to extract any possible hidden or subconscious memory. People could and can lie under hypnosis. Hypnosis stood upon shaky ground as far as it's use went on UFO abduction witnesses. The UFO world was divided on it's role on abductions, and that there would always be, no matter what, a division of opinion on the validity of it being used. However, I explained to both Garry and Colin, that as a researcher, it was my job to get to the truth, and in doing so, I felt that I should get to that truth by using any manner of means available to me. It would not be professional to throw out any means of assistance to a case study simply because a number of people say that it shouldn't be used. I strongly accept that hypnosis has it's pitfalls, it may not be the best means of finding out what a witness experienced, but at the end of the day I do honestly believe that the use of hypnosis can unlock certain doors of the mind of which can release previously suppressed information or memories which are too painful for the conscious mind to recall, and in effect, forces it back to the recesses of the mind. None of us wish to remember events in our lives which proved painful, and the human mind has a great capacity for suppressing these memories. The point is though, those memories are still there, they will never go away unless in perhaps extreme medical conditions, a severe knock to the head for instance of which has happened to

7

numerous people when they totally forget their own family and friends.

I went on to inform Garry and Colin that some police authorities the world over, use hypnosis and recognise the importance of doing so. That they have used it sparingly in cases in which they felt would benefit the case they were working on. At the end of the day, I told both men, I felt that whatever information we can provide to assist in the uncovering of the UFO phenomenon, 'must' be for the good. As a researcher, it was my job to get to the truth, and if I felt that the use of hypnosis would assist me in getting to the truth, then I certainly would use it. However, it should only be used by people who knew what they were doing, and by people who were qualified and were not 'fly by night' 'back street' practitioners. It would be a sad day indeed, if we kicked into touch a means of enquiry which might show us the way in the understanding of the UFO abduction phenomenon.

Having discussed then the whys and wherefores with both Garry and Colin regarding the use of hypnosis, I asked them what they felt, would they like to try it? Or would they rather they left this avenue alone, particularly as if might indeed lead to further recall, and that recall might well cast up images and information of which they might not like. The choice was thier's. I did not at any time force them or put any pressure on them whatsoever to go through with hypnosis, I left it for them to decide. Again a silence followed, after which Garry broke the silence by stating that, if hypnosis helped him find out what was the cause of his experience, he was more than happy to go through with it. Colin nodded and said, *"Me Too"*. I again asked if both of them were really sure that they wanted to tred down this avenue, to which they both replied that they were, all that was left, was to find a hypnotherapist.

HELEN WALTERS

My first thoughts on who to use, was a colleague of mine, and someone of whom I trusted implicitly, her name was Helen

Walters. Not only was Helen a qualified hypnotherapist, but she was also a gifted psychic and someone of whom our society had used in numerous case Investigations. I approached Helen and gave her as little information as possible about this case ensuring that she would not be knowledgeable about all of what happened, whereby she might be fore-armed and use leading questions. Helen was more than happy 'not to know' any main facts about this case, other than the obvious fact that 'something' strange had happened to these two men on the night of the 17th of August 1992. A date was set, and both Garry and Colin travelled over to the small town of Alva in Clackmannanshire Central Scotland where Helen lived at that time, (she has since moved to Spain) to have what would be the first of many hypnosis sessions. Garry recalls his first hypnosis session as not what he expected, he burst out into tears and was emotionally distraught. On the other hand, Colin seemed to handle this first session better, and remained calm throughout, with only the occasional movement of his head and body. At this first session, Garry recalls seeing only vague shapes but it was clear to him, that 'something' was trying to surface, and that 'something' just had to come out. Prior to the hypnosis session, I had asked both men not to read up on any UFO material, but to keep their head's away from any UFO literature which might colour or invalidate what might come out under hypnotic regression. This they agreed to do.

I remember those early hypnotic regression sessions well, each man went separately into a back room in Helen's house in which Helen carefully guided them through an introductory explanation which gently eased them back to that August night. Both men, although they were under hypnosis, were still very much aware of where they currently were and who was in the room, a common feature of most people who go under hypnosis. I not only audio taped and video taped most of these sessions, (I couldn't attend some sessions due to work commitments) I also took notes as well, and monitored the reactions of both men whilst they were under hypnosis. Many times both men's bodies jolted on the hypnotherapist's chair, this was in direct response to their recall of an event that 'surfaced' under hypnosis. The following weeks saw more visits by both Garry and Colin to be placed under hypnotic regression, and I shall now go through and inform you the reader, exactly what came out under hypnosis. It makes for harrowing reading.

HYPNOTIC RECALL. MORE MEMORIES SURFACE.

Firstly, let me make it quite clear, that both men under normal recall, only ever remember witnessing this large black object as it hovered above the road, followed by the unusual curtain of silvery light which descended down onto their car. They do not recall any 'aliens' or seeing inside what could be termed a UFO. The following information was gleamed purely from hypnosis and is presented here in depth.

Both Garry and Colin had a number of hypnotic regression sessions with hypnotherapist Helen Walters, I'll now go through a couple of these sessions and bring forward some more pieces of information that both men relayed on those occasions, starting off with Garry Wood, and a regression session that we conducted with him on the 14th of June 1994. Firstly, Helen took Garry back in his mind, through the years to the time just after the initial UFO abduction experience. Garry remembers finding himself outside his home clad only in his underwear but can't understand what he was doing out there, especially as all the doors were locked and he couldn't get back in the house. Sadly, no matter how Helen prodded, she couldn't get Garry to go back to that point and we never did find out any more about that.

THE ABDUCTION

Helen then took Garry backward through the years until she reached the year of August 1992, suddenly Garry explained that he felt that he was 'going away' and that he would never come back. (This was in direct reference to him being taken towards this UFO call it what you will). He had the very strong impression that 'this was it', he wouldn't see his family and friends again. He also remembers that he was crying whilst being taken. He remembers that he kept looking for Colin, but couldn't find him. Whilst he was being taken towards 'an object', (he states that he was definitely moving and felt as if he were lying down), he remembers seeing three strange shapes. Garry found it very hard to put into words exactly how these shapes looked like. *'They looked like people'*, he said, and the only way that Garry could describe them, was to state that the outline of their bulky bodies, were like American football players, like as if they had large shoulder pads. He only saw the outline of their body and their head, of which their head was extremely round. He got the impression that he was looking at the backs of these 'beings' (or whatever they were), in fact one of them actually floated down towards the ground and joined the other one which was already walking forwards.

Further on, towards the object, he saw a small 'being' of which Garry said looked as if it was hiding behind something, and that it was 'peeking' out to have a look as to what was going on. The surprising thing Garry said, was that this small 'being' had sort of zig zag lines under it's eyes, red and yellow and green markings, like women's make up he said. He only recalls seeing the one eye of this 'being' as it 'peeked' out from behind some structure. Garry recalled to me after coming out of hypnosis, that he felt extreme anger towards these 'beings' that were taking him, but he couldn't do anything about it, and this, for Garry, was the most worrying thing of all. Eventually he found himself in a large and spacious room which was filled with bright white light. He also saw a strange shape that was up against a doorway. Another unusual aspect to come out of this session, was when Garry later related that night to Helen and myself, that when Helen had asked Garry whilst he was under hypnosis, to look around and try and see as much as he could whilst in this strange room, Garry opened one eye (in Helen's room) but quickly had to shut it again, the reason being was, as he looked at Helen, Helen's face began to change, into what, he doesn't know, for he quickly closed his eyes again!

A MORE FULLER ACCOUNT OF THE ABDUCTION

In another hypnosis session, Helen our hypnotherapist dug a bit deeper into both men's account, taking them both back to the start of their encounter and asking them (individually) what they saw, and here is what transpired. Under hypnosis, both men state that the car was stopped on the road, after which both the driver and passenger doors were opened by three small entities. Colin recalls that he saw Garry being placed on what looked like some kind of stretcher, but with the major difference that, none of these three small entities appeared to be holding it! One entity stood at the front of this stretcher, whilst the other stood at the back. Garry it must be noted, cannot recall himself being placed upon this 'free floating stretcher'. Garry also experienced at this point, tremendous pain in his abdominal region, he described it to me as if all his internal muscles were being pulled in all directions, this caused him considerable discomfort and was quite distressing to him. Garry also recalls another entity which appeared to be lurking or hiding behind part of this UFO. Garry also recalls seeing 'underneath' this hovering object, and described it to me after he had come out of hypnosis as, 'having a round metallic shiny dome'. Colin recalls being led up a ramp into this object by some of these entities which took him direct into a bright white light. He also recalls at this point, being led around a curving corridor which eventually led out into a round room. This room was devoid of any furnishings or instrumentation of any kind, apart that is, from one unusual chair. This was a curved chair which featured what appeared to be an arm rest. Colin was stripped naked and placed upon this chair, after which, some form of medical or clinical examination was conducted upon his person. Colin also recalls looking up at the ceiling in this room and noticed that it was not flat like a conventional ceiling, rather it appeared corrugated (curved) and there were some kind of diffused lights shining through it. Garry also remembers being taken into a round room which was devoid of any furnishing or instrumentation of any kind, apart that is, from a raised table, (not a chair, as in Colin's case). Garry too was stripped naked and placed upon this table during which words came into his head, words stating that no harm would come to him. This brought no relief, for by now Garry was terrified. Garry informed me that he was brought up in the Niddrie, a working class area of Edinburgh and he knew how to handle himself. Garry had never looked for trouble in his life, but when it happened he knew how to protect himself. This situation however, was a different ball game, and he found himself in an environment of which he had no control over, and one in which he found extremely distressing. And as much as Garry wanted to strike out to these small beings, he found that he couldn't. He couldn't move a muscle, he was totally immobile, the only thing that he could move, were his eyes as he watched these horrible beings surround his raised table.

In another hypnotic regression which again took place at Helen Walters house in Alva in Clackmannanshire, Garry related the following. He found himself flying or floating above a crater, a very large and open crater. He was slowly moving up from it's base and up the sides, but he felt as if he wasn't in control, for he was being moved every which way. He had no control. When he tried to look at something, he was moved around, nothing was actually holding him. He had no free will of his own to move. At this point he remembers seeing jagged rocks, many jagged rocks, very sharp and slate like. He also saw other rocks of which there were a number of 'beings' standing behind them. Garry likened his flying experience as similar to that as one could experience in a small light aircraft as it swooped and dived, twisted and turned, that was the best way that he could describe it.

SANCTUARY

Another strange aspect of this particular session, was when Helen Walters kept on asking Garry to ask 'them', what they wanted. After a moment's silence, Garry continued with one word which was totally unexpected and surprised everyone in the room, for Garry replied, *'Sanctuary'* We didn't quite know what to make of this. Later on after Garry came out of hypnosis, he stated that this was indeed what was said to him by

13

one of these Grey 'beings', it said it wanted *'Sanctuary'*. Garry couldn't understand this, and neither could I. Why would it have said something like this! More of this in a moment. Garry also recalls seeing what he described as, a short fat and podgy small girl with long dark hair running towards a taller Grey, whereupon the taller Grey put it's arms around her to comfort her. Garry believes that it was he, that somehow scared this little girl. Garry kept going on about how podgy this small and naked girl was. He estimates that she was around 8 to 10 years of age. Garry also recalls seeing one of the greys that performed a movement which really surprised him. He stated that one of the Grey's actually moved it's neck in a snake like manner! It was moving all around, this way and that, and twisted behind itself to more or less look over it's shoulder. This really surprised Garry and gave him quite a start. Garry also recalls seeing one of the Grey's wearing a black suit, and looked decidedly out of place.

The main thing that came out of this particular session after it was concluded, was when Garry said to us all, that he now knew that he would not be frightened any more. From now on he said, he knew that things would be O.K. with him, and that he would be able to handle further regressions. Helen and I were most pleased with this, and Helen I recall, stated that this was a tremendous step forward and made it much more easier for Garry to continue with further regression sessions. Garry also said that he knew, that these 'beings' were not going to harm him, but the most amazing statement that Garry kept saying repeatedly, was that *'They want to come here'.*

CLOSE BY!

Garry further reiterated that these 'beings' definitely want to come here. He further stated that they were not too far away at the moment, and were somewhere near Earth. Garry also stated that he is sure that there will be many more abductions occurring all over the world, *"They need us"*, he said, *"We are very important to them"*. *"They don't want to destroy us, they just need us"!* One final point that I should mention about this hypnosis session, was that after coming out of hypnosis and discussing with us what he recollected, he calmly stated that he had the distinct feeling that 'something' was in the room with him whilst he was under hypnosis, he felt that most strongly.

GARRY'S HYPNOTIC RECALL

Most of Garry's recall have him describing scenes only from the point of him lying on this flat raised table which was the only feature in a round room. Garry states that as he was lying on this flat table unable to move, he became aware of a black lens shaped device which was free floating in the centre of the room. Garry explained to the author, that it appeared to be 'folding in on itself', it was turning and twisting, and he couldn't for the life of him, fathom out what it was or what purpose it served. Garry described the device as around 5 to 6 feet in width and was roughly 2 and a half feet in breadth. This device was also making some kind of 'whooshing' sound as Garry lay there totally in awe of this 'thing'. As Garry lay there mesmerized by this object with his eyes totally fixed upon it, a small and thin translucent grey arm with long fingers suddenly came into his line of vision and dropped onto his chest near his head. At this point, Garry shot out of hypnosis such was the fright and that this small grey arm gave him.

Garry stated that not only did he observe the commonly reported 'grey' being, which was small grey skinned, roughly four and half feet tall with a child like body, with a large pear shaped head with large black inky almond shaped eyes, but he also saw small brown beings as well, with heavy folds of skin which folded all over their faces. Garry was extremely frightened of one of these brown 'beings' but doesn't know why, as it never harmed him in any way during his experience. Not all of the grey beings were the same height, some were slightly taller than the others. Some were roughly six feet tall, whilst the others were roughly four to four and a half feet tall. Incredibly though, Garry also related to the author, that in one of his recollections, he remembers seeing a small man dressed in a black suit complete with tie. This puzzled him somewhat and was totally out of place in this already strange environment.

POOL OF LIQUID GEL!

Another recollection that Garry had, was again when he was on this flat table. He recalls seeing what appeared to be like a pool of liquid gel which suddenly appeared on the floor of this room. Whilst he was watching this, a can shaped device rose up from the floor and appeared at the right hand side of his head. It was roughly three and a half foot tall, and one and a half foot wide. This device was making some kind of motor noise and was spinning around slowly. Suddenly a part of this can shaped device rose up and extended from the main part of the device until it was horizontal with Garry's eyes. At the tip of this flap, were situated two small red dots. At this point, the pool of liquid gel on the floor began to vibrate, then suddenly a small thin grey 'creature' started to pull itself out of it. Garry states that this 'creature' was very frail looking, it looked like a skeleton with the thinnest of flesh around it. It was fairly tall and had long arms. The 'creature' was predominantly grey, but the flesh over it's ribs seemed bruised and red. Garry's best description of this 'creature' to me, was,

"It appeared as is it had a really hard time"!

Garry also explained to the author, that he felt as if there were 'more' 'creatures' in this pool of gel, although he only ever saw one. He also thinks that this 'creature' was somehow controlling this can shaped device, but for what purpose he couldn't imagine. Probably what could best be described as the most amazing aspect of Garry Wood's recall under hypnosis, and something which even surprised him, was when again he recalls lying naked on this flat raised table with two small 'creatures' standing at the foot of this table, one of whom was holding a bright diamond shaped object which was pulsating orange light. This 'creature' then began to move this diamond shaped device over Garry's body. Garry recalls being very frightened at this point and somewhat angry as well, but again

16

found much to his annoyance, that he had no control whatsoever over his situation, he wanted to lash out at his captors, but found that he just couldn't. Garry also noticed down to his right hand side, an arched doorway of which a tremendous bright light source was glowing, but he was unprepared and astonished at the sight which then befell his eyes.

THE GIRL ON THE FLOOR

For down to his left hand side and sitting on the floor with her back to him, was a completely naked female. She was sitting with her knees up to her chin with her arms grasped tightly around her legs. She was softly crying and was shivering with the cold. Garry also noticed that she had shaggy loose permed hair with blonde highlights. Suddenly and very gently, she slowly moved her head around in the direction of Garry, whereupon Garry noticed that she had tears running down her face, she looked so sad and forlorn. She then moved her head back to look at the wall. No words at all were spoken between the two, and Garry stated to the author, that if ever he came across this woman again he would immediately recognise her.

SANCTUARY, THE CAVE, AND STRANGE SMALL CREATURES

We mentioned earlier, that when Garry asked in his mind (as he found that he couldn't talk) why these 'creatures' were doing these horrible things to him. The strange and totally surprising reply that he got, was the word, *"Sanctuary"!* Another unusual aspect of Garry Wood's abduction, was when he related that he found himself standing beside rocks in a cave. *(October 17th 1994 hypnosis session)* This was a huge open cave of which he saw a strange craft just off to the left hand side. There was not much light in this cave and it was quite dark, although Garry recalls that the cave itself was quite warm. On another occasion, Garry found himself in some kind of built up environment, a very strange looking place. Looking up into the sky. he saw

17

within the confines of a circle, around 12 faces of the Greys. Then there was another occasion, again under hypnosis, when Garry recalled a number of strange looking shapes which were roughly six feet in length they looked like some kind of sea animal with a boxed tail, oval shaped body and a pointed nose. They moved in a strange manner towards him, they completed a short turn circle, and went back the way they came. All this, was observed through a red mist! At the beginning of 1998, I once more interviewed Garry Wood and asked him several questions pertaining to his case and how he reflected upon it today. The following are but some of the points that came out of that session.

GARRY WOOD ON HYPNOSIS.

I asked Garry if he regretted going through with hypnosis in the respect that it had now brought to the surface, memories of which he might have preferred not to know, (and I was referring to his recall of finding himself naked on a table, with strange looking creatures operating on him). Was hypnosis something of which he now regretted? He replied that he was very glad to have gone under hypnosis, for he desperately wanted to learn what had happened to him. Prior to Garry going under hypnosis, (before the time of the first session) he had read a few books about hypnosis, the good points and also the bad points. Garry mentioned the fact that he had never been hypnotised before. I asked him if he was aware of his surroundings whilst being under hypnosis, (ie, being in the hypnotherapists room), he replied that he 'was' aware of being in the room, but sometimes when the visions became so strong, he felt he was 'somewhere else', ie, inside the object that had taken him. When asked if he felt that all of what he recounted under hypnosis was true or was false, he replied that he is convinced, that 99.9% of what he recollects under hypnosis, 'really happened', and that it is not the result of an over active mind. What he saw under hypnosis, was unlike anything else that he had ever seen in his entire life, nothing came close to it, not even scenes from science fiction or UFO films! I asked Garry if at any point under hypnosis, he had experienced the feeling of pain, he stated that there was one point when these small creatures were doing things to his stomach, whatever they were doing gave him excruciating pain, he was in total agony. He also recalls the discomfort he felt when things were being prodded into his ear, at no time did he see what these things were. Garry described the noise in his ear as 'pulsating', which strangely grew louder each time hypnotherapist Helen Walters spoke to him. Garry said it was as if he wasn't meant to listen to Helen! And from an earlier interview that I conducted with Garry, he explained that when he was being 'taken', his entire stomach felt as if it were being pulled in every direction, that all his internal muscles were being pulled every which way. Garry went on to explain that after hypnosis was conducted upon him, he found he could sleep better at night. He began to come to terms with what had happened to him, indeed, the whole thing had made a big difference to his life.

I was keen to know from Garry, if he felt that hypnosis had given him the 'answer'? What had he learned through participating in all these hypnosis sessions? He pondered for a bit, and replied that hypnosis had given him the pieces of the puzzle. It had given him something to think on.

A LIFE, JUST LIKE OURS!

He went on to relate that on one occasion whilst under hypnosis, he remembers that one of these small 'creatures' said to him, (in his head), *"I have a life just like you, but only different"*. This statement stayed with Garry throughout the following years. Garry believes that these creatures, (or whatever they are) are really not out to harm us, and although they are taking people throughout the world, their purpose is not for harm, but for something else? Garry himself, is unsure as to what 'they' want, and there are a number of thoughts on this matter of which various UFOlogists throughout the world agree and disagree on (of which I'll come to shortly).

19

I also asked Garry how his family and friends had reacted when the story of his experience started to become widely know. He stated that his wife didn't like him talking about it, as she was frightened of the whole thing, however, she had been very supportive of him of which he was extremely grateful. Some of his work mates had had a laugh at him, (which Garry explained to me he would have done the same thing prior to his own event if someone had have told him all this). But in general, not much had changed. The people who really knew him, knew that he would not make up a story such as this. He only ever wanted to get on with his life, and make a home for his wife and family. UFOs and abductions were the furthest thing from his mind, he didn't have the time for any of it. 'He didn't need this in his life' as he kept telling me.

The following, is what Colin Wright remembers after hypnosis was conducted upon him.

COLIN WRIGHT'S HYPNOSIS SESSION

Let us now take a look back at some of what Colin Wright also recalls under hypnosis. The following is taken from an earlier hypnosis session conducted with Helen Walters on the 4th of August 1994 at Alva in Clackmannanshire, Scotland. Under hypnosis, Colin stated that he found himself on a strange curved and very smooth chair, he was naked, and was extremely cold. One of the smaller beings came towards him whereupon Colin asked why they wanted him, he was startled by the reply which was, *"It is Garry we want"!* This left Colin thinking, why then was he sitting naked in this strange curved chair! A short while later, whilst still in this chair, a small being came towards him and gently touched him on the face. This touch felt extremely cold and gave Colin the impression that it was 'cold blooded'. Colin felt that he was left sitting in this cold chair for quite a long period of time. During this time, he noticed that the walls of the oval shaped room that he found himself in, appeared grey and metallic. He had the impression that there was a room behind him, but he couldn't look round to find this out for sure. In this room, he heard strange noises,

noises of which he couldn't explain, they came no-where near to anything that he has ever heard before. One thing which he found most interesting, was the fact that these small 'beings' did not have flat emotionless faces, for he recalls seeing their facial muscles move, from a frown to some kind of smile, so much so, that when they did this, they would create furrows on their scalp just like humans.

THE GLASS OR PERSPEX CHAMBER

Another recollection that Colin had, was when he found himself contained within a large glass or Perspex chamber. He was totally naked and was strapped and held by the wrists and ankles. As he looked out of this chamber, he observed that there were many other chambers all situated around him, each containing people (male and female) old and young who were also completely naked. Colin found that he could not move any parts of his body, he could only move his head very slightly. Blowing around outside his chamber, was what looked like mist, (it reminded him of dry ice, he stated). He also observed one tall 'creature' who was standing next to a doorway and there were three other 'creatures' who were looking in at Colin from outside his chamber. Suddenly and quite unexpectedly, this glass or Perspex began to frost up. At this point Colin began to get alarmed and started to cry, no sooner had Colin begun to cry, than this frosting effect stopped, and he could once more see with ease outside this container. It was at this point that Colin observed a strange looking device which rose up from the floor and became level with his eyes. This was different from what Garry Wood experienced when a can shaped device rose up from the floor to become level with Garry's eyes. Colin stated that this device featured a long rod with a triangular shaped part at the top with two red lights at the front of it. There was also some appendage in the middle of this rod, and the rod itself was joined at the bottom with a box like effect. This device continually moved up and down and rotated from left to right. This went on for around two minutes, whereupon it then slowly descended back into the floor again. An unusual aspect of Colin's recollections were his descriptions of the 'creatures' that he saw. Some of them appeared to have indented heads and did not resemble the round pear shaped heads so commonly reported by many other abductees. However, having said that, he did also observe other 'creatures' who did have this pear shaped head. A short while later, he actually felt quite warm in this chamber, indeed, at this point, Helen during the regression, actually noted a warm glow on Colin's face, as if it was a hot flush.

In UFO researcher Yvonne R. Smith's book, Chosen, *(Recollections of Abductions Through Hynotherapy) Bachstage Entertainment 2008. USA).* She presents an abduction case, which to some degree, had some of the same hallmarks to Colin's situation in his glass or prespex chamber. Yvonne is detailing the case of a lady called Mary who is descibed to Vyonne about seeing people in some glass cases. She wrote,

Yvonne: *"What do the cases look like"?*

Mary: *"They're glass, a kind of scratched glass, and where the panes come together is a white sort of frame. And there's like a mist in them, but I can't really see. For some reason, I don't like those! I think there is someone sitting in it".*

Mary went on to say that these glass cases were at least six or seven feet tall. (The same height as reported by Colin) However, the difference with these cases as to what Colin experienced, was the fact that the cases that Mary saw, were two or three feet sticking out from a wall. Mary further stated that she saw an adult woman in one of these cases completely naked and that there was a fog or mist in the case. So, some similarities there with the fog or mist, but different in the sense that Colin was surrounded by other cases or cannisters, whilst this one appeared to stand alone. Mary herself had her own ideas as to what these aliens wanted. She wrote;

"I get the feeling that they are trying to manipulate our genetic material to create bodies fully adapted to our planet but

22

which can also house their own kind of consciousness, their souls, if you will. They are trying to create a body into which both species can incarnate and express their own styles of consciousness. Even as our bodies are not adapted to life on other worlds or permanent residence in spacecraft, their consciousness is not adapted to life in our stormy bodies and brains. They may not have much time left to create a life form adapted to this world, a world which may ironically change out of their design parameters."

Some very interesting thoughts there.

COLIN UNDER HYPNOSIS. 4TH AUGUST 1994

This abduction featured a number of differences in regards to other world wide UFO abductions, and I will be coming to these shortly, for now though I'd like to present the transcript of part of an actual hypnotic regression session that was audio recorded by myself back on the 4th of August 1994 at Alva in Clackmannanshire Central Scotland. Colin Wright was the subject of this hypnotic session, and I hope that this will give you the reader, a feel of the emotion and turmoil that Colin felt as he recalled these events. There were a number of pauses and silences during this session, but essentially this is what was said as SPI's hypnotherapist Helen Walters took Colin back to that night in question.

HELEN: "I want you to relive that night Colin, see it, feel it. Where are you"?
COLIN: "No where."
HELEN: "Where is no where!"
COLIN: "Just no where, complete blackness".
HELEN: "Are you at Katrina's yet"?
COLIN: "No".
HELEN: "Are you far from Katrina's"?
COLIN: "Complete blackness".
HELEN: "What are you looking at, what are you trying to see"?
COLIN: "I feel I'm going up"!

23

HELEN: "Going up"!

COLIN: "Uh huh".

HELEN: "See it, feel it. Can you hear anything"?

COLIN: "Nothing".

HELEN: "See it Colin, nothing can harm you at this moment, listen to the sound of my voice". **[Strong body reaction].**

COLIN: "Creatures, I'm telling them to get lost".

HELEN: "Where are you"?

COLIN: "I'm in a bright room".

HELEN: "What are they doing"?

COLIN: "Trying to undress me".

HELEN: "Tell me what is happening Colin, speak to me, it will help you"?

COLIN: "I'm just sitting with no clothes on".

HELEN: "Where are you sitting"?

COLIN: "A metal chair, it's smooth and cold".

HELEN: "How do you feel"?

COLIN: "Just cold".

HELEN: "Tell me what is happening Colin".

COLIN: "Something's in my right eye".

HELEN: "What is in your right eye"?

COLIN: "I don't know. It's uncomfortable, like a red hot poker in the middle of my eye. It's sore".

HELEN: "Who is putting this red hot poker in your eye"?

COLIN: "I can't see anything".

HELEN: "Is your left eye open"?

COLIN: "Uh huh".

HELEN: "Why are you shaking your head"?

(At this point Colin was shaking his head from side to side).

COLIN: "I'm trying to get a good look at this thing, the thing that is doing this to me. I'm trying to look at this bloody thing, but every time I look at it, it puts this thing in my eye".

HELEN: "Can you see now? What is happening"?

COLIN: "Just took it out of my eye. My right eye's burning, my eye is really watering, it's gushing".

HELEN: "What kind of material was it, what did it feel like"?

24

COLIN: "It felt like there was something clamped on it, that there was something going into my eye".

HELEN: "How did you get there Colin, I want you to relive the journey. Relive the journey, what can you see"?

COLIN: "The car is in a big bright metallic room".

HELEN: "How did the car get there"?

COLIN: "It was lifted".

HELEN: "How was it lifted? Try and see how it was lifted, what was lifting the car"?

COLIN: "I don't know, I just feel it juddering and being lifted".

HELEN: "Listen to the sound of my voice. O.K. go back to the beginning of your journey and describe it. Talk to me".

COLIN: "Just passing the reservoir on the left hand side, just passing the farm house on the right. This doesn't make sense. There is no road, nothing, the car is definitely off it. There seems to be some kind of force, there is nothing physical that I can see".

HELEN: "How high was it lifted"?

COLIN: (Author's note. Couldn't make out what Colin said on the tape here) I'm cold, I'm getting carried along at some rate." *(Strong body movements).* "I'm in that chair again, something looked at me back in that corridor, it was ugly".

HELEN: "Describe it Colin".

COLIN: "It's an ugly thing, it comes and goes".

HELEN: "See it, try and see it".

COLIN: "It's lurking in that corridor. It seems ancient to me. Ugly, it's really badly deformed, so ugly. I'm not scared of it any more." *(At this point Colin began to laugh).* "Its quite funny. Its so ugly its unbelievable. It seems as if this thing has been in a fight and it's the loser. I think it's trying to manipulate me".

HELEN: "In what way"?

COLIN: "I don't know. I think that I am really pissing it off because I'm not scared of it any more. I'm laughing at it, it's weird, it's away. I think I got the better of it. I see lights now, something built into structure of the walls. Massive, fluorescent lights, but its not, there is quite a few of them". *(At this point Colin stared to his right).* "I can hear a noise behind me, I can't think of a word to describe it", *(Strong body movement)*. "I'm now staring at a wee one".

HELEN: "A wee what"?

COLIN: "A wee creature. It's not very happy with me, I don't think that I was supposed to look behind my chair for some reason. It's looking at me with those black eyes, but I'll not give in".

HELEN: "You won't give in to what"?

COLIN: "It's trying to out stare me. It's away. I don't think it was very pleased with me. It just doesn't want me to see what is behind me for some reason. If I try to do anything, they'll come round the corner and try and stop me."

HELEN: "What do you have on Colin"?

COLIN: "Nothing, the chair is freezing, I keep wanting to get out of my chair but I bet it will be a big mistake".

HELEN: "Is any one else there"?

COLIN: "Not that I can see, but I bet if I get out of this chair they will be there".

HELEN: "Did they speak to you"?

COLIN: "No, but I could tell that it was 'pissed off'. My eye keeps watering. I'm looking at something. It looks like some kind of surgery tool or something, I think that this is what went into my eye."

HELEN: "Can you describe it"?

COLIN: "It sort of comes down and bends towards the left, and then bends down again, it's hard to describe. I've never seen anything like it. It separates into four, and there's all just things hanging from it, tubes".

HELEN: "What's it made of"?

COLIN: "It's metal"

HELEN: "What kind of metal"?

COLIN: "Grey, finely polished"

HELEN: "How big is it"?

COLIN: "Three feet in height, it just seems to be hanging there and not connected to anything".

HELEN: "How broad is it"?

COLIN: "Thin, it's just weird"

HELEN: "Why weird"?

COLIN: "Just the shape of it. I don't know the purpose it serves. All different tools, all different shapes".

HELEN: "What does the one in your eye look like"?

COLIN: "It's snake like. It's a wee oblong shape in my eye, but there is some kind of point, some kind of clamp mechanism. Oval, like a gripping kind of thing clamped on my eye, the shape of my eye, gripping it".

HELEN: "What is the gripping thing made of"?

COLIN: "Just the same as the rest of it, highly polished metallic stuff".

HELEN: "How long have you been seeing this"?

COLIN: "No idea".

HELEN: "Look at your watch Colin"

COLIN: "Not got a watch, I don't wear a watch".

HELEN: "Anybody there with you now"?

COLIN: "Nobody, I'm freezing though"

HELEN: "Move on from there Colin". *(Strong body movement)*, "What's happening Colin"?

COLIN: "Two of them have got me by the feet and are dragging me towards a small archway".

HELEN: "How did you get out of the chair"?

COLIN: "They grabbed me by the feet, I think I pushed them off".

HELEN: "What's happening now"?

COLIN: "They are dragging me back to the car, they are not fussy at hurting me". *(Strong body movement)*.

HELEN: "Where are you now"?

COLIN: "In the car, back in the seat".

HELEN: "Do you have your clothes on"?

COLIN: "Yes".

HELEN: "Go back to when you put your clothes on, what's happening"

COLIN: "Putting my clothes on".

HELEN: "Who"?

COLIN: "The wee aliens".

HELEN: "How many are there"?

COLIN: "Four". *(More strong body movement)*. "There is a big alien in front of me doing something, my head is pounding. I don't know if it is giving me something, or

27

taking something out of my head. My mind goes black, then lighter. My head feels numb, it feels massive, it feels as if I've a big forehead. *(Colin was rubbing his forehead very vigorously at this point).*

HELEN: "What are you doing"?

COLIN: "Putting my shoes on. I'm sitting with my clothes on".

HELEN: "Where"?

COLIN: "In the same chair".

HELEN: "Have you asked them why you are there? Talk to me Colin, what's happening"?

HELEN: "What's happening to your head now"?

COLIN: "Shooting pain, I don't know what they have done, but it's weird, my brain feels as if it is swollen and pushing my head out like it's going to burst. I can't handle this. It's stopped. It's weird".

HELEN: "Can you move on, where are you now"?

COLIN: "Back on the road".

HELEN: "How did you get there"?

COLIN: "Big bang, thud".

HELEN: "Anyone in the car with you"?

COLIN: "Garry's looking at me bewildered. Garry's asking me, did you see what I saw".

HELEN: "What are you seeing now"?

COLIN: "Garry's asking me, 'did you see what I saw'? Garry knows what I'm thinking".

HELEN: "What"?

COLIN: "That we saw a UFO".

HELEN: "Did you see Garry on your travels"?

COLIN: "No, just now.

HELEN: "Was he in the car before you"?

COLIN: "No. I felt the car banging down on the road. Garry's driving like a maniac".

HELEN: "Where are you now Colin"?

COLIN: "In my bed, in my mum's house"

HELEN: "When is this"?

COLIN: "The same night, Garry just dropped me off. I can't sleep, my head is buzzing. Feels weird, can't explain it".

HELEN: "What is the buzzing with"?
COLIN: "I don't know, feels weird. My brain feels swollen".
HELEN: "How do you feel?
COLIN: "Strange".
HELEN: "In what way, how strange"?
COLIN: "My brain feels half empty, pounding. I'm glad to be home"

At this point Helen slowly began to bring Colin out of hypnosis, saying that this was now the present, and that no part of him will remain in the past. We retired back to the living room in which Helen instructed me not to ask Colin any questions at all, but just let Colin freely begin to talk about what he felt and experienced under hypnosis. The following, is what Colin said and is taken from notes at the time.

COLIN: "I got a big 'buzzing' through my ears, like the sound of a television that is not on a station. I can't think of anything, I feel weird, I don't feel myself. I can't get my head to stay still. Its like my brain is floating about. I want to speak out, but I can't be bothered. I feel mentally drained. My head feels funny at the front. The car definitely got lifted off the road. I remember sitting on a chair, and something was in my right eye. I felt that I was in this chair for a long period of time, and when I did get up, this 'thing' came up to me and I tried to out stare it. I got the impression that it was mad at me. I feel mentally drained. My brain went black to dark grey then to light grey when this large alien/thing, touched my head".

This then, was but one of many parts of the hypnosis sessions that I had taken down. As I mentioned before, I am aware of the pitfalls of using hypnosis on cases such as this, but when all is said and done, I firmly believe that hypnosis is yet another tool which might hopefully extract more hidden subconscious memory. We can liken it to a workman who goes on a building site. That workman will not just carry one tool onto the job, he will carry a number of tools, all to get the job done, and this is basically what I am advocating with hypnosis.

It is just another tool to get the 'job done'. I saw the trauma that both men experienced, I felt their pain. I was totally convinced that these men did not make this story up, far from it. They wanted no publicity at all, that publicity eventually came, and it came purely because I advocated that it should do so.

The following week, I interviewed Colin about that previous week's hypnotic session, and this is what he had to say to me.

INTERVIEW WITH COLIN WRIGHT AUGUST 11TH, 1994. ALVA, CLACKMANNANSHIRE.

Abbreviations. (CW) Colin Wright. (MR) Malcolm Robinson.

(MR) "Colin, we are here tonight, to do further hypnotic regression on yourself and Garry Wood. First of all, tell us briefly about the night in question when you were in the car, driving to Tarbrax, and after you have told us about that journey, tell us what you have learned so far from your own hypnotic regression"?

(CW) "Basically we were heading off to Tarbrax to drop of a satellite system and we went around a blind bend, and right in front of the car was a UFO craft which was about 20 feet above the road. It seemed to throw down some sort of shimmering curtain. Garry crashed the gear box and tried to go as fast as he could underneath it. To my knowledge I thought we did. And then we came out the other side with a bit of a judder. We got to Tarbrax, a bit flustered, and basically just told the people when we got there, what had happened. I think they believed us, I can't recall what we were saying to them at the time to be honest"

(MR) "At one point in our discussions about this event, you explained to me that when you reached Tarbrax, that you looked down and found to your surprise that your seat belt was unbuckled. How sure are you, that your seat belt was buckled when you left Edinburgh"?

(CW) "100% certain, because Garry is a maniac driver *(laughs)* I always have my seat belt on".

(MR) "OK. So you arrived in Tarbrax, did you notice at this point, any time difference at all when you got to Tarbrax"?

(CW) "Eh no, I didn't bother to look at the clock after it happened. I couldn't tell you what time it was when we went into it". *(Author's note. Colin is of course referring to this shimmering mist)* "The time didn't enter into my mind If I'm honest. Later on we acknowledged that we lost an hour or more which I found pretty amazing".

(MR) "OK. Since this event which occurred in August 1992, you have tried to get UFO organisations involved with your case, to hopefully provide you with an answer. You were not successful until SPI replied to the communication to us from Garry. Now here we are, in August 1994 and we have had three or so, hypnotic regressions with yourself and Garry. Could you tell me what you have learned in regards to your own experiences under hypnosis. What has come out, and what have you learned of that event that night"?

(CW) "Well as I say, we went underneath the craft, everything went black, and the road just disappeared. To my knowledge, I thought we just drove underneath it and it lasted only a few seconds. Under hypnotic regression, it seems that we were taken on board the craft. Garry was taken from the car first. For some reason I was led away, rather than carted away, that was under the first hypnotic regression that I got. I remember sitting in a metal chair with no clothes on and I was freezing. I definitely didn't have any clothes on. At that time, nothing seemed to happen to me. The aliens kept saying to me that it was Garry that they were wanting and not me, which I found rather strange sitting with no clothes on. A small alien, like a child, came around the side of the chair I was on, and touched me. I was cold at the time, but this thing was freezing, like cold blooded, that's the only way I can describe it. Like

31

rigor mortis, really cold. The room was really bright, and I felt that I was sitting for a long period of time. Nothing happened. Later on, I found myself sitting back in the car, no sign of Garry. I must have fell asleep, because there was a period of time that had passed because I got woken up with Garry being placed back in the car and slamming the door, and that was what happened in the first hypnotic regression. The second one, it seems that I was worked on myself. It seemed that something was put in my right eye. I'm still in this metal chair with nothing on. I remember them taking my clothes off this time and dressing me later on, but they were also working on my right eye. There was some kind of clamp over my right eye and there was some kind of red hot poker in the centre of my eye. I've no idea what they were doing, or what the purpose of this was".

(MR) "You mention in this regression that you saw, what can only be described as, for want of a better word, 'aliens'. Could you describe them in more detail to me".

(CW) "Basically some people call them 'greys'. Funny shaped head, big eyes. A lot of people make out that they are stone faced like a robotic face. But I found that they could pull features, frown, and their forehead would wrinkle and all the rest of it. I found that different. I saw a really old one, well it seemed old. It was wrinkly, really wrinkly. It was slightly different from the rest of them. Its head was more sort of caved in at the top, elongated and oval looking. I just got the impression that it was an old wise one, like a top gun, a leader, I don't know why. To my knowledge, there were three different sizes. I would say that the smallest one was around three feet. They were like soldiers, they are the ones that don't take any rubbish from you, if you know what I mean. Then you have the ones at six foot or over, which are the ones that deal with your mind. They are the ones that do all the damage to your mind".

(MR) "Now having a look around this object that you were inside. Could you describe what you saw when you were actually on this chair. Looking around you, what did you see, if anything"?

(CW) "Sitting in the chair, I could tell that the room was oval, and it had some kind of florescent lights built into the actual structure of the ceiling. They were like florescent lights but they weren't. I mean, they were just a pure beam behind some kind of glass or something. I remember a thing that was in my eye at the right hand side of me, floating, about five feet at the side of me. It didn't seem to be fixed to the wall, it just seemed to be floating there. It had different gadgets on it, I couldn't tell you what they were for though. I was looking for handles, switches for the lights but I couldn't see anything at all other than grey metallic walls".

(MR) "So there were nothing else at all in this room that you were in".

(CW) "No. I couldn't see anything. I don't know why I looked about. Under hypnosis, I seemed to be looking around a lot, looking for things like switches etc".

(MR) "Now during the regression of which I attended, at one point you sat up in the chair and turned your head and stared to the right. Later on, we learned that you were staring at one of these creatures, could you go ahead and tell me more about this"?

(CW) "Basically what it was, was that I heard a noise from behind me. I knew that there was some kind of room behind me. I heard noises, I can't describe these noises. I've tried, but I just can't seem to describe these noises. I've never heard the likes of them before. So I was trying to sit up and look round to see if I could see anything. Then this alien appeared from nowhere and it seemed to try and out stare me. It came across to me as if it was cross at me as I shouldn't be looking. So I just sat and sort of out stared it, and eventually I got the better of it".

33

The interviewed was curtailed at this point as Helen Walters, our hypnotherapist, had softly called Colin to come into the back room for a further hypnotic regression.

GARRY AND COLIN EXPLAIN TO MALCOLM, EXACTLY WHAT HAPPENED ON THE NIGHT IN QUESTION.

On the 8th of January 1995, I invited both Garry and Colin to my then home in Tullibody, Central Scotland. This was to film both men where I would go through step by step with them, their experience. It provided an opportunity for them to recall as much as they possibly could. This filmed interview, was recorded a few weeks after hypnosis was conducted on both Garry and Colin. Here is what transpired. First up, was Garry Wood,

Abbreviations: (MR) Malcolm Robinson. (GW) Garry Wood. (CW) Colin Wright.

(MR) "Garry you are aged 31 and reside in the city of Edinburgh. Could you take us back to the day in question, what sort of day was it?"

(GW) "Well I finished my work quite late that night and I was a bit dirty with the job I do. Then I went home, got washed and changed, and planned to drop a satellite system off at my friend's house, Katrina. Colin helped me put the equipment in the car. This was late, about the back of nine or ten o clock. Colin said to me was it not a bit late to drop this equipment down, and I said, well I promised to take it, so we will head off and get down there. So we put the equipment in the car and headed off to join the A70 towards Tarbrax. We were driving along the road, it was a clear night, the Moon was out, and it was really bright and it was quite cold. Colin and I were just chatting away then we went round this bend, and Colin pointed up in the air, and said, *"What's that"?* So I looked up, and floating about 20 or 30 feet above the road was, to me, a UFO.

34

It was a simple as that. I was panicking with fright, and I banged the button down on my driver's door. I didn't want to stop as we had went round a bend. I was too scared to stop. I couldn't pull off the road, the only way I could go, was to go underneath the object. So what I did was, I dropped a gear, floored the accelerator of the car to go underneath it. And just as we were going underneath it, a shimmering curtain fell, and just as the shimmering curtain fell, everything went black. It seemed that no time had passed at all. There was like a shunt from the back of the car. I'm not sure what side of the road we were on, I was just driving along the road like a mad man with the fright of what we saw. When we got to Ian and Katrina's, Colin went to undo his seat belt, and found that it was already undone. We ran out the car, then we were banging on my friend's door to tell them what happened. They actually came out to us saying, *"God what time is it, it's bloody late, its quarter to one, what are you doing here at this time"?* We had no recollection of the time that had passed by".

(MR) "Now Garry, I would like to take you back to that morning in question, and go through with you the day's events and also the events as you travelled down the road. Was the day just like any other day, a normal working day"?

(GW) "A normal working day".

(MR) "Nothing untoward then"?

(GW) "Nothing untoward. Just went in, done my work. Had a couple of things to do at night, I knew that I had the satellite system to drop off, so got changed and headed out".

(MR) "Now can you remember what time that you went for Colin"?

(GW) "Well I never actually went for Colin, Colin come round for me at the house, and I reckon it was late, the back of nine when Colin came round".

35

(MR) "And have you any idea of the time that you actually set off from Edinburgh to this journey to Tarbrax"?

(GW) "I couldn't be specific on that. I reckon the time was after ten, late after ten".

(MR) "Now you are travelling down this road, the A70. What was the scenery like, could you describe that particular stretch of road what it was like"?

(GW) "Well we were really talking, we weren't paying too much attention to the scenery. Colin was talking away and I was just keeping my eyes on the road. It was a nice clear night, the stars were out. Everything was quite clear. We were just talking away, not really interested in anything else".

(MR) "Now in an earlier conversation that I had with you, you said that there was music playing within the car. Was that a C.D. or an audio tape."

(GW) "I've got a C.D. player in the car, but I had the radio on, and it was down low, because we were trying to have a conversation with each other about things".

(MR) "Now about this conversation. What were you saying to each other in the car, can you remember"?

(GW) "Oh just general things about what we had been doing during the week, just the usual things people talk about".

(MR) "How often, if at all, had you travelled this stretch of road before. Was it a road that you had travelled before. Or was this the first time"?

(GW) "I've travelled the road a couple of times before, but its not a road that I particularly went along".

(MR) *(Author's note. I now showed Garry a map of Scotland, and confirmed with him the area where he saw this*

36

object) "Garry, could you now describe the location where you saw this object".

(GW) "Well Colin and I were travelling down the A70, through Currie, and through Balerno. We were travelling down in my Astra, doing About 40 miles per hour, it was a nice easy drive. We come along past Harperrig Reservoir then we came around one bend, and as we were coming round, passing the reservoir, we came to a small blind bend. Just as we entered the blind bend, Colin put his hand in the air, pointing up to what I could only describe as a UFO".

(MR) *(Author's note. At this point Garry allowed me to show a video that he had taken of the actual area where the incident occurred)* "The following text is spoken by Garry transcribed from that video. On the video Garry states: This is the bend that we were driving round at the time of the incident. It is a blind bend and there is a hill at the side to block any view. On the other side of the road there is a field. Loads of farm animals, a small burn and trees". *(Garry then speaks to the camera stating that this is where the incident occurred)*

(MR) "Now Garry, how long from your home should this journey to Tarbrax normally take"?

(GW) "Approximately 30 minutes".

(MR) "About 30 minutes. Now, moving on to when you actually saw this object. Who was first to actually see this object in the sky"?

(GW) "Well I was keeping my eye on the road for driving, and Colin, he actually noticed it, and pointed with his arm saying, *"What's that in the road"?* I looked up and panicked".

(MR) "Now what did you think? You know, your first thoughts of what this object could be. Did you think that it could be an aircraft in trouble, or a helicopter. What was your early impressions of this object"?

(GW) "Well I know that it was nothing that we have, like aeroplanes and helicopters that just float there in the middle of the road. And this thing was stationary, just floating 20 feet above the road".

(MR) "Now the actual description of this object. Could you go over again with me, how you saw that, describe it"?

(GW) "Well actually it all went kind of quick. Colin pointed up and made me aware. I looked at it, it was definitely a UFO. It was in three pieces, like in three segments. It had a dome top, then it had a middle body part to it, then a big body part to the bottom. It looked round, but I couldn't be specific to the exact shape of what the craft was for the simple reason that I only saw the craft from the front. I never saw the craft from underneath or from the back. For when we actually drove underneath the craft, everything went black".

(MR) "Now we have the actual drawings that you made of the object. *(Author's note. I showed the drawing of the object to the camera and also Garry's UFO sighting account form that he did for me. I also showed Colin Wright's drawing)* Garry, as far as you can recollect, what time was it when you saw this object, and can you be sure of the time"?

(GW) "I reckon the time was around 11:30/11:36. Because we left late, the back of ten by the time we loaded the satellite dish into the car, we took off some nuts and bolts which took about 15 to 20 minutes. Then the time that we headed off on our journey, I would say late, the back of eleven, half eleven".

(MR) "Now moving on again to the time that you saw this object. I'm quite interested to find out about this silver shimmering curtain effect. Did it resemble anything? How would you define these silver shimmering particles, was it like anything you have seen before"?

(GW) "I've never seen anything like it. But the thing that looks very similar to it, is a television station which is not properly on the station and you get like a shimmering effect off the telly. It looked similar to that. But the funny thing was, that the shimmering curtain was the exact width of the road and the UFO object was actually bigger. I would say the UFO object was around 30 odd feet. I know for a fact that the road was 22 feet, and the shimmering curtain was the exact width of the road".

(MR) "Now earlier on when you spoke, you said that initially you were quite frightened and alarmed by the viewing of this object whereby you quickly tried to speed under and get away from this object, is this correct"?

(GW) "Yes".

(MR) "OK. Now, you've encountered this silver shimmering curtain. Was this curtain dropping when you were going directly underneath it, or did it just come down around the car when you were driving towards the object"?

(GW) "Well, what actually happened was, I saw the UFO above the road, I was too scared to stop and I couldn't turn off the road. So, I saw a gap, and I went to accelerate under the gap. Just as we hit underneath the UFO, the shimmering curtain just appeared and then it was just total blackness".

(MR) "Total blackness! Now we spoke a short while ago about the music that was playing in the car. Did you notice any difference in the music playing in the car. Did the sound go up and down for instance, were there any crackling interference"? *(Author's note. I was aware that sometimes when a vehicle is in close proximity to a UFO, sometimes there can be electrical interference either on a car's radio or lights etc.)*

(GW) "No, there was nothing, I couldn't even see my friend Colin in the car. I couldn't see nothing. It was just like I was in total blackness, and there was nothing at all around me other than complete blackness".

(MR) "Now, did you have any bodily sensations other than the visual sensation that you couldn't see anything. How was your body at this time, were there any affects on that"?

(GW) "Not to my knowledge. I just remember blackness and then there was this big shunt from the back of the car and then we were on the road again".

(MR) "Now, how can we define this shunt. Was it quite a severe jolt to the vehicle".

(GW) "It was like something hitting the back of the vehicle".

(MR) "Was it like, more or less another car bashing into the back of your car"?

(GW) "Yes, very similar to that yes".

(MR) "Now you have gone underneath this object and then you find yourself further down the road. Could you talk to me about the events 'after' you had observed this object. So you are further down the road, you are further down the A70. What are you and Colin discussing at this point"?

(GW) "Well I'm driving like a mad man at the sight of seeing this UFO, and Colin was shouting and balling at me to slow down, saying you are going to kill us, slow down, you are driving like a maniac, slow the car down now. He actually got quite abusive about it because I was driving in a dangerous manner. Then when we got to our friends, Katrina and Ian, Colin went to undo his seat belt and found that his seat belt was already undone. He just sat there looking at me. We both left the car pretty quickly and we were looking about outside in case the object had followed us, and I was banging like a mad man on Katrina and Ian's door".

(MR) "Now Garry, when you finally arrived in Tarbrax, what happened when you turned up at the house with the satellite system, and can you remember the time when you arrived"?

(GW) "I cannot initially remember the time when we arrived there. Ian and Katrina actually came down and Katrina was in her dressing gown and said *"What are you doing here at this time? I thought you were not coming".* And from that, we sort of worked out that we actually got there a lot later than we should have done".

(MR) "Can you remember the actual time when you arrived in Tarbrax, were there a specific time that you can recollect seeing"?

(GW) "Well I cannot recollect the time, Katrina specifically said that the time was quarter to one".

(MR) "And what were Katrina's impressions of both you and Colin when you arrived"?

(GW) "Well we were both in a state of shock and panic. We were banging on the door, she opened the door quick, and we ran into the house and explained to her that we had seen a UFO. Her husband found it a bit funny and started laughing, which I would have done myself. Katrina could see that we were distressed and was worried about us. Colin sat at one end of the room and I sat at the other, and we both drew what we saw, and Katrina looked at the pictures and she said they are the same drawings. Colin was in shock with it and I was a bit distressed. And we sat there and had a cup of tea, and it was a good long while before we started our journey home. We were thinking of contacting the police but seeing something like that, they might think that you are not quite all there, you know".

(MR) "Now talking about your journey back to Edinburgh, do you remember that journey"?

(GW) "No. I cannot remember the journey back".

(MR) "You can't"!

(GW) "No, I can't remember the journey back home".

(MR) "That's quite unusual. OK when you did eventually arrive back home Garry, did you tell your wife what happened"?

(GW) "I woke up my wife and I told her what happened, and she seemed a little bit distressed about it but she was more interested in sleeping".

(MR) *(laughs)*

(GW) "So I had to run Colin home, and I was a bit worried in case this thing had followed us. So Kim's sister Liz, actually lives with us. I woke her up and asked her if she could come with me and run Colin home, and we explained what had happened and she said, *"I'll run him home then"*.

(MR) "Apart from your wife and your wife's sister, did you tell anyone else about what you saw from that day and over the next few days"?

(GW) "Well we told a lot of local people and a lot of people got to hear about it and we got a lot of ribbing and slagging about it. I actually tried to contact some places like BUFORA (The British UFO Research Association) and other places. I phoned them all and they just were just not interested".

(MR) "They weren't interested"!

(GW) "No, they didn't phone me back. I never got any messages from these places, they were moving offices at the time and I never heard anything from them. And I found your name in a book (SPI) I gave you a phone and you were good enough to phone me back that night and send me out some forms the next day, and I explained to you all of what happened and what had gone on".

(MR) "Now I spoke to you earlier Garry and you told me that you went back to that area and visited some houses nearby and you actually distributed leaflets through their doors, asking if they had seen an object in the sky".

(GW) "Yes. Well we had made up some leaflets on my computer saying that a UFO investigation team was investigating that area to find out if anyone had seen that object so we made up these leaflets and popped them through everyone's door in that area, which we never got any reply from".

(MR) "None at all"?

(GW) "None at all".

(MR) "So this was done in a desperate effort to see if perhaps if there were any other witnesses and find out if anyone had seen it".

(GW) "We dropped off 15 to 20 leaflets in every single house in the area and even went down by the reservoir".

(MR) "And nobody contacted you"?

(GW) "Nobody contacted us".

(MR) "Now I believe Garry, and correct me if I am wrong on this, that your health suffered not long after this episode. Would you like to discuss about your health matters in regards to what happened after this incident"?

(GW) "After the incident I started to get pretty bad headaches, all the time, it was real painful headaches. It got that bad, that at night I couldn't sleep, and I signed myself into the hospital, the Royal Infirmary in Edinburgh. And the doctors had a look at me, and they could see that I was in some form of distress. They did lumber punctures on me, they gave me brain scans. They basically tried to find out what was wrong with me. I think myself that it was to do with stress, but I'm not a doctor, they had other ideas on what it was. But we never really got to the bottom of it".

(MR) "So you never got an explanation as to what was causing these problems with the headaches then"?

(GW) "Not at the time no".

(MR) "Are you still attending your G.P. or going back for any check up's regarding this initial discomfort"?

(GW) "Well now I have a bad sleeping disorder. I went to my doctor to see about that. The doctor was quite good, I explained to him what actually happened, and the doctor looked at it from this point of view, and I was really surprised, I thought he would have laughed at me. He was quite understanding and took the matter quite seriously".

(MR) "Now I believe that you went back to the scene of this incident, and you found something. Would you like to tell me what that was"?

(GW) "We found markings on the grass at each end of the road. We were wondering to ourselves what it was. It was just odd, like charred burned markings. But equally on each side of the road. We were basically looking around the area to see if we could see find anything at all in connection with the UFO we saw. And we found these actual markings but we are not sure what they are, we've no idea".

(MR) "How long after this incident did you go back. Was this a good while after the event"?

(GW) "Yes, it was a good while uh huh".

*   *At this point in the interview. I held a piece of the charred grass up to the camera. I then stated to the camera.*

(MR) "Now we actually have a sample of a piece of grass that you took from the area which has some discolouration, or stains on the grass, which basically could be some kind of oil, which means, that it could have a natural answer to explain these stains in the grass. How do you feel about that Garry, do you think that there is a natural explanation for the discolouration of this sample"?

(GW) "It could well be, we just found it odd for there to be two big markings on the road at each end. There were actually 3 burn marks on one side, and 3 burn marks on the other. So we just took some of the grass and put it in a bag and basically sent it to you".

(MR) "These samples are still to be analysed, and SPI will shortly be sending them away to be tested. Now Garry, I believe that you also found something else at that area in question. Could you tell us what it was you found"?

(GW) "Well, it was one of the dusters out of the back of my car. I knew it was one of mine because its like a certain type of duster that I use. And I had about 15 or 20 of them in the back of my car, and it was unusual to find one outside. And I cannot remember throwing one out of the window I just don't know how it got there".

(MR) "Are you sure that this was your cloth"?

(GW) "Positive. Because its a specific make of cloth and its the only kind of cloth that I use".

(MR) "Now was this the same occasion when you went back and collected the grass sample"?

45

(GW) "No, it was a different time and occasion when I went back to look about the area to see if I could see anything".

(MR) "Do you find it surprising that you didn't find on the occasion you were there checking for the grass sample, that you didn't find the cloth then"?

(GW) "Well it was actually a wee bit further up the road. I didn't actually go that far up the road, but I did at that point, as I was trying to look further afield to see if I could see anything else, any other markings or things lying about".

(MR) "Now we spoke a moment ago about the trouble that you had after the encounter and that you were in hospital for a short period of time. Now I believe Garry that you are also having trouble sleeping. Would you like to tell me about that"?

(GW) "Well I keep waking up all the time during the night. I have trouble sleeping at night because I think that something is watching me. I especially keep waking up at twenty past three in the morning and I don't know why. And I find myself running out the room. I seem to be wanting to get away from the room and turn the lights on all the time. I've actually moved house now, but where I used to stay, at one point I was knocking on the door about 4 or 5 in the morning and I wasn't aware of it, and my wife opened the door and I was standing at the door in my underpants. I don't know how I got outside, or where I was or what I was doing".

(MR) "The question must be asked, and that is, have you a problem with sleep walking"?

(GW) "Not to my knowledge. I don't think I sleep walk. Its unusual for me to open doors, and go outside somewhere and then bang on the door to get in. I mean all I remember was waking up outside the stair door and then banging the door like mad to get back into the house because I was so embarrassed as to how I was dressed in case anybody saw me. I don't know how I got outside".

46

(MR) "Now what time Garry do you go to your bed normally, for instance what time over this past few weeks have you gone to bed"?

(GW) "The back of three in the morning. I never go to my bed early now".

(MR) "You mentioned about the time as three twenty. Do you find yourself trying to get to sleep after this three twenty"?

(GW) "Usually yes, that's the truth. I try and avoid the time and go to sleep after it. Sometimes I might go to bed early, but I wake up at that time".

(MR) "When was the last time that you went to bed early, and for instance, did you wake up at three twenty"?

(GW) "Sometimes when I go to bed early it's alright. Then when I wake up at three twenty it will happen for the next few days and then it stops again. And then another time it will happen again, I start waking up at three twenty".

(MR) "Now when you do wake up at three twenty, obviously you are waking up out of a sleep. What can you recollect when you wake up, do you get dream imagery coming in. Or is it just a case of you wake up at this time? Do you have any problems perhaps sweating? I mean, how do you feel when you wake up at three twenty"?

(GW) "Well waking up at three twenty its like I am dreaming. I know, because I am actually out of the bed. I was doing something one night, it was that bad, the shuffling about and whatever, it woke my wife up, and she actually threw a lid at me saying, what the hell are you playing at, get in the bloody bed. She was pretty upset about it. And from there, she is starting to get used to this, which is of me waking up at this time of the morning and getting up and turning lights on and all that".

(MR) "Now Garry, its obvious to me and my colleagues at SPI, that you are very keen to find out what happened to you on the night in question. How keen,

would you say you were to find out, to get an answer as to what happened to you"?

(GW) "I would like to know what's going on. Before all this I was an ordinary guy just living a normal life, and from what I've seen, its upset my wife severely. I now realise that there are more things that meet the eye and I am interested to find out what happened to me and why".

(MR) "Does your wife share your quest to find out what happened to you. Is she supportive to you"?

(GW) "My wife thinks that I should drop this as it worries her. She thinks that it is a bad idea that I continue with this and that I should just put it behind me and let it go, which I cannot".

(MR) "Now is there any aspect of this incident Garry that I haven't mentioned and which you might like to expand on before we move onto the hypnosis evidence".

(GW) "No, there is nothing else. All I would like to say is that I did see a UFO, clear as day. It was a clear night and I know what I saw, and it was a UFO".

(MR) "Now who was it Garry that suggested that you should have hypnotic regression to perhaps unlock any hidden memories of that particular night"?

(GW) "Well after we had filled out your UFO report forms we gave you everything, and told you about the story. It was yourself who said, do you think that there is more to this than meets the eye. And you thought that hypnotic regression might be a good key factor".

(MR) "And were you quite happy to go ahead with this hypnotic regression"?

(GW) "Oh yes, definitely to see if I could find out anything and why it had happened".

(MR) "Now just before we move onto discuss the hypnosis, one of the questions which I failed to ask earlier, was just after this initial incident, the sighting of this object, you found yourself desperate for an answer. Did you read at all, any books or magazines on UFOs"?

(GW) "I did. I went out and bought some books to try and find out about UFOs and what was going on. Before that, I had never really given UFOs a thought, it was one of the things that I never thought about. When I read about these things in the paper I used to laugh at these people, and now, well the jokes on me eh"!

(MR) "OK so you were quite happy for the hypnosis"?

(GW) "I was just trying to find out anything I could about the UFO phenomenon".

(MR) "Now, about these books. Were there any books on abductions that you read? We have plenty books on UFO sightings, but any books on abductions"?

(GW) "Some of them had paragraphs and bits in them about abductions and when you buy a book it has all the various packages in it".

(MR) "You realise obviously that this is a question that I must ask? OK so you were very happy to be subjected to hypnosis along with Colin Wright who agreed as well. And we used, as you know, a qualified hypnotherapist, a lady called Helen Walters. Helen as you know, is also SPI's psychic and we take her on various cases. She is a qualified hypnotherapist and we took you and Colin over to her home to put you and

49

Colin under hypnosis, to see if we could find any answers to this. Now what can you remember Garry from that very first night".

(GW) "The first night when I went up for the hypnosis, I was a bit worried. She asked me questions for two hours, all different questions. Everything, about my age, times places, basically everything. Then, later on after that, she started the hypnotic regression procedure on me. And she worked through dates, going backwards and forwards through that month. And then she said to me that there was something to do with a certain date, and I just started to cry, I couldn't control myself, I was just in an awful state. The day was the 17th, and I had a lot of trouble dealing with that date, as if something had obviously happened to me. So she pushed me a bit further into the date on the 17th, and it felt like my whole body was locking up. I could see images around the car. I couldn't see clear at that point, but I was terrified. I know that I couldn't control myself, because I was crying and I tried to stop crying. It's a funny weird sensation hypnosis".

(MR) "Yes I have been put under myself, but not like that. It was a stage hypnotist, but I can agree with you on that, its a weird sensation".

(GW) "She asked me if I had been hypnotised before and I explained to her that I had never been hypnotised before".

(MR) "So this was your first time"?

(GW) "Yes, this was my first time".

(MR) "You mentioned about something moving around the car".

(GW) "I saw three vague images in front of the car, and it was like my whole body was pulling inside itself. All my muscles and everything went all tight and were hurting me. I was terrified. I couldn't move, and I was really crying and worried that I just couldn't move".

Author's Note: In Yvonne R. Smith's book, Chosen, (Recollections of Abductions Through Hynotherapy) Bachstage Entertainment 2008. USA. She gives the account of one UFO Abductee by the name of Laci, who, after coming out of hypnosis, stated to Yvonne, that she was feeling pain in her abdomen. Yvonne went on to state that one of her clients continued to feel pain in her legs months after her regressive sessions. Was Garry feeling the pain of some procedure that was done to him?

(MR) "Continuing on with the hypnotic regression sessions. How many have you had since that first one"?

(GW) "I would say five or six now".

(MR) "Now just to discuss with you Garry about all these sessions in general, obviously there is information that has been provided through hypnosis. So through this hypnotic regression, can you piece together for me, the events from where you were sitting in the car. So this is now under hypnosis. What do you remember from the car on-wards".

(GW) "I can remember from the car on-wards, to the shimmering curtain and then blackness, and then the whole scene sort of changes. I don't know if I am on something, or where I am. I haven't a clue where I am, just that I am somewhere, I know that. And I know that I am lying down, and I know that there are things going around me. I can see like entities moving about very odd shaped ugly looking entities doing things round about me. I looked for Colin, and apart from being in the car, I can't seem to find Colin anywhere at all and that's worrying me as well".

(MR) "And this is at the point outside the car"?

(GW) "Well I know that I am not in the car, I know that. I don't know where I am. But I know that I am in some kind of room somewhere, and there are creatures moving about doing things, definitely. The things that I have seen I couldn't have picked up in a book, they were terrifying me".

(MR) "Initially when we spoke before about this initial recollection that you had under hypnosis. Your first impression was, that you saw three or four different images or entities, something 'peeking behind something', how was that"?

(GW) "I reckon I saw three different images all together. I saw these great big ones they were about five to six feet high, I'm not entirely sure. I know they are big with long necks, and they are sort of white translucent. And I saw smaller ones, and they were a grey colour. And I also saw, it's funny, I saw these things, like working things over to my right hand side. And I couldn't see any arms, it was just like they were moving about but they had no arms. But the two other creatures, the small ones and the big ones, they had arms and limbs. I couldn't see hands, it was hard to describe what they were like, they had three fingers and they were really really long, their arms were really really long. It was like skin and bone and they were translucent".

(MR) "In a moment, I will be showing the drawings of these creatures (call them what you will) that you and Colin drew for SPI, but before that, let's first of all talk about the smaller entities. Describe again for me, the height, the shape, the skin texture etc".

(GW) "They were quite small. They were about two and a half to three feet high, and they seemed to be doing all the work, moving about doing things all the time. The bigger ones, seemed to be the ones that were just looking at us, well just me, as I couldn't see Colin at this point, they were doing things to me, but I've no idea what was happening or what they were doing to me. Something was happening to my leg, and they were doing things to other parts of me and my chest, but I have no idea what they were doing I just saw things coming away from my chest".

(MR) "We also discussed earlier before this interview, about a strange kind of buzzing sound that you had felt in your ear. Are you any idea what that was"?

(GW) "At one time I felt I couldn't move. I know that under hypnosis Helen was telling me to get up out of the chair, and I just couldn't get up out of the chair. I couldn't move at all. And it was like something was in my ear, and took up the whole width of my ear, and it was like a humming noise all the time, and it got really really loud and it got that loud that I couldn't hear Helen speaking any more I could just hear this severe noise in my head".

(MR) "Was this noise similar to anything else that you might have heard before"?

(GW) "It was just a humming noise going high and low, high and low all the time".

(MR) "Could it be something like the noise of a hand drill, something like that"?

(GW) "No it was nothing like the noise of a hand drill. I work with a lot of tools in my job, and its not like a noise that I have really heard before. It was just basically a loud humming noise".

(MR) "And what ear was that"?

(GW) "It was in my left ear".

(MR) "OK, going back again to these small creatures. You have mentioned about them being translucent, what was the actual colour of these entities"?

(GW) "The big ones seemed to be a more lighter colour than the small ones. They looked sort of different to me. When I was looking at one of them then looking at another, I was saying to myself, is that what I'm seeing, or is that what I'm seeing. Because I'm just expecting to see just the one thing and I just don't know where all these things are coming from. I'm seeing like this other thing doing something, then this other one, and there were lots of activity, and I was having trouble with it. And I saw this really old looking thing, its face was like map contours, and it came right up to me, and was looking all around me and then it just went away. I was seeing all these different things and I was starting to wonder myself".

(MR) "Now I take it that these creatures touched you to some degree on various parts of your body. If you can remember, what was that touch like, was it a cool touch, a cold touch, or a warm touch"?

(GW) "When I was under hypnosis, for some reason I felt freezing cold. I didn't seem to feel anything touching me because my body felt that it was all numb and I can't move, so I am not really aware to be honest with you of anything touching me. I seen them actually doing things to me, but as for like touch, I couldn't feel any touch".

(MR) "Were you lying down or standing up"?

(GW) "To my knowledge I was lying down"

(MR) "You were lying down". Did you look at yourself, and if so, did you have your clothes on"?

(GW) "At one point I was moving, I don't know why. Under hypnosis you seem to be more aware, and I could feel myself lifting off the chair, and I was like, what am I doing, why am I getting up? And I felt my whole body starting to raise off the chair. Its like I was being controlled, and when I was up in the air, I am positive that I saw my foot and my leg, and I had no shoes or clothes on my leg at that point, and that was the only time that basically I really saw myself up to now".

(MR) "Now when you found yourself in this room or whatever it was, of which we will come to in a moment. Were there any verbal communication to you from these entities? Did you know what they required of 'you'? Was anything said"?

(GW) "To my knowledge yes. There were no speaking involved. I'm not sure what you call it, telepathy or what, I don't know what it was. I just seemed to know what they were saying, it just came to me, you just seemed to know. I know that one of them was explaining to me, it's funny, because I never thought about it at the time, it said to me, that 'they' have a life as well, and 'they' have their up's and down's, not like mine and what's got to be done has got to be done".

(MR) "And were you angry or surprised at this"?

(GW) "I found it kind of funny, because I never once in my life thought of it in that way. I always thought UFOs and aliens, and that's it. My mind never seemed to go any further than that until under hypnosis, and now I've found a different outlook on it altogether, I can see it differently".

(MR) "OK, this room. Or this area, is it clear to you in your mind's eye right now, and if you can, can you just go through and tell me what you saw, if anything, in that room"?

(GW) "I can go back into my mind easy and pick out the pictures of the things that I saw yes. It's basically a room, there are things in the room, I'm not sure what they are, I don't know, its hard to describe. I mean how can you describe something that you don't know what it is, to describe what it is, the basic colours and things like that. I'm more concerned with these entities that are walking about because my eyes are trained on them all the time and wondering what's going on and worried trying to work out what the reason is if they are going to let me go or what's going to happen to me. I'm just basically worried to death. And they kept saying, *"It's alright, don't worry"*. But I've still not come to that decision of what the reason is, or what's happening".

(MR) "You mentioned about telepathy, now this has been reported by other witnesses. Now was it a fatherly figure voice, or was it a young voice? Was it a strong voice regarding these words that were coming into your head, or was it a feminine voice coming into your head"?

(GW) "It wasn't words. The words were coming from me. I was just thinking and the words were my own thoughts, you know when you think to yourself"?

(MR) "Yes"

(GW) "Well I could just think, and the words were there. It was just all coming out like that. There was concern in the talk, I know that. But when it was put into my mind and I was thinking of it, I knew that the words were coming from me, but not from me, it's hard to explain. But there was a lot of concern the way it was talking. Saying, "Don't Worry, it's OK" like it was reassuring me all the time".

(MR) "Now, what about the temperature in this room, was it warm, was it cold"?

(GW) "It was quite cold".

(MR) "Now, did you see any signs of visible interior lighting within this room"?

(GW) "I could see an archway to the right of me. And it was really bright, really really bright. It was brighter than the room I was in. The room I was in was bright, but not as bright as the room that I could see ahead. The archway was just to my right hand side. And there was something going on in there, but I've no idea what. I saw things walking towards me then going back again".

(MR) "Was this a bright white light or was it a coloured light"?

(GW) "To me it was a bright white light".

(MR) "Now moving on again to these wee fellas. How did they walk. If you were lying on this bed and you looked around and saw them coming and going. Did they walk in any peculiar manner or anything like that"?

(GW) "I only saw one walking, and it did walk kinda funny. I find it hard to explain. It seemed in a hurry, as it walked up to one of those big things and it went away in a rush. It's difficult to explain".

(MR) "You mentioned about the thoughts coming into your head. Did you pick up any thoughts between the small entities and the larger ones while you were lying on that bed. Did you know what they were saying to each other, or did you not get that much"?

(GW) "I never got that much. I could only sort of understand these big ones when they were looking down and directing on what was what"?

(MR) "How close were these bigger entities to you, and I'm talking about coming to your face, how far away were they"?

(GW) "One came right up to my face and I would say it was two or three inches away from my face. That was the one that was explaining everything to me, but I didn't understand what it was explaining".

(MR) "So you are not quite sure what it was trying to say"?

(GW) "Well under the regression that we are doing just now, we are trying to piece it together, we have never questioned what's going on or that".

(MR) "Yes, we are still trying to reach that point, that's very true. There are certain elements of this case which hopefully will provide answers. OK, this entity which is two to three inches from your face, describe for me Garry, how it looked. Its eyes, its nose, its ears, the face".

(GW) "Its eyes seemed to be the thing that your eyes are trained on, you don't seem to be looking at the rest of it. This is the thing, because I want to see the face clear as day but you seem to focus on their eyes, and that's the only thing you seem to pay attention to".

(MR) "What colour were the eyes of this entity"?

(GW) "The eyes were dark black".

(MR) "Was it a shiny black, or a dull black or......"

(GW) "It seemed a shiny black".

(MR) "Did there appear to be any membrane, ie, something resembling an eyelid which came down over its eye, or was it constantly just a black eye you saw"?

(GW) "It was pulling a facial expression, but I was more concentrating on its eyes than the rest of it. I was worried and panicking and was too concerned about other things to be worried about looking all around it. I was just trained on its eyes, and that was that"

(MR) "Yes, I understand. Do you feel that it was trying to impart some knowledge or some communication by being that close to you, that there was a purpose being served there, but you are not quite sure what that was"?

(GW) "Well I was trying to explain to it, I was trying to communicate with it, like, *'Why have you got me here, let me go' 'I've got a wife and kids and I have an important job, I don't want to be here, what's happening'?* To me it was just like a scary monster. Like something I have never seen before, and I was just worried to death about it. And it was trying to reassure me that it was OK, but I thought that they were going to take me away and not let me come back again, that's what I thought".

(MR) "Now your a fit man Garry, and a healthy chap, were there any inwardly signs of anger from you. I mean, you are in an environment in a situation which is totally out of your control. Did you feel that at any point that I am going to do something here, if I can do something then I'm going to do something".

(GW) "If I could have done anything at the time I would have done it. If I had seen anything coming at me, and I had the free will to do something, I would have had a go at it and destroyed whatever it was, no matter what it was, then run away definitely. The fact was that I couldn't move, and I couldn't do anything. I was powerless and totally helpless, so you haven't got a lot of choice in the matter at what's happening. At one point I was raging and annoyed that bits of my body, my head, and my whole body, were moving and I had no control over what I was doing. And I don't know if I was raging because of that, or raging at it, or it was making me feel like that, I've no idea, I'll never know".

(MR) "Were you being held down by any restraints on this table"?

(GW) "To my knowledge, I couldn't feel any restraints around me, I just couldn't move. The only movement that I could make, was movement against my will. I was moving against my will".

(MR) "Now again, when we spoke earlier, you mentioned about these small creatures and also these taller ones. There was also someone/thing else that looked as if it was in control of the situation, a type of elderly figure. In your own words, how would you describe this"?

(GW) "Brown looking alien, it was sort of in between sizes of them all. It was really really old, and it seemed to come round as if it was somebody in charge. And it had a look here, and a look there, then it went away. It sort of looked up and down at me. It was horrible looking and I was really scared".

(MR) *(Author's note. At this point I showed a drawing of one of these creatures that Garry had drawn for SPI and asked him to discuss it more fully with me)*

(GW) "This was only the brown coloured one there. It looked very old. It had like wrinkles all over itself, like map contours. I only ever saw that one entity, and it looked all over me and just went away. It really scared me".

(MR) "Do you think that in some manner or means, that it was in charge of the situation or not"?

(GW) "It looked like to me that it was in charge. But I wasn't aware of what was going on, but it just looked very important".

(MR) "And this one did not look like the smaller or larger ones"?

(GW) "It looked slightly similar to one of the larger ones, but it didn't look like the smaller ones, the ones with the rounded heads".

(MR) "Was this mainly because of the colour and the actual way the skin texture, if we can call it that, was on this one"?

(GW) "Yes. With a lot of them, their skin looked really tight, like tight translucent skin over bone. On this one though, the skin seemed to be like wrinkled, like loads of map contours piling up on each other. And they were all around it's face, neck and body".

(MR) "Now Garry, talk to me about this other drawing that I have in front of me. What does this represent"?

(GW) "This object here, *(Author's note, I held up a drawing of a black lens shaped device free floating above Garry's head)* I have no idea what it is. I was really concentrating on it. It was making a whooshing noise and it was folding inside itself, like something was going around in it. It was just making this funny noise and it had all my attention. But the noise and the way it moved was totally and absolutely perfect. It was an absolute perfect movement. And as I was watching this, I just saw this arm appearing, coming across my chest and coming to my head. It frightened me that much, that I actually jumped out of the hypnotic regression that I was under".

(MR) "The colour of this arm that fell on your chest, did it have any specific colour"?

(GW) "It never fell on my chest, it came across my chest slowly. It was whitey grey translucent, and the skin was tight over bone. I could actually see it coming towards my eyes and at that point it frightened me and I jumped out of the regression".

(MR) *(Author's note. At this point I showed Garry another one of his drawings that he did for SPI, and asked him to explain in greater detail. The drawing showed one of these small creatures lifting itself out of a hole, or a pool of gel! Here is what Garry said)*

(GW) "I know that I am lying down and I cannot move, but my eyes were trained over to the right hand side. I saw something bobbing about. I'm not sure if this was a pool, like a pool of something or a hole, and I saw something bobbing up and down. So I trained my eyes across looking at it, and this entity started to appear out of this hole. As it appeared out from this hole. There was a device to the right of me, and I could hear a turning motor noise, so my eyes looked across here *(Author's note, Garry points at a section of the drawing)* I saw this round cylinder type of device, and this flap on it started to open up towards my head. So I was looking at that, then looking at that. Then I was looking back at this device again, and it had two eye things on the end. It was like when this creature or entity came out the pool thing, this device started to work. And as this flap eventually started to lift right up. I jumped out of the regression again, something happened, but I am not sure what".

(MR) "Now this is you lying on this bed or whatever it was. Could you move any parts of your body, were you free to move your arms, your legs"?

(GW) "I know my eyes were moving, I know that. I think my head was slightly to the one side. I wasn't aware of any head movements, but I know I was really straining my eyes looking round about me at what was happening. But I could see that device to the right of me clear as day and this entity coming out of this pool, clear as day and it really frightened me".

(MR) "Now this is another drawing of this particular device. Could you tell me any more about what you felt this was or if it served any purpose at all"?

(GW) "It was to the right hand side of my head. I'm not sure what it was. I know that this actual device spun on its axis and came round towards me and had this flap which started to slowly lift up towards my head. The minute the actual flap was at head level with me, I actually jumped out of hypnosis. But I know that the actual object was say, two and a half, to three feet big, and I reckon a foot to a foot and a half wide. I'm not sure what these eye light things are that are on the panel *(Author's note. Garry pointed to what appeared to be two small red led lights of the tip of the flap that rose up from the body of this object)* but I know that they really frightened me".

(MR) "Was it making any noise at all"?

(GW) "It gave off to me, like a sort of motor noise of something actually turning. It's hard to describe the noise but you could actually hear the thing turning".

(MR) "What colour was this, did it have any specific colour"?

(GW) It was like a grey, yellowy colour, and that's what I saw, I can only tell you what I saw. I want to tell you the truth of what I saw. It just spun on its axis, and then it stopped, and then this flap started to slowly lift up to my head, at the same time that the entity was coming out of the pool. When this thing actually came to head level it done 'something', and I actually jumped out of hypnosis again".

(MR) "Were there any small lights attached to this device that you saw, or was it just basically as you described".

(GW) "As described. I didn't notice any lights on it. It was doing something, but I came out of hypnosis".

(MR) "Are we saying here, that this device was free floating, or was it attached to anything"?

(GW) "It seemed to me like it was on the floor. I don't think that it was free floating because I heard the turning noise in the flap, but I couldn't actually see the floor. I basically saw it up to that point, but with it actually turning and it being fixed, I presume it was on the floor".

(MR) "Now the drawing that we are currently looking at, was drawn at your last hypnotic regression which was just over a week ago. Could you tell us something about this drawing Garry"?

(GW) . "Well with this drawing here, I saw all this happening at the same time. These two creatures *(Author's note. Garry points at the drawing)* I saw them standing at the bottom of whatever it is that I am lying on. I'm not sure what I am lying on. I'm not aware of what it is, it looks like to me just a table. And this big creature on the right hand side, is holding an object which is pulsing now and again, and it seems as if its controlling me, because my head was moving about all ways. I was moving my head back and forward and from side to side. The thing that I didn't expect to see, was when my head was turning from side to side, I saw a female sitting on the ground, and she looked very distressed. She had brown, mousy brown shaggy hair, with like blond highlights on it. She actually looked round at me. She looked like she was crying, and she was shivering with the cold. Her arms were clasped around the rest of her body, she was trying to hide or cover herself. I could see her back, her spine which was protruding out of her back, I could see all that. She was really distressed and worried".

(MR) "How old roughly, would you say she was Garry"?

(GW) "I don't know exactly how old she was, it just came into my mind that she was like, just 22, 23 years old. I don't even know her name. She looked right at me though".

(MR) "Did she say anything at all to you".

(GW) "To my knowledge, no, she didn't speak any words or nothing. She looked really distressed. This actual drawing I saw all at the one time as it was happening. I saw these two entities and this female, she was actually sitting on the ground. The only reason I saw her, was because I was being controlled somehow or I don't think I would even have seen her, but it was the last thing in the world that I expected to see which was a female sitting on the ground distressed like that. I know to the right of me was a very bright room with that bright light again. These two creatures here *(Author's note, Garry points to the two creatures on the drawing)* well this one here, seemed to be doing everything and the other one was watching. At one point this other smaller entity walked up to the two, that's when I said earlier about the one walking which had difficulty in walking and walked away again. But this female here, was really distressed and scared".

(MR) "Now the entity on the right, has in its hands, an orange kind of diamond shaped object whatever its purpose may be. Did it move this object towards you, and if so, did it move to any part of your body, or was it just the way its depicted here in the drawing that its just stationary"?

(GW) "It was moving the object about, but it never moved it to any part of my body at any time at all. It just flashed now and again. Just before this drawing, when I was lying down before I was being controlled, I saw two things coming away from my chest. One of the objects was like a container of some form, I've no idea what it was, and the other object was a round object which lifted away. And then, this entity here, I think was controlling me, and it was like my head was moving from side to side, up and down, and I was getting really really annoyed. I was very angry because I couldn't understand why I was moving when I didn't want to move".

(MR) "And were there any communication from them to you, again in your head, were they saying anything to you".

(GW) "At that point under hypnosis I don't have any recollection of anything being said to me. The only worry in my mind, was this female here, she was really distressed and I was panicking with worry for her. It was just like seeing her crying I was really worried and angry with what was going on".

(MR) "Now talking about this woman. Did she look European, did she look oriental, or did she look like you and I"?

(GW) "Well, she had this very light permed hair which I would think that she was somebody of this time, or modern day. I saw her face clear as day, I think that if I saw her again, I would recognise her. She had a very slight tan. From where she was, or what origin, I've no idea. She just looked like to me, a normal girl who had a slight tan, mousy brown shaggy permed hair with blond highlights in it and she was really distressed, really worried".

(MR) "It was soon after this that you came out of hypnosis again".

(GW) "Well Helen actually took me out of hypnosis at that time".

(MR) "Right OK. Garry, thanks for the moment for reliving these memories for me. I really appreciate it".

(GW) "Your welcome".

TRANSCRIPT FROM A VIDEO INTERVIEW WITH COLIN WRIGHT. 8th JANUARY 1995, AT MY FORMER HOME IN TULLIBODY CENTRAL SCOTLAND

Abbreviations (MR) Malcolm Robinson. (CW) Colin Wright

(MR) "This is the 8th of January 1995, I have with me this afternoon, Colin Wright, one of the gentlemen who had a strange experience on the A70 back in August of 1992. Now Colin, you are here today to talk to me specifically about the strange experience that you had. So can I first of all, take you back to the actual morning in question, right from when you got up out of bed, what did you do".

(CW) "Got dressed, had a shower, not really much to tell you".

(MR) "So it was basically it was just an ordinary day"?

(CW) "An ordinary day yes".

(MR) "Now what was the reason for your journey to Tarbrax"?

(CW) "To take a satellite system to Garry's friends in Tarbrax and fix it for them to keep".

(MR) "Now do you remember the actual time when you left the house".

(CW) "The back of nine".

(MR) "Do you have an exact time"?

(CW) "About 20 past nine"

(MR) "And what was your actual journey like to Tarbrax"?

(CW) "It was a nice clear night and I was just talking to Garry about things in general".

(MR) "And what was the scenery like on this particular route"?

(CW) "Just fields, and a couple of farm houses, just fields and hills for miles".

(MR) "Were there much traffic on that night in question"?

(CW) "No, it was quiet"

(MR) "It was quiet!"?

(CW) "Quiet"

(MR) "Now I believe that there was music playing in the car, was it a CD or cassette".

(CW) "It was a CD and it was down low"

(MR) "What was the weather like on that night"?

(CW) "It was a clear crisp night, touch of frost but clear"

(MR) "Was there much cloud in the sky"?

(CW) "No cloud at all, no".

(MR) "No cloud as far as you can remember"?

(CW) "It was all clear sky, just the stars"

(MR) "Now how often have you travelled this stretch of road, was it a stretch of road that you have travelled many times before, or occasionally"?

(CW) "I think this was the second time".

(MR) "Now, have you travelled this road with Garry before, or have you travelled this road yourself"?

(CW) "It was with Garry".

(MR) "And that particular journey with Garry, how many months or years was it before this particular night, that you had the strange experience on the road with Garry".

(CW) "About a month before".

(MR) "A month before this event"?

(CW) "Yes".

(MR) "Now how long from Garry's house to Tarbrax do you think that this journey should normally take, any idea of the time limit involved to get from point A to point B

(CW) "Not long, 30 minutes, half an hour, it depends on how quiet the road is".

(MR) "And of course, how fast you, or in this case, Garry was driving. OK, now we have established the fact that this was just a normal journey to deliver a satellite system. Now who was first to see this strange object in the sky, and how did this come about".

(CW) "It was me, myself. We went round a bend, and it just caught my eye above the road. Garry was busy driving, he was concentrating on driving, and I was looking about and I saw it first and I pointed it out to Garry".

(MR) "And could you describe for me as best as you can, the shape and colour, if colour was there, and any lights? Indeed, anything at all about this object. What did it look like"?

(CW) "It looked like a UFO. It had three tiers to it. It was all blacked out, it was like a silhouette, there were no lights, it happened that quick, I never had much chance to have a proper look at it. It was just there, and we were under it".

(MR) "Now where was this object in proximity to the road"?

(CW) "It was straight above, about 20 feet above the car, right in front of us as we went round the bend".

(MR) "And at this point in time, roughly how many yards from the car to this object would you say you were when you first noticed this, how much of a distance are we talking about"?

(CW) "It was practically right in front of us as we went round the bend it was there".

(MR) "Had you any idea or impression that it could have been some form of aircraft or a helicopter. I mean, what did you think it was"?

(CW) "I had never seen anything like this before. I didn't know what it was".

(MR) "How would you describe your feelings when you saw this. Were you excited, frightened, nervous, what state of mind were you in? What did you feel when you saw this object, even if it was a threat"?

(CW) "I was amazed more than anything. Seeing something that I had never seen before. I didn't have time to be scared".

(MR) "Now you said there that you informed Garry about this object. I take it that Garry hadn't initially saw this? What was Garry's reaction when you pointed out this object to him, what did he say"?

(CW) "I think he swore, then put the foot down and tried to get underneath it and get away as quick as possible".

(MR) "OK. Now you have sighted this object in the sky, the car is travelling at speed. How fast would you say the car was travelling at this point considering that you are approaching a blind bend"?

(CW) "Well it was a pretty tight bend, probably 30 to 35 miles per hour"

(MR) "OK, so you have gone round this blind bend. Tell me what happened next as you approached this object".

(CW) "As I said, Garry tried to go underneath it, and it threw some kind of curtain down on the road as we tried to go underneath it, and then everything just disappeared. Sound the lot".

(MR) "Now you say disappeared, could you be a bit more clearer on that. How did things disappear"?

(CW) "It was like we went into a black hole I suppose. There was just nothing there. No road, no surrounding area, no fields. Nothing, I couldn't even see Garry".

(MR) "You couldn't see Garry"?

(CW) "I couldn't see Garry"

(MR) "You couldn't see the interior of the car"?

(CW) "Nothing"

(MR) "Now we mentioned the fact that it was the back of nine when you left the house, have you any idea or speculation at what time it was when you encountered this object above the road, roughly"? *(Author's note. It was actually the back of 11)*

(CW) "I didn't really look at the time. I didn't expect something like this to happen to you. You don't pay attention to the time"

(MR) "How long did this effect last for, when you entered this shimmering curtain like effect and then this blackness. How long did it seem to you that you were in blackness for"?

(CW) "Just seconds".

(MR) "Seconds"

(CW) "Yes just seconds".

(MR) "Could you tell me what happened once you came out of this blackness. What was the first thing you saw. Were

71

you looking directly ahead or were you looking to your left or was you looking to your right"

(CW) "Just a big banging coming from the back end of the car, banging onto the road, then I noticed that Garry was on the wrong side of the road".

(MR) "There was a bang"?

(CW) "A banging from the back end yes, as the car hit the road's surface".

(MR) "Did the car go into a skid, or was erratic when you regained your vision so to speak".

(CW) "No, just that the car was on the wrong side of the road. We went in on the left, and came out on the right".

(MR) "Now, you are on the wrong side of the road, your vision is back. How did you feel bodily. How would you say you were feeling at that point in time"?

(CW) "Eh, just confused as to what had happened for a few seconds till Garry was on the wrong side of the road. Nothing made sense".

(MR) "Did you feel that you had to perhaps stop and say, *"Well what was that"?* I mean, was there any time when everything came back. Did it go through your mind to say that we must stop the car, how did you feel about that"?

(CW) "Well Garry was just too scared, and had put the foot down and drove away up the road as fast as he could. The car was going everywhere he could have wrote the car off. We never thought about looking back".

(MR) "But did you want to stop, did you consider stopping, or were you just in the same frame of mind as Garry".

(CW) "I was just confused".

(MR) "Did you look and turn round and look through the rear window of the car".

(CW) "No"

(MR) "You never looked back"?

(CW) "No"

(MR) "Did you notice anything at all, further down the road".

(CW) "Nothing at all, no, it was just a case of getting to Tarbrax as fast as we could".

(MR) "So you have now entered Tarbrax, you've got to your destination. What happened when you turned up at your destination, can you remember as far as you can recollect"?

(CW) "We just basically got out of the car as quickly as possible. I went to take my seat belt off but it was already off".

(MR) "It was off"?

(CW) "Yes"

(MR) "Are you sure about this Colin"?

(CW) "Garry is a great driver and you have to wear a seat belt"

(MR) "Because this is important. You had your seat belt....."

(CW) "I definitely had it on yes"

(MR) "I take it that it was a chest one and not a waist one"?

(CW) "A chest one yes"

(MR) "So is the seat belt easy to get on and off. You know, some seat belts with any jolts will free themselves. Was it a tight lock"?

(CW) "Tight locking grip yes".

(MR) "And were you surprised at this, that your seat belt was unbuckled"?

(CW) "I was yes"

(MR) "Did you mention this fact to Garry"?

(CW) "I didn't have to say anything, he saw my reaction but didn't say anything. I think he was just as surprised as I was".

(MR) "Did you notice if Garry had his seat belt on or off at that point when you were ready to stop the car".

(CW) "He always wears his over his shoulder".

(MR) "OK. Now at this point in time, you have got out of the car, your going to drop this satellite system off. Talk to me again about what happened when you knocked on the door".

(CW) "Basically we got them out of their beds, which was a surprise as we had left early enough. Garry was still excited as to what he saw. I don't think I said anything, I was just numb. Basically we just told them what had happened".

(MR) "Did the householders say anything to you. You mentioned that you had knocked them up out of their bed.

What was their words to you, can you remember what they said"

(CW) "I remember what the woman said, she said we thought you weren't coming. I never clocked onto to the time period at this point either".

(MR) OK, so you have entered the house, did you at that point go back to the car to take the satellite system out of the car or did you leave it in the car and just go straight into the house".

(CW) "No we took the satellite system out of the car first, and then we had a cup of coffee inside, and basically told them both what had happened, what we experienced"

(MR) "You told them your experiences"?

(CW) "Yes".

(MR) "At that point in time, did you draw any drawings"?

(CW) "Me and Garry got some bits of paper and drew what we thought we saw above the road. I sat at one end of the room and he sat at the other, and basically they were quite similar".

(MR) "Have you any idea how long you were in this house for. How long did you spend in the company of these people before you left"? *(Author's note, I couldn't make out on the audio tape what Colin's response to this question was).* Do you recall the time that you arrived there, did you look at a clock in this house"?

(CW) "I don't recall".

(MR) "Did the occupants of the house say, "Look, it's such and such a time"? Did they mention any time at all"?

(CW) "Not that I was aware of. They might have done, but I might not have taken it in, I was still traumatised at the time".

(MR) "But you mentioned earlier that someone did say that they didn't expect you to be coming at this time"?

(CW) "I never checked the time, it never entered my mind".

(MR) "OK, what was the journey like back to Edinburgh, and did you go the same route, or did you use an alternative route back to Edinburgh".

(CW) "To be honest, I can't remember the journey back".

(MR) "You can't remember it"?

(CW) "I remember being up the town after it". *(Author's note. Colin is referring here to Edinburgh)*

(MR) "I spoke with Garry about this point, and Garry said that he couldn't remember the journey back. But you remember yourself back in Edinburgh"?

(CW) "That's right, yes. Up the town".

(MR) "Up the town. What was you doing up the town in Edinburgh considering that it was early morning"?

(CW) "We went up to Carlton Hill. There were a lot of people hanging about Carlton Hill and we were looking for one of Garry's pal's called Stevie, then we were going for something to eat, try and get a pizza".

(MR) "So you did converse with other people"?

(CW) "No we never spoke to anyone, we never saw his car there *(Author's note. Colin is speaking about Stevie's car,*

Garry's pal) so we just headed for something to eat, and went back through the town up Lothian Road".

(MR) "Have you any recollection when you arrived back in your own home. Did you look at a clock".

(CW) "It never entered my mind to look at a clock".

(MR) "Now when you went to bed and woke up the following morning, well in effect it would be the same morning. Did you tell anybody about this incident"?

(CW) "Nobody, there was nobody to tell"

(MR) "Nobody! Well at some point, who was that first person that you told. Surely there would have been someone that you spoke to this about"?

(CW) "I didn't"

(MR) "You didn't. Did you have any further conscious recollections of that night and that journey, did anything come back in your dreams or maybe you were doing a household chore and something just snapped back and you remembered an extra bit about the incident, about the object"?

(CW) "No, nothing entered my mind at all no".

(MR) "The object you said was tiered. How many tiers"?

(CW) "Three tiers".

(MR) "And the colour was....."

(CW) "The object was a shimmering black".

(MR) "You mention black, was it a dull black or a shiny black"?

(Author's note. My front door bell went and I had to get up to answer it. When we resumed, I back tracked and asked Colin some questions that I had asked before, purely to see if I would get a different answer)

(MR) "Now Colin, when you arrived back home, did you tell anybody about what you saw".

(CW) "No, I never told anybody".

(MR) "You never told anybody! Any friends or relatives"?

(CW) "Just Garry's girlfriend and his sister, she dropped me off at my house. But I never told anybody else".

(MR) "Did you report it in an official capacity, later on, I'm talking weeks

(CW) "No".

(MR) "You never? Now I believe at a later stage you and Garry went back to the scene of the incident and you found some marks or oily deposits at the side of the road. Would you like to tell me about that, and how long was it before you went back".

(CW) "About two years. Garry got the car one day and said let's go back and look through what happened and there were marks either side of the road".

(MR) "Do you not think that this could have been anything rather than be associated with the incident that you both had"?

(CW) "Yes, it could have been anything"

(MR) "And that was two years later that you found these marks. Surely you must have travelled back down that road before that. Apart from that incident did you go back down that same road again"?

(CW) "Not for the first year, it was the year after that. Garry got the notion to start looking into it".

(MR) "Now I also believe that you went back on another occasion, I'm not quite sure if it was the occasion that you saw these marks in the grass, these oily deposits in the grass. But from Garry's testimony, he also found a car cloth that he thought belonged to his car, and that was found in that location".

(CW) "That's right yes. It was one of Garry's work cloths that he used, we knew it was Garry's and had come out of his car".

(MR) "Is it a possibility that a firm or a similar firm may have used those type of cloths, was it a J Cloth"?

(CW) "It was a wool effect kind of cloth. I know that Garry's work used them, I don't know about anybody else. I believe it was from Garry's car".

(MR) "Now the first two weeks after the event, did you have any trouble sleeping at all"?

(CW) "No nothing was bothering me no"

(MR) "Did you have any strong strange dreams that you can recollect"?

(CW) "No, I just put it all to the back of my mind and tried to forget about it"

(MR) "So your dreams have been fine and OK, nothing at all"?

(CW) "Nothing at all no".

(MR) "It's obviously fair to say that you are quite keen to find out what happened to you that night, that goes without saying. In your own words, how keen are you to find out an answer to what you saw that night"?

(CW) "I want to find out exactly what it was. I want an explanation as to what was above the road that night. I know that it was nothing that I've even seen before".

(MR) "Are there any other aspects about this incident that perhaps I haven't covered in this short discussion. Is there anything else that you would like to discuss about that night, speak freely about any new points that you feel that maybe I haven't covered or you want to extend on, about times, or anything like that"?

(CW) "Eh, nothing really, I think you have covered it all"

(MR) "I spoke to Garry earlier about his experiences, and he showed me some of his drawings that he did after he came out of hypnotic regression. Now you too Colin have been hypnotically regressed back to that date. What has the hypnosis sessions done for you? And can you tell me your very first recollections through hypnosis. What did you learn through hypnosis of this event as far as you are concerned"?

(CW) "Basically that there were more to it than a few seconds. It turns out that there was quite a period of time. And it seems as if I was aboard some kind of craft, and different things happened to me over the different sessions that I had".

(MR) "Now from the first hypnotic regression session. In conscious recall you remember that there was a blackness, everything was black. Under hypnosis, where did you find yourself when Helen Walters put you under hypnosis. Did you find yourself still in the car, or did you find yourself out of the car. Where were you"?

(CW) "Well the first time I was put under I was in the car, and we were going round the bend, and I seen the craft as it happened that night, and then there were complete blackness, and the car was lit up by a bright light and then I was in some kind of metallic room, and the car seemed to be in there as well".

(MR) "The car seemed to be in this room as well"!

(CW) "We were definitely inside whatever it was yes. I saw some kind of being in front of the car about six foot, that's the first thing I can remember seeing".

(MR) "Could you describe this being, what was it like"?

(CW) "Six foot in height, light grey in colour, with big black eyes, quite thin".

(MR) "Did he approach you? What happened when you found yourself in this room, where did you go next"?

(CW) "Garry was still in the car. There were smaller beings about three feet to about five feet, they opened the doors and carted Garry off on some kind of stretcher thing, metal, metallic looking, it hovered by itself. He was taken away, and I seemed to be led out of the car rather than carted away for some reason, and I was taken up an elevator".

(MR) "You say you were led away, was it forceful or just natural"?

(CW) "No, just natural".

(MR) "I take it then that they touched you to lead you away, or did you go of your free accord"?

(CW) "Just my free accord yes".

(MR) "Did you touch these beings at all?

(CW) "No, I just followed them".

(MR) "OK, you were led somewhere, can you describe where you were walking, what you saw"?

(CW) "Well I was in the craft or whatever it was. It was round, oval inside. The car was in the bottom tier and there was an upper level, a second tier, and it was like there was some kind of conveyor belt. You went on it, but it didn't move as such, you just somehow seemed to go up it. I didn't understand that. There was definitely more than one level to it".

(MR) "After this point, did you find yourself anywhere"?

(CW) "My next recollection was that I was in a chair. I had no clothes on. There were a few of the smaller beings around me, they had taken my clothes off".

(MR) "Now this is the drawing that you did for SPI Colin. To your best recollection, are you happy with this as a representation of what you saw"?

(CW) "Its along those lines, it's not 100% accurate".

(MR) OK, we have what looks like a kind of heart shaped head with these black eyes. These appear to be very broad shoulders *(Author's note I was pointing to Colin's own drawing that he drew of one of these creatures which appeared to have broad shoulders. See photographic section)*. With a thin narrow body. The shoulders seemed bulged here, is that correct"?

(CW) "Its along those lines yes"

(MR) "This is the hovering stretcher drawing that you said Garry was placed on. Now this being, for want of a better word, that we have here, is different. How did you see this as being different"?

(CW) "It was later on under hypnosis that I was on a stretcher at one point as well, and this one appeared over me. The only way to describe it, is grotesque. It was right old looking. I only seen it that once. It appeared over me, and it seemed to be commanding the rest of them to, like, take him there, and you take him over that way".

(MR) "Were there any verbally spoken words at all. I mean, how was communication relayed at this point"?

(CW) "Through telepathy. I just heard the words in my head of what they were telling me".

(MR) "When you heard these utterances in your heard. Did they have any kind of dialect, you know, soft English, Scots, were there any 'twang' so to speak. Or could you fully understand what they were saying. Were there any edge to the words that they were saying, like a robotic sound of voice, or just a plain natural voice"?

(CW) "Just a plain natural voice. There was nothing strange about it".

(MR) "OK, this smaller one which you have put down as a child alien, has marks underneath what we will term eyes. Could you talk about these marks here? *(Author's note. This particular drawing showed these small creatures with what appeared to have coloured lines under their eyes. Something of which I have never ever encountered in any UFO abduction case that I have read about anywhere in the world)*

(CW) "It was the only one that I saw with these marks below the eyes. It was like colours, three colours, red black and yellow, which was strange. It was the only one I ever saw like that"

(MR) "Was it straight lines or wavy lines".

(CW) "It was zig zags"

(MR) "Zig Zags".

(CW) "I don't think it was like make up. I think that it was actually part of it's face. It wasn't drawn on or anything like that. The colours were actually in the skin".

(MR) "Well I have tattoo's, and I've got to ask, but do you think that it was like a kind of tattoo in the skin"?

(CW) "Yes, possibly yes".

(MR) "I'm looking at a drawing of these fingers which appear rounded at the top, with a bulge there, is that the best way that you can remember it"?

(CW) "Yes, quite long and knobbly at the end".

(MR) "Now you found yourself in this situation, in this condition, what happened next? You mention about this metallic chair"?

(CW) "I was sitting in this chair for quite a period of time. There was one point under hypnosis that I was getting worked on, in my right eye. Something was in my right eye and felt like a red hot poker. I don't know what it was doing there, but it was definitely doing something".

(MR) "Do you remember your clothes being taken off you at all"?

(CW) "At one point I was thrown into the chair and they were ripping my clothes off".

(MR) "They were forcibly ripping your clothes off"?

(CW) "They weren't bothering how they were taking them off".

(MR) "How were you reacting at this point. Were you struggling and resisting, or were you just going along with it"?

(CW) "I was just going along with it"

(Author's note. We now discussed the instrument that Colin drew for SPI which came down from the ceiling which was a long thin needle which was inserted into his eye.)

(MR) "Now this is the instrument Colin that you have drawn for SPI. You mentioned a moment ago that something came down and went into your eye. Was it your eye or just at the side of your eye?"

(CW) "It was actually in the centre of my eye. This thing went over my eye and inserted into my eye".

(MR) "Was it your right eye"?

(CW) "My right eye yes".

(MR) "Where did this device, this instrument come from"?

(CW) "It was at the right hand side, three feet above me, just floating there. It wasn't attached to anything".

(MR) "It wasn't attached to anything!"

(CW) "No, just free floating".

(MR) "Now obviously this would give you cause for concern. Did you try and move yourself away from this chair here when you saw this coming towards you"?

(CW) "Every time I tried to turn to look who was doing this to me *(Author's note. I couldn't make out on the tape what Colin said at this point)* The pain was unbearable. I just lay back, but couldn't see who was working this thing".

(MR) "How long was this in your eye for roughly"?

(CW) "It seemed to be a long time, but probably wouldn't be that long".

(MR) "Once this came away from your eye, do you remember what happened next"?

(CW) "I think it went away after that and I was left sitting in the chair. My eye kept watering all the time. I couldn't stop it watering. At one point when I tried to get out of the chair, one appeared behind me, one of the smaller ones touching me. I was freezing at the time and when it touched me it was cold".

(MR) "Were there anything else in this area that you were in, any form of equipment, seating arrangements whatever. How would you describe this room for me"?

(CW) "Basically just this chair that I could see. There were lights actually built into the actual structure of the room. I found that unusual. There were no switches or anything like that".

(MR) "Now you have since had further hypnotic regression with Helen Walters, could you now discuss with me, some of your other recollections that came out of these further hypnotic sessions"?

(CW) "There was a point when there was some kind of a clear chamber. I was strapped and sitting in some kind of seat. It got really cold at that point. I was sitting there frozen. Helen tried to move me on from that but she couldn't get me out of that chamber for some reason. She had a lot of trouble getting me out of there. Later on, it felt like it was defrosting. I went from cold, to red hot".

(Author's note. I then spoke to camera showing the drawing that Colin did of him sitting in this glass or perspex chamber)

(MR) "Could you just go through with me Colin, about this particular drawing that you did for SPI".

(CW) "Basically that's me sitting in the chair. I was stripped and in some kind of harness. I was inside this chamber and it was clear. It was going cold and it was frosting up"

(MR) "Was it hard to make out if it was glass or perspex".

(CW) "I couldn't really determine what it was, but it was clear. It could have been glass or it could have been perspex, I'm not 100% sure. I couldn't touch it. I was strapped in, so I couldn't touch it to see what it was made of. There were hundreds of other ones around me. At one point I could see a whole lot of other people, different nationalities".

(MR) "You saw other people"!

(CW) "Definitely. There were loads of other people".

(MR) "In the same position..."

(CW) "They were all getting put into these chambers yes. I saw the backs of them, I couldn't see their faces".

(MR) "Were they naked or clothed"?

(CW) "They were all naked, the same as myself. I found it really weird, there were a lot of people. There were coloured, Chinese, young and old"

(Author's note. At this point I drew Colin's attention to his drawing where he drew what appeared to be mist at the foot of these chambers) Colin stated.

(CW) "Yes the only way I can describe it, is like that cold ice you get (dry ice)"

(MR) "Did that effect move upwards, or was it always at the foot of all these chambers"?

(CW) "It was always on the floor yes, like a small cloud on the floor".

(MR) "You mentioned at one point that this glass or perspex started to frost up, what happened then"

(CW) "Basically the only way I can describe it was getting frozen. I was getting colder and colder and the next thing I know I was red hot, and you were heating up again. I just can't understand it".

(MR) "I'm looking at a drawing here where we have one tall alien standing at a doorway and three aliens looking at you outside the chamber. What were these beings like"?

(CW) "They were just the same as the other ones I saw, along the same lines. There was always a tall one there, and I think he was telling them what to do. The smaller ones were like helpers, and they had to do what they had to do, and big ones had the higher authority as far as I could make out".

(MR) "This is another drawing which is similar to what we saw a moment ago. This is this old being that seemed to be in authority, is that correct"?

(CW) "Yes that's correct. He was the top gun I suppose, telling all the rest of them what to do".

(MR) "These ridges, if we can call them ridges, how would you describe these effects on the neck *(Author's note. I was referring to these rippled line like effects on these creatures necks)*

(CW) "Just like ours, our windpipe. Theirs were more on the outside, where ours are on the inside. They were more outstanding than ours, and they were further down than ours" *(Author's note. Colin was pointing to his drawing where the windpipe of one of these small creatures actually extended 'onto' their chest"!*

(MR) "Now what other recollections from this area that you were in can you recall? Have you any other experiences and recollections of that recalled under hypnosis"?

(CW) "No, not from the last time I was under and being in that chamber. I've never been under since, it frightened me. I couldn't move on. I seemed to be stuck in there".

(MR) "I believe that after the hypnosis and Helen brought you out of the hypnosis. You went back home that night and had trouble with your eyes. What was happening there"?

(CW) "Basically my eyes were getting worse and I was getting back ache, repercussions I suppose. It just started off again, so whether that was because they were working on the right eye and I was reliving it again, I'm not sure".

(MR) "OK, we have subjected both you and Garry to hypnosis as a tool to hopefully fully extract further recall from that particular night. Are you happy to go through this hypnosis"?

(CW) "Oh yes. I want to get to the bottom of it just to find out if there are any bits missing. There is definitely more to it than I remember. I'd like to get the whole picture".

(MR) "Do you think though, that hypnosis is a good tool for 'you', in bringing forward recollections, or do you think that what you have spoken about through hypnosis, is perhaps some form of dream, or do you feel that its a reality, that its all true. How do you feel about what is coming out of hypnosis"?

(CW) "To me it's real. I couldn't make that kind of stuff up. I'm not the type of person to look at alien books, to read about them, or anything like that. I couldn't just make this up".

(MR) "Had you any interest prior to this event about UFOs, were you an avid reader of books and stuff"?

(CW) "No. I actually had the micky taken out of me".

(MR) "And has this experience changed you in any way"?

(CW) "Well I've got to believe that there is something out there after what had happened to me. Whether I will get to the bottom of it I don't know. I'd like to, but whether I will get an answer I don't know, it's yet to be seen".

(MR) "Well Colin thanks very much for speaking with me today about this particular incident, and hopefully one day soon, preferably sooner, we can get that answer for not only yourself, but also Garry. Thank you".

(CW) "Thank you"

Colin speaking on camera.

Colin Wright & Gary Wood (c) Malcolm Robinson

Colin Wright in passenger seat

Colin Wright

Garry Wood Driving his car.

Garry Wood outside Malcolm Robinson's UFO caravan in Alloa

onetribeTV.

BBC ONE

Debunked: Aliens On The A70
Tuesday 7th May
BBC One | 19:00

the **one** show

Michael Douglas investigates the mystery surrounding an alleged alien abduction outside Edinburgh in 1992. As Garry Wood and Colin Wright were driving along the A70 towards Tarbrax, they encountered a disk-shaped object hovering above their car. Michael meets paranormal investigator, Malcolm Robinson who reveals how - under hypnosis - both described being examined by grey, translucent creatures in a featureless room. Some argue what the pair say they saw was the result of false memory syndrome. Others have suggested the lights in the sky might have been the military testing a new kind of aircraft, but the interview tapes and their original drawings of what they saw, suggest this could be the most significant UFO incident in Britain.

Presenter	**Director**	**Assistant Producer / Camera**
Micheal Douglas	Matt Waddleton	Tom Parry
Production Manager	**Second Camera**	**Editor**
Jessie Anderson	Sonny Mackay	Samuel Webb
BBC Exec. Producer	**Exec. Producer For One Tribe TV**	**Production Assistant**
Michael Armit	Owen Gay	Francesca Barbieri

With thanks to Bath Spa University

The Glass House, Charlcombe Lane, Lansdown, BA1 5TT
www.onetribetv.co.uk | @onetribetv | +44 (0) 1225 469507

Flyer for the BBC One Show Episode on the Incident

Helen Walters. The Hypnotherapist (c) Malcolm Robinson

Malcolm with the BBC One Show presenter Michael Douglas

Intended A70 Movie Poster 2011

Malcolm Robinson and Garry Wood

On the way to Tarbrax, down the A70

THE 'THING' ON THE ROOF!

One of the questions that I asked Garry during the many times that I interviewed him, was, 'Had anything strange happened to him when he was younger'? Had he witnessed a UFO or seen anything peculiar which might be of interest to me? Garry replied that there was one particular incident which stuck out in his mind, and that was the time when he was around 11 or 12 years of age, he was with some friends approaching Duddingston School in Edinburgh to attend a Scout meeting, when one of his friends pointed out something that appeared to be hiding on part of the school roof. Whatever this thing was, it looked hideous, and to all intents and purposes, looked like a 'monster'. It had a humanoid shaped body, in the sense that it had arms and legs, but it's head was very peculiar. It did not look like the now often reported 'Greys', but was something entirely different. By now they were all terrified, and began screaming, which actually brought the scout master out, however this 'thing', or whatever it was, had vanished by the time the scout master had come out to see what all the commotion was. I asked Garry if he felt that this may have been someone in fancy dress, out to scare the people attending the scout meeting that night. To which Garry was extremely adamant that this was not the case. Whatever he saw, he said, it was real, and it was not the result of someone 'dressed up and clowning around'.

FACING THE MEDIA.

As this was a major UFO Incident, I was of the opinion that there must be other incidents of this nature, the thing was of course, that this type of event can be very personal, and one might not want others to know what they had experienced, and so therefore tend to keep quiet. As a researcher, it is important to me to ascertain if indeed other Scottish people had experienced a UFO abduction. The reluctance of people to come forward is obvious, but I had to find out if indeed there were others out there that might have had a similar experience to both Garry and Colin. And to this end I asked both Garry and Colin if they would be prepared to go forward publicly with their story, in the hopes of making other UFO abductees come forward. It was a gamble of course, but if Garry and Colin did go forward publicly, I hoped that someone out there, may decide upon reading Garry and Colin's story, to get in touch with our society whereby we could offer some kind of support. It was a big decision for Garry and Colin, but they themselves recognised the importance of coming forward, for they too, wanted to know if there were others out there who had had this experience, or if indeed they stood alone. By now they were well aware of the countless thousands of people world-wide who had also experienced a UFO abduction and both men wanted to have personal talks with those who shared the same gruelling experience as themselves.

THE SCOTSMAN NEWSPAPER ARTICLE

One of the major Scottish newspapers that picked up on this story when we went public, was the Scotsman Newspaper, where staff writer Brian Pendreigh interviewed Garry Wood. The article appeared in their 15th of September 1994 issue. Here is how the Scotsman covered that story.

Everything is silent. The moors are empty. Nothing stirs except the wind, sending little waves across the cold grey waters of Harperrig Reservoir and pushing dark rain clouds across the landscape. A watery sun poked feebly through the heavens. There is nothing else in the skies. Just the clouds and the sun. No flying saucers. Sometimes Garry Wood drives out along this road and stops at this same spot. But there are never any flying saucers, not since that first time, two years ago when he saw one above the road. Maybe he imagined it, but it would be easier to say that if he had been alone. His friend Colin Wright saw it too, two mature family men and they both saw it. *"I was frightened to death"* says Garry Wood. *"I was really scared, the only thing on my mind was getting away from it, getting away as far as I could"*. They reached their destination unharmed, it seemed. But a journey from Edinburgh to the village of Tarbrax, just off the A70, which should have taken half an hour, had taken them about two and a half. That was just the beginning. Both men are currently undergoing, a series of hypnosis sessions to try to release hidden memories of that night, memories they may have buried in the subconscious. Both independently recall being on a spaceship with alien beings.

Malcolm Robinson, founder of the Scottish based SPI, Strange Phenomena Investigations says, *"Nowhere in the annals of Scottish UFOlogy, has there been an abduction case like this".* Helen Walters, the hypnotherapist who conducted the sessions says, *"I believe that they've had a genuine experience on a UFO"* Garry Wood and Colin Wright just want to know what happened, *"If I could get an answer to this, I could come to terms with it",* says Wood. *"As it stands, I can't come to terms with this because I can't get an answer".* Neither has spoken to the press before. They know they are risking ridicule, but Wood is desperate to find an answer and seems ready to try anything that might help. I spoke to Wright on the phone, but he failed to turn up for two interviews and cancelled a third, saying he was under pressure from his girlfriend. Wood is 31 now. He seems an ordinary guy, a little nervous at first, but seemingly pleased to have someone promise serious consideration for his story, a story that begins on a clear, starry night, just over two years ago, 17th August 1992.

The two men set off at the back of ten from South Edinburgh in Wood's blue Astra. They were taking a satellite television system to a friend in the village of Tarbrax about 15 miles outside of Edinburgh. It was a journey that would change their lives.

"I was driving about 40, 40 odd miles an hour, just chatting away", says Wood. *"Then, going around this blind bend with barriers on either side, Colin put his arm up and said, 'What the hell is that'? I looked up and got an awful fright. I never seen nothing like that before, but I knew it was a UFO. It resembled the classic flying saucer of sci fi films".* Woods reckons it was 30 feet wide, wider than the road, and black in

colour, with no signs of windows. *"It looked like a solid metallic substance of some sort. I work in the ambulance service. I'm a mechanic. I work with a lot of metals and different types of things. I put the foot down on the throttle to go underneath it because it was floating 20 feet above the road. Just as we were going underneath it, a shimmering curtain fell and we went into total blackness"*. He describes the curtain as looking like the picture on an untuned television set. *"I couldn't see anything, and then there was a shunt on the back of the car, and then I'm on the road again. I put the foot down on the gas. I must have been doing 80, 90 miles an hour up the road"*. Nevertheless they did not arrive at Tarbrax until about 12:45am.

Wood did not contact the police for fear that they would think he was a 'crackpot' though he did report it to the British UFO Research Association. He wanted to forget about it, but was unable to. He developed severe headaches for the first time in his life and has had brain scans and spinal taps to no avail. He started buying books on UFOs. *"It's not the kind of thing I was ever interested in. I was more interested in cars, going out, and just the usual everyday things in life"*. He came across Malcolm Robinson's phone number and it was Robinson who suggested hypnosis to try and account for the 'missing time' on their journey to Tarbrax. Hypnotic regression is a tool therapists use to help subjects come to terms with painful memories they have buried in their subconscious but which are affecting their current mental well being.

"My first regression wasn't really what I expected", says Wood. *"I burst into tears. I was really emotionally distraught. Colin seemed to react a lot better to the hypnotic regression. Colin has come out with all sorts of things, pretty heavy stuff. She, (the hypnotherapist) says I seem to fight it, I don't want to actually go there to that time. She says there's something I'm terrified of"*

At his first session, Wood saw only vague shapes, but later sessions provided more vivid 'memories'. *"This long arm extends over my chest towards my head and it frightened the shit out of me that much that I jumped up out of the chair. It was a translucent bone shaped arm with long fingers coming towards me over my chest".* On another occasion, he saw fluid or gel in a hole in the floor. *"I saw a head appearing out of it and I saw a body and two arms. The creature I saw must have been pretty big, bigger than me. It was like a skeleton with flesh round it. It had long arms, really long arms. It had a long body, really skinny, with the skin tight to the bone, and it was actually getting out"* Wood says it had a large head with two black eyes. It was predominately grey, but the flesh over its ribs seemed bruised, brown and red. *"It looked a really frail creature. It looked like it had a really hard time"* He saw other creatures, similar but smaller. Wright saw similar creatures during his sessions and believes they were examining him and communicated with him telepathically.

Helen Walters is a commercial hypnotherapist more accustomed to using hypnotherapy to help people give up smoking. There is some controversy over its use in unblocking memories. Some people have claimed to have remembered being abused as children leading to allegations of 'false memory syndrome'. I underwent two sessions for a feature on reincarnation and the mind certainly came up with powerful and appropriate imagery. Walters believes Wood and Wright are telling the truth. *"They're completely sincere",* she says. There seems little doubt that they saw an unidentified flying object. The question is what. There is no doubt that, under hypnosis they appear to remember meeting aliens. The question is, are these memories or imaginings. *"To me it's real enough and that's enough for me"* says Wood. *"Colin is a stand up guy. Colin doesn't believe in any of this muck. He doesn't read books. He's not really interested in it. Colin isn't the sort of guy to come out with these kind of things at all. I'd say he is telling the truth"* Wood's workmates call him 'Starman' and his wife thinks he should drop it, but he cannot get over the experience. *"I'm frightened at night",* he says. *"It frightened the shit out of me and I'm feared in case it comes back again. The question is, what is 'it'"*?

It's fair to say that the Scotsman article above, opened Pandora's box, and as soon as that edition featuring Garry and Colin's story hit the streets, I was inundated by the media, all wanting a piece of Garry and Colin. Of course I had to protect my witnesses, it's alright trying to find out more UFO abductees from stories in the press, but the last thing I wanted to do, was for both Garry and Colin to be ridiculed in the press. That unfortunately did happen with the News of The World story sensational heading, *'Aliens Took Me To Meet Naked Woman In A Spaceship'*. Dated October 2nd, 1994. Typical gutter press headlines, knowing that a heading like this, will undoubtedly draw the reader in. The thing is, I should have known better! I was promised by staff writer David Leslie that he would do an honest piece on the incident, and that he wouldn't take the micky. Unfortunately the powers that be at the newspaper, decided that his piece needed to be spiced up, and as such gave it the stupid headline. To be honest, the rest of the two page article was pretty decent and told it as it was. The late Professor Archie Roy (70) who at the time was working at Glasgow University in the Physics and Astronomy Department gave his feelings to the paper when he said.

"UFOs are very real and we are experiencing a phenomenon we know little about. Strange things happen and we simply cannot rule out the possibility of other intelligent species in the universe. The sheer number of people coming forward with what they see and experience is too great for us to turn a blind eye".

The paper went on to state that SPI's hypnotherapist Helen Walters had done eight hypnotic regression sessions with both Garry and Colin, and she was quoted as saying,

"I am satisfied the story they tell has the ring of truth. The evidence so far leads us to dig deeper to find out what really happened. I do not believe that Garry and Colin are fantasising. They are sincere men of solid character. If they were making it up, I would have been able to detect it from the

first session.   They are desperate for answers.   They are troubled".

The News of the Wold showed a photograph of Garry holding up the drawing that he did for SPI, which shows the naked female on this craft. It goes without saying that both Garry and Colin were none too pleased with this headline, and it was soon after that, that they both decided not to be featured in any other newspapers. Although, as the years went by, the story did see the light of day again, but I ensured that any further newspaper who wanted to discuss this story with its readers, had to truly promise me in writing, that they would treat the incident, honestly and without any journalistic pomp! Sadly one newspaper that I didn't have any dealings with about the A70 case, was the Sunday Express, who, in their November 19th 1995 edition, featured another ridiculous and demeaning headline. It read, *'Did Aliens Beam Up Pals For a Car Trek?'* Garry was interviewed again, but by this time, Colin was refusing any newspaper interviews. Garry came across honest, and the story was pretty accurate, well, other than the fact that they showed a photograph of Colin Wright, which wasn't him? It was another UFO witness by the name of Andy Swan, who himself had an incredible UFO sighting which was also featured in this article. For the first time ever, the lady who Garry and Colin were going to see that night in the village of Tarbrax, Katrina Philip, was herself interviewed, and she was reported as saying;

"Garry had phoned at 10pm to say he and Colin were coming over. When they didn't arrive, I went to bed. It was well after midnight when the knocked loudly at my door. Both appeared shocked and were chattering excitedly about aliens. They drew identical diagrams of the craft and the little men that had seen".

Of course it wasn't just the newspapers that got in on the act, many radio stations and Television stations did as well. Garry and Colin appeared twice on the popular London Weekend Television programme, Strange But True? Hosted by seasoned television presenter, Michael Aspel. Garry and Colin also appeared with me on the Grampian Television programme, 'We The Jury' and in 1996, Garry appeared with me on the Mysterious North programme which was recorded at Castle Fraser near Aberdeen. Simon Biagi was the presenter. This interview almost didn't happen, but before I tell you why, let me set the scene for you.

RIGHT, WE'RE LEAVING GARRY!

Prior to the show Garry Wood and I (along with other participants in the show) were treated to a slap up meal in a lovely restaurant in a small town near Aberdeen. It was here that I was fortunate enough to meet up with the famous Scottish Bram Seer, a mystical and charismatic man with an enormous white beard, put him in a red suit, and he was the double of Father Christmas. This chap was famed as was his family before him, for predicting (before they happened) many events from not only the U.K. but overseas as well. I had a very interesting lunch with him I can tell you. After lunch we were all taken to the castle and it was there that I met up with a memory man (I can't recall his name that's how bad my memory is?) Anyway, I came across this man staring at a very large board that had row upon row of playing cards. What he was doing, was remembering the lay out of these cards, as he would later be asked by the host of the show, what card was where. In other words, what was the card that was on the 6th row down and was the 35th card across? Incredibly this chap, when it came to his appearance on the show, got them all correct!

The show's host Simon Biagi who also worked on Good Morning Britain, a breakfast television show, changed his jacket with each new recording, so that one would think that it's a new week, a new show and a new jacket, clever eh!). (In point of fact they were recording several shows that day due to be broadcast over several weeks) Anyway also on the show, were a number of vampires. I kid you not. Young teenage men and women all dressed up and looking like vampires and warlocks, they really looked the part. One confessed to me that she lived in a council house but slept in a coffin, *"Didn't everyone"* she asked!

The room in which the filming was being held, was a large room with suits or armour all around. There were also shields, swords, and lances stuck on the wall, all very impressive looking. At the end of the room where the interviews were taking place, was a large fireplace and a massive fire was burning in the hearth all very cosy stuff. Garry had agreed to come on the show with me and relate his experience. However, as Garry and I sat in on the recording sessions with other people before us, we could see that the presenter Simon Biagi was not taking these subjects seriously, and the guest he had on whilst we were watching, a lady talking about colour healing, was more or less getting the micky taken out of her. At the time both Garry and I were all miked up as we were next to go on. But when I saw the treatment that Simon was dishing out to his guest, I was disgusted and turned round to Garry and told him that I would not put him through this and that *'let's get the hell out of here'*. No sooner had those words left my lips, that I noticed a stage technician looking at me and waving his hands frantically as if to say *'noooo'*. Both Garry and I looked at him puzzled, at which he came over and said that because we were miked up, he could hear every word that we were saying, and that we shouldn't leave the building. I stated that I wouldn't put Garry through this treatment, as we were here in all seriousness to discuss a subject that demanded respect. The technician promised that Garry's experience would be treated seriously, and true to his word, as soon as Simon had finished with his last subject/victim, this sound guy had words with him. He came back and told us that Simon had promised not to take the Micky out of us, and I'm pleased to say that he was true to his word. The interview went off well and without any Micky takes. If that technician hadn't heard my conversation about taking Garry off that show, Garry and I would have walked, of that I have no doubt.

Garry and Colin also appeared in a German T.V. documentary, Pro 7. In a sense, we were showing to the world, that these UFO abductions not only occur in the United States and other countries, but they sure as hell occur in Scotland as well, and, as unwanted as they are, it is a sad fact of life. At the end of the day however, this television exposure did not bring forward the response that I had hoped for, only three people came forward with similar tales of UFO abduction. However the exposure did highlight the seriousness of the UFO enigma and more so this particular aspect of it.

There were numerous radio interviews around this period, and the following is a short piece that Colin Wright did with BBC Radio Scotland which was broadcast on the 20th of September, 1994.

BBC RADIO SCOTLAND. 20th September, 1994.

The lead in to this piece, was done by the BBC Scotland presenter Mark Connolly who stated.

"UFOs have arrived in Scotland to, with what could be this country's biggest abduction case yet. Colin Wright from Edinburgh is undergoing hypnotic regression organised by the Central Scotland based, Strange Phenomena Investigations. He claims, that along with a friend, he was abducted while driving near Edinburgh".

Colin Wright then stated;

"All I remember was a big alien in front of the car and there were two small ones at the side of me which helped me out of the car. At the other side of the motor, was another three, which carted Garry away, and he was off. The next thing I remember, was sitting in a kind of metal chair. I knew that I didn't have any clothes on because I was freezing. They said to me, "It's OK, it's Garry we are wanting" for some reason. But I don't understand if I didn't have any clothes on they did not do nothing to myself".

A SIMILAR CRAFT NEAR THE A70!

In August of 2013, I received an e-mail from a Scottish gentleman by the name of Phil Fenton who wrote to me about a chap who had experienced a strange looking UFO not so far away from the A70. Here is what he wrote to me.

Hi Malcolm

"I have recently been talking to an individual called Richard Harrison who claims to have witnessed a large triangular shaped UFO near the village of Kirknewton whilst travelling back from Edinburgh. I have no doubt his claim is genuine and he really did see what he saw. He says he reported the incident at the time but never heard anything more about it. He also says others must have seen it as well as there was traffic behind him. His wife also witnessed what happened".

"This happened around 1999 or 2000. We know this, because he had been to the cinema to see a James bond film featuring Pierce Brosnan called 'The World is not enough' which came out in November 1999. He described the object as an extremely large triangular shape but curvy. Much bigger than an aircraft such as the Vulcan bomber. It was 'duck egg blue' underneath (which is a military aircraft camouflage colour) but this object was not flying like any conventional aircraft he knew about. It seemed to be hovering and moving very slowly (about 25/30 mph) and he could see what would appear to be riveted panels making up the hull of the craft. On the top was a large bubble canopy as seen on fighter aircraft, but much larger. The three corners of the craft had lights that were white when it was stationary, and glowed red when it moved away".

"My own thoughts on this is that it must be a military flying machine. Most likely a rigid airship but incorporating stealth technology. This would explain it's ability to hover and move very slowly as well as the strange shape. I put this to Richard and he agreed that this could be the case, but he went on to explain that when it left, it accelerated away very quickly, much

quicker than a cumbersome Airship could hope to achieve. It also manoeuvred and changed direction very rapidly in ways that are well beyond any aircraft's capabilities".

"What also interests me is that there is an old RAF station (RAF Kirknewton) near where this occurred, it's now used as a base for gliders and the ATC (Air training corp). It's also very near the A70 and the Harperrigg Reservoir where another incident took place which you have written about in your book UFO Case Files of Scotland (Volume 1). And I wonder if the cases are related? A secret RAF Stealth Airship would be a very useful device. It could hide in the clouds and take off and land undetected in foggy conditions. And (assuming it was stealthy and undetectable to radar) it could creep up on the enemy undetected and land in any open space without the need for runaways, allowing troops and armaments to be deployed. When you think about it, if the military don't already operate such craft, then they really should develop one for the reasons just described?"

"What puzzles me though, are the rapid speeds and changes in direction also described, that are beyond our current understanding of technology".
Phil Fenton.

Needless to say, I quickly sent an e-mail to Richard Harrison and here is his reply, dated, 21st January 2014

Hi Malcolm,
"Apologies for the time taken to respond, hectic life! Our story is a little different as to how Phil has explained it, so I'll write it below for you from fresh".

Summary.

Date: *"Driving back from the UCI Cinema in Craigmillar Edinburgh after Michelle (my wife) and I watched James Bond (the one with a single seat stealth boat down the Thames").*

(Author's Note: This would be the movie, 'The World Is Not Enough' which came out in 1999)

Time: Late Evening.

Location: *"Along A71. Start - Edinburgh Airfield, Linburn War Blind on A71, end - Field between A71 and Kirknewton Airfield".*

Witnesses: *"My wife and I, a second car behind us on the A71 which had at least two occupants".*

Object: *"Larger than a RAF Tornado. Two level centre section. Large equilateral melted triangle. RAF camo. Pale blue underside too. No markings. Large panels (saw shut lines). Extremely fast. Also totally Static at one point at about lamp post top level"*

Time Duration: *"Guesstimating ten minutes, but not measured".*

What happened:

"My wife and I were in our car driving back from the Cinema. It was dark outside, and we were on a high talking about the movie and about general life stuff. We were driving past Edinburgh Airport on the A71 parallel to the Airfield where an aircraft was taking off. We could see the lights as normal, and this lit up the side of the normal aeroplane which was clearly seen, but I also noticed a craft between us and the obvious Aeroplane. Weirdly though this second craft had three red lights only. The three red lights were all on and there were no white lights at all. Between the lights was just darkness (but this may be down to the fact that I was driving and trying not to crash etc. so my vision was on the object then looking ahead then back, etc.) The two craft took off at the same time in line with each other".

110

"I said to Michelle immediately "Look at that. Something's not right!"

Michelle "What do you mean?" Me "red lights..... that's closer to the road... there's two aircraft there...."

"Needless to say, we were both looking out at the craft as it sped forward and out of sight at an aeroplane speed. As we drove along the winding A71 we saw the red lights zoom from right to left and then from left to right a few times. We were gobsmacked with what was happening. Then the craft came directly toward us through cloud and the clouds lit up red and then the lights got sharper as it came closer out of the cloud. "It's coming straight for us! Woh!"

The craft came down to almost touch the silhouette of the trees and then it shot directly vertical at an obscene speed and was gone! We slowly drove along, totally freaked out, and discussing what had just happened. We passed 'Linburn' which is a residential area for the War Blind. We were looking everywhere to see if we could see it again. As a field opened up to our left, there it was. Totally static, just above ground. No metal engine noise, no movement from it AT ALL! It was fixed in the air solid. There was no landing gear and it was at lamp post top level in the far corner of the field beside a telephone pole and line of trees. This lies right beside a railway track".

"I could see the shape of the craft, the colours, patterns, panel shut lines and the lights. All three lights were now only white and stuck on. I panicked as I realised I was driving at just under 30 mph on the A71 which was a 60 mph road at that time. I looked in my rear view mirror to see another car looking over to the object too! They were also driving the same speed as us at a safe distance. We could see their silhouette's in the car. It was a large equilateral triangle with melted down ends, a large top central canopy area. The wings were thick and rounded which weirdly reminded me of the Vulcan bomber because of the curve on the wing edges. Just to let you know, I was an Air Cadet. I had been around aircraft a lot, either by attending ATC Camp on RAF bases, or also by attending Leuchars air show's. I was a qualified Glider Pilot

111

(Kirknewton Airfield). I think this is relevant and hope it helps give a little credibility to our account"
Kind Regards, Richard Harrison.

So, what are we to make of this account? The A70 is less than a half mile from the A71 at its shortest, but as the road progresses south, the two roads distance from each other quite considerably. This account is from 1999, seven years after both Garry and Colin had their strange experience on the A70. Could it have been the same craft still flying about that particular area, and if so, why! The shape of the craft was different to what both Garry and Colin saw. This object had more rounded wings with a cupola on top, a marked difference as to what Garry and Colin saw. I present this sighting here, simply because of the very nature of what was seen, and it's close proximity to the A70.

A70 THE MOVIE

Of course being Scotland's biggest UFO Abduction case, it wasn't long before it came to the attention of an Independent film maker based in London, (due to confidentiality issues, I can't disclose that person's name or her company). The film maker made herself known to me, and I travelled up to London to have talks with her in a plush London hotel. It was clear that she was a very knowledgable lady, and someone who clearly loved the UFO subject and held a deep fascination for it. Before I go into the why's and wherefores of how the movie never saw the light of day. Here is an article that I wrote for UFO MATRIX about the film maker, and her desire to get this movie made. (Please note, names have been changed due to confidentiality)

Drivers' UFO tale is beamed on to the silver screen

By Oliver Farrimond

THE tale of two friends who were beamed aboard a UFO as they drove by a reservoir on the outskirts of Edinburgh is to be made into a movie.

Garry Wood and Colin Wright, now 46 and 42, who claimed to have had a close encounter in 1992 near Balerno, have always stuck by their story and even passed a lie-detector test on TV.

Now DBR Entertainment, based in London and Los Angeles, is financing the production of the film after almost two decades of controversy over the encounter.

Film producer Dionne Rose, who is financing the film through the company, said: "It's such a fantastic story and I was attracted to it from the first time I heard it.

"I had seen the film Fire in the Sky, which has similarities, but Colin and Garry's experience did have unique elements to it."

In what became famous as the "A70 Abduction Case", the pair were driving to Tarbrax village, near Balerno, when a "disc-shaped object" appeared in front of their car.

In fear, driver Garry attempted to flee the object, but they claim that, as they passed underneath, they were enveloped by a shimmering energy beam.

Although initially unable to remember anything between this and arriving at Tarbrax some 96 minutes later, hypnotherapy sessions brought back some of the memories.

Both men eventually re-

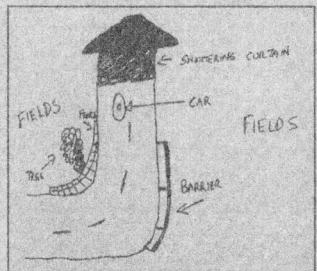

membered being surrounded by small creatures on the road.

Other snippets recalled by the pair include being carried on a floating stretcher, and having experiments performed on them by a translucent, skeletal, grey alien.

Edinburgh-based car mechanic Garry, pictured below, went on to pass a televised lie-detector test about his claims, and the pair visited paranormal investigator Malcolm Robinson, who is also working on the film.

Mr Robinson, who lives in Hastings, said: "I'm really excited about this project.

"We all know about the American encounters, so for DBR Entertainment to make a movie about Scotland's biggest incident of this kind is great news.

"Both Colin and Garry were desperate for anything that could explain what happened to them. Garry

told me that he was strapped to a table with these things prodding him and he desperately wanted to take a swing at one of them.

"It's such a great premise for a film and we're currently going through script negotiations with both Colin and Garry on board to make sure they're happy with everything.

"I hope they don't add too much salt and pepper to it and make it another Braveheart, based on fact but 80 per cent inaccurate."

Mr Robinson, who has just published a book chronicling Scotland's UFO case files, added: "Different people have asked me who I would like to play me in the film.

"I usually answer Ewan McGregor, although I had a moustache in those days so he'd have to grow one.

"Colin and Garry are such down-to-earth guys it's hard to imagine any famous actors playing them."

The two friends were unable to comment on ongoing plans for the film version of their alien encounter, as both have signed confidentiality agreements to remain silent until the release of the film.

Sketch, left, illustrates the UFO encounter of Garry Wood and Colin Wright near Edinburgh

Daily Express October 2010

113

MORE ARE COMING, SAYS MAN IN FLYING SAUCER MYSTERY

Garry Wood on the A70 Road Sunday Express 1995

Film maker plans close encounter of the A70 kind

■ A poster for the film.

CAMERAS are set to start rolling on a film about Scotland's most famous alien abduction case.

The movie is due to begin filming in February and could be touching down in cinemas by late next year.

Producer Dionne Rose, of DRB Entertainment, has also signed up a top Scots sci-fi heartthrob to play one of two men who say they had a UFO encounter in 1992.

Pals Garry Wood and Colin Wright claimed they were driving in West Lothian when a UFO hovered in front of them before they were beamed on board and examined by strange creatures before being sent back to earth.

By Bob Smyth

Garry said he saw a small being with a child-like body and a large pear-shaped head with black eyes.

He recalled lying naked with two small creatures at the foot of the table, one holding a diamond-shaped object. The creature then began moving it over him.

Colin found himself in a large glass or chamber, naked and strapped by the wrists and ankles.

He was then dragged by "wee aliens" back to the car.

Both men came back from their close encounter with scars that were not previously there.

The amazing story, known as the A70 Incident, sparked a sensation — and put the pair under a critical worldwide spotlight.

But they stuck to the details of their stories, which came out under hypnosis, and Garry even passed a lie detector test.

He's to be played in the film by Paisley actor Paul McGillion, Dionne has revealed.

Los Angeles-based Paul has plenty of sci-fi fans after starring as Dr Carson Beckett in the TV series *Stargate Atlantis*. He was so popular fans launched a protest to stop his character being killed off.

Dionne, originally from Merseyside, says she is

chasing *Lord Of The Rings* star Billy Boyd to play Colin.

She says she's had great help from the real-life pair, who've signed confidentiality agreements to stop them speaking about the movie, to be called A70.

She said, "Both men and their families received so much upset, it was unfair to them all.

"All these guys wanted to do was to look into what happened to them and seek answers. Instead both suffered immensely.

"Garry and Colin have been really supportive," added Dionne, speaking to *UFO Matrix* magazine, which is out now.

Sunday Post Talking about A70 Film

114

Rapimento alieno sull'**A70**

UN CASO CLAMOROSO PASSATO ALLA STORIA
IN UNA STRADA DELLA SCOZIA NEGLI ANNI NOVANTA

di Umberto Visani

WEST LOTHIAN, SCOZIA
11 AGOSTO 1992

Italian UFO Magazine

KIDNAPPED: Ambulance mechanic Garry Wood claims that he was kidnapped by aliens travelling in a spaceship while he was driving along the A70 to Tarbrax

Did aliens beam up pals for a car trek?

By David Hamilton

AS EXCUSES go, "Sorry I'm late, I was abducted by aliens" has to be one of the more inventive ever offered.

But Garry Wood is deadly serious when he says he was nearly two hours late arriving at a friend's house because he was kidnapped by aliens.

Ever since his close encounter, Mr Wood, 32, an ambulance mechanic from Edinburgh — his workmates have nicknamed him Starman — has suffered flashbacks, panic attacks and sleepless nights.

It began the night he and friend Colin Wright set off by car to deliver a satellite television dish to a friend.

The journey along the A70 from Oxgangs, Edinburgh, to the West Lothian village of Tarbrax should have taken only 30 minutes.

They arrived two hours later, ashen-faced and shaking. Both told uncannily similar versions of an encounter with a flying saucer crewed by

SAME STORY: Companion Colin Wright

two "skeletal" aliens with large heads. They said they had turned a corner near Harperrigg Reservoir to be confronted by the spaceship hovering 25ft above the ground.

Identical

Mr Wood recalls "I put my foot down and accelerated. I was thinking 'These sort of things are not supposed to exist. As we were going underneath it, a shimmering curtain fell and we went into total blackness I couldn't see anything."

Catriona Phillip, the friend who had been waiting for the TV dish, said: "Garry had phoned at 10pm to say he and

> 'They seemed able to look into my life'

Colin were coming over. When they didn't arrive, I went to bed.

"It was well after midnight when they knocked loudly at my door. Both appeared shocked and were chattering excitedly about aliens. They drew identical diagrams of the craft and the little men they had seen."

Both are adamant they didn't stop during the journey.

To discover what happened in the "lost" 90 minutes, Mr Wood, who has been the worst affected of the two, agreed to regressive hypno-therapy — which can be seen in a BBC1 documentary tonight.

He describes to Glasgow-based psychiatrist Dr Prem Misra the aliens he met on the night of August 18, 1992.

While under hypnosis, he talks about "a wee man" coming up to him as he lay on a stretcher or platform. He recalls two aliens, like "thin, translucent, fragile-looking skeletal beings."

"They seemed to look right into my life," recalls Mr Wood. "I didn't think these things existed but whatever they are, they have a life like me and you. They are here and I know more are coming."

Dr Misra has no doubt Mr Wood genuinely believes he had a close encounter. His advice to Mr Wood is to learn self-hypnosis to help his anxiety attacks.

Science fiction writer Stewart Campbell is more sceptical. Although he has not fully investigated the case, he believes the men may have encountered an astronomical mirage and simply became confused about the time.

Mr Campbell said: "Most UFO sightings are mirages of astronomical objects or aircraft. You can generate a wave of sightings if you tell people you've seen a UFO."

Also featured in the BBC Scotland documentary, called Close Encounters, is the Stirlingshire village of Bonnybridge where more than 2,000 UFO sightings have been reported since 1992.

Gateway

No one can explain why the village with a population of 9,000, two pubs, a hotel, social club and a dozen shops has had so many sightings.

UFO experts believe the village may be a "window area", a gateway between our universe and another which allows UFOs to be seen.

The programme also tells the story of Andy Swan, 27, a cable layer with Scottish Power who saw a "Toblerone-shaped object" over Armadale, West Lothian. Police confirmed seeing an orange light at the same time.

Inspector John Mackinnon, who attended the July 1994 incident, said: "We always take these sightings seriously. We have neither proved nor disproved any of these stories."

● *Cracking Stories: Close Encounters* is on BBC1 Scotland tonight at 8.30pm.

The Sunday Express 1995

A70. THE MOVIE. An interview with the film maker Marie Bell (pseudonym) By Malcolm Robinson.

Big cases of UFO abduction are few and far between in Scotland, so when I was contacted by two men who claimed to have been abducted by aliens, I was both mightily surprised and interested. There was no doubt in my mind as those early days of my investigation into what's now known as 'The A70 Incident,' that I was dealing with a very major case. A case which stood head and shoulders above anything that I had previously researched before. A case which taxed my brain, my belief systems, and basically everything to do with the world we live in. It soon became apparent that these guys 'were telling the truth'. Absolutely without question they were telling the truth. Indeed a few years later, one of the abductees, Garry Wood, passed a BBC TV lie detector test with flying colours a test assessed by a trained and professional assessor.

When this case eventually hit the big wide world, it caused a sensation. It was the first 'reported' UFO abduction of its kind to have occurred in Scotland. I participated in many U.K. and overseas television documentaries explaining to viewers the complexities of this case, and how it contributed to the growing world wide phenomenon of UFO abductions. Never in my wildest dreams did I think that one day, this impressive case would be made into a feature film, that was until one day in 2008 when I received an e-mail from one lady, who I will call Marie, (not her real name) Marie explained that she had read about the A70 incident on the internet and was absolutely fascinated with it, so much so she said, that she wanted to make a full length feature film about it. She went on to say that as I was the principle investigator who had worked on the case, could we set up a meeting where we could sit down and have a proper chat about it. Needless to say I was more than happy to oblige, and a date was set where Carole my partner and I, travelled up to London *(Author's note, I was living in Hastings at that time)* for a meeting with Marie and her colleague at the Charring Cross Hotel.

I saw at that meeting, how passionate Marie was on the A70 project. She was full of questions, full of energy, and had an incredible drive to see through to completion this film project. I sat there mesmerised and captivated by her sheer enthusiasm and knew immediately that I was dealing with a woman of purpose and integrity. As the weeks rolled by, the lady and I communicated by phone and e-mail and her enthusiasm never waned. She kept me up to date with how things were progressing on the movie, and as things stand, things were looking good. My main concerns with anyone who would have done a movie on the A70 UFO abduction, was, how well they would cover it! Admittedly money comes into it. If you pay for a five bob TV that's what you'll get. Funding is ever so important with any movie, and this one is no different. My fear, would be that the movie may (because of limited funding) not have the strength and power to convey to the viewer, how deeply shocking and traumatic an experience like this really was. However, my fears have been allayed by Marie, for at the end of the day, her reputation as a film maker is also involved, and there is no way that she would want to be involved with a turkey! She has convinced me that A70 the movie will be graphic, not only in its design, but also in its pictorial vision. It will leave the viewer under no illusions that we are dealing here with a bona fide phenomenon of immense proportions that warrant's everyone's attention. In order to keep the readers of this UFO publication up-to-date with what is happening regarding this movie project I recently took the opportunity to conduct a brief interview with that lady, who, as I've stated, we are calling Marie Bell.

(Author's note. This was a series of questions that I put to the lady in an e-mail, and she responded accordingly)

Abbreviations: (MR) Malcolm Robinson. (MB) Marie Bell.

(MR) "Marie, could you tell me a little bit about yourself, your hobbies interests, music TV etc"?

(MB) "I am a Film Producer, Casting Director, and I also run my company, representing actors, film directors and Screenwriters including my production company. I absolutely love fishing, whether it is sea or course fishing, although I would love to try fly fishing at some point. I love horse riding, keeping fit, photography, movies and going out for dinner, and having fun with my lovely daughter, friends and my family. I love my music even when I'm working. I really love tracks from the 60's, 80's, 90's and I love my Rock bands such as Muse, Kings of Leon, Foo Fighters and Queens of the Stone Age. I'm also a huge fan of Fleetwood Mac and The Beatles. I love watching anything on wildlife, history, Science and the paranormal even Eastenders (although that is my daughter's choice!)"

(MR) "Now you have had your own UFO encounter, would you like to tell me about it"?

(MB) "There was an incident when I was 14 years old during November 1980. We lived on a very quiet road and there was a row of houses opposite us. In fact this road was roughly a mile long. It was around 2am / 3:30am and I was woken up by my sister screaming and shouting. She was sitting upright on the bed looking out of the window and really stressed out. I was confused, and wondered what was happening, and thought she might have been unwell and I was asking her if she was OK. Everything at that time happened really very quickly. My sister stated that there was something outside of the window and shouted at me not to look outside. Naturally I was really intrigued to why she was freaking out, so I looked out of the window. Not sure if that was a good move thinking about it, as I then witnessed this very large dark oval shaped craft hovering on the opposite side of our house. It literally was hovering over 4 houses, and these where built and laid in an L shape as part of the road. This was just a few meters away from us, and we could see every single detail on this thing. It was just hovering above these houses and not a sound could be heard. It was really, really scary. I just felt physically sick. I had just turned 14 years old, but I certainly knew what it was, and I just wanted it to go away. I was so scared that something really bad was just going to happen. Suddenly, lights appeared on this thing, and I do remember seeing strange patterns cut into the craft, also the

118

colour and just the whole appearance of this object was incredible but also disturbing. Then these lights just appeared in a formation on this craft and then my parents dashed in and within a blink of an eye this thing just moved. I witnessed how it moved which was really scary, it moved at such a speed, it is far more advanced than anything we could possibly imagine. Within a blink of an eye it vanished, it was gone and it left no traces of dust, just nothing. I sometimes wonder if it was watching us, maybe that was why it moved. I really have no idea. This craft appeared further up the road by which we could still see from our window, and my entire family by this point was watching. And then it just moved, it was gone. Our house was filled with panic and my father wanted to go and knock on the neighbour's house. Of course that was not a good idea at that time of the morning to ask your neighbour *"Hey you just had a UFO hovering above your house and I just wanted to check to see if you're OK"* This certainly would not go down well. And as we never had phones, my dad wanted to call the police, he even took a knife with him because he was really scared himself which was not like my dad. He then went for a 10 minute walk to a phone box. I don't remember anything after that. But I do know he called the police and made a report on what had just happened and what we had witnessed, and gave them his details. I had been looking out for this report, I know the government stated they would release all files that were reported, but I could not find anything. I even went to The National Archives to look at the files that were not available online. Nothing could be found".

(MR) "What do you think is behind the UFO enigma, have you your own thoughts"?

(MB) "These things do exist without a doubt. There are some strange stories out there and we have to push them to one side and focus on the good evidence. We have seen hundreds of witnesses and stories over the years and I certainly did whilst I was researching for a documentary I was working on. We even have witnesses from celebrities, the public, even those with a professional background, such as Navy, Army and RAF Pilots.

We have strong evidence and well over a decade on UFO encounters. I believe that there must be an underhand government that is certainly fully aware on these UFO Encounters and why they won't come forward is beyond me, and completely outrageous to why they cover this up.

(MR) "What is your favourite UFO movie of all time"?

(MB) "Close Encounters is such a classic, although I loved Fire in the Sky, and I would have loved to remake this film and get the full story told".

(MR) "What is your favourite book on UFOs (apart from mine that is)"?

(MB) "I have only read yours Malcolm. Oh, and I'm just reading Philip Mantle's as he wants me to work on a documentary, but nothing is yet confirmed".

(MR) "What drew your attention that very first time, to the A70 Incident"?

(MB) "I first came across the A70 incident back in the late 90's. The story is very unique, powerful and emotional, and the amount of research that has taken place into this story by Malcolm is incredible. When you look into this story, there is no ending, and it was very difficult writing a screenplay trying to find a closing to this. Both men Garry and Colin including their families, received so much upset this was unfair to them all. All these guys wanted to do was to look into what happened to them and seek answers. Instead both guys suffered immensely".

(MR) "Why did you want to make this movie"?

(MB) "I was working on a documentary at the time, and I was researching other stories that had taken me a couple of years to put together and I secured these stories in Australia, Europe, U.S. and the U.K. and of course the A70 case in Scotland. Without doubt the A70 case was unique, and I had known about this for many years. I could not film just 15 minutes on the A70 case by re-enacting this, I wanted to make this into a movie and tell it how it is, and it is an incredible true story. Both Garry and Colin have been really supportive including you Malcolm".

(MR) "If you had the millions, who would have been your top actors to play the lead roles in the movie"?

(MB) "Billy Boyd and Paul McGillion".

(MR) "Who do we have actor wise at the moment for the film"?

(MB) "I am currently in-talks with Billy Boyd and Paul McGillion. And at this stage and I cannot state who the actor is that I am in-talks with in regard of playing you Malcolm Robinson".

(Author's note. It later transpired that Scottish actor Dougray Scott was contacted to play me, Malcolm Robinson.

(MR) "When do you expect (once you get the funding and all is tied up) that the movie will eventually hit the cinema screens"?

(MB) "We are currently aiming to begin filming in February 2011. I am currently in talks with Co Productions but I cannot disclose this information just yet, but it all is very exciting. Post Production can take many months so at this stage I would say late 2011 early 2012".

(MR) "Are there anything about you that would surprise us"?

(MB) "As my friends and family would state, I am always full of surprises. Yup full of surprises indeed".

(MR) "What movies have you been associated with previously"?

(MB) "I met up with Stan Anderson when I was a producer and a casting director, alongside my company, where, I also represented screenwriters, Film Directors and actors for TV and Movies in the U.S. and the U.K. Stan had worked on some fantastic movies as an editor, and Stan and I seem to work really well together. We have now completed a couple of films including 'Toby's Odyssey' which is on the international film festival circuit including Los Angeles and the Venice Film Festival. We have a Psychological thriller 'Selective Amnesia' which is looking very exciting and I'm looking into other projects which I would like to produce and cast. And I have now been approached in collaborating alongside a production company in the U.S. with my production company here in the U.K. which I'm discussing but nothing yet is confirmed".

(MR) "Will this be the start of you doing any more UFO movies"?

(MB) "Never say never. I would love to have an opportunity in working on another UFO or alien abduction movie for sure. I have a documentary I will be working on again after A70 which I am looking forward to, and I am planning on going to the U.S. and of course I have other projects and a backlog of screenplays".

(MR) "Would you like to do a movie based on a true paranormal case"?

(MR) "Absolutely, and I know you have stated something to me so who knows"?

(MR) "What would you like to be doing in 5 years time"?

(MB) "Being a mum to my lovely daughter, and continue making movies on a job that I absolutely love doing".

(MR) "Finally what do you hope to bring to the A70 movie"?

(MB) "A fantastic cast and a strong and powerful movie that simply tells truth of course".

So, through this UFO magazine the story was out. There was going to be a movie made about the A70 Incident. Soon after, I started to receive phone calls and e-mails from the media who were keen to learn more, and although all I could say at this point was that the movie was in its early stages, which was of course factual, they were still keen to print 'something' about it.

SCOTLAND'S BIGGEST UFO ABDUCTION INCIDENT BEING MADE INTO A MOVIE

This was the headline from the Scottish Television's web site from the 7th of October 2009. I won't go into all of what this story related, as it is pretty much covered throughout the book. What I will do though, is take out some quotes from the article which I feel are quite poignant.

"I'm ever so pleased that is going to happen, for the Scottish public to realise they have their own recognisable phenomena in their own backyard." says paranormal investigator Malcolm Robinson. *"We may laugh and joke about this subject, but there is something very, very real and very mysterious ongoing in the skies."*

The A70 incident was a pivotal moment for Malcolm who's new book *UFO Case Files of Scotland*, gives investigative information on various sightings across Scotland. Previously a sceptic of UFOs and alien activity, Malcolm firmly became a believer after hearing from Garry and Colin about their experiences. *"I was an ardent sceptic,"* says Malcolm. *"I really didn't think that there was any validity to these tales of machines flying about the Scottish skies". "But it is like anything else in life, once you physically get involved in investigating these subjects, then you come off the fence. I found that after a few years of investigation, there's enough*

123

substantial data to validate the people that have been seeing these things."

FILMMAKER SET TO REOPEN LOTHIAN'S VERY OWN X FILES

This was the heading from one of Scotland's newspapers which sadly although I have the report, I don't have the name of the paper that it was featured in. The reporter was Mark McLaughlin, and the feature was printed on the 9th of October 2009. This is how Mark reported it.

It has already become Lothian's most famous X-File and now it's set to feature on the big screen. The claims by two Edinburgh friends that they were abducted by aliens while driving in 1992 have become the stuff of legend and fierce debate. In what has become known as the 'A70 Abduction Case' Garry Wood and Colin Wright have stood by their incredible story ever since.

The pair are now working with a London production company which is finalising a script to turn their close encounter into a film."*It's such a fantastic story and I was attracted to it from the first time I heard it,"* said film producer Marie Bell, who is financing the film through her company.

"I had seen the film Fire in the Sky (based on the experiences of American logger Travis Walton who was purportedly abducted in 1975) which has similarities, but Colin and Garry's experience did have unique elements to it."

The two friends have told over the years how they encountered the flying saucer on the A70 near the Harperrig Reservoir, a few miles west of Balerno. The pair drove beneath it in an attempt to get away, and were enveloped in a shimmering energy beam. When they arrived at their destination in Tarbrax village, about five miles from Harperrig, they were an hour and a half late and could not account for the time. Medical checks failed to find a cause for the memory lapse, or the severe headaches both men had developed, but hypnotherapy sessions brought forth memories of alien experiments conducted by a translucent-grey, skeletal creature. Gilmerton mechanic and car-enthusiast Garry, whose workmates took to calling him 'Starman', went on to pass a televised lie detector test, and the men's experiences pre-date the spate of alien abduction claims which were sparked by the X-Files television series in the mid-90s.

Shortly after their experience the pair visited paranormal investigator Malcolm Robinson, who was based in Alloa at the time but now lives in London, and he convinced them to go through hypnotic regression. *"These guys were desperate for anything to explain what happened to them,"* said Mr Robinson, who is also working on the film.

"Under hypnosis they described tall grey creatures quite unique from standard abductee descriptions of five-foot childlike aliens. "Garry, who's from quite a tough part of Edinburgh, told me that he was strapped to a table with these things prodding him, and he desperately wanted to take a swing at one of them. "It's such a great premise for a film and we're currently going through script negotiations with Colin and Garry to make sure they're happy with everything. I hope they don't add too much salt and pepper to it and make it another Braveheart, based on fact, but 80 per cent inaccurate. "People have asked me who I would like to play me, and I usually say Ewan McGregor, although I had a moustache in those days so he'd have to grow one. Colin and Garry are such down-to-earth guys it's hard to imagine any famous actors playing them." Neither Colin nor Garry wanted to comment on the film plans due to contractual reasons.

PROMOTING THE A70 INCIDENT ON STV'S THE HOUR.

After the newspapers got wind of this incredible tale being made into a movie, it was time for Scottish Television to get in on the act as well. I was contacted by a researcher at Scottish Television and asked if I would like to come to Scotland, (I was living in Hastings, East Sussex, England at the time) and appear on their live TV lifestyle magazine show called 'The Hour'.

125

Needless to say, I said I would be delighted to. And in October 2009, I set off for Scotland, where I also managed to squeeze in a visit to family and freinds. 'The Hour', was broadcast every weekday at 5:00pm and presented by Michelle McManus and Stephen Jardine from the STV studios at Pacific Quay in Glasgow. They also asked if I could bring along a UFO witness, and as I was staying over at my good friend Brian McMullan's house at Lennoxtown near Glasgow, I asked Brian if he would be happy to come on the show with me. He heartidly agreed.

After a enjoyable breakfast and a chat about UFOlogy, we were met by Fraser, a family friend of Brian's who then drove us to the new Scottish Television Studios on the South Side of Glasgow by the River Clyde to meet up with the staff and presenters for the STV's 'The Hour' programme. In the car on the way to the studio, Brian produced a wee silver hip flask which contained rum and coke and passed it to me. Now I never have a wee drink before I go on the television, but on this occasion I decided to take one wee sip. I was tempted to take more but didn't! Arriving at the studio we signed in and went and sat in a room adjacent to the studio. We were then briefed by the programme's producer, afterwhich I got talking to another of the show's guest's, a chap who has been described as Scotland's answer to Victor Meldrew for his complaining. This chap was on the show to talk about his household garbage bin not being collected by the bin men because it was slightly open, and not closed properly. Now this gentleman showed me the photo of the bin lid in question, and it looked shut to me. But, if you looked closely, it was just a tiny centimetre open. Brian and I congratulated the chap for going on the telly to complain, its great that the ordinary man and woman in the street can be seen and heard in this manner when it comes to standing up for your rights. I bet the binman are not happy with him now!

'THE HOUR'
After a short while we were taken through to the studio for a short rehearsal, and on this rehearsal they showed Brian's drawing of the UFO that he saw a few years back. When it was time to do the show live, we were again taken through and sat down on a settee in front of the presenters Steven Jardine and

Michelle McManus. As soon as I sat down Steven Jardine said, *"Hey, I know you don't I"?* I replied that he surely did, as he and I worked together for GMTV (Good Morning Television) on a haunted house case in Kilsyth Central Scotland back in 1994 (I'm glad he remembered it) His co-presenter Michelle McManus was a former winner of Pop Idol back in 2003 and she had made occasional appearances on the show, but this show was to be her first show as a permanent presenter and I was to be her first guest. The studio was much like any other TV studio that I have found myself in over the years, and before too long we were live to the Scottish Nation where Brian and I spoke about my book and some of the better sightings of UFOs over Scotland. Sadly, they didn't show Brian's UFO painting that they had done in rehearsal, which was a shame as this is a classic case. Another disappointment was that they didn't show the front cover of my book (UFO Case Files of Scotland Volume 1) Admittedly the producer had already said to me earlier in the day that I was not to mention my book too much for commercial reasons! What! Surely that was why I was on their show. Thankfully Steven did mention the book so it wasn't that bad. I would have also liked the TV folk to have mentioned the fact that Brian McMullan (Snr) has not only assisted SPI in our research over the years, but that he is the guitarist with the UFO Rock band CE IV, but they wanted to stick mainly with the movie. We also spoke about the A70 case and that we were in the early stages of turning this impressive case into a full motion picture.

Anyway before too long our brief interview was over, and we were ushered out into the foyer where we met the next guest on the show, Ruth Madoc who was in the hit TV programme Hi De Hi. Anyone who knows me will tell you that I'll speak to anyone and I quickly looked over to her and said, *"Hi Ruth nice to see you in Scotland"* and soon we were in deep conversation more so because she spotted my book under my arm and wanted to know more about it. Brian also engaged her in conversation as Ruth's husband looked on. Nice lady.

SO, WHAT HAPPENED WITH THE A70 MOVIE?

Firstly I was ever so proud to be associated with this movie. I knew that this movie would show the world that Scotland as a nation, has also been touched by the UFO presence. There has been many a documentary on some of Britain's UFO cases, but never a full length warts and all movie, and I hoped that the A70 movie would make even the biggest sceptic sit up and take notice. But it was not to be. After many script changes both Garry and Colin started to draw back from the project. Their heart was in it from the start, but as we progressed through the scripts, it became clear that both men wanted to steer clear from it and it was decided to drop the project. A great shame, as I firmly believe that someone 'out there' should make this movie, maybe some day, who knows.

2021 THOUGHTS BY FILM MAKER MARIE BELL.

A70? I was beyond devastated to close this project down and not one month will go by when I think about 'what if' if I'm honest. A70 is an incredible and powerful story and so unique. I have never come across anything like this story ever (besides the film 'Fire in the Sky'). I remember very well meeting up with you and Stan in London, and our meetings, even the struggles with Skype was interesting at times. I miss those days and the talks we had. I still have the file you gave me. It kills me to read the background on this A70 project it really does. I worked so hard to get this project up and running and gave it everything. I tried to work out a way that it could work every time. So many times I thought about contacting you and Stan to discuss if we could consider this project with a different direction perhaps. Would I consider this project again? Never say never as they say.

OTHER WITNESSES (SIMILAR ACCOUNTS)

I mentioned that other Scottish people came forward when they heard about the A7O Incident, (I always ensured that the press agencies gave my address as a contact source for other possible UFO abductees to get in touch). I would now like to mention a few other cases whereby you the reader, will see that Garry and Colin's case is certainly not isolated. This case comes from a lady from somewhere near the town of Campbeltown in Argyll Scotland. The lady wishes to remain anonymous, but her identify is on file with the author. This is what she had to tell our society.

ANOTHER WITNESS COMES FORWARD.

"My earliest recollection would be about the age of 9, myself and several friends noticed lights in the sky that appeared to follow us. They would move when we moved, stop when we stopped, and then suddenly speed off. This went on for some time but being so young, it seemed like a game and did not go beyond childish curiosity. Between the ages of 10 and 13, I had quite a few odd experiences, I would quite often wake in the morning with the feeling that something had happened during the night but couldn't remember what. I often had dirt on my hands and feet, and sometimes scratches on my legs and arms. Very often as I was trying to get to sleep at night, I would hear a soft droning noise that would very slowly get louder until my bed would be vibrating with the noise. Sometimes it would suddenly stop or gradually die down as it had started. I did ask my parents what it was, but they said that they hadn't heard anything which I found difficult to understand as it seemed so loud".

"I often slept with my curtains open, and was awakened one night by bright lights shining into my bedroom. I got up and looked out of my window, straight into the window of what I can only describe as a space craft hovering outside the house, there were faces staring back at me. The next thing I remember, is morning. I have always believed this to have been a dream. I awoke one night to find a large cat with huge eyes sitting on my wardrobe, it jumped down and went to the bedroom door, and for some reason I felt that I must follow it. I opened the door and was blinded by a brilliant white light. I stepped through the doorway and remember nothing else until I

awoke in the morning. At around the same time, my father found a black cat sitting on my bed staring at me, he chased it out of the house. No one knew how it had got in".

"During this period, I started hearing noises and voices as though someone was playing with the tuner on a radio. I could hear parts of conversations that were being held several doors away. I could read the registration numbers of cars that were passing outside. I also started 'seeing' in quite graphic detail, events that were about to take place, such as motorway accidents, train crashes, etc. Between the ages of 13 and 16, all the above continued, but now with the addition of electrical appliances switching themselves on and off, and taps turning themselves on. There would be knocking on internal doors, always 3 knocks, usually 3 times. A friend was once disturbed to see my sister's doll's pram wheeling itself up and down the hallway".

"When I was 17, we moved to a new house a few miles up the road. A few months later, I was drifting off to sleep when I suddenly felt very strange, I felt as though I was floating. I opened my eyes and was shocked to find myself hovering above the planet. I realised that 'something' was with me, and suddenly I felt very calm. We turned towards a bright light in the distance and seemed to be floating towards it. As we drew nearer, I could hear the most beautiful sound, I couldn't possibly describe it, but the nearer we got, the louder the noise became. I realised that 'my' voice had joined in with this strange choral music. All of a sudden I was whisked backwards and found myself lying in bed looking up at a large glowing orb hovering above me. It seemed to be transparent with particles moving within it. It reminded me of a jelly fish. It then shot through the window just as my mother ran into the bedroom. She had evidently been awakened by what she called 'the most awful inhuman sound' coming from my room".

"I married when I was 19 and moved to Yorkshire. A few months later, I awoke early one morning in pain. I had a circular mark at the bottom of my leg. Over the next few days,

130

my leg swelled horribly. I went to the doctor who told me that it must have been some sort of bite. I still have a circular scar three quarters of an inch in diameter. Within the next two years we moved house again, (still in Yorkshire) and I had my daughter. During this period I had odd experiences, but cannot remember anything specific until a year or two later, which brings us to 1985."

"I had several troubled nights waking in the morning, remembering that during the night I had experienced being totally paralysed and had tried to move and shout to my husband, but that was all I could remember. I was very disturbed by this. This went on for a couple of months, then one night some friends came over. I went to bed about 11:30pm and the others stayed up to watch television. I had just turned the light out and snuggled down in bed, when I became aware that there was something in the room and I again became totally paralysed. I tried to scream for help, but couldn't make any noise. I thought that if I could somehow manage to reach up and pull the light cord, it would go away, or if I were dreaming, I would wake up".

"I managed somehow to reach up and switch the light on, I was still unable to move or shout, and the room was full of an indescribable substance, it reminded me again of jelly fish. I could see my bedroom furniture through it, but everything was distorted. I remember thinking, "What are you"? "What do you want"? "I don't understand, I'm frightened". It then slowly disappeared through the open bedroom window. I got up and went downstairs and our guests were concerned as I looked in shock. Then one of the men said, "That's odd, the T.V's O.K. now"! Evidently whilst this had been happening to me, the T.V. reception had gone. It is worth mentioning that the aerial was right outside my bedroom window".

"There seemed to be an awful lot of odd things happening during this time. For example, I was speaking to a friend on the telephone when suddenly the receiver shot out of my hand, the lights flashed on and off, and the T.V. went off. I tried to

131

redial, but the phone wasn't working, so I went into the kitchen to use the one in there and found the kettle boiling and the cooker full on. I finally got through, and before I could say anything, she said that 'her' phone had jumped out of 'her' hands and something had whizzed past her head down the hallway. She was quite hysterical and I had to contact her husband to get him home. We both asked our neighbours if they had a power cut that night, they hadn't. We lived quite a distance from each other and, as it turned out, were on different electrical grids. There had not been any storms that night".

"I was divorced a year later and moved into a cottage with my daughter. The experiences carried on. Baby-sitters refused to sit for me as they thought the house was haunted. Things would move about and something kept knocking on the cellar door. I was standing in front of this door brushing my daughter's hair before taking her to school, when we heard a strange sound coming from behind the door. We both jumped, and I noticed two screws holding a bolt on the door were unscrewing before my eyes. We dived out of the door. When I returned, I screwed them back in again. I was sitting in my car at traffic lights a few weeks later when everything outside seemed to distort. The road looked as if it were 'rippling'. I was still sitting there long after the lights had changed".

"In 1988 I moved with my daughter back to my parents house in Milton Keynes. A few weeks later, these nightly visitations resumed with a vengeance. They were occurring two or three times a week. Shortly after this, I remarried and moved to Windsor for a year. A few weeks after moving, things started happening again. My husband was witness to much of what was going on, such as the knocking and tapping, time slips etc. I once walked from the kitchen to the living room, picked up a tea towel that I had left in there, and walked back to the kitchen. This two minute activity took '35 minutes'! I had looked at the clock as I had walked out of the kitchen and it was 9:55am, I looked at it again as I walked back in and it was 10:35am".

"I remember being told things and seeing symbols and shapes. As a child I was terrified to go to bed, now it is just certain nights. It's as though I can sense that something is going to happen now, but I am still caught out from time to time. This may or may not be connected, but for years it has been commented on that I speak a strange language whilst asleep. When I remarried, my husband (who is Scottish) recognised this as Gaelic. I have no knowledge of this language, and certainly cannot speak or understand it."

"I would like to mention at this point, that I have seen ghosts or spirits, (or whatever you wish to call them), and have no fear of these. The other experiences induce a totally different feeling, I have no conscious understanding as to what they are or why I feel the way I do."

In further communications, this witness went on to provide details of observing what are now commonly know as the 'grey's' in her bedroom, and believes that her daughter has experienced contact with them as well, although the daughter is very reluctant to speak about it.

The people who contacted me after Garry and Colin's story was featured in the media, were not just from Scotland. I had a lady who wrote to me from Farnborough in England with her UFO abduction accounts. This lady claimed to have witnessed many strange objects in the sky above Farnborough, all of which she claims were not man made. These objects performed manoeuvres out with the capabilities of what is current in modern air-craft today. Of course the town of Farnborough is famous for it's Air shows, and has hosted many displays and open days throughout the years. There is of course an R.A.F. Air base at Farnborough which obviously sees a lot of air traffic on a regular basis, but again, this witness claims that what she has seen over the years, is certainly not conventional. I have on file many accounts relating to these sightings, one of which actually mentions the time when she saw a strange being! For now though, I'd just like to mention briefly some of her accounts in relation to our A7O case, and in regards to the reader's understanding that the UFO abduction phenomenon, is certainly prevalent in the United Kingdom. The following is taken direct from the witness's own written testimony.

THEY COME AT NIGHT!

"In the late 1970's, my daughter Sandra (pseudonym) and myself lived alone in the highest house in our high tech area of mid Southern England. So much goes on here, much we do know about, and much we don't. Sometimes I would be suddenly aware of a pair of eyes boring into my back and feeling very frightened sometimes to the point of rushing out of the house into the garden. This happened many times." "At this time, something else was happening to my little daughter and myself. We would be in our bed (we slept together) we had quite bright street lighting but then I was aware of more than this. It was an orange/red glow over by my drawing board. I then became aware of a figure, all dark standing there. Now I would normally scream, but somehow I could not do this. Then suddenly tiny figures came out of the glow towards my bed. They were small thin and grey in colour approximately three and a half feet tall, there were about six or seven of them, they were splitting up to go towards Sandra and myself, I couldn't do a thing about it, I couldn't even move. For some reason I had no fear, I think 'they' must have taken away my fear, for I know that I would have gone absolutely crazy with fear".

"It was at this point that I think we must have been 'put out', but before we were, I remember being poked and prodded all over with fast moving hands. There was one occasion when I was aware of them coming round to Sandra's side of the bed, my first instinct was to protect this tiny child beside me, but I could do nothing. I was lying on my side powerless, then I was 'put out' for I remember nothing more. When the "greys" move, they remind me of tiny children in some ways, sort of skipping and hopping, their over sized heads would bobble about. I tried not to look into their faces by closing my eyes when they came up close to me."

"The after effects at that time were not something that I immediately connected with what was happening, for much of the night before would be wiped, I just had a vague remembrance, and in those days, I had no idea that UFO abductions were taking place, only UFO sightings. The physical effects were for me, a weeping navel, this happened on many occasions, it was very sore and red. My daughter Sandra is a handicapped child, and she was to my knowledge, never interfered with 'down below' as she has always had special nappies to keep her dry at night. For myself, I remember another occasion when I got up one morning feeling unwell, I found that I was swollen and very sore down below, (pubic region). I got Sandra off to school then made an appointment with my doctor as I was very worried as to what it might be. Upon examination my doctor (female) looked at me with shock upon her face and said, "How did you get this mutilation, you are all wounds with sore red patches. I'm sure you will heal in a while, but I've never seen anything like this". I told her that I hadn't a clue as to how this had happened. (I felt as if 'she' felt that I was lying and she wasn't so nice to me after this point). She then asked if another doctor could be present. Another doctor came in and his expression told me all I wanted to know, and I wish I hadn't gone. She said that if this ever happened to me again that I was to go to her. She gave me some cream but I had the impression that I had something awful and I thought I may well die. I lived with this for ten and a half years until I was told I was perfectly alright by my new doctor."

"Then there was the time when I awoke with a sore arm, and I was shocked to find that I was literally black on my right forearm (inner part). I believe that it was the Greys that did this. On the night of October 11th, I went to my winter wardrobe to get my favourite white jumper (cardigan), and to my surprise and annoyance, I found that it was covered in a brown and orange stain all over the forearm in the same location where my bruise had been. I found other stains of the same kind on the right hand side of the cardigan. I had not worn this cardigan since the spring, and I would never have put it away in this mess. I tried to see if resin had come off the

wood (of the wardrobe) which might explain it, but nothing. I tried everything to wash it out, but to this day it's hanging there ruined, bleach didn't remove the stains either. I am not as frightened as I once was, neither is Sandra, but she still looks at the corner of the bedroom when she's had a bad dream, but being autistic, she is not able to tell me just how she feels. I 'know' that she remembers the taller dark figure and the small grey ones that we saw in the room".

One would feel that the terror of being unable to help not only oneself but one's daughter in a situation like this, must have been very terrifying, but the witness relates that her fear, was taken away from her. This was also the case with Garry and Colin, they were both told 'not to be afraid, that no harm would come to them'. Of course this is a ridiculous statement to make in the light of what must be a traumatic experience. Being taken against one's will is no laughing matter and certainly it is abhorrent to this author, but the above testimony is very similar to the testimony that is coming from all parts of the globe. Let us now look at yet another account that was presented to me by a witness who had heard about the A7O Incident. This young lady got in touch with our society looking for answers, she too, had experienced a UFO abduction and wished to relate what happened to her. The following is a condensed account of what she told us. The witness lives near Alexandria Dunbartonshire Scotland.

I WAKE UP WITH SCARS ON MY BODY

"My name is Cathrine Mitchell (pseudonym) I am 14 years old and I think that I may have been involved with the UFO abduction phenomena. I am interested in UFOs and things to do with the paranormal, but what I am about to tell you I swear that I have not invented it to get some attention. My dreams started when I was about 7 or 8 years old, although I vaguely recall having a few when I was a bit younger."

"Every three or four weeks I have recurring dreams of little grey 'beings' with large black eyes and small bodies, then

136

sometimes the dream goes on and I find myself in another room which is brightly lit and I am lying on a cold metallic table. (Similar to what Garry Wood found himself on). *The 'beings' surround me and are doing things to me, sometimes I feel pain and other times I don't. When I wake up after these dreams I sometimes find scars on my body. I don't know how they got there and this troubles me very much. Most of them are on my right calf, I also had one just below my left thigh, the scar is pretty thin and long. I have woken up with scratches but I don't toss and turn or have any sharp points on my bed. Usually the dream starts with a light shining into my room. I feel paralysed and I can't move or speak, then I feel as if I am floating then I feel sick. When I am lying on this cold metallic table, I can see symbols on the wall, but not very well, as the room I'm in is brightly lit. There is also a stand behind the table that I am on, it has strange looking instruments on it. There has also been a few times when one of these 'beings' has stared at me so hard, that I have passed out, then I find myself back in my bedroom. I have began to keep a diary of these dreams, but sometimes these dreams are so bad, that I just cannot write them down. A recent dream that I had, was really frightening. I can remember feeling paralysed and felt the sensation of floating, then I experienced really bad pain. I woke up and discovered that I had a cut on my right forearm. I am finding that these dreams are beginning to affect my social life, my private life and also my school work. At one point I actually broke down in the Maths class, I wanted to tell my teacher but I just couldn't bring myself to do so."*

This young lady went on to inform me about another strange experience, this is what she had to say.

"I had a dream on my birthday but I can't remember all of it, what I can remember was that I was flying across water, I don't know why, but I was. When I went to school the next day, my friend asked me if I had seen the strange lights across the loch near Greenock. I answered no, but then wondered about the fact that I had flown across the water"

137

I kept in touch with Cathrine over the next few years and learned that she was still having these unusual dreams, dreams of which were now entering a new dimension. They were becoming more traumatic and were certainly taking the same course as the many other reported world wide UFO abductions. The following account, taken direct from one of Cathrine's letters to the author, details more dreams that she had experienced. This is what she had to say;

"On the 25th, 26th, and 27th of June 1997, I had more dreams, they were similar to the other dreams, but instead of being in my house, I was walking through the woods about 50 yards from my home. I felt uneasy, but relaxed at the same time. I then felt as if I was passing out but had my eyes open so that I could see what was happening. I couldn't move, and three 'people' not taller than myself, seemed to lift me off the ground. I don't remember anything else from these dreams. These three days in a row were all the same, walking through the woods, feeling as if I had passed out. I should point out, that when I woke up, I found grass at the bottom of my quilt and my feet were dirty"!

"On Sunday the 29th, I woke up at 07:00am feeling very panicky. I felt very uneasy and I felt as if I was suffocating. My eyes started to close, but I didn't want to go to sleep, and I tried to fight it off as much as I possibly could. I couldn't, 'something' made me go to sleep. I felt totally unable to move, I was having difficulty breathing and I felt as if I were floating upwards. I wanted to shout out but I couldn't. The next thing I knew, I was in a really bright white room, it was really cold and I seemed to be on some sort of 'floating table' (The reader should remember that Colin Wright recalls seeing his friend Garry Wood being placed upon a 'floating stretcher').

"I seemed to be floating up towards some sort of metal grid or cage, my legs hung over the edge of the table on a sort of reclining bit. I still couldn't move. I could only move my eyes". (Again the reader is reminded that during Garry and Colin's abduction, they too found that they could only move

their eyes, with a very slight movement of the head). *"In the far end of the room seemed to be some sort of television screen. The walls were curved, and a metallic hum seemed to be coming from 'inside' the walls. As I floated towards the grid/cage, two side flaps which were in grid style, seemed to come down on either side of my body at my arms. Another cage like bit came over my face and I could hardly breathe. It seemed as if I was getting locked into this thing. "I could see two or three 'people',* (Author's note. Cathrine writes in her account of them as people, but she draws them as small grey 'beings'). *Looking at me, but I couldn't make out their faces at all, but when one of them looked at me, I seemed to relax".* (Author's note. This is quite a common feature of most UFO abductions, just when the experiencer is in total despair, these small 'beings' seem to somehow take away the fear and anxiety of the abductee).

Cathrine went on to inform the author that she had experienced witnessing what could be a UFO when she was on holiday in England. This is what she had to tell me.

"In 1995 I was in Andover in England for my summer holidays, I was staying with an auntie, and one night I heard a commotion (noise) in the next door neighbours garden, this was about half past ten in the evening. I looked out and saw the neighbours looking at a bright white object in the sky, the object was darting about the sky. I came back in and went to bed shutting the window as I did so. About 01:30am I woke up feeling really frightened and there was a light outside my window. The next thing I know, I was walking into the back garden, there were 'people' 'beings' waiting for me. That's all I can remember, but the next day I woke up and found mud on my feet, I don't know how it got there because I had taken a shower just before going to bed."

"People have said that the marks on my body are psychosomatic, but I have never wished for any of them to appear. I would now like to tell you about the latest dream that I had (30th June 1997). In this dream, I can see the faces of

the 'people'. I was pinned to my bed, something was holding both my feet and something was holding my left arm. My right arm was free, but I could not move it. There was a really bright light coming through the curtains which was hurting my eyes. I could hear the words, "First Table" in my head, that's all I can remember from that dream. But on my right leg just above the knee to the outside, is a small bruise with what looks like one or two puncture marks on it".

Cathrine continues to have her strange dreams to this day, but are they really nothing more than dreams? or are they happening in our 'reality'? Many witnesses think of their own experiences as nothing more than strange dreams, that is until they wake up to find scars on their body which previously were not there, or wake up to find that they have mud on the soles of their feet (as what happened to Cathrine). In some cases, people have woken up to find that they have different clothes on! Clothes that don't belong to them! There is no denying that the UFO abduction experience is strange, far stranger than perhaps we can ever imagine. Not every UFO abduction follows the same pattern, but nearly all of them have people being taken against their will, and placed on some kind of table, where some form of medical or clinical examination is conducted upon them. This can prove quite traumatic for those involved, and this was certainly true of both Garry and Colin.

As we have learned from the cases above, there have been similarities between those and certain parts of Garry and Colin's experiences. Cathrine mentioned that she found herself on some kind of 'floating table'. This was a feature in the A7O case. I hadn't heard of this effect anywhere else in the UFO literature, that was until I gave a lecture to BUFORA (The British UFO Research Association) at their International UFO Conference which was held in Sheffield England. I recounted the A7O Incident, and a few weeks later a UFO researcher from Doncaster, wrote to me to inform me of a case of which he was working on which also featured a floating stretcher. The following are brief details from this case which happened somewhere in England.

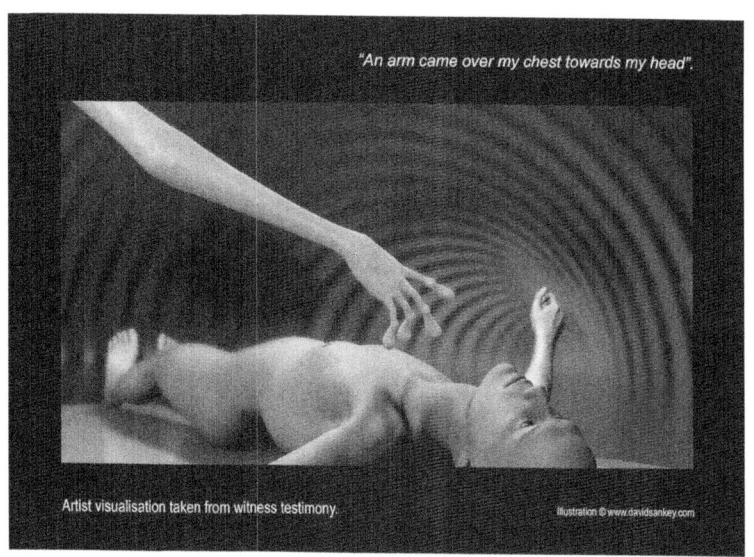

A thin grey arm came over Garry's chest. (c) Dave Sankey

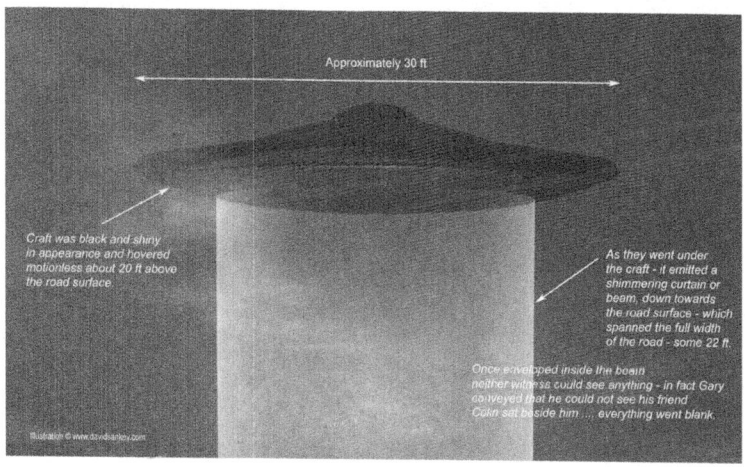

A70 UFO above the road (c) Dave Sankey

Artist rendition of view down corridor inside craft

Illustration © www.davidsankey.com

Alien in corridor (c) Dave Sankey

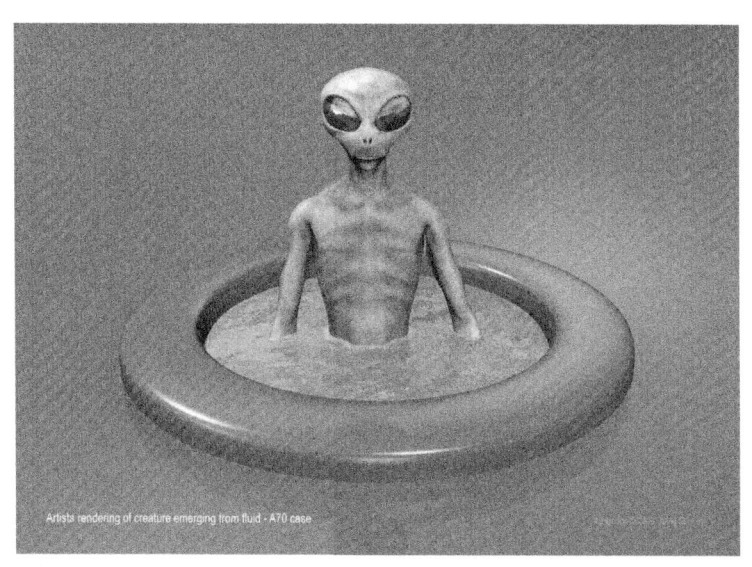

Alien in Liquid (c) Dave Sankey

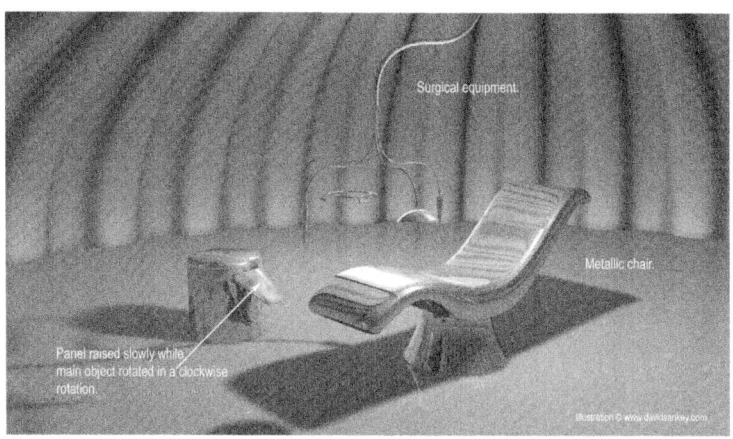

Tableau of what Colin saw (c) Dave Sankey

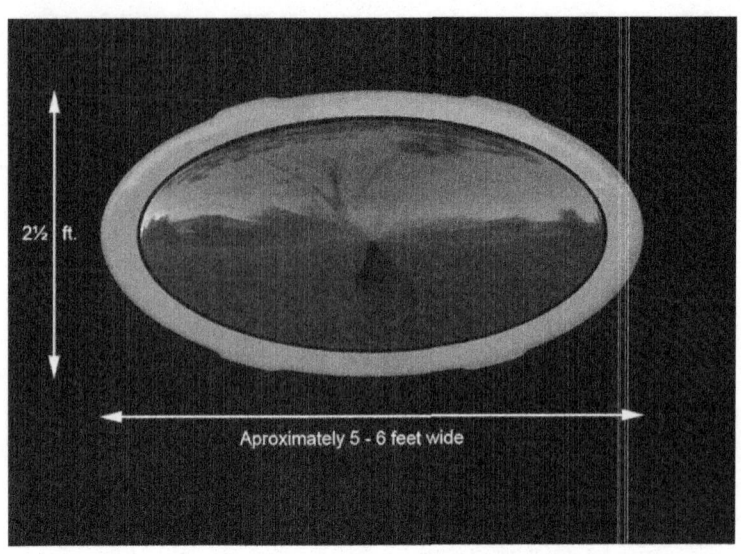

Free Floating Lens Device near Garry (c) Dave Sankey

FREE FLOATING TABLE

The incident occurred in 1967 when the lady was 28 years of age. In fact the whole events that were recalled were remembered at a time when the lady was currently under going an emergency caesarean section brought about by foetal stress of her yet unborn child, consequently, this was to become her only child, a baby daughter. The researcher of this case assumed initially that the whole event was either a 'NDE' (Near Death Experience), or an 'OBE' (Out Of Body Experience). It wasn't until he interviewed the lady in more depth that he was of the opinion that the event's remembered may have predated the caesarean operation and were consciously remembered at that time due to the stress involved. The researcher found much to his surprise, that this particular case did not feature the usual 'Greys', but instead featured another well reported aspect of 'beings' being seen, that of the Nordics. Tall blond haired human looking men which were often reported back in the 1950's. The lady was told by her captors, that the one's who would follow (!) had intentions not quite what they seemed. This particular case is quite extensive, and for the point of our study, we are only concerned with this free floating table.

The room in which the lady found herself in, gave the impression of being some kind of examination room. Medical equipment was suspended above each 'free floating' bed area. All the beds were identical, non metallic, more glass like in appearance but white in colouration. All were certainly 'self illuminating' with insets for head placement. The overall design was undoubtedly for 'humanoid physiology'. The lady felt that the equipment was not 'permanent' and could be removed or folded up in an instant. The medical type of equipment comprised of a needle or probe, an object similar to an anaesthetists face mask and a third instrument which can only be best described as looking like the suction devices used in modern day milking of dairy cattle. This equipment was also 'free floating', but gave the impression that it could be 'stretched' and 'extended' to where ever needed once used returning back to it's original position and alignment. (An associated smell of almonds was also evident within this scenario.)

The illustrations done on computer from the Investigator who researched this case, certainly look similar to the free floating table/bed that witness Cathrine Mitchell described, even to the part of this table that sloped down. (Like a dentists chair). In the A7O case however, the 'free floating' stretcher that Colin saw Garry being placed on, was flat, and Colin is unable to remember any more features about it. At the end of the day, there are many people who will not accept any testimony gained through the use of hypnotic regression, I accept this. I fully understand, as I have said many times before, that hypnosis has it's pitfalls, that it may not be the best tool to obtain any further possible hidden subconscious recall, but in my book, it should still be tried, whereupon any evidence gained, should be laid on the table for any other respective researcher to look at. Hypnosis is another tool in the study of the UFO phenomenon.

The A70 Incident was a most peculiar case. It had in part, all the hallmarks of similar tales throughout the modern world. That said, above the similarities of the case, there were differences as well, and in that regard, let us not take a look at some of those similarities and differences.

SIMILARITIES.

1. Device In Colin's Eye. There was a device that inserted itself into Colin's eye, similar it must be said, to the device that was seen in the movie, 'Fire In The Sky'. This film was about the abduction of a forestry worker Travis Walton. Colin assures the author, that he had not read the book of this incident neither had he seen the film. (The film came out in 1993, a full year after the A70 Incident) Admittedly, and for the record, hypnosis was not undertaken with both Garry and Colin till 1994, so although the film was out a year before the hypnosis, but men still claim not to have seen that film prior to hypnosis being used.

2.   Similar Creatures.   Some (but not all) of these 'creatures' that were witnessed by both men, were similar to what other UFO abductees have witnessed, in that they were small in stature, between three and a half to four feet tall. Some were larger at around six feet tall. Some of the 'creatures' had bluey grey translucent skin, with pear shaped heads. Again, consistent with other world wide encounters.

3. Coldness. Both men experienced a coldness in the room that they found themselves in. Again, this is consistent and common with other UFO abductees recollections.

4. Flat Raised Table. Garry found himself being placed on a flat raised table in a round room, again, yet another similarity to other UFO abduction accounts.

5. Curving Corridor. The curving corridor that led out into a round room, this has also been a feature of other UFO abductions.

6. Scars. Both men came back from their encounter with scars on their bodies   which previously were not there. Colin had a strange scar at the base of his penis, whilst Garry had a strange mark at the back of his neck.

7.   Misty Fog/Mist. One of the major similarities that I found with this case and which has been a feature of many other world wide UFO abduction accounts, concerns this strange misty fog like effect that people encounter. Let us now take a look at but a few of these similarities before we look at the differences.

THE AVELEY ABDUCTION. *(Fog on the road)*

This incident occurred to a family from Aveley in Essex England on the evening of Saturday August 14th 1977. This case is quite extensive and is too much to go into here, however, the salient point in regards to our study, is the fact that this family which comprised of three children accompanied by their mother and father, were travelling in their Vauxhall Victor estate car nearing the town of Aveley. As they were approaching the town, one of the children noticed what appeared to be a large bright star which seemed to be following them. Then just as their car was about to turn round a bend, *(Author's note. Remember the blind bend in the road in Garry and Colin's case!),* They encountered a large fog or mist which appeared in the road about 3O yards from their car. *(Author's note. Again let us remind ourselves with the misty sparkling fog like effect that both Garry and Colin encountered which descended from beneath the object that they saw!).* However, the fog or mist that the Avis family saw they described as green, different it must be said, to the white sparkling fog that Garry and Colin saw). The fog that the Avis family described, was about eight to nine feet in height. The top of this mist was flat whilst the bottom of this mist touched the road's surface. As the Avis's car entered this misty fog like effect, the car shuddered very violently as the mist curled around it. As the car entered this fog, the family experienced a total and unearthly silence. They couldn't even detect if the car was even moving! Then after what appeared a second or two, *(Author's note. Both Garry and Colin felt that as their car went into this mist, the effect only lasted a few seconds)* they experienced the car jolting again. *(Again Garry and Colin felt their car jolting as it came out of this mist).* The Aveley case was Investigated by Andrew Collins, Andrew Walmsley and Philip Mantle, of the then (IUN) Independent UFO Network.

Clearly then, there are strong similarities with the Avis case in regards to the A7O case. Let us recall the moment when Garry and Colin entered their mist. Because as we have learned, as soon as this mist touched the car, both men were enveloped in total and inky blackness. This blackness was also a feature of another famous British UFO abduction case, that of Mrs Elsie Oakensen.

ELSIE OAKENSEN. *(Velvety Blackness)*

Another strange UFO encounter, occurred to a lady called Elsie Oakensen on the evening of the 22nd of November 1978 as she was heading back to her home in Church Stowe near Northampton England. For our part though, the interesting feature which bears a striking similarity to the A7O case, was the point when Elsie mentions that her car was stopped on the road, it lost all it's power, and she was left sitting in what she described as, *"Velvety blackness'.* She knew that she was sitting in the car, she felt her hands on the steering wheel, but she couldn't see the inside of the car, or the road, or the trees which had been a feature of both sides of the road. This blackness as we know, was a strong feature of the A7O case.

Another case which features a 'mist like effect', was related by author and researcher Jenny Randles in her 1993 book, *'Aliens, The Real Story', (Robert Hale Books).* She tells of the experience that occurred to three people on the remote Island of Mull in Scotland back in October 1981. The widow of a colonel who was a deeply committed Christian, was driving with two American tourist friends over the remote Salen forest, when suddenly a strange mist surrounded the car which solidified. With this mist, came a heavy pressure and a vibration that shook the metal body of the car. Suddenly this instantaneous mist just 'vanished' and everything returned back to normal. However, they did notice that something else was not quite right. They noticed that the sun had moved quite a distance in the sky from it's original position. They were all disorientated, and they noticed that the digital watches worn by the American couple had 'stopped' at the precise moment that this strange mist had appeared. The car's electrical clock had also stopped.

THE BEAGARIE CASE.   *(Strange bank of fog)*

Another interesting case, again from Britain, concerns the Beagarie family from Dunstable in Bedfordshire. This family had a strange experience on the 8th of August 1992. They were driving from their home in Dunstable to Milton Keynes, a familiar journey of approximately 12 miles. As their car was turning right towards the small town of Hockcliffe, about four miles into their journey, they encountered a strange bank of fog or mist which just 'suddenly' appeared before them, (surprisingly, Mrs Beagarie didn't see this, she only saw a heavy down pour or rain, Mr Beagarie didn't see this rain, he only saw the mist. Again we must reflect on this strange instantaneous mist, a feature of the A7O case. I should point out however, that no structured object (UFO) was seen by the Beagarie family. (This case was Investigated on behalf of BUFORA by Judith Jaafar)

THE PATRICK FORSYTH CASE. *(Strange bank of fog)*

In my first book, UFO Case Files of Scotland (Volume 1) available on Amazon. I presented a case, which, in part, has similarities with the A70 Incident. It concerns the Forsyth family. In that case, witness Patrick Forsyth had left his home in Denny Stirlingshire Scotland, and was travelling in his car accompanied with his two young children heading towards the Scottish town of Stirling. As he was driving along the A872 at roughly 45 miles per hour, his children alerted him to a black disc shaped object roughly 1OO yards away from his car on his left hand side. This object was hovering roughly 3O to 4O feet above a field. Suddenly the family witnessed, the formation of an instantaneous mist or fog bank which just suddenly appeared in front of his car. Mr Forsyth likened it to a large sheet of milky white cardboard with the difference being that it was made out of fog. The edges were sharply defined and it was roughly ten feet in height. This fog bank stretched from the left hand side verge of the road, to the middle of the road touching the white marker lines. He slammed on his brakes and looked around to notice that this fog bank had disappeared. Patrick has no recollection of anything else strange happening at this point, and when asked by the author if he got to his destination on time, he replied that as far as he could recall, yes, he got to the town of Stirling on time. I was of course trying to see if there were any time unaccounted for.

In UFO Experiencer Elsie Oakensen's book, *'One Step Beyond, (Regency Press, London & New York')*, who we heard of above. She states that she heard of one man's experience whilst driving down a country road (sadly this is just from her recall and she does not give the man's name or what country road he was driving on) but she went on to state that as he was driving down the road, he stopped and noticed what seemed to be a fog bank with thousands of small lights sparkling through it. He didn't stay around to see any more, and he quickly sped away from the area. Again, this description of a fog with sparkling lights throughout, smacks of what Garry and Colin experienced as they observed this jet black object hovering above the road.

THE STRANGE CASE OF THE ILLUMINATED CAR!

Our next case provides yet another similarity to the A70 case where that massive burst of intense sparkling light descended down onto Garry and Colin's car. A similar effect was seen in the following case. Before we begin, let me set the scene. The following statement comes from the driver of a car who was taking his friends home from a party. The witness was not at the party, and as the driver, he did not consume any alcohol, he was just there to collect his friend from the party. This event occurred in Fife Central Scotland near the small town of Ballingry The witness stated the following.

"It was the week before Princess Diana had died". (Author's note. Princess Diana sadly lost her life in the early hours of August 31st, 1997) *"It was 03:15am on the Monday morning. James and I were about to leave our mates house, he was lying slumped in a chair, the combination of alcohol and heat had induced a coma like sleep, so we left him to it. Before we left the house, we had a quick discussion and decided to head up and onto the back roads of Perth for a spin in the car. We often did this, especially when we were younger. We would drive around the dark winding roads listening to the stereo. Even though it was the early hours of the morning, we were past caring. The thoughts of sleep had come and gone with my*

second wind, for I was raring to go, and despite being fairly drunk, James was keen to go on the run".

"The dark fresh night was a real contrast to the heavy heat of the house. I heard James take a few deep breaths and give a few coughs. There was some broken cloud in the sky, but everything was dry. It looked like a real good dark night for a drive. As I drove, we reminisced about the laughs we had earlier on in the evening, but it wasn't long before James's contribution to the conversation began to wane. That few seconds of cold fresh air had began to take its toll, and seemed to heighten the effect of the alcohol. His diminishing words were now slurred and his head seemed to roll excessively whenever the car moved one way or the other."

"We were now passing by the Gas Plant at Costains Open Cast Site, we came to the junction where turning left would take us to Ballingry or right towards Loch Leven. We turned right. When I think back to this point in the journey, I can remember how still and quiet things were. We had the radio on, but it was very low. I can remember looking towards the farm on our left and thinking how dark and peaceful it looked. I can't remember what I was talking about, but I do remember every now and again glancing over to see if James was still awake. He appeared to be fading fast, only the occasional grunt let me know that there was some cognitive activity, but not much. We passed by the farm on our left, the massive dark bulk of the Bishop Hill loomed in front of us, just inky blackness, and then it happened."

"The light was a deep golden yellow, but very bright. It appeared to come from above and slightly behind us. I can remember being completely shrouded by it. All I could see was the white lines in the centre of the road which was directly in front of me. I can remember my eyes darting all around the car, where ever I looked there was this bright thick yellow light. I could not see out of my side window, it was as if someone had turned on a real powerful light in the car. I then glanced towards James. It was strange, but in that brief glance his

profile was just visible against the window on the passengers door, the rest of his features seemed to be shrouded in light. I remember holding my breath, I had never experienced anything like it. It lasted for approximately a few seconds then it was gone. I was dazed, as stupid as it seems, I tried to keep on talking because James's head was looking down. I did not know if his eyes were open, I can't remember what I was saying, I can just remember stumbling over my words as my mind tried to make sense of it. I began to feel disorientated. I did not know it at the time, but Garry did have his eyes open and was actually looking down to the side of the chair (at his left side). He told me days later, that it was so bright, that he could clearly see the floor which was festooned with chocolate wrappers. I continued to try and talk, but by now I was feeling quite strange. It wasn't a sickening feeling, quite the opposite, but it started to effect my driving. I suddenly had real concerns about my ability to drive. I could feel the panic rising in me. I noticed that when I blinked, my head seemed to be full of the yellow light. My head was swimming with a thousand different things. I no longer tried to speak. My whole body seemed to tingle with this heavy heat."

"The road had now turned to the right; I didn't dare take the sharp turn to the left which would take us towards Scotlandwell. As I tried to make sense of things, it happened again. The exact same thing, the whole of the inside of the car filled up with this bright yellow light which totally engulfed us. For some reason, this time it did not seem to last as long as the first time, but it was only a fraction of a second shorter. This time I was terrified. When it disappeared I could not move. I gripped the steering wheel and tried to focus on the road. I then became aware that James was mumbling something, I turned to him, his head was still down but I could clearly hear him say, "What was that back there"? "That was brilliant, I feel amazing". I then realised that Garry had also seen it. I could not contain myself, I blurted out, "Did you see that fucking' light, did you see it"? He kept saying, "What was that"? "What was that"? "That was amazing"! I was frantic, it's not that the sensations were unpleasant, it was that they

were so strong that I had to slow down because I felt I could not drive the car. It turned into the worst drive I have ever had. The warm heavy sensations were such, that my body felt numb, but what was worse, I started to forget where I was, I could not remember what road I was on. I would remember, then forget, remember then forget. I knew I had to get to Leslie (a small town) *in between the relapses. I knew that it was a relatively straight road to my friend's house."*

"To be honest, I did consider stopping the car, but I didn't think I could handle sitting there in the pitch black, besides, I knew if the police came along they would just have to take one look at us and they would know something was up. And even though I had not been drinking, my gibbering appearance would certainly have meant sometime in the cells that night. So rightly or wrongly, I continued to drive. A few cars passed just minutes after the second 'contact', it was real scary stuff. I was speaking out loud, forcing myself to remember the road. I knew I had to turn left and cross Auchmuir Bridge, then turn right towards Leslie. As we crossed the bridge and headed towards Leslie, there were outside lights on a pub. As we passed them, the car was temporally lit up. Despite what was going on in my head, I knew that there was no logical explanation for it, the light did not even come close to replicating the light that we both saw and felt. It was about ten minutes to get to Leslie. I can remember the sweep of relief as I stopped the car, we virtually stumbled out. I remember closing my eyes for a few seconds, this bright yellow light was still inside my head. Ironically, once we were out of the car, the sensation was really pleasant and very relaxing. We awoke my friend and she could instantly see that there was something up with us. The effect of the alcohol had seemed to be temporarily lifted from James, we blurted it out about this light that had hit us"

"We sat there for about three hours before heading home. My thoughts seemed to be covered in this deep yellow light, whenever we shut our eyes, it seemed to 'well up' inside of us. Once the effects of the alcohol started to wear off, James had more difficulty in making sense of it than I did, especially that

154

night. We spoke about it over the next several days. James described it as a 'cloud of light' inside the car, which is a very apt description. He was looking down at the floor the first time it happened. It was so bright that he could actually see the floor clearly. It's worth remembering that there are no lights of any kind on this road, even when we passed those cars, there is no way that these lights can illuminate the interior of a car and not once on the journey were there any cars behind us. Besides, it was the incredible sensation that the light left us with, that was just as amazing, as the light was still with us whenever we closed our eyes, it was in our heads as was this warm heavy sensation on our bodies".

Robert Ashberry.

Well, what an incredible story. What on earth are we to make of that! As you have read, this tremendous burst of light that came from above and 'entered' their car, was, to a degree, similar to that intense burst of light that descended from beneath the UFO that both Garry and Colin witnessed on that lonely A70 road. Let's take a look at this particular case and go through some possibilities. Firstly, was this light the result of a helicopter which perhaps was searching the countryside with a powerful searchlight? No say our witnesses, this was in the early hours of the morning, with no traffic on the roads, they did not hear the sound of a helicopter, and even if it was a helicopter, this bright intense light would have shone not only in the car, but all around outside of it as well, moreover, the helicopter would have needed to be directly in front of the car in order to shine it's light straight into it. What about the Farmhouse? Robert states that when the light first hit the car, they had just passed a Farmhouse, could a farmer working in the early hours of the morning have shone a light, even a tractor light which might have been turning further up the road, into their car? Again the witnesses state that when they had passed the Farmhouse, there were no lights on the Farmhouse at all, the whole area was covered in blackness. We have to remember, that we are dealing here with a tremendous and powerful light. No object of any kind was seen by any of the men, all that they could see, was this brilliant yellow light and nothing more. Again I say that 'light phenomenon' be it seen near UFOs or as something which enters people's cars or bedrooms, is something which is part and parcel of the makeup of the whole UFO phenomenon. Many researchers the world over, have case after case of these type of events which makes us wonder, *"Why"!* What purpose is served by these lights? Fellow Scottish researcher Brian Allan and I, interviewed both witnesses at the site of their encounter, and it's fair to say that the area is certainly desolate, with open fields and countryside all around. Both men are sure, that this was all that happened that night, they have not had any strange dreams, or marks on their bodies that they cannot account for. And as far as they can tell, (although they can't be positive), there is no evidence of 'missing time' which is usually a feature of worldwide UFO abduction accounts. All we have is this unusual incident which cries out for an explanation and which to me, is extremely puzzling and frustratingly difficult to understand.

OK, so, as we have seen above, there are certain similarities to a number of other so called UFO experiences. This misty fog and complete blackness, to the penetrating light coming down into cars. But let us now take a look at some of the differences that were experienced in Garry and Colin's case.

THE DIFFERENCES.

1. The Heads. Some of the 'beings' heads, that both Garry and Colin witnessed were similar to other world wide UFO Abduction events. Witnesses relate to them as being pear shaped. However, whilst both Garry and Colin saw these 'beings' as having pear shaped heads, they also saw what appeared to be 'indented heads', or, in other words, heart shaped heads.

2. Free Floating Stretcher. The free floating stretcher that Colin saw Garry being placed on, this is most unusual, and I have never seen any reports of this type of thing anywhere in all the UFO literature that I've studied. Colin apparently was led by these small 'entities' into the object and was not placed on a stretcher. One may ask why Colin was also not placed on one of these stretchers? This may not seem an interesting question, but again we have to ask ourselves why. Why Garry on the stretcher and not Colin?

3.   The Necks. From the drawings that both Garry and Colin completed for me, one can clearly see that the 'beings' necks, extend out onto their chest region. Usually in overseas cases this is not the case, and the neck sits firmly on the torso. Furthermore, as stated earlier, Garry stated that one of the Grey's neck's moved in a snake like manner! It was moving all around, this way and that, and twisted behind itself to more or less look over it's shoulder. This really surprised Garry and gave him quite a start.

4.   Perforations Under The Eyes. Some of these 'entities' had what appeared to be perforations under each eye that were coloured red, yellow, and green. Again, I am not aware of any other case which features this effect. If any readers do know of a similar case, please contact me at my address at the end of this book.

5.   Wrinkled 'entity'. Garry saw a very brown wrinkled 'entity' of which he felt was very old and wise. Garry also had the distinct impression that this' entity' was somehow in charge of what was going on. These wrinkles on these creatures, are not really a feature that witnesses mention. In the main most, if not all witnesses, describe the beings as either being grey translucent, with tight skin. At the moment, I've only come across one other case of which the entities are described as having wrinkled skin *(If you the reader know of others, then do get in touch with me at my contact address at the end of this book)*. And that case was the Pascagoula entities which Calvin Parker and his friend Charles Hickson encountered back in October 11th 1973. They had their own abduction experience off a pier near the South Mississippi's Pascagoula River west bank. Admittedly, these creatures were markedly different from what Garry saw, both in size and stature. It was only the heavy folds of wrinkly skin on the Pascagoula creatures that I found most intriguing.

6. Ribs! All of these 'entities', according to both Garry and Colin, had what appeared to be like ribs sticking out from their chest region. When I quizzed Garry more on this point and asked him if 'he' felt that these were indeed ribs, he paused for a moment, and suggested that they might not be, that they could, in point of fact, be heavy folds of skin. However, he wasn't entirely sure about this. Whilst we are on the subject of 'alien ribs'! I came across a case in the book, *'Alien Identities'* written by Richard L. Thompson, published by Govardhan Hill Inc, P.O. Box 52, Badger CA 93603, U.S.A. 1993. Which mentions ribs. It told the tale of a 28 year old woman and her six year old son who witnessed five UFOs near a cow pasture. This occurred near the town of Cimarron New Mexico. She was hypnotically regressed by Dr Leo Sprinkle, a University of Wyoming psychologist, and under hypnosis, she stated that she not only saw small 'alien' creatures who were surgically removing organs from the cows in the pasture,(another aspect of UFOlogy which is not the scope of this book), but she also described these small 'beings' as having a thin waist with many ribs, (more ribs, than what we humans have). Is the A7O and the Cimarron case just isolated incidents of this nature, or are there other cases 'out there' which also have these same features? Incidentally Dr. Leo Sprinkle, himself became intrigued by the abduction phenomenon in the 1960s. After looking into the subject closely, he was of the opinion that, here was something real, indeed, Sprinkle has told others that he believes that he had been abducted by aliens when he was younger.

7. Fingers. Many witnesses in UFO abduction cases very rarely mention the hands and fingers of their captors, and when they do, there appears to be a difference of opinion on how many fingers/digits, these 'entities' have. Some state that they recall seeing four fingers, whilst others claim to have seen three. In Colin's case, he clearly recalls seeing three fingers (no thumb). Each finger had a bulbous segment to it. Where one's knuckle would be on a human finger, there was a deep circular piece of skin, this was also a feature at the end of the finger.

WHY THE ROAD?

When we look at the similarities and differences that the A7O case provides, it strikes me on how many times that I personally have come across accounts in the UFO literature of this strange mist or fog like effect that just suddenly and mysteriously 'appears' in front of the startled witnesses. Also, this bend in the road, that too has been noted, not only by myself, but by many other UFOlogists, as a big feature in some UFO abductions. What we have to ask ourselves however, is why? If we are dealing with an alien technology and culture, why were Garry and Colin abducted from this lonely stretch of road? Why couldn't they have been abducted from the safety of their beds, as has been the case with countless other UFO abductees? To me this doesn't make any sense, and I have puzzled over this for many a night.

INVESTIGATING THE A70 INCIDENT

As with any UFO Investigation, our society ensured that all avenues of Investigation were followed. We checked with local and National Airports to see if perhaps there were any aircraft in that vicinity on that particular night, there were none. Neither were there any helicopter activity in that area that night. No members of the public had telephoned the police to report any unusual objects in the sky. Even although both Garry and Colin specifically stated that what they saw did not appear to look like a conventional aircraft. We nonetheless had to find out if the possibility was that there might have been an aircraft in the area, and as I mentioned above, there were none.

I also wrote to the British Ministry of Defence in London England asking them if they had any UFO reports from that night, or indeed nights leading up to, and after, the 17th of August 1992. In a reply dated 17th February 1994, Miss Kerry

Philpott, Secretariat (Air Staff) 2a, Room 8245, thanked me for my letter and stated, and I quote;

"I have looked back through our file which contains details of unexplained aerial phenomena reported to the MoD, and can confirm that we were notified of only one sighting on the 23rd October 1994, and that sighting occurred in the south of England. The MoD is not aware of any evidence that the U.K's air defences have been breached, which as you are aware, is our only concern in this connection, and I am afraid therefore, I am not able to shed any light on the sighting to which you refer".

It was the tired old MoD statement that I had received many times over whilst doing research on a number of UFO sightings and I wasn't really surprised at her closing comments. I guess that I shouldn't have expected anyone to report a UFO from that stretch of road on that particular night, for as we have read, it was a very desolate stretch of road with very little traffic about. Various other avenues of research were undertaken, all of which proved fruitless in providing a rational explanation for the A7O case.

So, we had a major UFO incident that had no corroborating witnesses, this however, isn't that uncommon, and this in no way should be seen as a black mark on this particular incident.

ATTACKING A GREY!

Garry did say that there were times just after the incident, that gave him cause for concern, and he told me about the time when he woke up one night and found 'something' in his room! Garry said that he woke up one night (an evening during 1996) and saw a small grey standing at the far end of his bedroom. He tried to wake his wife up but found that he couldn't do so. This again seems to be a relevant factor in UFO abductions, that of either the man or woman trying to alert and wake up their partner for them to see what is going on, but find out must to their astonishment, that they are unable to awaken them, 'no matter how hard they try'! This was the case here. At this point Garry felt extreme anger, it was bad enough for him to have the experience of 1992, but for them to come back again into his own home, was too much. He threw the bed covers back and raced over to confront this small being, as he did so, Garry noticed an element of surprise on the 'creatures' face, as if it were startled at being seen. No matter, Garry was determined to let 'it' know that he was there and he threw the most hardest punch into the face of this small 'creature'. At this, the small 'creature' shot backwards at a speed which surprised Garry, for he told me later, that although he definitely contacted his fist with it, it really wasn't that hard a punch, and yet this small 'creature' fell back with a speed which was quite amazing. However, the small 'creature' after getting up from the floor, raced at Garry at which point Garry lost consciousness and cannot remember another thing about that night. Garry explained that he spent many a sleepless night after his experience, and when he did go to sleep, he experienced terrible nightmares. On one occasion he actually ran out of the bedroom after waking up from one of these nightmares. These nightmares were also getting to Garry's wife, and she was becoming increasingly worried about her husband. At this point in my interview with Garry, I asked him if anything strange had 'recently' happened to him whereupon he proceeded to explain to me about quite an alarming event that had transpired a few months earlier.

THE STRANGE LIGHT SURROUNDING GARRY'S CAR.

It was around the middle part of 1997, and Garry was returning in his car back from visiting his mother in law. In the car with Garry, was his two young sons aged 8 and 11. They were travelling along the A198 coast road at about six thirty in the evening approaching the town of Gullane. The road at this point is bordered by fields on either side. As they were driving along, suddenly the whole interior of the car lit up with a tremendously bright white light, it was like a magnesium flare Garry said. This was totally unexpected and totally out of the

161

ordinary. This effect only lasted a few seconds, and upon looking out of the car, there was nowhere from where this strange light could have come from. (Shades of the Robert Ashberry case mentioned earlier) During the time when the light was illuminating the car, both of Garry's son's were screaming in the back seat. Indeed one of Garry's son's was violently sick in the back of the car. Thankfully this strange light didn't return, and Garry and his two sons eventually returned to the safety of their home. This was an unnerving experience for Garry, and something of which he couldn't explain. There were no helicopters or aircraft outside his car, nor were there anyone flashing any torches of bright spot-lights.

COLIN WRIGHT'S 2019 THOUGHTS.

Back in 2019, I was working with One Tribe TV who were making a short piece on the A70 Incident for the BBC One Show. I decided to get in touch with Colin Wright to see if he would take part but knowing that he probably wouldn't, as Colin had taken a back seat with this experience and no longer wanted anything to do with the media. Nonetheless, I asked him anyway, and I also asked him how he was generally feeling, and how, if at all, this had, or still was, affecting him. He replied on Facebook messenger with, and I quote.

"Hi Malcolm"
"It's my skin, it's mostly my groin area legs and hips and other parts, all the areas that they were doing experiments on. I've had 5 biopsies and nothing's come back. My specialist admitted he has never seen it before in all the years he has been a skin specialist. He took photos so many times as it kept changing. This was to put in a medical book for the next generation of specialists to view. It's a new skin condition, but unless three people come forward with the same thing it can't be diagnosed as such. Have tried everything, nothing helps. Doctors can't help me either.
I've also became hypersensitive to everything with a smell, and have flare ups on my face. Even paint, I can't go near it yet. I've done decorating for about 30 years. I have problems with

162

my right eye again. As you know I had something done to it. It even watered under hypnosis. If you remember it goes so blurred that I can't make anything out, yet the next day it can be back to normal until it happens again. My life is ruined haven't seen my kids or grand kids for about 18 moths can't tolerate the smells, have become very isolated".

I replied to Colin with.

"Oh Colin I am so very sorry to hear all this I really am. The effect that it is having on your life is shocking. No wonder you want nothing more to do with this, I don't blame you. Daft question, but have they come back! In dreams or at night? Have you had any flashbacks from the original event? Would medical hypnosis somehow tell your mind that this skin condition will ease away to nothing, and that your sense of smell will be fine? Sounds daft I know, but maybe, just maybe, deep hypnosis on just getting you back fit and healthy might work. Just a daft thought my friend".

Colin replied with.

"It's not daft Malcolm. I was actually thinking the same, would hypnosis make my brain and immune system go back to normal by making my body believe everything is OK again and I have no issues with smells or my skin. I meant to say that I had a C.T. scan and they asked me to go back for a second one as they found scarring on my lung and asked if I ever had an operation. How do you explain that one, I was shocked to say the least".

I replied with.

"That is weird Colin. Apart from the needle in your eye, can you remember any other medical type of procedure that 'they' did to you which might have caused this scarring? Has anything come back to you recall wise over the years"?

Colin stated.

"They were doing all sorts to me. I was more focused on trying to get away, and angry that this was being done against my will. Fear quickly changed to anger which unsettled them somewhat".

I continued with.

"You were placed on a different chair to Garry, he was on a flat table and you were on a curved chair of sorts. Do you think that what was done to you, was when you were in that see through glass or Perspex chamber thing, of which next to you were similar people all naked?. Do you think that being in there caused the problems, or was it just when you were on that chair"?

Colin replied.

"On the chair. The glass chamber was later on, that was to either to freeze you or protect you, or possibly both"?.

I then asked.

"Did you hear in your head them saying, 'we are not here to hurt you'. Did you hear anything at all from them"?

To which Colin replied.

"No. I just remember thinking, how can all these people go missing and not be missed by family or friends".

As I didn't want to take up too much of Colin's time. I wrapped it up by saying.

"Thanks Colin. If you have anything else that you feel is relevant to your condition then do let me know. Best wishes my friend".

I BELIEVE HIM NOW!

One thing that I never mentioned about the A70 case in my first book, was the astonishing fact that Garry's wife also encountered some of these small 'beings'. It all started one night as I was sitting watching T.V. back at my home in Tullibody Clackmannanshire Central Scotland. The telephone rang and I picked it up. It was Garry's wife. She proceeded to tell me that whilst she supported her husband to a point in regards to his strange tale, she never truly believed him. She went on to say that the previous night, both her and Garry were at home and lying in bed. Garry was sleeping next to her, and she was finishing a chapter of a book that she was reading. After a short while, she closed the book, and carefully placed it down on the bedside table beside her. She then switched off the bedside light, and the room was enveloped in darkness. That said, there was a shaft of light coming into the room from a street light outside which allowed her to see some of the bedroom. Then, around 20 seconds later, she suddenly experienced small fingers grasp both her ankles which then pulled her forcibly down the bed. And whereas her head had been situated on the pillow, her head was now halfway down the bed. She pulled back the covers, and was astonished to see three small 'beings' at the foot of her bed. As soon as she stared as these 'beings', they immediately released their grip on her ankles and wobbled backwards to the bedroom wall. Garry's wife noticed that the wall took on a 'rippling effect', similar to a mill pond where after you throw a stone into the pond, there are concentric ripples that spread outwards, this was what she was seeing. As soon as these three 'beings' wobbled backwards into this 'rippling effect', the wall closed and all was back to normal. Garry's wife's parting words to me on the phone that night were,

"I believe my husband now".

Science writer and author Steuart Campbell from Edinburgh, felt that the real cause of the A7O Incident, was the direct result of both men witnessing an astronomical mirage and simply became confused about the time, an explanation that didn't go down too well with both witnesses.

GARRY WOOD INTERVIEW. 23rd May 2021.

Abbreviations. (MR) Malcolm Robinson (GW) Garry Wood. Garry Wood's 2021 thoughts on his UFO Abduction

(MR) "Well firstly let me say that its great to speak to you again Garry, its been a wee while, and the purpose of this telephone call is to go over with you some of the things that happened to you and your friend Colin Wright on that eventful night of August 17th 1992. I'd like to first of all ask you about those dust deposits that you found on your car 'after' your encounter with that black hovering disc above the A70 Road"

(GW) "Well my car started to somehow chemically change. You know how if you have a faulty battery and it starts growing those crystals, like a discharge, and parts of the body around the car started to form those white crystals and they started to come through the paint in different areas, not so much on the outside, but more on the inside, and it was starting to grow, and I had to rub it all off and paint it, but it kept happening. It was like a chemical reaction in certain bits".

(MR) "Is that a natural thing then Garry"?

(GW) "I don't know. Its natural to happen to the battery. I mean you have two earths on an engine one from the battery to the engine, and one from the battery to the chassis. My car was quite a new car at the time and everything was fine with that. But it was coming up on bits of the inner valance, bits at the back. It was just unusual that was all. If it was a natural occurrence, it is difficult to say".

(MR) "Did it have a colour this dusty deposit"?

(GW) "It was like a crystallized white, and when you rubbed it down it was powdering. So I treated it all and painted it, but it just kept coming back in places, and not long after that I got rid of the car".

(MR) "And did this only happen after the event Garry"?

(GW) "It happened 'after' the event yes".

(MR) "And do you remember how long after the event that you sold the car, the Vauxhall Astra"?

(GW) "I cannot remember, its hard to say to be honest with you. I'm not sure".

(MR) "A couple of years maybe"?

(GW) "It would have probably have been about a year later. Because I lent it to Colin, and Colin blew the head gasket on it. And I fixed it. And after I fixed that I got rid of it. I was on holiday at the time and I lent Colin the car. I don't really see Colin at all now. The last time I saw Colin he came up to the college to visit me as he had a problem with his car and I fixed it for him, and that's going back eight or nine years ago. Although he is still on my Facebook".

(MR) "See when you were over in Alva to get hypnotised with Helen. Now, I want you to be honest. Do you really, really think that you were hypnotised, were there a change in your mind so to speak, or do you 'not' think that you were hypnotised!"

(GW) "I definitely think I was. I've got all the tapes remember, I have them all stuck away somewhere, every single tape. Because I recorded the sessions, every single one of them. I don't know what condition they are in, but I've got them somewhere in the house. Helen spent weeks and weeks working through dates and time. She said its your birthday, what did you get for your birthday. It's now Christmas time,

167

and these flashbacks, Christ I cannot even remember that I got that bike and it was red. And that's how she worked. Through dates. And what she would do eventually, was that she gradually took the dates up to the time that the event happened. And she would go to that date and ask me what I was doing, and I said that I was taking a satellite system out to my friends. And that's how she did it. There were no leading questions. Once we got to that point, I started to come out with stuff. She told me what was happening, and said that now I am going to emphasize on things that you have told me that's happened, and you can emphasize on that. And she said 'right, you told me that you were in such and such area and you saw this thing, what was it doing'. Whether its right or whether its wrong, I definitely know that something happened. I was definitely totally aware when I went into that empty blackness looking about and there was nothing. I have every single tape of how she did the hypnosis. People will say there were leading questions, but that dissolves that. As I've said before, all Helen would work on were dates and times, and she explained that to me. She didn't want to talk about aliens, she didn't want to talk about any of that"

(MR) "Yes, that's right".

(GW) "And the good thing about Helen was that she was trying to help us".

(MR) "Yes, that's right".

(GW) "I did at one point though Malcolm. She had to stop. Because when I was getting the hypnosis, I did at one point think that I was going to have a heart attack. It was a crushing pain in my chest. It was really bad and she had to stop and she was really worried".

(MR) "Wow, that's a concern in anybody's book if you were getting a feeling like that. She was quite right to take you out".

(GW) "It was a crushing pain. I honestly thought that I was going to die. Tears were running down my eyes with it. I thought I was having a heart attack".

(MR) "I know that we are many many years down the line now from that event. But have you had any strange dreams or has anything else happened since then"?

(GW) "Now that I am aware of. It's difficult to say, as these things are that clever. I don't know. It was a long time ago. Of course the other thing that happened with my laddies *(Author's note, Scottish word for Children)* was really upsetting".

(MR) "A bright light"?

(GW) "Yes, that thing that flashed over my car and we were at the side of the road and my youngest laddie was being sick in the back. My oldest laddie said that it was like being in heaven".

(MR) "Wow".

(GW) "That's what happened. It was this 'white stuff' coming up over the car. It came up over the metal, and came 'through' the windscreen".

(MR) "It came right into the car this light"?

(GW) "Yes. There was a big flash in the sky, and this thing was just above us. And that was heading up by the carton place coming back from Gullane".

(MR) "Was this a quiet road Garry, or was this a Major road".

(GW) "It was quite a quiet road as you took a left up a vennel, up a country road heading up towards a carton place. I know a couple of ambulance drivers that saw a UFO up there and that's where it happened".

(MR) "And did this effect last only a few seconds or was it longer Garry"?

(GW) "Well it was at the side of the road, and me and the bairns woke up and one of my kids was retching in the back seat"

(MR) "Wow, that must have been scary".

(GW) "My wife at the time was in hospital, and her mum was looking after her in Gullane, and I was down there collecting the laddies because she looked after the laddies because I was working, so I was bringing them up the road, and I was in a bit of a state worried about things".

(MR) "So how did this start? Was it just a light that came from the front of the car through the window or what"?

(GW) "There was a big flash in the sky, and there was a big object above the car. And then this white stuff just started to come up over the bonnet of the car and then just came straight through the windscreen".

(MR) "Jesus. Did you see an object above in the sky"?

(GW) "Yes I did, but I couldn't make it our properly, because it was directly above the motor. I can't even remember what car I had at the time".

(MR) "That must have been scary, more so for the kids. I bet your were saying, 'Christ, here we go again'.

(GW) "I've never ever changed my mind that something happened there, and on the A70 as well. What's the point of making something up, you've got to tell the truth about these things".

(MR) "Absolutely Garry".

170

(GW) "I've better things to do with my life than talk a load of s**t".

(MR) "And what about these marks on your body".

(GW) "Well the one thing that I had on my arm, that eventually vanished. I had a scar on it, and for some reason I cannot find it any more, it's gone".

(MR) "Is that your left or right arm"?

(GW) "Is was my left arm".

(MR) "Other than that, did you have any more scars or that after the A70 event"?

(GW) "Not that I am aware of. Because being a mechanic, you tend to cut yourself in all different areas. You know, when you are working away with a spanner"

(MR) "Yes, yes".

(GW) "It's difficult to say. There is no point in going looking for things, because you could make things up. Its best to stick to what you know and that's all I have ever done".

(MR) "Have either of your kids had any strange dreams"?

(GW) "Not that I am aware of. I think they get a bit embarrassed talking about it. I've also got a wee boy aged eight".

(MR) "Now I want to take you back to the time when you were a wee boy yourself when..............

(GW) "When I was four I went missing, I think I told you about that".

(MR) "What about the time when there was a small 'being' in the bedroom and you punched it. Is this correct, is my memory correct?"

(GW) "That was after the A70 thing. It was in my room, and what it was doing was it was going up to my partner at her side of the bed, and it was as if it was trying to pull her out of the bed or it was going to do something to her. And I looked at it, and 'it' looked at me, stared at me, and it just walked towards her again. And I punched it over and it fell against my bedroom wall. And then it flew at me and there was a big flash and then I woke up in the morning. Now whether it was a bad dream I don't know, but it didn't seem like a bad dream, it seemed real".

(MR) "And when you punched it, was it like punching a wall or like soft putty or something? I mean, what did it feel like to you"?

(GW) "No, it just went backwards I was obviously that far across the other end of the bed. She was sleeping on the side of the bed that it came up to".

(MR) "Right".

(GW) "And I was at the other end. So you can imagine just hitting this 'thing' to get it away. And then it kind of fell backwards and got up quickly and then there was a big flash. I remember the big flash, it switches you off".

(MR) "Did you jump out of bed to punch it or did you raise up on your side of the bed to punch it"?

(GW) "I just raised up on my side of the bed".

(MR) "Right, I've got you".

(GW) "Because I was looking, and I was saying, 'am I dreaming here'? What's going on here? What's that? And it must have thought that I was still sleeping. I can't remember shouting, but I do remember hitting the thing and I do remember that I couldn't wake her up".

(MR) "Do you think that it was surprised to see you, and was this 'thing' similar to what you had seen on the A70"?

(GW) "It was a bit surprised that I saw it, because it stepped backwards a bit, whatever it was".

(MR) "And was this 'thing' similar to the 'things' that you saw onboard the object on the A70, or was it different"?

(GW) "It was smaller, really quite small. It's difficult to say Malcolm to be honest with you. You know, these 'things' can get in your head. They can make you think anything. Is it what it wanted you to see! It's a story that goes down a million roads Malcolm, you know better than anybody".

(MR) "I know".

(GW) "I'm quite happy about people punching holes in things because if I had an answer to it, I would be happy. The fact is I haven't. But the fact also is that we will eventually find out and there will be some disclosure on some things. You just have to get on with your life. There is no good wasting your life on it, you have to make a choice. I don't mind keeping an interest. I sometimes look about, but very rarely. I'm a bit frightened to go looking up there because you feel like you are out of control" *(Author's note. Garry is referring here to the A70 Road)*

(MR) "Have you been back to the A70 recently"?

(GW) "No, not recently. I think the last time I went out there was probably myself, two years ago to have a look about. The rain was that torrential, I had my Volvo at the time, that I ended up coming home. But I remember taking a guy from

CSETI out there, and he reckoned something happened when a big owl flew right into the car".

(MR) "Right, OK".

(GW) "He knows you well Malcolm, he was at the last Scottish UFO and Paranormal Conference and he said to me, keep that to yourself (about the owl) I haven't been right since then".

(MR) "So an owl flew into your car"?

(GW) "Well, it used to happen quite a lot up there because I said that to him as we were driving up there. I said, you'll see the horse as you come round this bit and I said, for some reason there is this big owl, and I don't know if its the car lights or whatever and it flew at the car. And I remember standing outside the car with him looking, and then we got back in the car, but he says otherwise! and he told me to look up something to do with Whitley Strieber, the 'Unseen' or something like that".

(Author's note. The Unseen is Whitley Strieber's Unknown County website. I checked it out and found an owl looking at me from the top of the page. That page highlighted a book called, 'The Messengers' written by Mike Clelland of which author Richard Dolan had this to say about this book, and I quote).

"I would characterize very few UFO books as beautiful, but this one is. The owl has held a place of reverence and mystique throughout history. And as strange as this might seem, owls are also showing up in conjunction with the UFO experience. Mike Clelland has collected a wealth of first-hand accounts in which owls manifest in the highly charged moments that surround alien contact. His book explores the owl's connection to the UFO experience. It also includes profound synchronicity's, ancient archetypes, dreams, shamanistic experiences, personal transformation, and death. From the mythic legends of our ancient past, to the first-hand accounts of the UFO abductee, owls are playing some vital role".

(GW) "And he said that he does not really want to talk to people about this. And he said that it kind of changed his life a bit. He is quite a well to do chap, very nice".

(MR) "Are you still getting headaches, because you used to get a lot of headaches after the incident. Do you still get those, have you any problems with your health"?

(GW) "They are not so bad".

(MR) "Are you still waking up at 03:20 in the morning because I was going through some of the old hypnosis tapes that I've got, and you mention that in one of them"?

(GW) "I wake up most mornings at 04:00am now".

(MR) "04:00am"?

(GW) "Yes. Most mornings".

(MR) "Have you any idea why this might be, is it your body clock just waking you up at that time"?

(GW) "Maybe yes. I don't know. I look about me then go back to bed. Since my old cat passed away I've not been right. She was my best pal".

(MR) "Now you mentioned back in the day that you had a mark on the back of your neck or something, I don't know if you remember that"?

(GW) "Yes, that's right. I've never really checked to see if there is anything still there. You know, I've kinda put a lot of things to bed. I don't go out of my way to do things or get too involved with things and that".

(Author's note: Garry is referring here to UFO matters)

(MR) "As I say, I was listening to all the old audio tapes and……….."

(GW) "I mean, I don't know. You can look up things and get paranoid, check your body, and you don't know if something happened to you when you were small, or if you have just found this thing. You kind of have to experience a pain or something happening to you after and say, 'this is what happened to me'. It's that long ago, it's nearly 30 years ago"

(MR) "I believe it's the 30th anniversary of your encounter next year, 2022"

(Author's note. Garry and I then discussed the time when a movie was going to be made about his encounter on the A70, and he told me that at the end of the day, he didn't feel comfortable about signing the contract, and that for me, is perfectly understandable)

(MR) "Now Garry, when you came back from Ian and Katrina's house after your encounter on the A70, you went home a different way"

(GW) "Yes, that's right, we went home a different way".

(MR) "And you went back to Edinburgh up to Carlton Hill to see a friend but he wasn't there".

(GW) "Yes that's right".

(MR) "And you ran Colin home".

(GW) "Yes, and I got Kim's sister to come with me in the car because I was that scared. I remember going out with her one time, and she could verify this herself, and we saw this blue light thing shooting about up there. Like a ball of light, shooting about up there. I used to go up there all the time to get some filmed proof or evidence. That's really it you know. Hard solid evidence. And even if you got it nowadays, nobody would believe you. You could be showing it live, and there would be somebody saying, 'ah it's just a man in a suit'

(MR) "I totally agree Garry. I mention this in my talks actually. I say you don't need to believe a word I have been saying ladies and gentlemen, go out and look at the evidence yourselves. And even if we did have the best evidence known to man, the best photograph, the best video, people would say that I manufactured it up on computer, you cannot win sometimes you know"

(GW) "No, that's right".

(MR) "So do you think that hypnosis, I'm not saying it harmed you, but did it help you or make it worse"?

(GW) "I would say the opposite. I would say that it completely helped me. It made me realise, because I was so terrified at night sleeping, it made me realise that whatever it was, it wasn't going to hurt me, or I thought it wasn't going to hurt me. Whatever it was, seemed to have some kind of understanding. It wanted to take me away, but it let me go when I was pleading with it, saying things like, 'I've got kids, I've got this and that".

(MR) "Yes. Because of course the major stay with the hypnosis, or the major thing that came out of your hypnosis, was the word, 'sanctuary'"

(GW) "That's right".

(MR) "And you said at the time that you felt that 'they' were really really close, that they were here, so to speak".

(GW) "Yes, that's right. I asked if they were hiding from something, or they need to be here. I mean, they could be in a different dimension from us, it could just be slightly off. You know how atoms work. It could be a world within a world. It could be anything Malcolm. It could be a billion different things"

(MR) "Yes, I agree".

(GW) "I mean you look it, it's just like the Bible, which goes off in a million different stories. It's so vast. It could be just something that is projected into our minds. Could it have been an American project which is mind altering. Where do you draw the line with it all. I can only draw the line with what I think I saw. I know it definitely happened, up to the shimmering curtain of light to looking about it blackness. I remember that distinctly, that's what I remember. After that, it's difficult to remember anything, it's like a jigsaw puzzle"

(MR) "There is a small air base at Kirknewton on the A70 road, I believe its now used for gliders. Somebody said to me a few years ago that it could have been an experimental aircraft that was being test flown from that base, and that's what you saw".

(GW) "Yes, there was an air base near the A70, an American one. I know they did the Blackbird aircraft and I know they did the Stealth Bomber in 1971 and all that. Scotland was a quiet place at the time, whose to say that maybe there were some spaceships there and they could have been messing around with it. I don't know. I don't think it was that. Because when I drove around that bend, it was like it was waiting on us, and there was no way you were getting out of it. It was like a trap, and I've always maintained that"

(MR) "Have you seen the model that Jason Gleaves did for me of your encounter, the craft and your car and the road etc"?

(GW) "I did yes, it's quite good. I put a thumbs up on Facebook about it. And Mike Mitchell my friend said that it was a pity that the model didn't show all the cans of coke that I had in the foot well of the car (laughs)

(MR) "It was a blue Astra car".

(GW) "Yes it was a dark blue Astra. When I bought the car, it was a year old at the time. I didn't buy it brand new, I bought it a year old. And that's what I was thinking as well, that this was a fairly new car, why was this corrosion happening. It was coming everywhere through the paint. I was hitting it with the steam cleaner, I was rubbing it down, I was painting it again as best as I could, but it kept coming through in patches in all different areas of the car. Like something had chemically altered the negative earth of the car. In the old days, they were positive earth and then they changed it to negative earth so stuff runs through the car, but it was like something had altered that".

(MR) "You said that when you were younger, you saw a strange being on a school roof, hiding behind a chimney or something".

(GW) "That's right. I was at Scouts, and I was there with Gavin Glendinning. We heard this noise and we looked up and we saw this thing looking down at us, and we both screamed and the thing vanished and I got a row off the Scoutmaster for it".

(MR) "What school was that, where was it"?

(GW) "Duddingston Primary School. And Gavin and a couple of other people saw it as well".

(MR) "That must have scared you. And what age were you when this happened"?

(GW) "I must have been about 12 or 13. Because I was a P.L. a Patrol Leader".

(MR) "Can you remember what that wee thing looked like at all, or is it too far back in your memory to remember"?

(GW) "It's difficult to say what it looked like to be honest with you. I didn't know much about these things at that time, I just thought that it was some kind of monster. At the time, it kind of looked like a luminescent dull but bright yellow colour. It was odd, just odd. It was like it was in a thing, like a shield, I don't know. I had no experience of things like this at that time. You had no internet back then, for me it was a monster. Even when that event happened to me and Colin, we didn't know where to look about things like this. Do you look in a f*****g phone book (laughs) No, but that's all you had Malcolm, (a phone book) You had no internet or computers then. It wasn't a thing I was interested it".

(MR) "Yes, that's true".

(GW) "I worked in the ambulance service. For me life was all about making money, having a job, having a wife and kids and things like that. I'd watch sci fi things. We would watch Star Trek and that, which was good, but you didn't believe any of it. If anyone saw a spaceship, you would say 'Aw f**k' till it happens to you, and that's when you change your mind on it. As you say Malcolm, the mind works better with an open parachute than a closed one (laughs)

(MR) "That's very true. I remember I used to say that at the close of all my lectures, still do sometimes. I think your first port of call after your encounter, was BUFORA (The British UFO Research Association) and I believe they didn't get back to you"!

(GW) "Yes, they never got back to me. I wrote them a letter. And what I did was that I went back to the area to see if anyone had seen or heard anything. And years later, when the first computers came out, I put info through their door". *(Author's note. Garry is referring here to some houses on the A70 Road)* "And I made up a flyer saying E.S.A., Edinburgh Sightings Association and put it through their doors to see if anybody had seen anything, but nobody got back to me"

(MR) "Yes I remember you telling me that. Because there are a few cottages as you go past Harperrig Reservoir".

(GW) "That's right. And there is a bit on the main road, and there is a house further down. And I put notices through all their doors".

(MR) "How would you say that your encounter has affected your life now, or is it something that you don't even bother about. I was there, and its now back in the past"?

(GW) "Oh I'm still interested. I would still like to know, who, what, why where! It's just so difficult. I still get tempted to go out and look, but because of my wee boy I don't. I said to Emma not long ago, we'll go out there for a drive one night for a look. I said, you never know, we might be able to leave this **** **** (laughs)

(MR) "(Laughs)

(GW) "They did say something that they would be back again".

(MR) "Right".

(GW) "Because that's where they wanted me to go, and I said 'no'.

(MR) "And was that them talking to you through telepathy or what"?

(GW) "Well that's what to me it seemed like".

(MR) "Did these words seem to formulate in your head"?

(GW) "No it looked into my mind and I could look into it's, but I can't remember anything. Because it was funny in what it was looking at. It was looking at things that I had experienced in my life. And it could feel that. It's like you looking into

181

your wife's mind and your wife is experiencing something and you do as well"

(MR) "So you knew what was going on, what was happening"?

(GW) "Well it couldn't stop me looking into its mind when it made that connection, but I can't remember nothing. I don't know if it wiped me or what, or if it allowed that for a better connection, but that is what it was. You have machines now that can read you, its only years ahead now that this kind of thing can be possible".

(MR) "When I was listening to one of the hypnosis regression tapes you were laughing, and Helen was saying, 'what are you laughing at' and you said to Helen, 'well they have a life just like ours'.

(GW) "Yes, a life like ours but different. And 'they' reckoned that we were more advanced than them but we were capped! I think the advanced bit was that they had a lot of trouble dealing with the pressures here. You know, like gravity. And I think that they had trouble with our gravity".

(MR) "That's a strange thing to say Garry. But then again, I guess it is so difficult to understand what they would experience when they come through to Earth, how they would feel and.............."

(GW) "Well I reckon that that fluid they were in, was a method in which they could travel", *(Author's note. Garry is referring here to what he saw onboard this craft, when a small 'being' pushed itself out of a pool of liquid gel in front of him)* "Because if you take something in a fluid, and its a gel like substance, its going to act as a shock absorber. You could do fantastic manoeuvrers, and do things and you are going to be held steady. You are not going to get blown apart. So if you are in that kind of atmosphere, as in like inside a ball or inside a craft and you are in like a wallpaper paste stuff".

(MR) "Yeah".

(GW) "You can move, but move slowly. But as like torsion, as like throwing a ball against a wall, if you are in that fluid, you are not going to like splatter off the walls, you are going to be kind of suspended where you are".

(MR) "That's an interesting thing that you are saying there Garry".

(GW) "So you could do fantastic manoeuvrers and great things, and possibly use that, especially if it could feed you as well. If this fluid could repair you, and feed you and help you with different types of gravity and things like that, you know".

(MR) "That's very interesting. And another thing that was said, I can't recall if it was by you or Colin, was that you were quite surprised when one of these small 'beings' moved it's head like a snake, like it was moving in all different directions".

(GW) "I cannot remember that".

(MR) "OK, it must have been Colin. Also in some of these small 'beings', their neck extended onto their chest, instead of a neck like ours which goes straight into your body, it was like small struts. And some of them had folds of skin as well".

(GW) "I remember seeing this small one at the back, and it had folds of skin. It looked like it was ancient, it had folds of skin like an elephant kind of thing. Tiny small folds on its body, and it was just looking. It wasn't doing anything. It kind of reminded me of something like the Devil, the folds of skin and it was brown in colour".

(MR) "Was it a dark brown or a light brown, I remember you drew some drawings of it".

(GW) "Probably going towards a dark brown".

(MR) "One of the unusual things that you mentioned, or it might have been Colin that said it, was that you also saw a man in a suit"?

(GW) "I can't remember that". *(Author's note. In Garry's original audio taped testimony back in 1994, he does mention seeing one of the grey's wearing a suit, on board this object and looking decidedly out of place).*

(MR) "It's mentioned in the audio tapes".

(GW) "I'm not embarrassed about what happened, I just wish that more people would stand up to the plate and be truthful about things. The state of this place (Earth) and everything that is happening here, with all this nonsense with Agenda 21 and everything else that is going on".

(MR) "I know, I know, its crazy".

(GW) "And all the inoculations. I mean, going back thirty years, you would never believe now that they are talking about depopulating the world and things like that. That is where its heading".

(MR) "You mentioned on the audio tapes that you felt that you were moving all the time, and that you were up high, and you saw lots of rocks, slate grey rocks and there were faces above you".

(GW) "At one time I thought we were under the ground, that's what I thought. And I remember seeing these three ships under the ground, just floating there. Or did I see it in a movie somewhere, or is it what I saw".

(MR) "I think one of the most interesting things was right at the start of the abduction so to speak was when you were taken out on a kind of stretcher. It was like a floating stretcher and none of these small 'beings' were holding it".

(GW) "Yes, that's right. It felt like I was being electrocuted in the car, that something was pushing me back in the car and I couldn't move, something crushing me, like I was having a heart attack in the car".

(MR) "Wow".

(GW) "Because I probably would have lashed out and had a go at whatever it was. That's why I didn't stop, because I thought, 'monsters', that's exactly what I thought. I'm not stopping my car. I was doing what I thought was right, which was driving underneath the thing and getting away, but that wasn't happening. If I know now, what I didn't know then, I would have stopped the car and got out (laughs) But I think I probably would have been a lethal force against anything because when you are threatening somebody's life you will do anything. And I felt that my life was being threatened. I thought, something's going to get me. I was on high alert, all my adrenaline was going. I pushed the button down to quickly lock my car door, I crashed the car out of lower gear to go underneath this object when it dropped this shimmering curtain of light".

(MR) "Do you remember 'them' taking you out of the car"?

(GW) "No. I just remember them coming up to the car and then being all crushed up into the car".

(MR) "Do you remember that floating stretcher at all"?

(GW) "No"

(MR) "I believe Colin mentioned it". *(Author's note. Again on checking my witness testimony records, it was only Colin that recalled seeing this free floating stretcher)* "Now Colin also mentioned that he actually saw the car on board this craft. Do you remember that at all"?

185

(GW) "No. I know that the craft was bigger than the road. The road was 22 feet wide. It splayed over the road, and I'm wondering, could a car fit in there you know. I don't know. It's funny, because why would they not just lift the car. If they could do that, why could they not just lift the car, or did they lift the car when we were in the blackness. I just don't know".

(MR) "Do you remember the actual road that you took back, I know that it was a different road"?

(GW) "We went through the town. Because we were both scared and I think we were kind of high about what happened. And I had to take Colin home, but what I did was, I went home first to Oxgangs and I woke up Kim's sister and got her to come with me to drop Colin off. Because I was terrified to be on my own".

(MR) "Quite rightly so".

(GW) "And that whooshing thing, that black eye thing, I'm sure was some kind of engine. It made a perfect whooshing noise and it was balanced. It was like a free energy device. It had four packs on it, and this thing was like a black eye and it made the most perfect noise, like perfectly tuned, and perfectly balanced. Was it an engine, or was it something else? But it was just the noise that it made. It was particularly spot on. Being a mechanic you listen to things, nuts and bolt things, and you hear when things are running right, and that thing, whatever it was, was running right (laughs)"

(MR) "I remember you saying about this big black lens of an eye thing free floating above your head".

(GW) "No, it wasn't floating above my head".

(MR) "It wasn't"?

(GW) "No, that was over to my left".

(MR) "Alright".

(GW) "And this floating eye thing was held, it was like four pacts, it could have been like magnets or something I don't know. But whatever it was, it was balancing and it was causing this eye to go round at a high speed whilst making this whooshing noise".

(MR) "Right, OK".

(GW) "So if you look at the eye, you will see four devices around it", *(Author's note, I'd refer the reader to the photographic section of the book to see this eye like device that Garry is referring to)* "And it was making the thing whoosh, and it would fold in on itself. So it was like an engine or a device. It wasn't above my head, that was to the left of me".

(MR) "And did this device effect your body in any way, or did you just hear this whooshing noise"?

(GW) "I don't know. It just made that absolutely perfect noise".

(MR) "What about that can shaped device that rose up from the floor when you were lying on this bed thing. A small flap opened on it".

(GW) "Yes, a small flap opened, and like two eyes things, and it just sort of got my attention, and it was like, just looking at me, like scanning or looking. And I remember that the 'things' were interested in my legs for some reason. Was it to do with this gravity thing, because I know that one of them got a bit ill, one of them didn't look well, and I thought it was to do with the gravity and pressure. Maybe they were looking at our physiology, trying to see if they could adapt our body to their body, as if to deal with the gravity, and how we deal with it. I know that its an advanced culture, but even if you are an advanced culture, you need specimens to see well how are these people managing this. It's like a fish in the sea, how does that

187

fish live in the sea for us to know that, we would need to take it out and look at it".

(MR) "Well certainly since the last time we spoke, you surely are looking at things in an out of the box way. And sometimes you do need to do that, ie, think 'outside the box' and think what it could be, or couldn't be. And that's all we can do, because we don't have the answers, nobody has the answers. I certainly don't have the answers, definitely not. Helen was there to help you. I was there to get the story out and find out if there was anyone else that could relate to your story, and could share in your experience, in that they too, had a similar experience".

(GW) "Helen helping me, was the best thing that could ever have happened. I don't care what anybody says. I slept better at night because of the hypnosis. I had this sense of not knowing, and it kind of settled things down a bit. So as for me getting hypnosis, I would say that I scored big time, because I think it helped me, it really helped me. And I genuinely think that Helen cared more about us and what we were going through, than the actual incident itself. And I think she took that on board and helped us. So, no matter what anybody does or says, she helped me".

(MR) "Uh Huh"

(GW) "And I'm forever grateful for that, I really am. More so for you introducing me to Helen. I know Helen likes her ghosties and that she was psychic and things like that, and there is nothing wrong with that, there is certainly something in it. As to what though, some people can pick these things up. It's like what these creatures said to me, 'we can do amazing things', but we are kind of capped. Have you ever had a pal who could play the guitar or have you ever had a pal that could do special things. Have you ever had a pal who was an athlete. Imagine you could combine all those special things into one person".

(MR) "Yes"

(GW) "And I think that whatever that was, that was a stumbling block to humans, and that 'thing', was kind of removed a small bit. But what would happen would be that some people would be good at things and those things would slip through the net".

(MR) "Yes, I'm with you Garry".

(GW) "If you took that as a collective, and added that, and put all that into one person, you would have an awful power on your hands with that one person".

(MR) "Absolutely, yes".

(GW) "You would have like a perfect specimen of a human being".

(MR) "And do you think that this is what they were trying to do with you and Colin, that they were either trying to put something into you, or take something out of you"?

(GW) "I don't know"

(MR) "I guess that's the one question that you and Colin cannot safely answer. Why, why, why".

(GW) "It was just unusual that they said that particular word, is that what it meant". *(Author's note. Garry was referring here to the word 'Sanctuary' that came into his head from one of those small 'beings')*

(MR) "Helen had her job, my job was to get your story out, and try and elicit more people to come forward. But a lot of people are embarrassed to come forward. Because we need to build this UFOlogical jigsaw and find answers".

(GW) "People think you have mental health issues when you come forward saying all this stuff".

(MR) "I mean there were a few differences from the conventional abduction, and I am referring particularly to the coloured lines under one of those small 'creature's' eyes. Red, green and yellow, or black. It was like perforations or something. Do you recall this, or was it mainly coming from Colin"?

(GW) "Yes, I remember drawing that in a picture, and it was like zig zags under their eyes".

(MR) "Yes, that's right"

(GW) "It was all odd, when it was first coming out. Because the first drawings I did, it was like robot things fixing the ship or something, these things with the markings under them. Was it a pattern thing? Was everything done to me to make me remember? Was it something they fed into me to make me see that? The only thing that I can categorically say 100%, although the hypnosis revealed that some of it was right, probably most of it, was simply because there were things that I have never seen before. And I was trying to think that have I ever seen these things on T.V.? Or if I had seen them in a book, or a comic when I was small, and I was trying to rack my memory on that, and I couldn't. But the thing I categorically remember, was seeing the craft, and seeing the shimmering curtain of light, and trying to get away from it, driving underneath it, and then being in the blackness and looking about. "Where's my car"? "where is Colin"? "Am I dead"? "What's happened to me?"

(MR) "Yes it's something that you will never ever forget. It's intruded into you and Colin's life. Something that you didn't want, I'm pretty sure of that. And it's just trying to find out the cause of it".

(GW) "Is it time travellers, and they do this kind of thing to you? Is it somebody from my future coming back to see me? and what we will do, is we will kid on that we are aliens and with their technology. They could do that, I mean, where do you draw the line?"

(MR) "I know, I agree".

(GW) "I could tell you a million different things of what I've been thinking and it would never stop".

(MR) "I know. It's a massive thing that has happened to you, and it was a traumatic thing as well".

(GW) "I mean I had Budd Hopkins come to my house, that was something you set up Malcolm, and we spoke about what happened to me and he showed me a lot of his stuff. Budd said to me, "You know what happened to you, you don't need to convince anybody, remember that". He went on to say, whether its a good thing or a curse, I couldn't tell you. He was a really nice guy, he genuinely cared about people".

(MR) "Yes, he was a sad loss to UFOlogy was our Budd"

Author's note: At this point in our conversation, we spoke about sceptics and their take on UFO abductions. We now pick up from that point.

(MR) "It's OK to be sceptical as most people are"

(GW) "Of course"

(MR) "But by the same token, some sceptics are more debunkers than sceptics"

(GW) "But Malcolm you need these people".

(MR) "Oh Yes"

(GW) "You take them with open arms, and you just tell them how useful they are. As in some cases, these people can bring you back down to Earth on a lot of things".

(MR) "Yes, I totally agree".

(GW) "We should never ever poo poo them. We can say, I know you are saying that, and I am taking that on board, because there could be some useful things in it. We should always listen to them and always take them on with open arms. Because with this jig saw, its going to take all kinds to solve it. Its going to take you guys (UFOlogists) who are coming up with these fantastic ideas of what it 'could be', because there could be something in it. Then you have to say, does what you say, fit into my piece of the jigsaw. And you could turn and twist it, and you might not get it to fit. So therefore, although the sceptic has said that, and it sounds promising, it just doesn't fit with that case, it doesn't fit with that part, but it might fit in another part".

(MR) "I totally agree with you Garry, I love the way you are thinking. And will we ever get this UFOlogical jigsaw finished, that's the million dollar question in our life time I wonder"

(Author's note) And that was that. It was great to speak with Garry again, as it had been well over a year since we had a proper chat about his encounter on the A70. He was more than happy to agree for his statements above to be a part of this book.

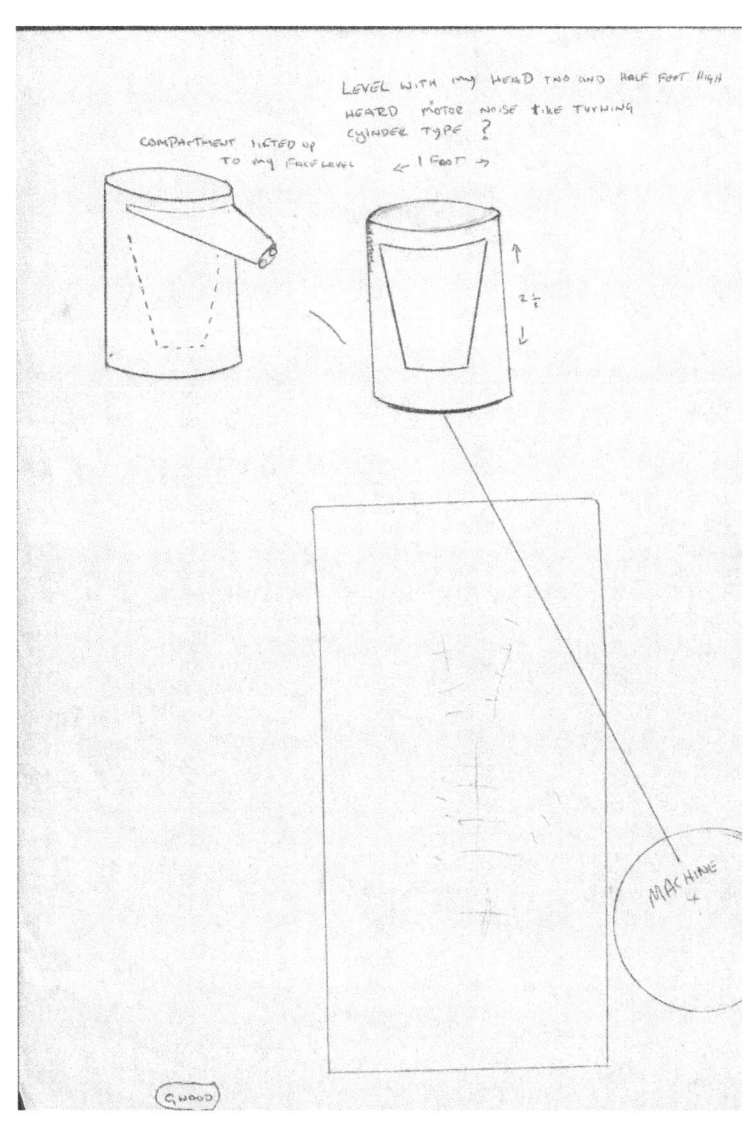

Can Device drawing 2 by Garry Wood. (c) Garry Wood

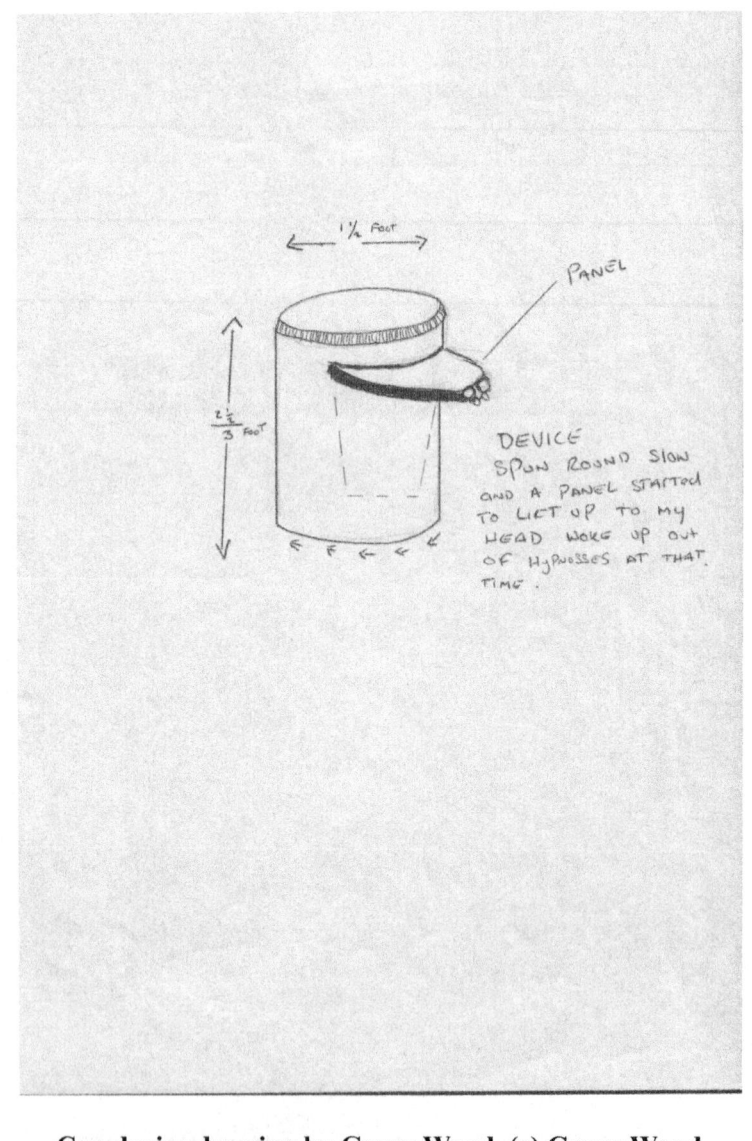

Can device drawing by Garry Wood. (c) Garry Wood

194

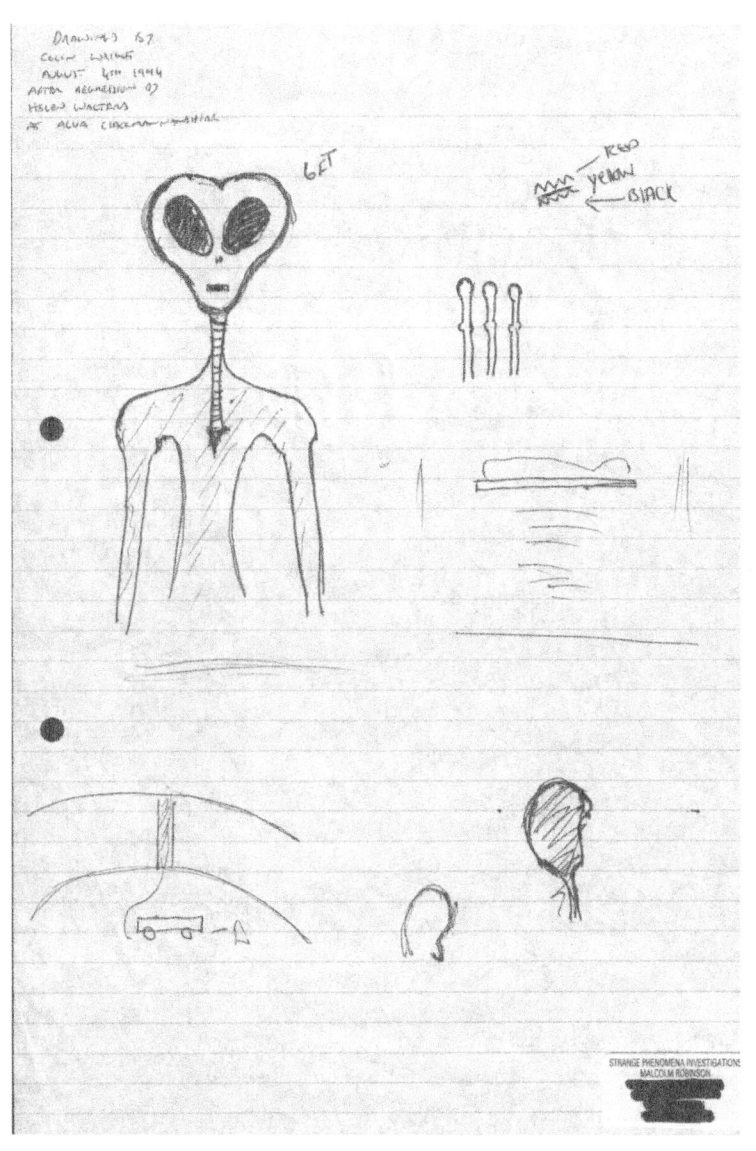

Colin Drawing from his hypnotic recall (c) Colin Wright

195

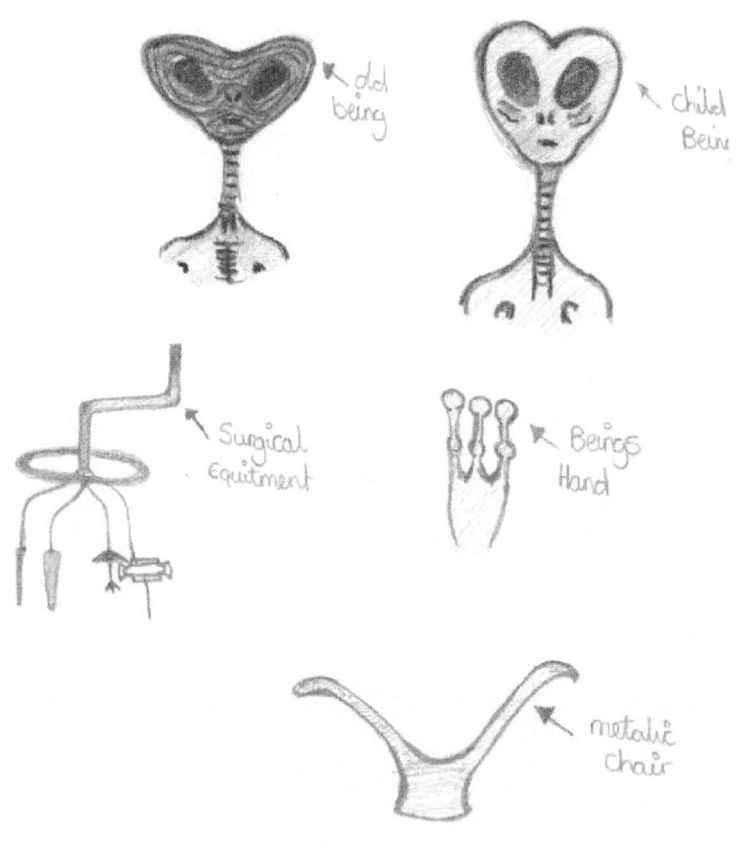

Colin Wright Drawing from his hypnosis recall. (c) Colin Wright

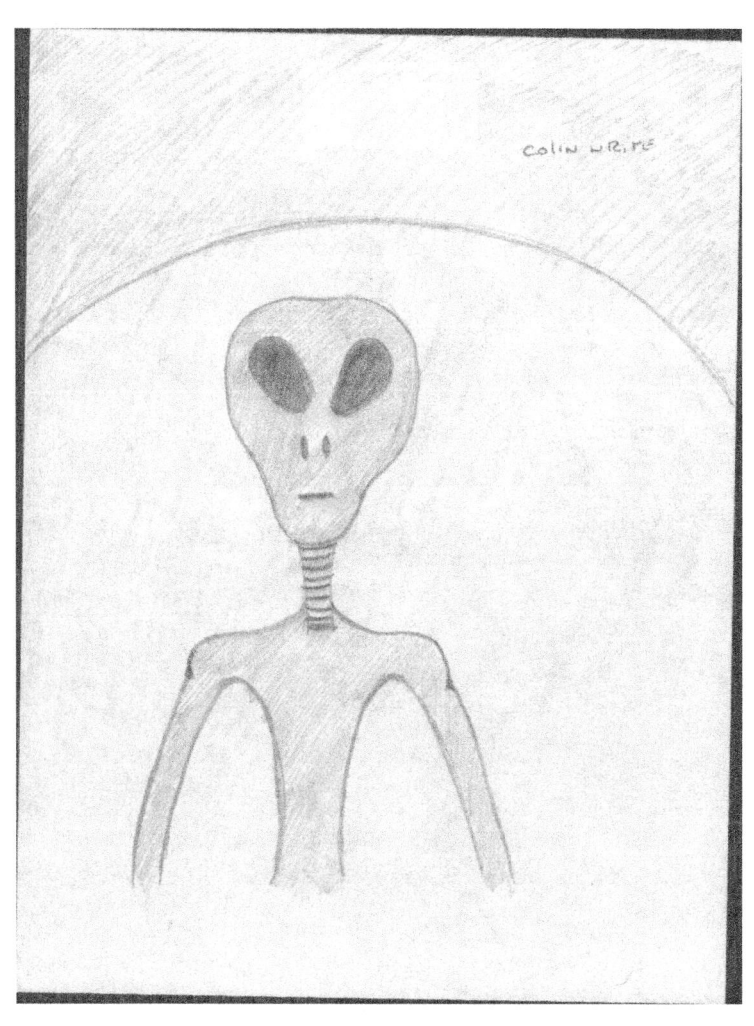

Colin Wright drawing of Alien (c) Colin Wright

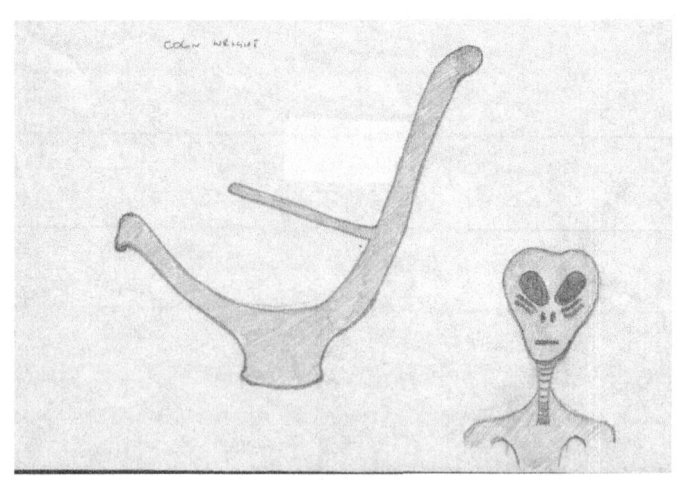

Colin Wright's Chair (c) Colin Wright

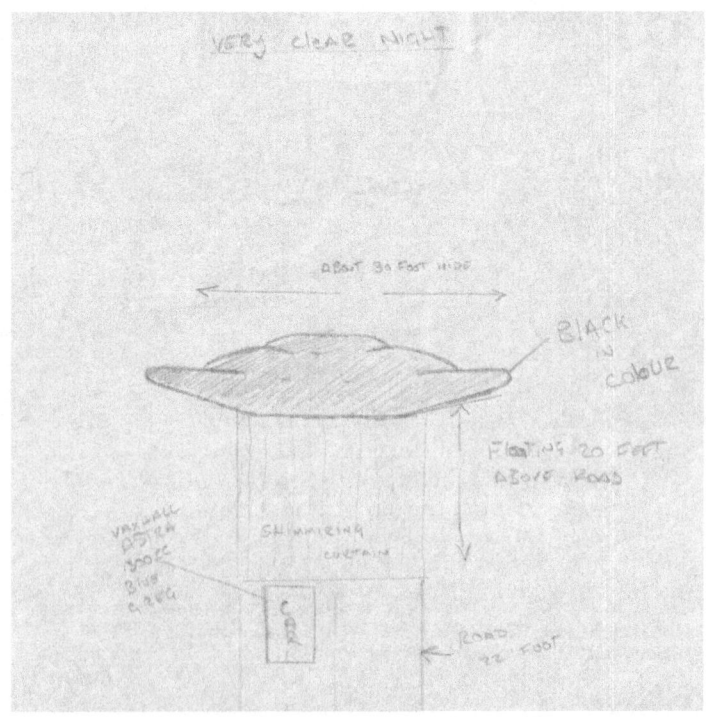

Garry UFO drawing (c) Garry Wood

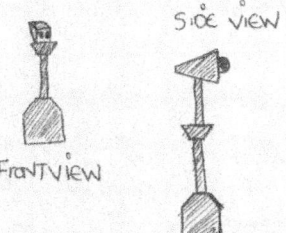

SIDE VIEW

FRONT VIEW

this object appeared in front of the chamber I was in, it came up from the floor and came level with my eyes moved up and down, then rotated left to right for about 2 minutes then lowered it-self back into the floor again

18.10.94   C Wright

Colin's drawing of device coming up from floor. (c) Colin Wright

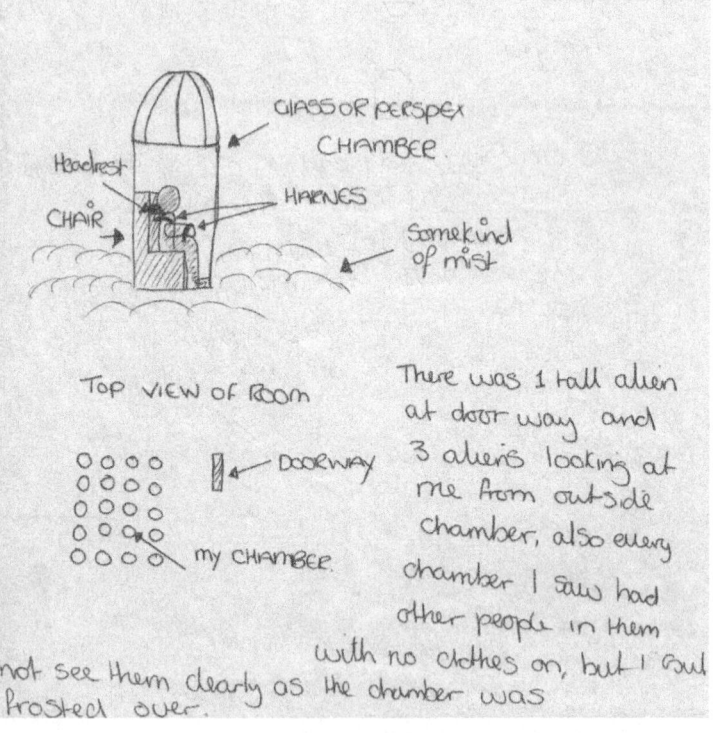

Colin's drawing of the chamber he found himself in. (c) Colin Wright

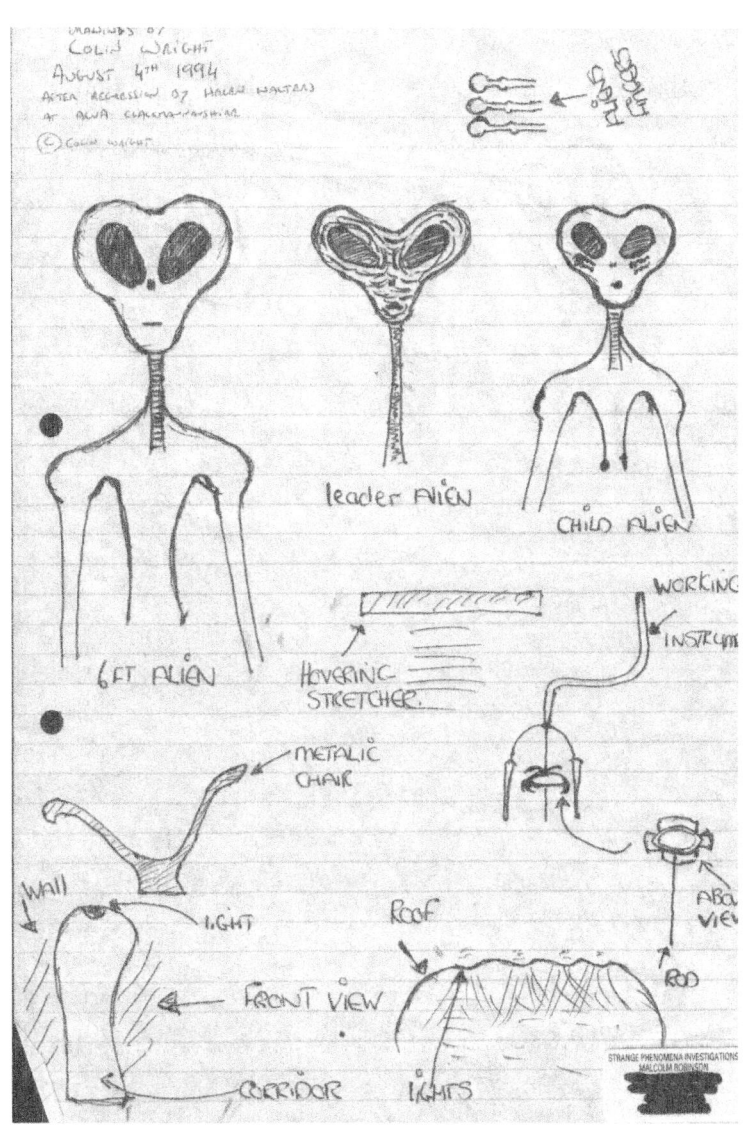

Colin's tableau of what he saw (c) Colin Wright

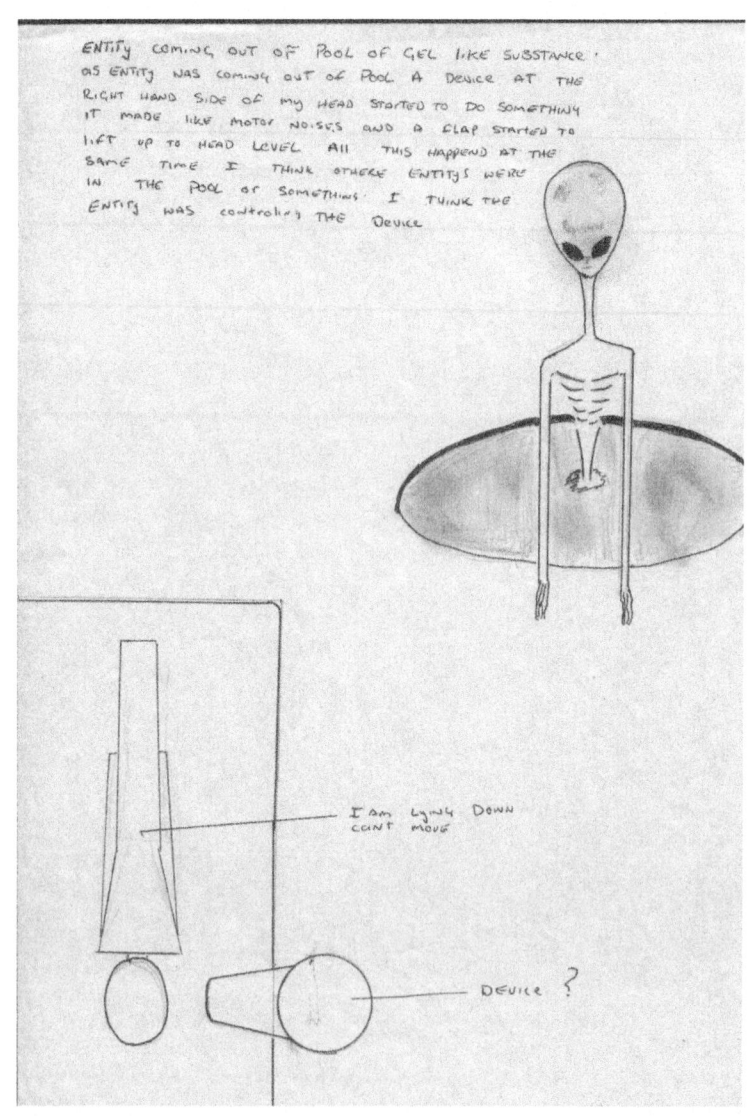

ENTITY COMING OUT OF POOL OF GEL LIKE SUBSTANCE.
AS ENTITY WAS COMING OUT OF POOL A DEVICE AT THE
RIGHT HAND SIDE OF MY HEAD STARTED TO DO SOMETHING
IT MADE LIKE MOTOR NOISES AND A FLAP STARTED TO
LIFT UP TO HEAD LEVEL. ALL THIS HAPPENED AT THE
SAME TIME. I THINK OTHERE ENTITYS WERE
IN THE POOL OR SOMETHING. I THINK THE
ENTITY WAS controling THE DEVICE

I AM LYING DOWN
CANT MOVE

DEVICE ?

Garry Wood and can device (c) Garry Wood

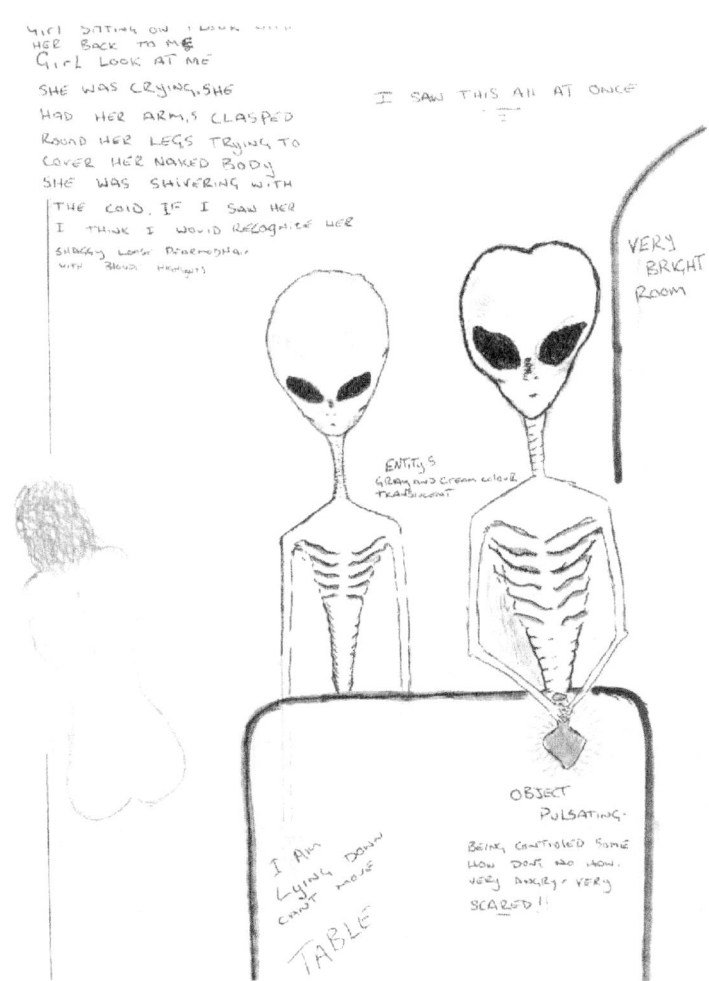

The handwritten notes on the drawing read:

GIRL SITTING ON FLOOR WITH
HER BACK TO ME
GIRL LOOK AT ME
SHE WAS CRYING. SHE
HAD HER ARM,S CLASPED
ROUND HER LEGS TRYING TO
COVER HER NAKED BODY
SHE WAS SHIVERING WITH
THE COLD. IF I SAW HER
I THINK I WOULD RECOGNISE HER
SHAGGY LOOSE PERM/MED HAIR
WITH BLOND HIGHLIGHTS

I SAW THIS All AT ONCE

VERY
BRIGHT
ROOM

ENTITYS
GRAY AND CREAM COLOUR
TRANSLUCENT

OBJECT
PULSATING.

BEING CONTROLED SOME
HOW DON'T NO HOW.
VERY ANXIOUS VERY
SCARED !!

I AM
LYING DOWN
CANT MOVE

TABLE

Garry Wood Drawing (c) Garry Wood

203

Garry Wood drawing of Ancient looking being. (c) Garry Wood

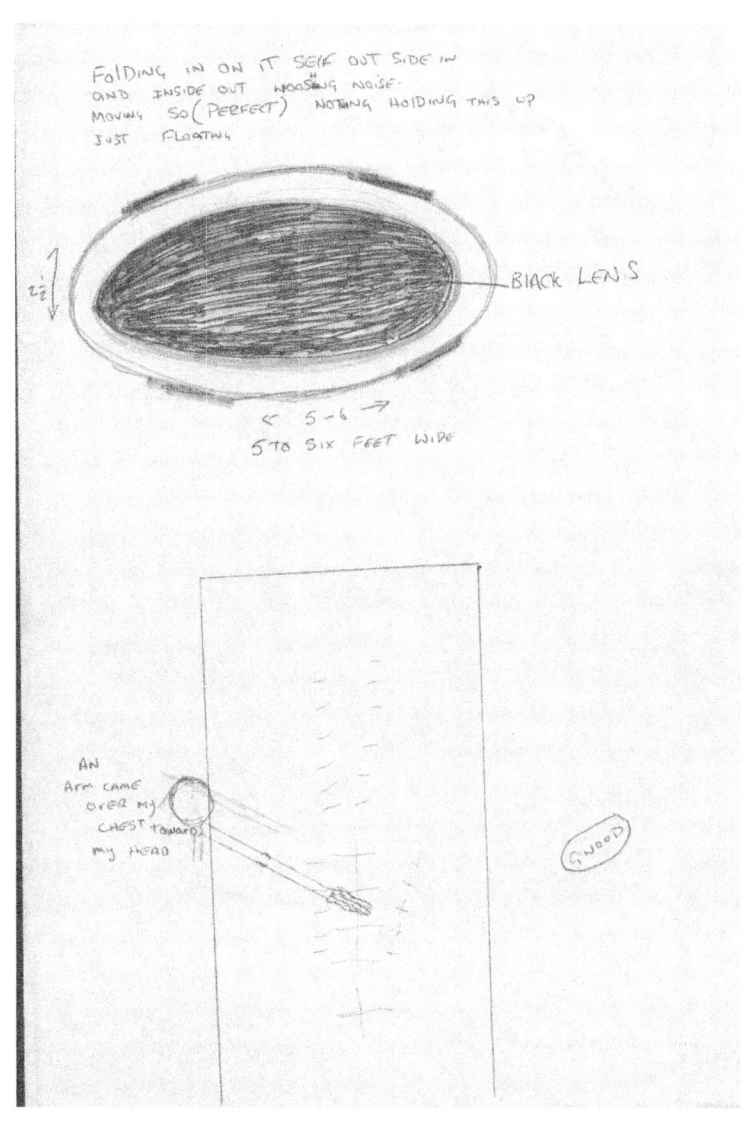

Garry Wood Lens device above table. (c) Garry Wood

205

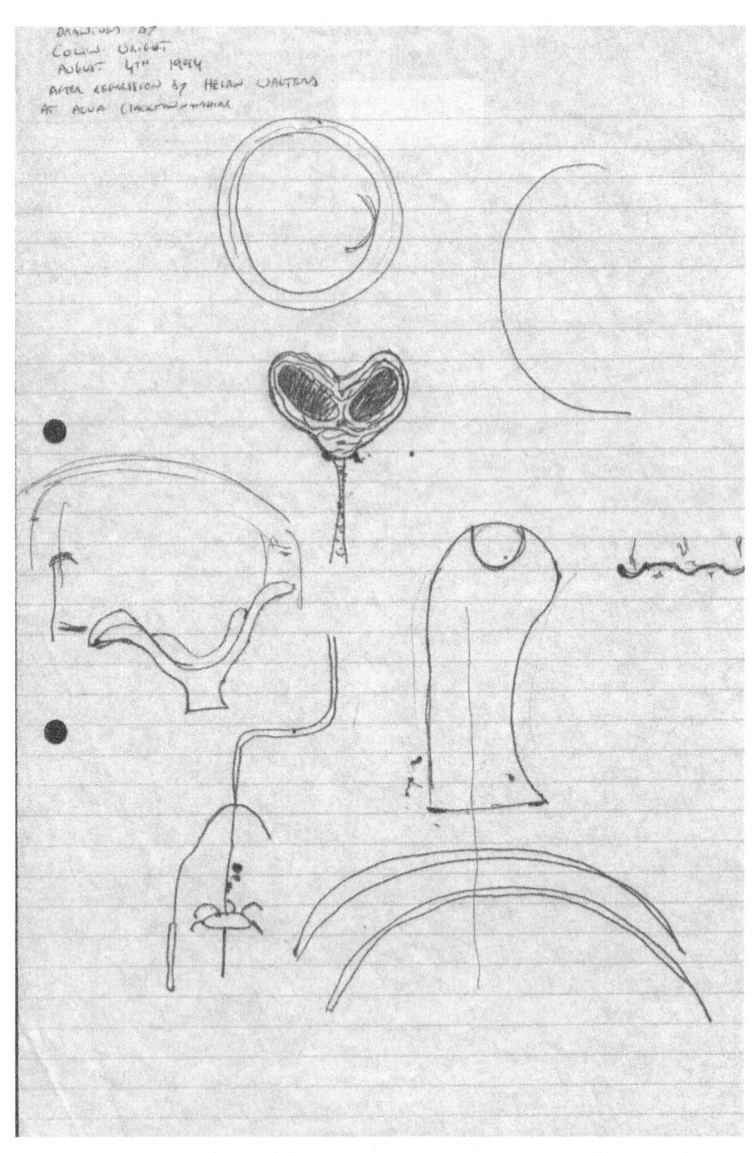

Hypnotic recall by Colin Wright (c) Colin Wright

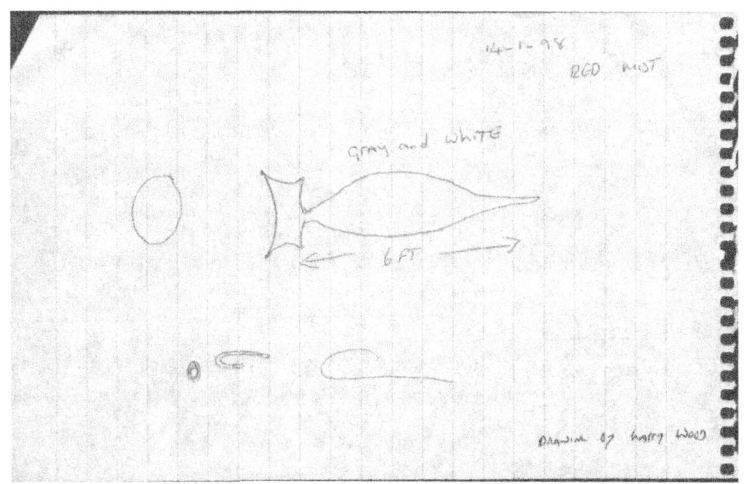

Garry's drawing of floating small bendy creature. (c) Garry Wood

CHAPTER TWO

THE THOUGHTS OF FELLOW UFOLOGISTS.

"I kept asking it, what do you want?...what do you want?
What is it? and it said 'Sanctuary'.
(Garry Wood recalls what these 'beings' said to him whilst
under hypnosis)

Needless to say all UFO researchers have their own thoughts as
to what may lie behind the UFO Abduction enigma, and I
decided to ask a number of Ufologists what their own thoughts
were. As you will see, there were some surprising answers.
First up, is Nick Pope. From 1991 to 1994 Nick Pope worked as
a civil servant within Secretariat (air staff). He undertook a
wide range of secretariat tasks, relating to central policy,
political and parliamentary aspects of non-operational RAF
activity. Part of his duties related to the investigation of
unidentified aerial phenomena reported to the Department to
see if they had any defence significance.

**NICK POPE (My thoughts on the UFO Abduction
Phenomenon)**

Like the UFO phenomenon, alien abduction sometimes
considered a sort of subset of ufology is multifactorial. There's
no single explanation for the wide variety of cases, and no neat
solution to the mystery. With UFO reports, one can say that
most sightings can be explained in terms of misidentifications,
hoaxes, hallucinations or psychological delusions, with a small
proportion of cases remaining unexplained. While sceptics and
believers alike have their theories about the unexplained cases,
even those of us who've investigated the phenomenon from
within the government, remain unclear as to the true nature of
what might be called the 'core phenomenon'. The same is true
with abduction reports, though there are differences too,
because the misidentification explanation doesn't really read
across.

Broadly speaking, abduction reports can be categorized as follows. Some reports will be entirely fabricated. Motives for this are varied, but can include attention-seeking, the desire for fame and fortune (unlikely outcomes, but the mistaken belief that this is possible may motivate some). The desire to test investigative methodologies of researchers and/or discredit researchers by getting a bogus account accepted. Hallucinations, psychological delusions and vivid dreams (especially if combined with sleep paralysis) may explain other reports. Hypnosis is a massive complication in abduction research, and may explain some abduction accounts. There's no absolute consensus on the true nature of the hypnotic state. Some say it's an altered state of consciousness, while others think it's really only a relaxed, concentrated state of mind. And despite the claims, it may increase suggestibility more than powers of recall. Furthermore, some believe that regression hypnosis can distort existing memories, or even create false ones especially where the hypnosis is done not by a trained hypnotherapist, but by a UFO/abduction researcher, where the use of leading questions can further complicate the issue.

Setting aside the conventional explanations, is there a 'core phenomenon' when it comes to alien abductions? And if so, is that phenomenon what the UFO community believes it to be, i.e. the literal taking of people onboard extraterrestrial spacecraft, without consent, possibly as part of some sort of human/alien hybridization program? The short answer is that I don't know. I keep an open mind and certainly don't rule it out, but neither have I seen any definitive evidence to support such a conclusion. However, as with UFOs, the sceptics have to be right every time, whereas the believers only need to be right once!

Notwithstanding the above, the vast majority of abductees, contactees and experiencers (the differing terms are interesting in and of themselves) I've met both while investigating UFOs for the MoD, and afterwards, in a private capacity have seemed sincere. They're ordinary people in extraordinary situations, mostly with little to gain and much to lose by speaking out. But unlike UFOs, where we have (at least within government!) good evidence in terms of things like MASINT, the abduction phenomenon is really just narrative. There's nothing wrong with that, and we should bear in mind that even in these days of forensics, DNA and CCTV, eyewitness testimony remains at the heart of the criminal justice system. But the lack of corroborative data makes abductions tricky in evidential terms. Until and unless we have something more substantive, like an implant analysis published in a peer-reviewed journal like Science or Nature, all this can only be categorized as intelligence analysts assess any fascinating-but-unproven information: "interesting, if true"!

In relation to the A70 abduction, I'm familiar with the essentials of the story, but haven't investigated it personally. Ironically, the events themselves took place while I was posted to Secretariat (Air Staff) the division where my duties included investigating UFO sightings. Frustratingly, however, the witnesses for whatever reason didn't report their sighting to the MoD in 1992, when it happened, choosing instead to contact a local university and the media, among others. It was 1996 by the time someone reported it to the MoD, and while there's a 2-page summary of the events in one of the MoD case files, no meaningful investigation was judged to be possible so long after the events, and my successor chose to take no further action.

This was Nick Pope's 2021 thoughts, but I thought I would share with you, what he sent me a few years ago about the UFO abduction phenomenon. This is what he said then.

"I started off feeling that genetic explanations centring on an extraterrestrial programme to create a human/alien hybrid race were the key to the mystery. But why should aliens whose technology is clearly light years ahead of ours bother with the logistical nightmare of thousands of abductions when they could easily remove the genetic material they wanted from our laboratories? Ultimately though, I discarded the genetic theory because it did not tally with the views of the abductees I met, many of whom had positive feelings about their experiences. This coupled with the abductees frequent and spontaneous development of interest in Spiritualism and the environment, seemed at odds with the idea of aliens using them as guinea pigs. I am the first to admit that my belief that the phenomenon is part of a campaign to civilise us, is only one more theory to join the ranks of competing ideas."

"The distress experienced by some abductees has been sobering, and has acted like a brake on the idea that my theory may represent some sort of New Age interpretation of the phenomenon. It would be nice to think that the motivation behind abductions is to prepare humans for entry into some sort of Galactic Network, but if this were so, why aren't the Extraterrestrials open with us? The covert nature of what is going on suggests that any alterations being made to our behaviour, are done for the benefit of the abductors, not for us, perhaps to remove the threat 'we' may pose to 'them'."

Nick Pope finished with.

"Having spoken to hundreds of genuine well meaning people, I believe alien abduction may be far more common than even many UFOlogists suspect. The purpose of this Extraterrestrial meddling, is I believe, to civilise human society. Most abductees are neither hoaxers or cranks, they are only too mindful of the adverse reactions to their claims. Many had their sanity questioned, were called liars and ostracised by family and friends. At the very least, they have risked ridicule" (Nick Pope).

Nick's statements are most certainly true, as both Garry and Colin found out when their UFO experience eventually came out. Both men had to endure the gauntlet of many a comment!

BUDD HOPKINS.

One leading light of UFO Abduction research, was the late Budd Hopkins. I only met Budd Hopkins once, and that was at a UFO Conference held in Sheffield England, where he and I were giving a talk. Budd Hopkins sadly passed away on the 20th of August 2011.

Budd was a strong advocate of using hypnosis, and wrote a number of books about UFO abductions. He clearly felt that hypnosis could, in the right hands, be a reliable tool in order to get to the truth. In his best selling book, *'Missing Time'*, *Ballentine Books New York 1981*, he mentions that the New York Times science page of October 14th 1980, carried an article by Jane E. Brody in which she wrote about how hypnosis could be used as a weapon to fight crime. She cited the following case as a prime example on the use of hypnosis in getting to the truth. This is what she wrote,

"The rescue of 26 schoolchildren kidnapped at gun point from a school bus in Chowchilla California in 1976, was facilitated by hypnosis of the bus driver who then recalled enough of the license plate number to enable police to find the getaway van. Last summer a Ballerina who had seen a man with a young cellist at the Metropolitan Opera House shortly before the cellist's brutal murder, was able, under hypnosis, to describe the man well enough so that a police sketch led to the arrest of a suspect".

In this same New York Times article, writer Jane E. Brody wrote;

"In the Los Angeles Police Department, eleven officers have used the technique in about 600 cases, with ninety percent of the hypnotic Investigations yielding information that led to the arrest of a suspect".

Budd Hopkins clearly felt that hypnosis was a valid tool that could be used by courts and police departments as an avenue to get to the truth.   However, he admitted that certain controls should be administered and that the use of hypnosis on 'any' subject, should only be done by a qualified practitioner.

DAVID M. JACOBS

Another advocate regarding the use of hypnosis on UFO abductees, is David M. Jacobs, Associate Professor of History at Temple University in America.   Jacobs is particularly well known in the field of UFOlogy for his research and authoring of books on the subject of alleged alien abductions.

In his book, 'Secret Life', Simon & Schuster New York, 1992, he stated;

"Hypnosis is an indispensable tool in unlocking the memories of an abduction. It is the best method available to gain detailed access to people's hidden abduction memories. Hypnosis however, is not foolproof, some abductees simply do not remember, when they do remember, especially details, it may be an incorrect memory that they are 'filling in'. In hypnosis, even asking questions about a specific event can put pressure on the subject to invent details of that event to provide the answers to those questions.   Even in deep hypnosis, the subject can consciously fabricate stories".   David M. Jacobs.

Despite David Jacobs misgivings on the use of hypnosis, he still believes that it should be used, but like everybody else, he maintains that it should only be used by professional and qualified practitioners. There are many other UFO researchers the world over who feel that hypnosis has it's place in the study of the UFO abductee, but it's fair to say that there are equally as many UFOlogists who feel that it has not.   It has not gone unnoticed by me the phenomenon known as 'False Memory Syndrome'.   Many people believe that certain individuals have a capacity to invent a story and somehow end up believing that their story is true, and even when pressed by authorities, or indeed under hypnosis, the invented story surfaces as large as life and told with conviction and honesty by the individual who invented it. We will be coming to the False Memory Syndrome shortly.

DENNIS HANNA

Next up to share their thoughts on UFOs and the abduction phenomenon, is Englishman Dennis Hanna, a fellow UFOlogist with an enquiring mind into the UFO subject. Here is what he had to say.

The Nature of the UFO Phenomena
Today, UFOs are a part of everyday culture. TV programmes, films and books are replete with accounts of spacecraft and aliens, not to mention abductions. The main flap began in the 1940s, but it's arguable exactly when. Ever since, the rate of abduction cases seems to have increased, but we seem no nearer to finding out for certain what it is we are dealing with. Some say it's the work of travellers from far-off planets, others claim our visitors are time travellers, and some say it's interdimensional in origin. For my money it is all three. interdimensional travel means that time and space can be breeched at will. The concept of time being a linear process no longer applies once the traveller moves between dimensions. This all seems rather hard to understand and it does require a complete shift in understanding. To grasp what is really going on requires a higher level of thinking and an admission that our human grasp of reality is fundamentally flawed.

Here's why:

What we humans perceive as reality is in fact a 3D model, manufactured by our brains. We get nerve impulses that our brain converts into vision, smell, sound, touch and taste, and that's when the brain conjures up a model that we can easily understand. The problem is we humans have very poor senses which only provide us with a fraction of what is really out there. In truth we see very little of the light spectrum and the same applies to our other senses. So, what is this interdimensional stuff all about? Imagine that reality is like a giant onion. There's an outer skin and many other skins that can be peeled back. Each skin is another dimension and another reality which is very slightly different from those adjacent to it. As you travel through the layers, the world seems to change more and more with each layer that is peeled back, until the traveller reaches worlds that bear no resemblance to home. These worlds are filled with 'alien' beings that are not like humans at all. However, the dimensions nearest to ours are more recognisable, indeed those closest are barely any different. It could be that we slip in and out of these nearby dimensions many times a year without realising it. Maybe that's the answer to those conundrums such as missing keys that turn up in ridiculous places, even the owner knows their keys could not have been placed there by them. The explanation may be a poltergeist but perhaps the key owner has slipped into another dimension and found their keys in a strange place, well, strange in this dimension!

Some of these 'alien' species from far-off dimensions may have perfected ways to travel between dimensions at will. This means they can travel to any time, any place in the universe, and any dimension they choose. Quite handy, don't you think? During their explorations, they may have come across our dimension and noted that we are close to interdimensional travel ourselves. When they look at our world, such a realisation must fill them with dread, given our violent nature. So, perhaps they are keeping an eye on us so that we do not drop in on them any time soon. These interdimensional beings may be from many different dimensions and have little in common, other than their advanced technology. This could explain the huge differences in appearance that startled onlookers report. Anything from small greys to Nordic races have been reported, not to mention those Reptilians. Some may be totally invisible to us, so one could be standing right next to you now! This could also explain the sudden appearance of Bigfoot, the Loch Ness Monster and other strange but illusive creatures. Perhaps the dimensions are kept apart by some unknown force that normally keeps them separate from each other. But perhaps these barriers are weaker at some points allowing startled onlookers to 'peep through the curtains' into another dimension. These witnesses may even drop into the interdimensional hole and disappear forever. Or they may return a few days later with tales of monsters and aliens that no one takes seriously. Perhaps these aliens routinely abduct people to have a look at them and equip these unwilling abductees for some task or other. Maybe these people are prepped to allow downloads of information that the aliens wish to transmit to humanity and have chosen certain people to act as a conduit in order to pass on the alien message. Stuff like look after your planet or you'll be sorry, or stop killing each other, or don't come to our dimension if you don't mind. Who knows? Well, perhaps some of us do, and are already being used as an information conduit to pass the alien message to our fellow humans. Makes you think, doesn't it?

PAUL SINCLAIR.

Paul Sinclair has held a deep fascination for all things weird and wonderful all his life. He began his research back in 2002 and is the author of several books on strange phenomena. He lives with his wife and family in the town of Bridlington in England. Paul stated.

As I see it, the abduction phenomenon is the holy grail of all human experiences, if you consider that seeing a UFO in the purest sense of the word can be a life changing experience. Imagine actually seeing the beings from within these structures or from another sphere of existence. That shifts the scenario on to a whole new level. A level that is difficult to deal with for anyone who has been genuinely touched by the phenomena. The reasons why these situations are so impossible to deal with are many, but the lack of proof is at the top of the list when attempting to validate an abduction. What people claim happens sounds impossible, and that is the reason so many people choose the path of silence over speaking about their experience. It is a no win situation where skepticism and ridicule rule. On the other hand we also have to realize that sleep psychosis, medication, prescribed or illegal substance can induce symptoms similar to those described by abductees. Our own

216

imaginations can produce false memories and scenarios not unlike those described in the abduction scenario. Add to that list, people who are lying, and you have the explanations often used by science and academia to dismiss the claims people make about being abducted by aliens. However none of that should detract from the fact that people all over the world have and are being touched by something outside of human understanding. My own experiences with the beings I called the night people, leave me in no doubt that they are real. If I were to give one example it would be my own. To wake in the early hours of the morning and see 'beings' that could only be described as 'alien' is nothing I can ever forget. Then in the light of day, discover marks on my body that were not there the night before is the only proof I need that these things are more than the products of our imagination. This is a silent pandemic touching every part of the world and does not appear to discriminate between color or intelligence.

NIGEL WATSON

English UFO researcher and author Nigel Watson, kindly gave me permission to use an article that he wrote on the UFO Abduction phenomenon. Here is how he sees the phenomenon.

THE REALITY OF THE UFO ABDUCTION EXPERIENCE.

The powerful combination of *Intruders* and *Communion* for good or bad, set the standard for abduction experiences. As might be expected, there is no such thing as an 'average' abduction experience, but we can outline their structure and format as reported in the UFO literature. First there is what I will call the trigger-event that causes the abductee to report it to the media and to UFO investigators. This usually takes place when the abductee is alone in their bed at night, or when driving late at night on deserted roadways. The trigger for someone to discover they have been abducted does not have to be an actual UFO or alien encounter. A series of strange nightmares or some other traumatic experience might make someone think that they have been abducted. Reading about the subject or seeing a film or documentary about UFOs can also trigger a memory of an encounter. Visual images of aliens seem to be particularly potent. The illustration of the alien head on the cover of Whitley Strieber's book *Communion*, has triggered many such memories. All these instances indicate that abductees have no control over how and when they are contacted, but there are cases of people making deliberate contact on their own initiative. This might be done through meditation, trance or even drug-induced states.

Bedroom encounters usually involve the person waking suddenly. They hear a buzzing or whizzing sound, and they are paralysed so they cannot get out of bed. At this moment they might see a strange figure or figures at the bottom of their bed. They are usually described as being human-like, with large heads, who wear one-piece silvery outfits. In the case of abductees in cars or outdoors, they usually see a light in the sky that comes towards them. They might then go through a fog or mist. Car engines and their associated electrical systems, and radio equipment have also been known to cut out or act erratically in the presence of a UFO. It is assumed that UFOs created an electromagnetic effect that stopped cars that got within their range, but studies of this effect have proved inconclusive. Everything in the area might seem to be silent and strange as if time or space has become distorted. This change has been termed the 'Oz Factor' by Jenny Randles and she thinks witnesses enter an altered state of conscious at this stage. She explains this in relation to a sighting by two fishermen of a large disc-shaped UFO:

"The witnesses said that they were not afraid. Indeed, they were strangely calm and subdued. They felt themselves isolated in time and space, as if removed temporarily from the real world and melded with the UFO above them; only they and it existed."

Minutes or hours later the person will 'wake' and discover that they cannot remember anything during this missing time period. Motorists who experience this, will suddenly find themselves miles down the road without knowing how they got there.

Entering the Alien World.

The trigger event causes the abductee to seek out why they cannot remember a period of missing time after witnessing a UFO, or they might want to know why they feel traumatized by 'alien' nightmares. It is usually when a UFO investigator hypnotically regresses a witness, that we learn about the person's abduction experience. In his 1987 study of 270 abduction cases, folklorist, Dr. Thomas Bullard, identified six major elements of abduction accounts:

1. Capture

2. Examination

3. Conference

4. Tour

5. Otherworldly Journeys

6. Theophany.

It is worthwhile to use these points to gain an understanding of what might occur during an abduction. First of all capture involves being floated up to a flying saucer or the abductee simply walks up a stairway that extends from the craft. Much to the disbelief of more hard-headed ufologists many abductees have reported being floated through solid walls or windows on their journey to a saucer hovering over their home or car. Often people do not remember how they got inside the flying saucer, this has been labelled 'doorway amnesia'. Inside, the craft has a clean, sterile environment with no windows but light is provided that emanates from no apparent source. The abductee is taken down a curved, white or gray, metallic corridor, which eventually takes them to the centre of the craft. This seems to be a medical centre. Working in a businesslike manner with great efficiency, the aliens strip-off the abductee and place them on an examination table where they are medically examined. Some people have even reported being put inside a machine, others have been put in a tank that's filled with fluid like Betty Andreasson. *(Author's note Betty is an America UFO abductee)* The aliens use strange looking surgical equipment to scan the subject and to probe their body. Needles are inserted in their abdomen. There is usually an intense interest in the person's genitalia, and they might extract blood, sperm, or ovum samples. Parts of the body, such as eyes or whole brains, have been removed and then returned without any damage. Others have reported having a tube placed up their rectum and faecal material sucked out of them.

They are also likely to place small implants into the brain via the nose, or inserted behind the ear, or other parts of the body. The spine or other parts of the body might be injected to extract or inject fluids. There are many cases of people being raped or forcibly seduced by the aliens. To encourage sexual intercourse the aliens have disguised themselves as celebrities, religious figures or even appeared in the guise of an abductee's dead spouse.

Female abductees who have been raped by the aliens and become pregnant suddenly 'lose' the foetus, later they are abducted and shown their 'lost' hybrid baby. Other abductees have seen on flying saucers or in what they believe to be underground bases on Earth, nurseries, containing such babies and human bodies in liquid-filled containers. There have been accounts of abductees seeing other humans on the ship being mutilated, flayed, dismembered, drained of blood and stacked in a heap. They are threatened that if they do not cooperate they will end up like these people. The procedures are conducted on the abductee whilst they are in a conscious yet paralysed or sedated state. More than one type of alien might be present during the examination, and they often induce great fear, pain and humiliation. Conference with the alien captors is usually limited. The aliens do not ask permission to operate on their victim, and there is usually no explanation for their activities. Rather than by verbal means, the aliens tend to communicate telepathically with the abductee. If other human abductees are present they seem to be in a trance, and it is impossible to talk to them or make any other form of contact with them. When the aliens communicate with each other, it is either in an unknown language or in a manner that is inaudible to the abductee. Abductees are sometimes given a tour of the ship, they might be shown a film or slide shows presented on TV monitors. There is an attempt to train abductees in the use of alien technology, or they are lectured on how this alien technology works. They might also see the ship's control room, which contain maps of star systems showing where the aliens come from. According to David Jacobs, none of the 50 abduction cases he investigated contained any reports of seeing the living quarters of the alien craft.

Some abductees are taken on what Bullard calls 'otherworldly journeys' to the home planet of the aliens, or they get a short ride round the solar system. Contactees of the 1950s were most likely to report such trips, usually garnished with detailed descriptions of alien civilizations on Mars and Venus. Since our own space probes have proved that life of this type does not exist in our solar system, supporters of the contactees contend that they must have travelled in a different dimension or astral plane. After this the abductee receives important information about the future of our planet and our species. They warn that we will be destroyed, and that only the chosen will be saved and taken to another planet. The aliens are either regarded as our spiritual benefactors or as the minions of the Devil. After an abduction experience, the abductee will want to spread the-word that they have come to save us or to destroy us. This could be because there are evil and good aliens carrying out these abductions, or it could be that they act the same towards everyone. In the latter case, it is how the abductee responds to them that conditions whether they are perceived as good or evil.

Ufologists have noted that the biases of the investigator seems to have a bearing here, as some investigators seem to only see abductees who have negative and painful experiences and others only get abductees that have been spiritually uplifted by their experience. Finally, the abductee returns to full consciousness several miles from where they are taken, if the incident involves a car, or they are dumped several yards away from where they were originally taken. Others wake up in their bed, and wonder if the abduction was a dream or not. Jacobs notes that abductees wake up to find themselves in odd positions, their clothing is re-arranged, or they find unusual stains in the bed and they feel they have not had a proper sleep. Abductees have a screen memory planted in their subconscious mind to hide their abduction experience. The screen memory takes the form of seeing owls, wolves, eagles, raccoons, mythical birds like the Phoenix, angels or devils. Yet, the memory of the abduction is never totally erased and most of it can be retrieved through hypnotic regression.

Post Abduction Experiences

After what I have called the trigger event, the person can suffer a multitude of physical and psychological signs that indicate that they have been abducted.

These indications can be listed as follows:

1. Amnesia or 'missing time' after seeing a UFO.

2. Nightmares, insomnia, and fear of the dark and enclosed spaces.

3. Scars, scoop marks, bruises, punctures will be found on the person's body without any immediate explanation for them. The abductee might have frequent nose bleeds and feel that they have got an unusual growth or implant inside them.

4. The health of the person deteriorates. Serious illness sometimes leading to death can occur in the months after an abduction. Terminal brain tumours can appear after abductions. Female abductees can develop serious gynaecological problems.

5. Behaviour Change. These can be for good or bad. Abductees might become born again Christians or become more spiritual and relaxed in general. They might become vegetarian and take up animal-rights and other charitable works.

On the bad side of the equation, they can take to drug, food and alcohol abuse. Their behaviour can become excessive and erratic. They get obsessive about their abduction experience and it's implications. They lose any meaningful relationship with their wife or partner, family and friends. They cannot deal with normal life any more and can become suicidal.

6. The abductee might become psychic and/or is plagued by paranormal apparitions or poltergeists.

One or a combination of these indicators will cause the person to seek help that will uncover their abduction experience. Hypnotic regression is used to recall this information, but sometimes this is not necessary, and it is spontaneously recalled. When recalling their abduction experience, the person often remembers that they have been in contact with aliens since childhood, it is only after the trigger event that they realize why they have had certain phobias or strange screen memories. Several of these indicators have been used by investigators to determine whether people have been abducted or not. There is an online survey (at: http://www.abduct.com/survey.htm) that asks you 28 questions of this nature and if you get a high score you could well be an abductee. I should add that I scored 3 points so it seems the aliens have left me alone so far. Ufologists have also come to think that abductees are chosen rather than randomly snatched away. This is indicated by the fact that whole generations of families have been plagued or blessed by alien abduction experiences.

Discussion

UFO researcher and historian, David Jacobs', survey of 60 abductees involving 300 abduction experiences published in his *Secret Life* book in 1992, and Harvard professor of psychiatry, John E. Mack's case histories of 12 abductees in his 1994 book *Abduction,* set the seal on the subject. They gave powerful support to Hopkins' view that thousands of U.S. citizens are being abducted, and confirmed that they followed a stereotypical pattern. John Rimmer agrees that 'there is strong 'family resemblance' between a great many cases, and, many uncanny details (are) repeated in case after case' Bullard's study equally conveys the impression that abductions fit a highly structured format that suggests that they are the product of real experiences rather than rumour or fantasy. Martin Kottmeyer puts forward the case that each abduction case seems to gain details from previous cases and other cultural images and sources, which would explain the consistency of abduction details.

The framework of abductions can be explained by the fact that Bullard takes his data from the UFO literature rather than from case files or other documents. The thrust of most abduction accounts and books is to place the often jumbled and confusing information gained over months or years into a structured form that fits a theoretical and/or chronological structure. Furthermore, many of the prime U.S. abductions, have been investigated and publicized by a relatively small group of individuals and organizations, who are likely to take an interest in cases that conform to their preconceptions. Since Hopkins and Jacobs are convinced of the literal truth that 'nuts and bolts' spacecraft are coming to abduct us, how do they account for stories full of magical happenings? Jacobs acknowledges that when he started hypnotically regressing abductees they recounted wild and impossible events. He regarded these factors as the result of false memories and

224

dreams that filled the vacuum of the 'legitimate memories'. Through continued work, he felt he was able to distinguish between the false and truthful memories, and, after two and half years of work, he was able to fit them into a three tiered matrix. His abduction matrix consists of physical, mental and reproductive procedures that the aliens carry out on a regular, less frequent and irregular basis.

The abduction scenario, although worldwide, is heavily influenced by U.S. periodicals, websites and books. This means that they broadly agree with the U.S. abduction accounts, yet they also introduce their own national and/or cultural biases. In Britain, Jenny Randles notes that when she conducted a study of 19 British abduction cases, between 1979 and 1986, none of them involved the stereotypical gray beings. Instead, British abductees saw monsters, robots or Nordic-type human entities. There were few medical examinations, and although abductees reported missing time lapses the investigators were able to account for these lapses. This made her wonder how they could recall abductions lasting minutes or hours when they had at best, time lapses of only a few minutes. More worryingly she found that abductees were more traumatized by the hypnotic regression process than by their abduction experience. It was her view that they had probably encountered a UFO that triggered their abduction experiences, but whether these experiences were real or not seemed highly suspect.

To answer the question of whether alien abductions are real or not, all we can firmly say is, 'it depends....'

PHILIP KINSELLA.

English researcher Philip Kinsella, is the author of several UFO/Paranormal books. He has appeared on national television and radio, and hosts his own radio show 'Twin Souls' with his identical twin brother, author and artist, Ronald Kinsella, and which is part of the Paranormal UK Radio Network. Philip was kind enough to send me what he believes is behind not only the greys, but UFO Abductions as well.

225

The Greys, Cloning & Interdimensional Time Travel

We seem no nearer in finding answers which could lead us in the right direction regarding what we are up against with these nightmarish intrusions and the reasons why these so called abductions are, seemingly, being inflicted upon a large number of people.

Although researchers have tried to come up with certain theories, I believe we have to look at the subject from a fresh perspective, and one which just might offer us clues as to what the Greys really represent and where they may come from. The Greys have become ingrained within the minds of society as diminutive, large-eyed, telepathically communicating creatures. Indeed, within the film industry they have been depicted as evil, with the intent of taking over the planet through the process of world wide destruction. This is typical of Hollywood. Because these stories which date back to the famous Roswell crash in 1947 in New Mexico, have excited masses through the media machine, a large amount of money is to be made from any sci-fi battle with 'Them' against 'Us' as the theme! This does little to help promote any consideration that we might be experiencing a very benevolent race of creatures that are anything but hostile!

But what is the real reason behind an abduction? Let's explore this question and see if we can look at the whole enigma in a completely different light. The reason why we are not finding the answers to those questions that baffle our senses, is that maybe, we are looking at the whole subject matter within a rigid mind set. A puzzle comes in many pieces. We have to find the right parts in order to fill in the mosaic, which hopefully might show us a clearer picture of what actually is going on. Many people assume that the Greys come from another planet. Most believe they are merely robots serving a higher power to further their exploitation of humanity! There is the hypothesis that these creatures are 'Us' from the future, making a return journey into the past to try to fix certain problems that threaten their very existence namely reproduction!

This might be the case, but for some reason I believe they represent something entirely different from our current level of understanding, namely because their '*modus-operandi*' appears to suggest a much more complex agenda, and one which has baffled respected Ufologists around the world. There also appears to be a 'Spiritual Connection,' and something which may offer us new clues as to what is really going on behind the apparent wall of silence from not only our own Governments, but the military too, who are quick to clam up about anything relating to UFOs or abductions. So, who now is there to help us try and understand this phenomenon? Not that the British Ministry of Defence are of any help to the public in the first case! The same is said for other clandestine military factions the world over.

The Abduction

Let's take a look at a typical abduction. Most commonly, a person is rendered powerless throughout their ordeal by a host of said grey alien beings who seem to enter the abductee's property by apparent super-human means. The Greys do not communicate verbally as one might expect, but by some method of telepathic exchange. Many people report that the large, black, wrap-around eyes of the Greys, which are so commonly reported do all the communication, somehow rendering their victim into an anaesthetised state. The subject is then '*taken*' through the walls of the house and transported onto some type of craft where a rather intrusive mental, physical, and sometimes spiritual investigation is performed. Although the abductee is aware of what is happening to them during the time of the encounter, their memories however are suppressed, and most often buried deep within the subconscious mind. This may indicate that the human psyche is temporarily and forcibly removed from its normal processing of data within this matrix because it has been shifted to an altogether different reality. Startlingly, the experience of an abduction is not that dissimilar to what is termed as a near-death-experience (NDE for short). Because the NDE is a natural progression beyond this Earth and into a different dimension of awareness, most people do remember their encounters with these types of experiences, simply because they are not deliberately forced. What is also of great interest, is the fact that the Greys are fascinated by human reproduction.

With regards to an abduction, the individual who has gone through this ordeal will sometimes find that they have had more than one encounter with these Greys, leading to the suspicion that certain individuals are selected for examination on a regular basis throughout their lives. This clearly indicates that the Greys' subjects are *'tagged'* rather like cattle to identify and catalogue not only the physical, but also mental attributes which have been stored throughout the person's physical life (reference: *Casebook: Alien Implants* by Whitley Strieber, Bantam Doubleday Dell Books, 2001). Implants have been well documented within UFO research. These are sometimes discovered as small lumps around or within the ear and nose cavity, arms, or legs or even within the brain itself. The main emphasis of the Greys is to hide these objects in areas of the human body, which makes them difficult to detect. These implants are usually clouded in a small membrane of tissue in order to cleverly conceal any indication whatsoever that the person has been marked for further abductions. This may also account for the fact that the foreign object will not be rejected within its biological host. It has been known that, while our doctors have tried to remove these implants from abductees through a simple medical procedure, they have mysteriously moved away on their own accord while the process of extraction is being implemented.

The easiest example to use here is the 'bar-coded system' that we apply to items to identify a product being sold. The 'tagging system' which we call 'implants' could be used by the Greys in a similar fashion to recognise their chosen human subject, along with a complete history of their psychological, medical and spiritual records downloaded into the implant throughout the individual's life experience here on Earth. In many cases, and where these implants have been successfully removed, the individual feels as though they have 'lost' something and many abductees prefer for the implant to remain in place. There could be a very good reason why the Greys seem intent in cataloguing their subjects, and we shall discover a startling theory, which lends credit to what we are actually dealing with here, and something that goes beyond the nuts-and-bolts syndrome of Ufology.

Many abductees also report that some type of reproduction program is being implemented as a covert part of the Grey's agenda. On almost all occasions, males have sperm removed and females are impregnated with some type of alien/human hybrid while these abductions are taking place. These have all been well recorded within UFO literature, but the question is, 'Why?' Are the Greys dying? Have they come to the end of their line where reproduction is concerned? We know that from the physical characteristics of the Greys, they have no means to reproduce themselves.

As far as we know, the molecular structure of the males' enzymes within the sperm must be tampered with by the Greys in order to change the DNA configuration to create their so-called 'hybrids.' Many female abductees report being pregnant after an abduction and then find they lose the foetuses normally about a few months afterwards! This is followed by those females who carried the 'hybrid' being returned to the alien craft to view her offspring, which are exhibited in either test-tubes, or presented to the female as weakly looking human/alien crossbreeds which have matured to about the age of two or three in our Earth years. It is obvious that some form of accelerated growth is initiated by the Greys for their hybrids to develop quickly. The female is then asked, on occasions, to bond with the hybrids in order that emotions are brought into the fray. Why is this important?

Firstly, we must look at what methods the Greys employ to get their subjects onto the UFO in the first instance. It would appear that the human, etheric body is being forcibly removed from its physical counterpart as opposed to the entire bodily mass. Most are aware that we have what is commonly termed a 'soul', which temporarily affixes itself into the physical vehicle through incarnation. Indeed, some religions throughout the world believe this to be the case, and once the soul has exhausted its Earthly life, it returns back to what is known as the spirit world where it continues on its eternal path, albeit in a different dimension.

There are those who are gifted in the ability to 'will' their soul away from the body through a process called 'out-of-body experience, (OBE for short.) In these instances, individuals are able to access other planes of consciousness by thought alone. It is reported that the 'etheric' body is still attached by what is known as the spiritual umbilical cord. This method requires a great deal of meditation on the practitioner's part and can sometimes be a frightening experience for those who have little understanding of the subject. However, this may be one of the ways that the Greys are able to retrieve the 'real you' in order that you be brought into their correct field of vibration.

We are aware that the common television set is designed to collect an invisible signal being sent out via stations across the world. This process of sending and collecting waves of information could also relate to how our human brain works. A physical body (i.e. the television set), is needed in order to catch signals, (consciousness), which the human eye cannot see, and the physical hand cannot touch, much like a radio or mobile phone. Within these signals being sent out, entire reams of data are being downloaded into these mechanisms for us to view, absorb and digest mentally. So, we can see from example that both the physical and spiritual body are two entirely separate entities.

The body is merely the mechanism within this dimension to carry the soul through these Earthly experiences. Death is a natural process, which releases our spiritual essence back to its original source of origin. It is believed that reincarnation is also an accepted part of our spiritual progression. It has been argued that in order for a soul to learn life's lessons here on Earth, it will invariably have to go through many incarnations. I believe the true essence of one's character/personality does not necessarily change, and that your life experiences are amalgamated from past lives to further progress to different levels of understanding.

We are natural products of evolution, able to reproduce and continue the cycle of creation in an effort to allow the soul of a person residing on the 'Other Side' to return when ready to take on new challenges. Our experiences might not necessarily limit us to the Earth plane, but other worlds and dimensions also. Some assume, as I agree, that our Genesis was implemented by extraterrestrials who had re-modified the hominid throughout its varied stages of evolution. However, the main emphasis here is to illustrate that the soul of a human does indeed encompass the material body, and that it goes through a process of reincarnation brought on by human reproduction.

The UFO/Abduction and The Greys

What is interesting about the Greys is their complete lack of understanding regarding age, taste, smell, and colour, along with emotions. It's as though they have come from a dimension which carries none of these essential ingredients which make up our entire physiology. This is suspect indeed when we also discover that the Greys seem to work as a hive-mind, or group-consciousness. Are we dealing, then, with a collective entity trying to understand more about itself through us? This would appear to be the case. If the Greys themselves have been on Earth since the dawning of our species as many assume, (and I am in no way disputing this), then these areas of reproductive investigations would be nothing new to them.

Understanding human emotions, along with their reproductive program, seems paramount to their goals, and they come at a time when it appears our planet is going through the most turbulent environmental shifts, rise in diseases along with political, economic, agricultural and scientific disasters and corruption. Are the Greys speeding their operations up because there is a feeling that our species might be on the verge of collapse? Are they aware as a hive-mind that we have little time left before real changes to our planet occur? Or are they themselves endangered? If we as a human species were to be wiped clean from the face of the Earth through some catastrophe, then they themselves would also be lost. As we shall see, they need us more than we are aware. The Greys also implement visions of world-wide destruction into the minds of their abductees while their operations are being carried out. Is this merely a psychological experiment to see how their captives react to such scenes through an emotional response? Or are they showing what is to come here on Earth?

The Issue of Cloned Greys

Let's assume through our hypothetical theory that the Greys were, indeed, once able to reproduce themselves. Through the art of cloning, could it be possible that these extraterrestrials had lost the ability to reproduce, (probably due to some environmental collapse on their world), and found that cloning seemed the only answer to their plight in order to continue their race? Or is it possible that the Greys had cloned an army to explore the Universe as many assume to seek out other lifeforms? Is it possible, even, that the Greys have deliberately engineered a program which would take them out of the loop of reincarnation altogether, throwing them into some type of spiritual devolution? Whatever the theory, we are in no doubt that the Greys represent some form of cloned entity. There are some researchers who believe that the Greys are advanced robots. Although I will tread lightly upon this idea, (and I fully respect other people's thoughts on this matter), this seems unlikely in the event of what the Greys are doing with regard to their so-called hidden agenda. Robots would need to repair themselves, however biologically advanced they were in terms of physiology. They would also need a programme to work towards, and depending upon the minds of their Creators, there would be limitations with what these machines were able to carry out. If these Greys were advanced mechanisms, the hybridisation programme would not benefit them in any way, seeing as they are not pure, biological creatures themselves. Which poses our next question! What exactly are they? And where do they come from?

The Soul

If, as we assume, the Greys are clones, then I feel the ethical question of the soul must be brought into question. As humans, many are in agreement that the physical body does indeed house the spirit: that its main purpose in this life is to experience this third-dimensional realm and that through reproduction we are able to continue this cycle of re-birthing as a means to bring the soul into the Earth's matrix from its natural sojourn. The cloned Grey once inhabited a physical form, but were only able to experience one, single life in that body. Once its corporeal self died, the question of where its 'soul' gravitates too is questionable: namely because clones, I theorise, reside outside the field of creation.

Unlike their masters, (the original copies), these clones would not, (to my mind), be able to return to a spirit world like we do, because they have not come into the loop of natural conception. Therefore, with only the experience of one, single physical life, these Greys would have no understanding whatsoever of the continuation of their soul. It could be argued that if millions of Greys were cloned, then their spirit, which would not follow their original masters, would gravitate to another dimension. They may well have grouped together as a one-mind-consciousness and have found a way to infiltrate this plane of reality through some form of psychic projection on their part. It would appear, then, that these cloned souls, (copies from the original), are interested in the concept of human reproduction, and this may be their answer in somehow bringing them back inside the loop of creation through us, as we shall see.

Spirits in a Material World

So, we can theorise that the Greys are indeed clones, that they were constructed to experience one, physical life, and are therefore outside the normal process of incarnation and reincarnation which our human souls experience. Once these Greys died physically, their souls, (unable to return to what we consider to be a spirit world), have grouped themselves together as a united consciousness and have penetrated our plane through a very powerful process of psychic manifestation. Let's explore how this may be possible!

The process of an abduction is not that dissimilar to a near-death-experience. These cases, whereby an individual has physically died for a brief period of time, find themselves removed from their material body. In many cases, they travel down a tunnel after seeing an incredible light, where they are met by loved ones within a higher dimension, which we call heaven. Communication from those who have 'passed over' are performed through a process of telepathy, and the individual who is going through such an encounter feels they are able to physically integrate within their new surroundings. Time has no meaning, and the feeling of 'belonging' is sometimes reported as something which goes beyond anything they have felt within their physical lives. This new world is reported to be more real than the one they left behind.

Now, let's look at an abduction. The individual is taken *'through'* the walls to their house or apartment. The Greys do not appear sufficiently able to literally 'beam' their subjects up without themselves having to be present during an abduction. It's as if the Greys need to be in close proximity to the abductee at all times, which I find puzzling yet fascinating. The person is then taken onto an awaiting craft of some kind where the Greys communicate through a process of telepathy. Because the Greys have temporarily removed the etheric body of the person away from its physical host, they are, in effect, bringing the spiritual body of the individual into *'their'* correct vibration frequency, which means they are able to 'physically' interact with the person, much like a loved one on the other side when death is imminent. In this instance, any medical procedures being carried out on the etheric body by the Greys onboard their ship, will invariably affect its physical counterpart which remains within the Earth dimension. If the Greys are working as one-hive-consciousness, then their ability to manifest themselves would be tremendous. Mental projection on their part would be achieved through a united effort, building a platform whereby they are able to penetrate our plane with relative ease. The UFO would then be created within the minds of the Greys in order that a fixed point of contact be established by them and their chosen subject. Much like the NDE, the whole experience would be tangible, and interaction is then achieved.

In order to understand a little more about the etheric body, science is beginning to accept that we have, what is commonly known as, an aura. This is the life-force of an individual and carries with it the sum of all that you have been and will be. In effect, it is the soul. What's interesting about the aura is its ability to change colour, depending on its physical, psychological, and emotional state. In some instances, healers are able to alter the ailments of a person's physical body while projecting energy through the more subtle layers of the aura. This proves that integration on a mental level does indeed have a profound effect upon the physical well-being of the person receiving treatment. In other words, the spiritual body acts as a conduit for the physical. Why, then, should this be any different for an extraterrestrial species who operate as one-mind-consciousness to penetrate these said layers of the human, spiritual body? With this in mind, we can now see why the Greys are interested in our ability to reproduce. They yearn to understand about themselves, being devoid of empathy. And they would come across like robots, having the experience of only one, physical life and no other memories with which to access. Is this the reason why the Greys are intent on looking within the minds of their subjects, collecting data on a monumental scale in order to best understand their plight and eventual, hopeful, freedom through us from the clutches of some manufactured creation?

The hybrid program could be their salvation. Because the Grey clones have no way to reproduce, and although they have the spark of a soul, (awareness), they have nevertheless come together as a group consciousness after physical death in order to find a new passage away from eternal, spiritual stagnation; that the cross breeding projects of theirs are a way for them to filter their souls into these abhorred mutations in an effort to sling shot their awareness back to their spirit world and thus redeem themselves from the ashes of their past. It is hard to consider that these hybrids are the forming of a new race, although we must be open to all forms of speculation. Through reports the hybrids appear as weak and sickly, not the type of super race one would come to expect! The Greys have never given any clear indication as to their true intentions, and although I have outlined a theory, it is a theory at that. In fact, the whole UFO enigma resides in the realms of speculation.

But it is important for us to try to draw parallels. I am in no way suggesting, either, that all Greys are clones. After all, there seem to be other factions of them that have been described within UFO literature.

Interdimensional Time Travel

One wonders, then, if the Greys are us from the future? That we, ourselves, have destroyed the means to reproduce, and in an effort to rectify this situation have returned to this time using some form of interdimensional time travel as a means to implement the breeding programme? There has been the suggestion that the Greys are, in fact, us, after millions of years of evolution! Somehow, I doubt this, but I cannot dismiss this theory entirely.

Although there has been much heated debate regarding the ability to bend space-time, I feel sure the Greys are able to do just this. The hypothesis is fascinating, to say the least, but I suspect that our very own secret governments, along with the military, know enough about the Greys and want rid of them. Perhaps the reason why there is a wall of silence is simply because much of the General Public who are not aware of the UFO phenomena (or those who choose to ignore it completely), would be shocked to learn that an extraterrestrial force have indeed penetrated our realm, and are using us in a bid to save themselves. The carefully constructed model of society would be toppled by just such a revelation. I also believe the Greys are able to shift themselves through any passage of time using the process of remote viewing, but on a much more powerful level. Remote viewers, (gifted psychics trained by the secret American military back in the 70's and onwards, instructed by the artist, author and psychic, Ingo Swann), are able to travel using their etheric body, penetrating beyond the boundaries of time and space in order to view not only the past and present, but future too. Is this how the Greys employ their method of time travel, one wonders? So, we can see, theoretically, that one faction of Greys are lost souls, yearning to reconnect themselves through a process of artificial reproduction in order to create a hybrid with which to mould their soul, (spark of awareness), into. By using a physical host, they hope to bring themselves into the cycle of reincarnation and back to their spirit world. But has it been successful? One can only postulate as to that conclusion. There is one thing for sure, they are using the hybridisation programme to their advantage, which they are not revealing to their chosen, human subjects.

Dire Warnings

We have to stop and think ethically about cloning. I'm sure scientists behind closed doors have been performing all sorts of experiments of this nature under the guidance of the military. And I am also convinced that humans have also been cloned. The spiritual ramifications would be enormous if we allowed our kind to clone men and women for war or, even worse, medical purposes. How would we even begin to explain to the cloned human that we are not sure about their 'spiritual' path? Is there a heaven for them? Or will they reside outside the natural laws of creation? As spiritual beings ourselves, we must understand that we are not masters of this Universe. There are other forces at work here, and instead of covering the facts, it would be better for us to all share in this knowledge.

The Greys have tried to conceal their operations. Perhaps they can see just how destructive a species we are and keep us at arm's length. We feel it our duty to experiment on the animal kingdom and proclaim this is right. Anything which cannot be controlled from our end must surely come under fire. Although many feel the Grey's agenda is dire, I would suggest that we could learn a lot from them. Their methods through our eyes would appear monstrous, but many who have undergone an abduction are changed by the experience, literally – as though some type of universal consciousness has connected with them.

If, for example, our species were under threat, I'm sure we would, ourselves, take drastic measures to ensure its survival whatever the cost. As a society, we seem to become more distant from one another the more we progress technically. Are we in danger of becoming like the Greys? Are they trying to warn us of what we may become if we do not change our ways?

Whatever the reason, we are truly on the verge of some type of revelation, and one that might just show us our place within this universe and answer that age-old question about not only UFOs, aliens, but also death and the journey of the soul.

(Author's note. Some wonderful speculation and insight from Philip there as to the possible reasons behind the greys and their cladstine UFO Abductions)

PHILIP MANTLE.
The nature and origin of the alien abduction experience.

Philip Mantle is a long standing UFO researcher and author from the U.K. He was formerly the Director of Investigations for the British UFO Research Association and the MUFON Representative for England. He is a regular contributor to Outer Limits Magazine and is co-host of Inside The Outer Limits Radio show available on the Paranormal UK Radio Network. He is the founder of FLYING DISK PRESS and can be contacted at http://flyingdiskpress.blogspot.co.uk/

One of, if not the most controversial aspect of the UFO phenomenon, is that of alien abductions. I think we can all agree that it was the Betty and Barney Hill account from the USA in 1961 that added the alien abduction ingredient to the relatively new recipe of the UFO phenomenon cooking pot. Ever since the Hill's went public the alien abduction experience the debate has raged concerning the nature and origin of such encounters.

In 1994, my colleague Carl Nagaitis and I, co-authored a book entitled 'WITHOUT CONSENT'. The book deals with alien abduction and missing time cases from the U.K. only. A revised edition is now available on Amazon. One thing that Carl and I did as part of our research for the book, is to ask the abductees themselves what they believed was the nature and origin of their experiences. Some were of no doubt that extraterrestrials were responsible, others thought that the experience was spiritual in nature, one young man blamed the

Russians, and others simply had no idea. In short, even the abductees themselves could not agree on the nature and origin of their encounters.

I have been involved in UFO research for over forty years and during that time I have come across UFO researchers of whom I have the greatest respect and who have made me think about this very topic. One such researcher who passed away some years ago, was in no doubt that alien abduction experiences had nothing to do with the UFO phenomenon at all, and the study of which should be left to professional psychologists. Another with whom I have spoken to just recently and who you would know, told me that he can accept the abduction accounts where a person has one encounter, but he totally discounts the accounts where the abductee claims to have had multiple abductions starting in childhood and even goes back to their parents and so on. On the other hand I have met and talked to other abduction researchers who were totally convinced that extraterrestrials were the answer and they could put an equally powerful argument forward to equal any sceptical theory.

When you try and sum all of this up, speaking with the abductees, reading the literature both pro and con and discussing the various cases with those researchers who have a wealth of knowledge on alien abductions, it is for me quite clear, that no one is right and no one is wrong. The short answer is if you take an open minded, objective look at alien abductions it is easy to see that no theory or hypothesis fits. None, zilch, zero. Pick any theory you like and you will find some abduction cases that fit it, but there will be others that totally contradict it. The problem we have is that there are so few UFO researchers that are open minded and objective. The theories behind alien abductions has and still is being driven by those who have their minds made up, and nothing or no one will convince them otherwise. In essence what I am saying is that if you are looking for the answer to what lies behind alien abductions then you are not going to find one simply because their isn't one. None of the theories fit all the data; it's as simple as that.

What I will say is that no matter what you think, one thing is for sure, these experiences still happen to ordinary, everyday members of Joe Public who are simply going about their everyday tasks. Walking the dog, driving to work, watching TV and so on. None of them want to be a member of the alien abduction club and a larger proportion of them are as puzzled and baffled as the UFO researcher who is trying to help them. All I suggest is that we keep an open mind and document such cases to the best of our ability and hopefully one day someone somewhere will solve the puzzle.

RON HALLIDAY

Fellow Scottish UFO and Paranormal researcher and well known author Ron Halliday, has published a number of books including Haunted Glasgow, The A-Z of the Scottish Paranormal, and McX: Scottish X Files. He lives with his wife Evelyn in the Scottish town of Bridge of Allan. Ron writes,

The abduction phenomenon is probably one of the more contentious aspects of the UFO mystery. Can we seriously believe that alien beings from other planets are randomly picking up human beings for some unknown purpose? It seems to defy common sense, and yet individuals are reporting that this has happened to them, and sometimes not just once, but on multiple occasions.

If it is indeed taking place, what is the reason for it? And why are certain individuals targeted? And why isn't it more widespread? Compared with the USA the number of reported cases in Scotland are miniscule, and few in number even within the U.K. taking population differences into account. Why should American citizens be more regularly abducted by alien beings than the Scots or English? It doesn't seem to make any sense. U.S. citizens may be more willing to talk about their experiences which may explain some of the difference, but not the extent of the difference. So we're left in the somewhat strange situation, in that there doesn't appear to be any logic either to the place where victims are selected and what type of victim is picked up, men, woman, adults, children, all have been alleged victims. Nor do the victims share an identical experience. Certiainly the theme of being subjected to a medical examination reoccurs. But even in the limited number of Scottish cases that was not true in every reported incident. However, it is generally accepted that an examination of some sort is a key motive behind abduction with implants of various kinds also a feature with some scenarios, resulting in even more extreme results including pregnancies.

So what are to make of the A70 case in this context, the focus of Malcolm Robinson's book? Having interviewed Garry Wood several times, I have absolutely no doubt that he is completely 'on the level' regarding his recollection of events. I've also no doubt that an incident of an inexplicable nature occurred involving both Garry and Colin Wright. The question remains though exactly what happened during the period of missing time? And there's no doubt that a period of time is unaccounted for. The details that Garry and Colin eventually gave were not the result of spontaneous recall. Their description of events came following hypnosis, a process which is criticised by some because of the 'false memory' syndrome, that is the possibility that under hypnosis an individual may be over-suggestible, or recall events from any source, for example, a film recently seen. These are factors that we have to take into consideration, but that doesn't mean that we have to dismiss the substance of the A70 event, that Garry and Colin were the victims of abduction by unknown entities of some description. I can't see what else can explain the strange series of events that occurred on the A70. The fact that we find it difficult to understand why it happened, who carried it out and may be unsure of the details should not detract from the fact that it was a remarkable and truly out-of-the-world event which even the most sceptical must find hard to dismiss.

JOHN E. MACK

Another stalwart of UFO abduction research, was the late John Edward Mack (October 4th, 1929 – September 27th,

2004) Mack was, amoungst other things, a psychiatrist and writer. He was also a professor and head of the department of psychiatry at Harvard Medical School. Mack authored over 150 scientific articles but it was in the late 1980's, that he took a deep fascination for UFO abductions. He wanted to find out what was behind this seemingly elusive mystery. And as such, he interviewed over 800 people, which culminated in him writing two books on the subject. Before his tragic death in London, at the hands of a drunk driver, he felt that the crux of the abduction phenomena lay in the psychiatric arena. Lots of cases that he studied showed evidence of post traumatic stress disorder. Mack is on record as stating that this would imply that the patient genuinely believed that the remembered frightening incident of the abductee, had really occurred. Mack was quoted as saying,

"It might be useful to restate that a large proportion of the material relating to abductions is recalled without the use of an altered state of consciousness, and that many abduction reporters appear to relive powerful experiences after only the most minimal relaxation exercise, hardly justifying the word hypnosis at all. The relaxation exercise is useful to relieve the experiencer's need to attend to the social demands and other stimuli of face-to-face conversation, and to relieve the energies involved in repressing memories and emotion".

Mack further stated,

"The furthest you can go at this point is to say there's an authentic mystery here. And that is, I think, as far as anyone ought to go".

THOMAS BULLARD

Another gentleman who has also contributed immensely to the subject of UFO Abductions, is folklorist Thomas E. Bullard. Born in North Carolina in 1949 Thomas took an interest in flying saucers after watching numerous 1950s science fiction movies. He started to read as many UFO related books as he could get his hands on, which led him to join UFO groups such as NICAP and APRO. Needless to say, Thomas went on to write hundreds of papers on UFOs and was mostly known for his research into the 1896-97 great Air ship wave which culminated in a book. His study however, into UFO abductions truly was something else. This was done with the cooperation of the Fund for UFO Research. This project was set up to catalogue and study UFO abduction reports. The study started in 1982 and was completed in 1987. The report entitled, 'UFO Abductions The Measure of a Mystery', featured over 300 alleged UFO abductions which were found in the UFO literature in the mid-1980s.

Whilst Thomas Bullard would accept the nature of the UFO abduction experience, he was still at odds with the fact that some abductees when returned to Earth, have found themselves in a different location from where they were taken. Some indeed are wearing clothes which do not belong to them! Indeed fellow UFO abduction researcher, the late Budd Hopkins, was quoted as saying that these mistakes were the 'Cosmic application of Murphy's Law' and that in his own personal research, he found that these 'errors' would make up around 4 to 5 percent of abduction reports. If we are talking about a superior race of beings, abducting humans from their safe environments, how is it possible that the abductors can make such a fundamental mistake of placing back their abductees in the wrong house, or even more bizarre, the abductee is wearing his clothes back to front! Makes no sense. But then again, some would say that as these 'beings' do not wear any clothes themselves, they might be unsure how to replace them on the abductees body.

What Thomas Bullard did find surprising, was how 'changed' some of these UFO abductees were when they came back from their encounter. Some had a profound sense of love. Some said it was like being 'high', like being on drugs. This sensation, was something that both Garry Wood and Colin Wright experienced at the very start of their abduction experience. Colin Wright stated;

"Both Garry and myself felt very high and hyper, something that I have never experienced before"

243

PETER ROBBINS

Peter Robbins is an investigative writer, author and lecturer whose writing and research are focused on the subject of truly anomalous UFOs and their implications for humanity. He has appeared as a guest and consultant to numerous radio shows, television programs and documentaries. Peter states.

It's generally agreed that the subject of so-called UFO abductions entered into the public consciousness in the mid-nineteen-sixties. The catalyst, the publication of an account in a popular American magazine of same involving a married American couple, Betty and Barney Hill, and following closely, the first book devoted to the subject, *The Interrupted Journey* by John G. Fuller. And a fine book it was. It was not until the nineteen-eighty-one however that the abduction phenomenon began to engender the serious attention of the greater UFO research community, this with the publication of *Missing Time* by UFO investigator Budd Hopkins. Hopkins' went on to distinguish himself in the years and decades to follow as the pioneer in the scientific investigation of UFO abductions.

But what is the *'true'* nature of this alleged phenomenon? Surely, individuals making such claims cannot possibly be asking the public at large to accept their well beyond-outrageous allegations that 'aliens,' 'other intelligences,' whatever one chooses to call them, have actually been *taken* and are actually taking, abducting human beings, as in floating them out of their bedrooms, cars or other locations, through walls, through ceilings, through plate glass windows, and then bringing them onboard their craft or other locations, examining them, preforming procedures on them, marking them with small, self-cauterizing removals of skin, in some cases inserting or surgically introducing 'implants' into the abductee's body, altering or eradicating their conscious recollections of the events in question, and in many instances, repeating the process with certain individuals throughout their lifetimes from the time the person is very young until they are considerably beyond their reproductive years.

Are such reports, the great majority of which being made by seemingly credible, same, responsible people somehow 'all in the mind?' Are they some aspect of a complex cross cultural, global psychosis made to seem all the more real by the experiencer's tendency to suffer from a condition termed 'sleep paralysis? Or, in facing the challenge posed by strikingly similar claims made by people from every corner of the world, are we in fact actually dealing with a highly advance non-human presence from parts unknown with a hyper specific agenda engaged in repeated acts with otherwise credible human beings that are as reported and in no way allegorical, nor manifestations of or presenting signs of an exotic psychological disfunction or an incredibly real seeming altered state of perception? If you're asking me, UFO related abductions are as real as the chairs that you and I are sitting in at this very moment.

How did I come to arrive at this conclusion? To the very best of my knowledge I have not had any such experiences, but one of my sisters did, and there was no ambiguity about it for her. Following her sharing her conscious memories of this with me many years ago, I began to immerse myself in the subject, much to the detriment of my career in the visual arts. Within a year another New York City based painter, Budd Hopkins, and I had begun a thirty-five-year friendship and professional relationship that would last until his death almost ten years ago. For about half of that time, I worked as his investigative assistant into many cases of UFO abduction. Few people I think, have had the privilege that I have had, to see, handle and evaluate so many types of corroborating evidence that I long ago passed the point where I have, what I would categorize as, 'the luxury of disbelief.' I only wish that you had the opportunity to come to your best informed decision regarding this paradigm-altering subject in the same manner that I did. That being, armed with decades of study, investigation and research, not to mention the many hours I have spent with so many of these courageous, honorable people.

Peter Robbins. Ithaca, New York, June 2021

SECTION B Written Account
Please write an account of what happened to you

ON THE 17 OF AUGUST 1993, BOTH GARY AND MYSELF
WERE TRAVELLING TO TARBRACKS. WHEN AT APPROX
11·36 WE ENCOUNTERED A UFO ON A BLIND
BEND, AS WE CAME OUT OF THE BEND, IN THE
ROAD STRAIGHT INFRONT OF US WAS THE SHIP
HOVERING APPROX 20ft ABOVE THE ROAD SURFACE.
THERE WAS NO NOISE NO LIGHTS JUST A
BLACKEND OUT SHAPE OF THE CRAFT AND A
BLACK AND GREY SHIMERING CURTAIN, WHICH WAS
THE WIDTH OF THE ROAD. AS THE CAR ENTERED
THE CURTAIN THE ROAD AND THE SURROUNDING
AREA JUST SEEMED TO DISAPEAR, I REMEMBER
SAYING TO GARY WHERES THE ROAD? THEN REALIZED
I COULD NOT SEE HIM, THE NEXT THING I REMEMBER
IS THE CAR JERKING FORWARD AND GARY GOING AS
FAST AS HE COULD WE DID NOT LOOK BACK. ALSO ON
ARRIVAL AT TARBRAK MY SEATBELT WAS   *Continue on a separate sheet of paper if required*

SECTION C Object Characteristics UNDONE WHICH WAS FASTENED
BEFORE.

Please use this space to sketch what you saw

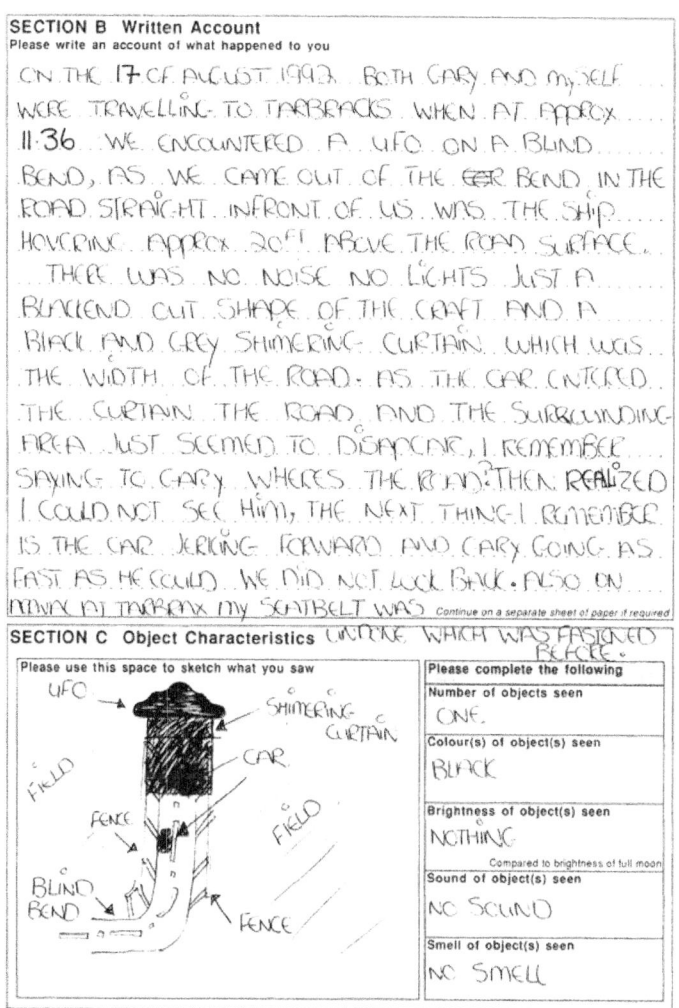

UFO → SHIMERING CURTAIN

CAR

FIELD

FENCE

FIELD

BLIND BEND →

FENCE

Please complete the following

Number of objects seen
ONE.

Colour(s) of object(s) seen
BLACK

Brightness of object(s) seen
NOTHING
Compared to brightness of full moon

Sound of object(s) seen
NO SOUND

Smell of object(s) seen
NO SMELL

Colin Wright UFO Form with drawn UFO (c) SPI

247

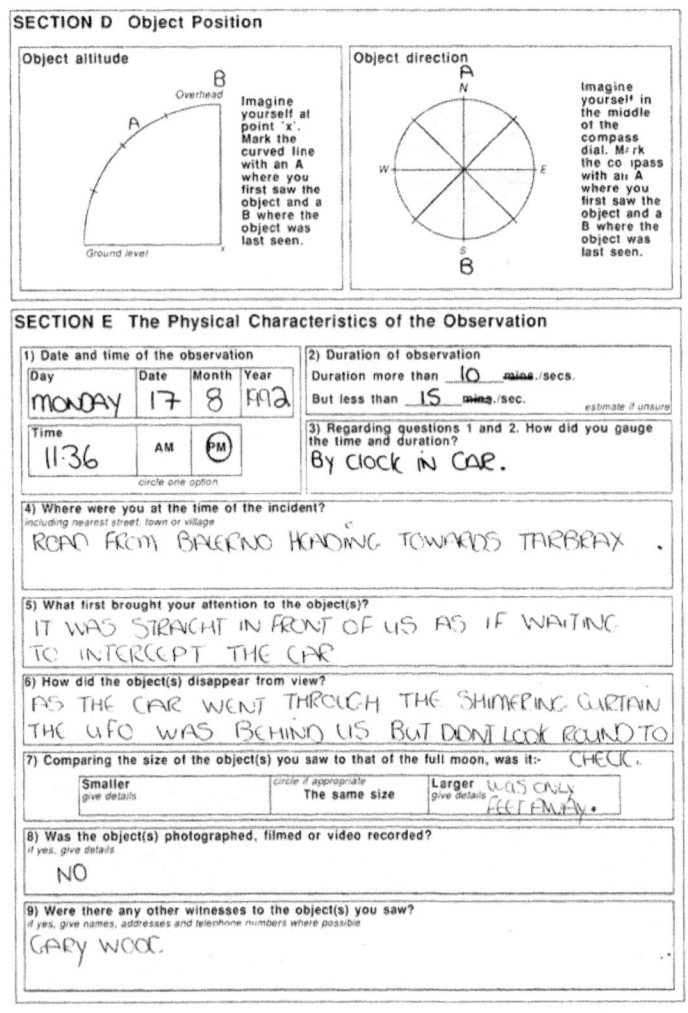

SECTION D Object Position

Object altitude

Imagine yourself at point 'x'. Mark the curved line with an A where you first saw the object and a B where the object was last seen.

Ground level

Object direction

Imagine yourself in the middle of the compass dial. Mark the compass with an A where you first saw the object and a B where the object was last seen.

SECTION E The Physical Characteristics of the Observation

1) Date and time of the observation

Day	Date	Month	Year
MONDAY	17	8	AA2

Time 11:36 AM (PM)
circle one option

2) Duration of observation

Duration more than 10 mins./secs.

But less than 15 mins./sec.
estimate if unsure

3) Regarding questions 1 and 2. How did you gauge the time and duration?

By CLOCK IN CAR.

4) Where were you at the time of the incident?
including nearest street, town or village

ROAD FROM BALERNO HEADING TOWARDS TARBRAX .

5) What first brought your attention to the object(s)?

IT WAS STRAIGHT IN FRONT OF US AS IF WAITING TO INTERCEPT THE CAR

6) How did the object(s) disappear from view?

AS THE CAR WENT THROUGH THE SHIMERING CURTAIN THE UFO WAS BEHIND US BUT DIDN'T LOOK ROUND TO

7) Comparing the size of the object(s) you saw to that of the full moon, was it:- CHECK.

Smaller give details	circle if appropriate The same size	Larger give details WAS ONLY FEET AWAY.

8) Was the object(s) photographed, filmed or video recorded?
if yes, give details

NO

9) Were there any other witnesses to the object(s) you saw?
if yes, give names, addresses and telephone numbers where possible

GARY WOOD

Colin Wright UFO Form 3 (c) SPI

248

SECTION F Other Characteristics Relating to the Observation

10) Did you, or the surrounding environment, suffer any physical effects which you consider to be attributable to the object(s) seen?
if yes, give details

I FELT VERY UNUSUAL lIKE I HAD BEEN ON DRUGS AND HAD THE FEELING OF BEING HIGH, I ALSO FELT I NEVER HAD A CARE IN THE WORLD

11) Were you aware of the passage of time around the time of the observation?
if no, describe

NO

12) If you have had any other 'unusual' experiences in your life please describe them
you may feel unable to describe such events, if so, please indicate that there are matters you wish to discuss in a meeting with the investigator

NO

13) Other than the event you have reported, did anything else 'odd' or 'out of place' occur around the time of the observation?
if yes, describe

NO

14) Did any other witnesses experience anything in relation to questions 10, 11, 12 and 13?
if yes, describe

GARRY. THE SAME EFFECTS AS MYSELF.

SECTION G Prevailing Weather during your Observation

i) Clarity of atmosphere	Clear	Hazy	Foggy		
ii) Cloud cover	None	Quarter	Half	Three Quarter	Total
iii) Atmospheric temperature	Freezing	Cold	Cool	Mild	Warm
iv) Precipitation	Dry	Rain	Snow	Lightning	Other
v) Wind strength	Still	Breeze	Strong Wind	Gale Force	
vi) Visible astronomical objects	Stars	Moon	Sun	Aurora Borealis	Shooting Stars

circle all appropriate responses

Thank you for completing this questionnaire. Now please return it to your local investigator at the address provided. If you require guidance in answering any questions included in this questionnaire, please contact your investigator.

STRANGE PHENOMENA
INVESTIGATIONS RESEARCHER
MALCOLM ROBINSON

investigator's address

Colin Wright UFO Form B (c) SPI

249

SECTION B Written Account
Please write an account of what happened to you

WHEN DRIVING TO TARBRAXIS. DRIVING ROUND
A SMALL BLIND BEND. I SAW A UFO IT WAS
FLOATING TWENTY FEET IN THE AIR NOT MOVING.
WHEN DRIVING UNDER THE UFO IT DROPPED
A SHIMMERING CURTIAN DOWN IN FRONT OF
THE CAR. WHEN DRIVING THROUGH THE
CURTAIN THE CAR WENT BLACK I COULD NOT
SEE. ENYTHING. I COULD NOT SEE MY
FREIND COLIN • IT WAS SO DARK.I SWERVED
AND SKIDDED ON THE ROAD TRYING TO CONTOL
VEHICLE • DROVE AWAY AT HIGH SPEED
VERY WORRIED. TOLD FREIND AT TARBRAX
WHAT HAPPEND. BUT WHEN DRIVING
THROUGH CURTAIN MIND WAS BLANK DID
NOT LOOK BACK.

Continue on a separate sheet of paper if required

SECTION C Object Characteristics

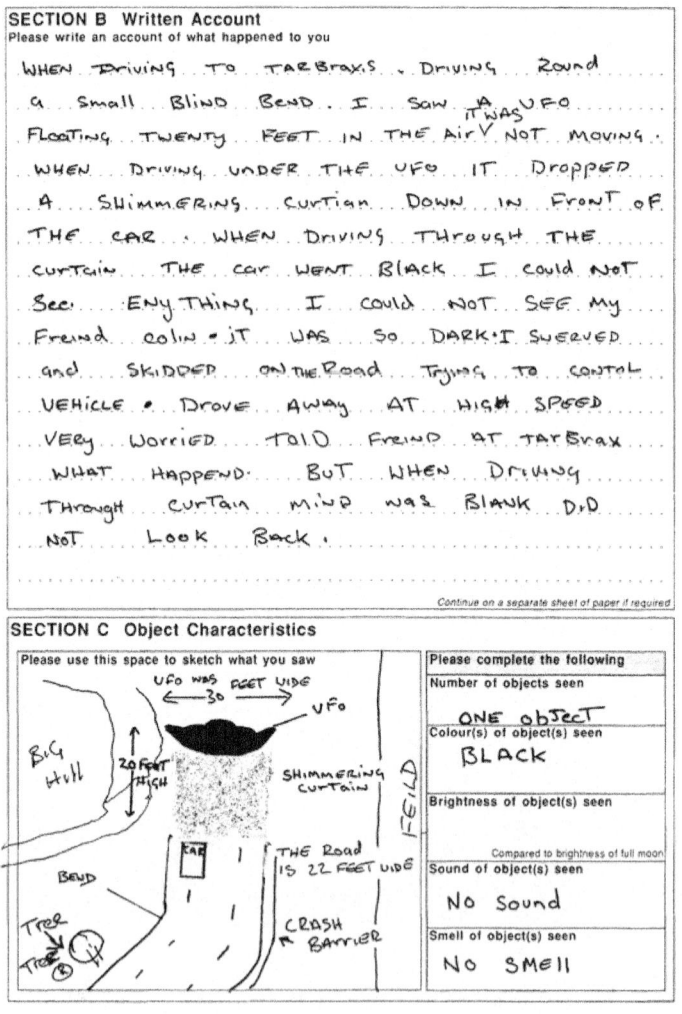

Please use this space to sketch what you saw

UFO WAS FEET WIDE
← 30 →
UFO
BIG HILL
20 FEET HIGH
SHIMMERING CURTAIN
FEILD
BEND
THE ROAD IS 22 FEET WIDE
CRASH BARRIER
TREE
TREE

Please complete the following

Number of objects seen

ONE OBJECT

Colour(s) of object(s) seen

BLACK

Brightness of object(s) seen

Compared to brightness of full moon

Sound of object(s) seen

NO SOUND

Smell of object(s) seen

NO SMELL

Garry Wood UFO Form 2 (c) SPI

250

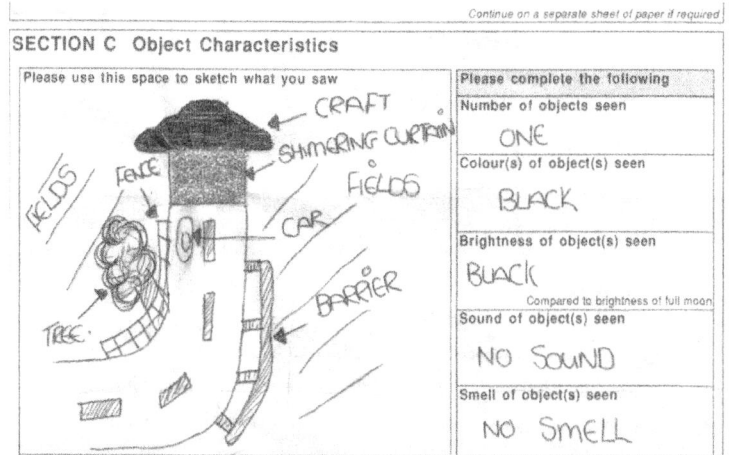

Colin Wright's UFO drawing of object he saw. (c) SPI

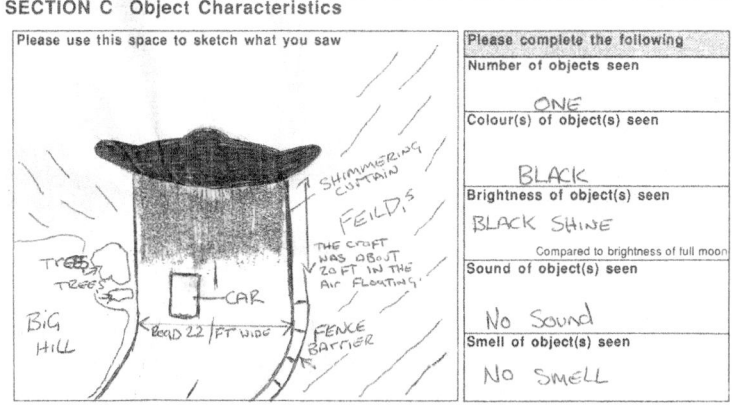

Garry Wood UFO Sighting Account Form With UFO. (c) SPI

251

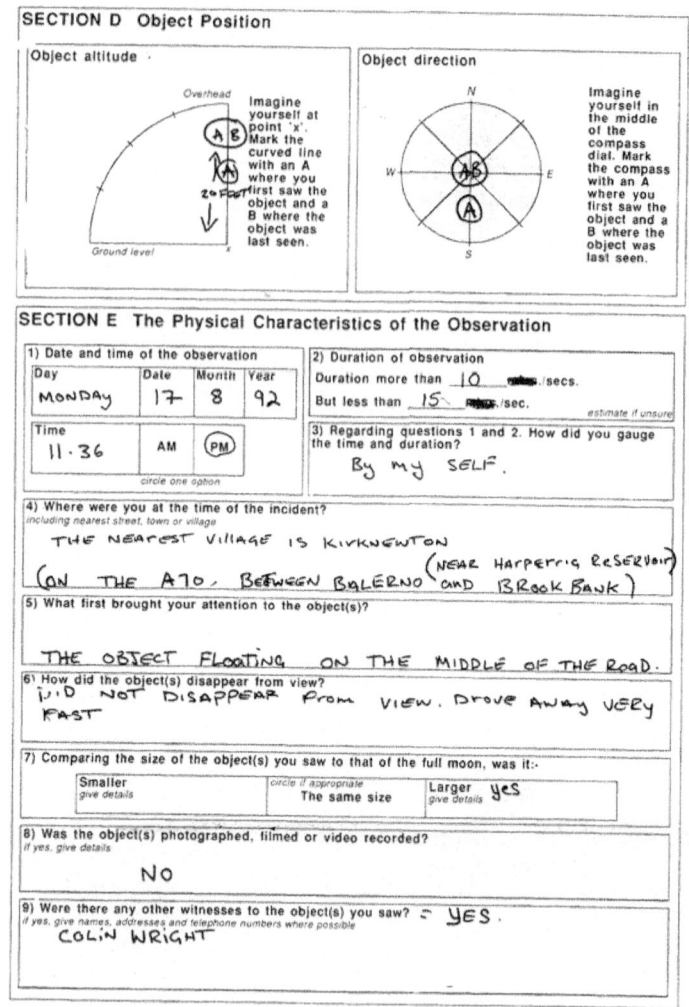

SECTION D Object Position

Object altitude

Overhead

Imagine yourself at point 'x'. Mark the curved line with an A where you first saw the object and a B where the object was last seen.

Ground level

Object direction

Imagine yourself in the middle of the compass dial. Mark the compass with an A where you first saw the object and a B where the object was last seen.

SECTION E The Physical Characteristics of the Observation

1) Date and time of the observation

Day	Date	Month	Year
MONDAY	17	8	92

Time
11.36   AM (PM)
circle one option

2) Duration of observation

Duration more than __10__ ~~mins~~/secs.

But less than __15__ ~~mins~~/sec.

estimate if unsure

3) Regarding questions 1 and 2. How did you gauge the time and duration?

By my SELF.

4) Where were you at the time of the incident?
including nearest street, town or village

THE NEAREST VILLAGE IS KIRKNEWTON

(ON THE A70, BETWEEN BALERNO (NEAR HARPERRIG RESERVOIR) and BROOK BANK)

5) What first brought your attention to the object(s)?

THE OBJECT FLOATING ON THE MIDDLE OF THE ROAD.

6) How did the object(s) disappear from view?

DID NOT DISAPPEAR FROM VIEW. DROVE AWAY VERY FAST

7) Comparing the size of the object(s) you saw to that of the full moon, was it:-

Smaller *give details*	*circle if appropriate* The same size	Larger *give details* yes

8) Was the object(s) photographed, filmed or video recorded?
if yes, give details

NO

9) Were there any other witnesses to the object(s) you saw? = YES.
if yes, give names, addresses and telephone numbers where possible
COLIN WRIGHT

Garry Wood UFO Form 3 (c) SPI

252

SECTION F Other Characteristics Relating to the Observation

10) Did you, or the surrounding environment, suffer any physical effects which you consider to be attributable to the object(s) seen? YES: FELT DRUGGED. VERY
if yes, give details
HIGH. VERY WORRIED. FELT lIKE I DID NOT HAVE
a CARE IN THE WORLD.

11) Were you aware of the passage of time around the time of the observation?
if no, describe NO. FELT VERY UNAWARE VERY WORRIED TRYING
TO GET AWAY.

12) If you have had any other 'unusual' experiences in your life please describe them YES
you may feel unable to describe such events. if so, please indicate that there are matters
you wish to discuss in a meeting with the investigator yes

13) Other than the event you have reported, did anything else 'odd' or 'out of place' occur around the time of the observation?
if yes, describe yes

14) Did any other witnesses experience anything in relation to questions 10, 11, 12 and 13?
if yes, describe YES

SECTION G Prevailing Weather during your Observation

i) Clarity of atmosphere	(Clear)	Hazy	Foggy		
ii) Cloud cover	(None)	Quarter	Half	Three Quarter	Total
iii) Atmospheric temperature	Freezing	(Cold)	Cool	Mild	Warm
iv) Precipitation	(Dry)	Rain	Snow	Lightning	Other
v) Wind strength	Still	(Breeze)	Strong Wind	Gale Force	
vi) Visible astronomical objects	(Stars)	(Moon)	Sun	Aurora Borealis	Shooting Stars

circle all appropriate responses

Thank you for completing this questionnaire. Now please return it to your local investigator at the address provided. If you require guidance in answering any questions included in this questionnaire, please contact your investigator.

STRANGE PHENOMENA
INVESTIGATIONS RESEARCHER
MALCOLM ROBINSON

investigator's address

Garry Wood UFO Form 4 (c) SPI

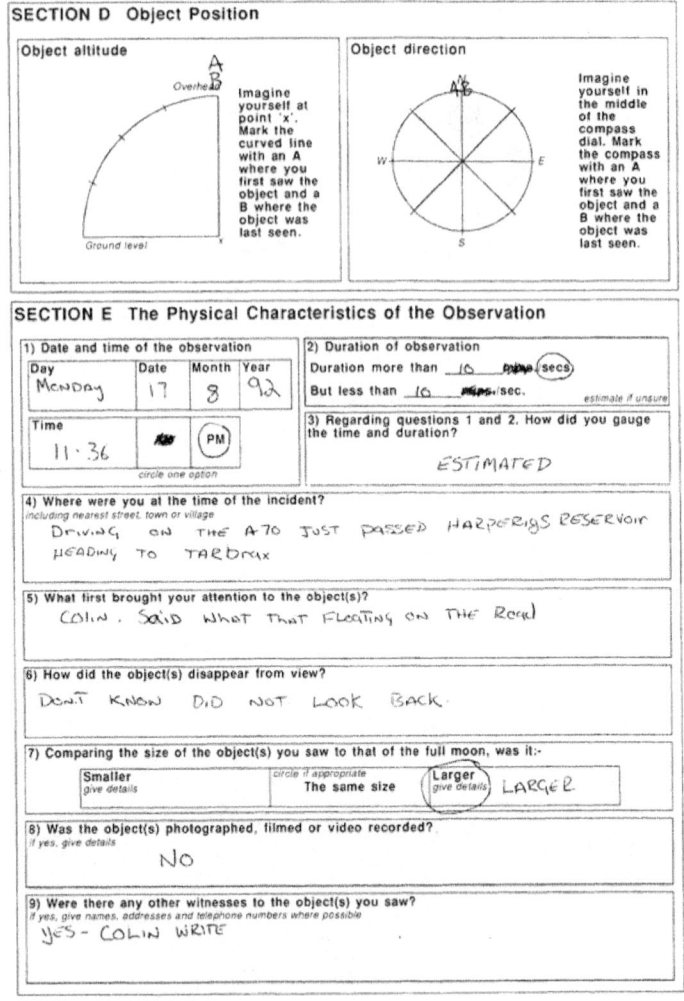

SECTION D Object Position

Object altitude

Overhead A B

Imagine yourself at point 'x'. Mark the curved line with an A where you first saw the object and a B where the object was last seen.

Ground level

Object direction

A B

W — E

S

Imagine yourself in the middle of the compass dial. Mark the compass with an A where you first saw the object and a B where the object was last seen.

SECTION E The Physical Characteristics of the Observation

1) Date and time of the observation

Day	Date	Month	Year
MONDAY	17	8	92

Time 11·36 AM (PM)
circle one option

2) Duration of observation

Duration more than 10 ~~mins~~ (secs)

But less than 10 ~~mins~~/sec.
estimate if unsure

3) Regarding questions 1 and 2. How did you gauge the time and duration?

ESTIMATED

4) Where were you at the time of the incident?
including nearest street, town or village

DRIVING ON THE A70 JUST PASSED HARPERRIGS RESERVOIR HEADING TO TARBRAX

5) What first brought your attention to the object(s)?

COLIN. SAID WHAT THAT FLOATING ON THE ROAD

6) How did the object(s) disappear from view?

DON'T KNOW DID NOT LOOK BACK.

7) Comparing the size of the object(s) you saw to that of the full moon, was it:-

Smaller *give details*	*circle if appropriate* The same size	Larger *give details*
		(Larger) LARGER

8) Was the object(s) photographed, filmed or video recorded?
if yes, give details

NO

9) Were there any other witnesses to the object(s) you saw?
If yes, give names, addresses and telephone numbers where possible

YES - COLIN WRITE

Garry Wood UFO Form (c) SPI

CHAPTER THREE

How can we explain the UFO Abduction Experience?

"I cannot offer the key to this mystery. I can only repeat, the search may be futile, the solution may lie forever beyond our grasp. The apparent logic of our most elementary deductions may evaporate. Perhaps what we search for is no more than a dream, that, becoming part of our lives, never existed in reality. We cannot be sure that we study something real, because we do not know what reality is. We can only be sure that our study will help us understand more, far more, about ourselves. This is not as worthless task."
Jacques Vallee. (Passport to Magonia)

OK, with any book that addresses an issue as controversial as this, it's always fair to point out, and agree to a certain extent with the sceptic, that there are possible alternative explanations to account for any given UFO sighting and abduction. In this chapter we shall take a look at a fair number of possibilities which some may say, provide the answer, and that its game over and time to go home. As a UFO researcher, it is my job to look at 'all possibilities' and not accept what some of my fellow UFOlogists believe the answer to be, that of an E.T. hypothesis. Some may say that the UFO abduction phenomenon is purely a medical problem. Perhaps some global psychosis! There may be the odd occasion in which an unbalanced observer witnesses something natural in the sky and misconstrues this as a fanciful 'flying saucer' but the vast majority of UFO witnesses are very much sound of mind, they relate sightings which in some instances, sound so incredible, that we have to take stock of what they say and try and understand that the subject of UFOlogy, is indeed a very complex arena with many wide and varied departments. Let us now take a look at 'some' of these departments.

This is not an exhaustive study, and the reader may find even more alternatives elsewhere as to what could be behind the

UFO Abduction phenomenon. But I hope at the very least, I have covered some of the main contenders. The British UFO Research Association (BUFORA), have put forward a number of possibilities to account for UFO sightings. So let us start by looking at them, before we enter the arena of UFO Abductions. Incidentally, (BUFORA) do not subscribe to any one theory, but keep an open mind to all possibilities.)

UFO HYPOTHESES.

1.   That the UFO sightings involve misidentifications of objects or phenomena which are man made or natural and are well known to experts.

2.   That the sightings involve natural events which are not observed often enough for scientists to have produced suitable scientific explanations.

3.   That the sightings are hoaxes or involve fabrications.

4.   That the sightings involve man made devices only known to their inventors.

5.   That the sightings are mental projections by, or received by, the witness.

6.   That the sightings involve devices produced by one or more alien advanced technologies which originate:

A. Elsewhere in our Universe, being (i) within our solar system.

or   (ii) Within our Galaxy.
or   (iii) Beyond our Galaxy.

OR.

B.   In a Universe which is not obvious to us yet using conventional techniques and which is,

(i)   Parallel to ours in space and time.
(Ii) Parallel to ours in space but not in time.
(Iii) Parallel to ours in time, but not space.

7. That the sightings are of intelligent processes beyond our space time continuum, not explicable in any of the aforementioned categories.

Then there is another avenue of which some of the more wilder aspects on theorising on what the UFO sightings could be.

1.   Somehow to do with a psychic realm, (whatever that may be)
2.   Somehow to do with dimensions.

I shall now carefully go through each of the above mentioned categories, we may be none the wiser for going through all these categories, but it will certainly bring to our attention the enormous difficulty we are faced with when we are trying to explain the UFO phenomena. I will present my own personal feelings as to what is going on at the end of this chapter.

MISIDENTIFICATIONS

The first hypothesis, is that of sightings which involve misidentifications of natural and man made objects which are well known. It is a well known fact that 95 out of a 100 sightings of what we would term as UFOs, can be found in this category, and that what people think are UFOs, are in fact only one of the following, Kites, Aircraft, Satellites, Comets, Wind Debris, Stars, Weather Balloons, Lenticular Clouds, Ball Lightning, Flares, Birds, Venus, and I've not even scratched the surface. There is no denying that people believe with sincere conviction, that what they were observing was some form of unexplainable phenomena.   But after research, it has been found that what they have in fact witnessed, was one of the afore mentioned possibilities. The true UFO phenomena, is really only centred on a 5% ratio, but this 5% is as yet not accounted for, and it is to this small 5% of unaccounted observations of UFOs that we must now look to and see where they might originate from.

NATURAL EVENTS

The second hypothesis is that the sightings involve natural events which are not observed enough for scientists to have produced suitable scientific explanations. Again, some might say, this is a strong candidate to explain some, if not all, UFO sightings.

BALL LIGHTNING

The UFO phenomena (or part of it) may turn out to be some form of as yet unexplainable natural phenomena, perhaps something along the lines of Ball Lightning (BL). (BL) comprises of a small round fireball roughly the size of a football (but sizes can vary). It has been observed to pass through walls, and sometimes a hissing or sparkling sound can be heard. The observation usually ends with a loud explosion, though not always. I am of the opinion, that some UFO sightings are in fact the misperception of Ball Lightning, but that the whole UFO phenomena is 'not' a result of (BL).

EARTHLIGHTS

Then of course there is the Earthlight Hypothesis. As late as 1987 after having read Paul Devereux's book, 'Earthlights', I was utterly convinced that the only solution to the UFO mystery lay in this theory. I began to realise that the E.T. hypothesis may be masking something of equal importance, and although I did not give up on the E.T. angle, *(as that was where my research was leading me)* I started to look into the Earthlight theory with gusto, I saw it then, (but don't now) as the answer that we had been overlooking for so many years. We were all (or at least most of us) pre-occupied in looking for

258

'aliens' that perhaps the answer was more closer to home. Basically what the Earthlight theory is, is that balls of light (BOL) can be produced by forces exponentially accumulating in seismic prone or fault areas, more often than not, in areas where there have been a high concentration of earthquakes, but these strange luminous lights can also be witnessed away from the main epicentres of earthquake activity. Researcher Paul Devereux and Canadian scientists, Michael Persinger and Gyslaine Lafreniere, have shown that during the strain of seismic unrest, pressure on rock crystals in a large area, produce electrical fields through a modification of what is known as a piezo electrical effect. Research has also shown that these pre-fracture electrical fields, can reach values of several thousand volts per metre, which in turn, can ionize the local area and give off balls of light which can dance and spin for periods of up to ten minutes or so before finally fizzling out. These effects, have generated a number of misleading UFO reports. Michael Persinger stated that basically UFO reports being luminous in nature, are caused by strain within the Earth, often this strain can be manifested by Earthquakes. Michael further stated that there appears to be a basic relationship between UFO reports, weeks to months before increases in Earthquake activity. Persinger believes that in the regions of localised faults, stress within the rock can cause these balls of light, these would consist of a plasma of hot ionized gases, and because of their electrical charges, they would move erratically around the landscape. Persinger also found that in some cases, such fields could reach up into the Ionosphere, where perhaps sonic energy could be produced, mainly during periods of seismic stress which could produce audible as well as infrasonic ultrasonic effects. Paul Devereux also shares Persinger's beliefs and stated in his book Earthlights that UFOs can 'shapeshift' which is one of the characteristics of Earthlights.

As most of us are aware, electrical impulses within the body can create various moods, it could be the case that an interaction may be possible between these balls of plasma lights with the witness, who not knowing the true nature of the phenomenon, and depending on the closeness of the witness to the phenomenon, they could be affected by the emissions of this ball of plasma light, and that the low level ionisation of the air, may give rise to what British UFO researcher, Jenny Randles coined "The Oz Factor". This refers to a quasi-conscious experience. A feeling of isolation, calmness, and sometimes sensory depravation. There are a number of locations throughout the world in which has witnessed a lot of Earthlight activity. Hessdalen in Norway for instance, was a major location in which strange luminous shapes cavorted about in the sky, some of which were captured on film. The late Dr J. Allen Hynek one of UFOlogy's pioneers, visited Hessdalen shortly before his death and recognised the fact that here was something very important, not only to the UFO community in regards to understanding natural light phenomenon, but to scientists as well. He felt that the scientific community should visit Hessdalen and see for themselves what was going on.

Then we have the Yakima Indian Reservation in Washington State. This area has also seen much luminous activity. Many UFO researchers now accept that Earthlights and Ball Lightning, do indeed make up a big percent of claimed UFO sightings. According to the Scotsman newspaper of August 31st 1992. An Edinburgh family had a narrow escape with Ball lightning. It stated that the families home was struck by a strange form of lightning which comprised of a 'ball of light'. At that time Edinburgh was being battered by severe weather conditions, torrential rain and howling winds and thunderstorms. (Just a normal day in Scotland I guess!) The story continues to state that Ciro and Camilla Esimio, and their 19 month son Antonio, were sitting down to their Sunday meal in their flat in Carrick Knowe Drive, when a 'ball of light' exploded at their window. The next thing they knew, smoke was pouring out of their television set. A neighbour had witnessed a huge 'ball of light' flying in the sky then hitting the Esimio's roof. Their roof was scorched and they were left without water and electricity for several hours. This 'ball lightning' strike also put their telephone out of order. So as we can see, not only is Ball Lightning nice to look at, it has destructive powers that we should be careful about as well.

HOAXES.

The next hypothesis is that sighting reports are hoaxes or involve fabrications made by the witness. This sadly is a feature of the UFO phenomenon. However, you will always find that certain people are out to gain publicity or monetary gain by fooling the public with tales of sighting a UFO. There have been countless hoaxes throughout the UFO history, and many interesting and what appear on the surface as very good UFO photographs, have eventually tumbled to the sophisticated computer. Some people seek publicity at any cost, their lives may appear dull and uninteresting and so they may wish to draw attention to themselves for a period of time. They will look to the UFO phenomenon as a way of attaining this. Thankfully, good UFO Investigators can easily spot the frauds and generally unmask their claims. But sadly, we will always have frauds, they will never go away.

UFOS. MAN MADE DEVICES?

The next hypothesis is that UFO sightings involve man made devices only known to their inventors, or devices that look extremely unusual and get mistaken for UFOs. The great American Air Ship wave of UFO reports back in 1896-97, is a prime example of this. Many American people witnessed strange boat shaped objects with propellers moving across the sky. In some instances they were observed at close range. Conversations were allegedly made with the occupants of these strange objects. Some of the occupants looked oriental and said that they were trying out new inventions. But not all looked oriental, there were Germans, Americans, and Scandinavians, (according to the witnesses who spoke with them). Other objects observed at this time, resembled the 2nd World War Zeppelins. The United Kingdom saw their own 'Air Ship' wave of UFO reports, this occurred during the years 1912 and 1913. And the objects sighted, resembled what the people over in America had witnessed. There are many people who still think that the American and British 'Air Ship wave' were Extraterrestrial, however, I'm not convinced that this is so.

Apparently it was difficult in the late 18th century to receive permission for tests on aerial flying machines, and so inventors took it upon themselves to do night tests. Also in this category for odd aircraft which have been mistaken for UFOs, is the 'Flying Flapjack', an American Military plane reputed to have reached speeds of 6ookpm. Then we have the Avro Canada VZ-9 Avrocar which had it's first flight in Canada back in 1959. It was reputed to have been able to stop in mid air, and hover at any height and was jet powered. This device wasn't successful and production was stopped, but it had the classic flying saucer shape and looked most peculiar. During the second world war, Germany produced a number of circular aircraft and some researchers even today, think that these circular aircraft were captured by the Americans at the end of the second world war and taken back to America in which modifications were made upon them and of which have been flown by the U.S. Air Force since then. There is no denying that Germany did indeed produce circular aircraft, most of which were unsuccessful in flight, but I'm still unconvinced at this time that what we are seeing in the skies of the world is the result of captured Nazi aircraft!

In America during the 1940's and 1950's, there were some weird patents registered from inventors for unusual shaped aircraft, so weird, that a lot of them were not taken very seriously. The circular shaped design did not prove to be very successful, but we have to bear in mind, that at this time during the 1940's and 50's, many inventors may have been trying their weird flying machines out, and any unsuspecting individual may have viewed these machines as something other than what they truly were. In August 1997, an amazing revelation came about through the C.I.A. (Central Intelligence Agency), in a report published at the Office of the Director of Central Intelligence World Wide Web Site, it was stated that the C.I.A. lied to the American public. Apparently they were happy to use the cover of UFO sightings to hide the fact that they were flying U-2 and SR-71 secret spy planes. These planes were developed in the 1950's and 60's to photograph enemy targets. They flew from secret bases mainly in

California and Nevada and on occasions flew to bases in countries such as Britain, West Germany, and Taiwan. The current day commercial airliners only flew at a height of around 3O,OOOft whilst the U-2 spy plane attained a height of more than 6O,OOOft and the SR-71 to an even greater height of 8O,OOOft which is roughly 15 miles from the edge of space. Rather than let the American public become aware of these highly secret spy planes, they were quite happy to feed the public with false cover stories some of which had to do with UFOs. The SR-71 which first flew in 1964, was painted black and it's fanciful nick name was the 'Blackbird'. These were painted black so that they would not be so noticeable in the sky as the sun struck off their shiny fuselage. This was all very well, and some felt that this was just another ruse by the American Military machine to throw UFOlogists off the scent, For after all, not all UFO sightings were of objects seen high in the sky. How could they explain the low level close proximity UFO sightings? It just didn't add up. Most UFOlogists now accept that the American Military and Government authorities will gladly tell people anything to steer them away from what is really going on. The 198O's and 199O's, saw even more unusual shaped aircraft mostly manufactured in America. The XB-7OA Valkyrie bomber was developed for the USAF but never went into production. In 1991, more reports surfaced of people claiming to have seen a strange aircraft which resembled the XB-7OA. The September October edition of Britain's *UFO MAGAZINE,* featured an article by Bill Rose, which went into graphic detail about this new American aircraft technology. It made for interesting reading, and showed it's readers that mankind was experimenting with new and different shaped aircraft. Again, some of these odd shaped aircraft could have been misconstrued by a watching ground based observer as a 'fanciful flying saucer'! Indeed, I am totally convinced of this, and would suggest to the reader of this book, that the vast majority of UFO sightings during the 1950's and 60's, were our own prototype aircraft.

Then we have some UFOlogists who believe that the wreckage retrieved from an alleged crashed UFO at Roswell

New Mexico back in 1947, was somehow 'back engineered' by the American Air Force (or a Government division thereof) and adapted into their own aircraft design. In other words, they tried to re-create a Flying Saucer. The way I see it, this would be like giving Christopher Columbus a nuclear submarine in 1492, and asking him to build one for his voyage to America. I mean, can you imagine it? The back engineering of someone else's advanced technology would be a terrific feat if accomplished, but I very much doubt that it can be done, that is unless of course, they got help from 'visiting aliens'! I'll be coming back to this point later on. As far as Scotland goes, there were reports of strange looking aircraft flying in and out of Machrihanish Airfield in Argyll Scotland during the early 1990's. A Norwegian Newspaper came to Scotland to investigate reports of this aircraft supposedly being seen at the Machrihanish Airbase. This was due to the fact that there had been a number of Incidents in Norway, in which strange sonic booms were heard thundering through the air. These mainly came from above small fishing communities between Trondheim and Narvik. In Narvik for instance in March 1986, after a sonic boom was heard, there was an avalanche of snow which killed 16 soldiers. The Netherlands had a sudden earth tremor which they blamed on this secret plane. Enquiries found that the plane in question, was the secret Aurora aircraft which apparently could fly at three times the speed of sound. Evan Wiley, a Military aircraft specialist, stated in the Scotsman newspaper in January 1996, that a north of Scotland RAF base tracked a very fast radar blip the previous year, but when the incident was reported to RAF Buchan, superior officers there, denied all knowledge of it. It's been said that the Machrihanish runway, which is 10,000 feet in length (the longest in Europe) would be an ideal place to test the Aurora aircraft. Not only is the runway suitable, but the isolation in this area is perfect for this clandestine work. The British M.o.D. deny that the Aurora aircraft exists, which was a statement that Bill Sweetman, the technical Editor of Jane's information group and a specialist in Stealth technology found most amusing. He was reported as saying in the Scotsman article,

"Put it this way, in 1988 the U.S. Air Force had 50 F-117 Stealth Aircraft operating in Nevada, and still they (The American Government) *denied they existed.*

The Stealth bomber was flatly denied as existing by the British and American Governments for years, before the cat was finally out of the bag. And let us not forget dear reader, that the Stealth Bomber also gave rise to false UFO reports for a time.

I do accept that the American and British Military powers, must to an extent, keep what they are manufacturing a secret until they are happy with the end result. But having said that, they should still at the very least, state the fact that they are in production of an experimental aircraft which is flying in and out of where ever. By doing this, this would clear the way and ensure that people 'knew' what it was they had seen in the sky. But on the flip side of the coin, one can see why the air force are more than happy to use the cover story of UFOs to ensure no-one gets to know about their secret experimentation.

Then of course we have those other strange airborne machines, the UAV's (Unmanned Aerial Vehicles) or drones as they are also called. Britain used several small circular shaped drones during the Gulf War. These were flown over the Iraqi positions in order to detect troop movements and obtain relevant information. I've seen a number of photographs of these strange devices, and believe you me, they look exactly like a conventional 'Flying Saucer'. It isn't any wonder that it's getting harder and harder to detect what is 'ours', to what is 'theirs' (!) The afore mentioned 'devices', are but some of the many 'man made' aircraft and machines that could quite easily be misconstrued as a 'Flying Saucer', and sadly it pains me to think that many UFO books and magazines may be carrying stories of fantastic UFO sightings, when all they really were, were just our own advanced aircraft. It certainly is 'muddy waters' out there, and this is why UFO Investigators must be on their toes to 'all' possibilities.

265

MENTAL IMAGERY & HALLUCINATIONS!

The next hypothesis is that the UFO sightings are mental projections by, or received by, the witness. This is yet another avenue that we must explore and consider. Part of this theory is that the human mind may impregnate on the human eye, a vision of various illusions to one who is unbalanced through severe illness. It's a case of seeing something which really isn't there. We may liken this theory to 'after images' in which we may (for instance), look at the centre of a light bulb which is switched on, then look away in a different direction. And, for that short period of time, that bright spot image can still be seen, but now in a new position. Some UFO sightings may be due to individuals looking at bright outside lights then looking up to the sky where they will now see a bright light zipping quickly across the sky. Sounds ridiculous I know, but I know of a few cases in which this has happened, and in those cases, those individuals were heavily into UFOs. People can and do, see things which are not really there. One might look up into the sky and observe the passing clouds and state that they can see faces in them, or a whole range of different images. The human mind can make images out of mostly anything. We see pictures in the flames of a fire, we may see faces in patterned hanging curtains. There is a whole range of natural things of which some people can make strange images out of. Then there is the other camp, those who would tell you that the E.T's, are putting imagery into 'your' head. That they might not be physically 'there', but are observing you and infiltrating your mind with their selected imagery! Sounds incredible, but then again so does the fact that the scientists of today, state that in just under 5O years time, they will be able to produce a chip with imagery on it which they will insert and attach to the human brain, this in turn will give it's recipient images which do not belong to them. People may laugh and scoff at what mankind hopes to achieve in science, this is wrong, science will always progress, people will be born who will turn out to be geniuses with a way of thinking way beyond the norm. Who can envisage the future at this point in time and the many wonders that it must hold. The cloning of animals was not thought possible until the 5th of July, 1996, when a cloned Scottish sheep by the name of Dolly was showcased to the world. Experiments were carried out by the Roslin Institute led by Sir Ian Wilmut. It was the first mammal that was cloned from an adult somatic cell. Of course, this makes us wonder how far cloning will go, will it progress into humans? And if so, what will be felt on the massive implications of such trials?

The human mind is an impressive organ, and it's incredible to think that we only use but a small percent of it, around 10%. Psychic individuals claim that they can tap into the remaining percent of the brain that most of use can't normally access, I believe this is possible. Hypnosis can make people believe that they are seeing things which are not really there, or feel heat on their hands when there is no heat being applied. We know so little about the brain, and indeed some might say that the human brain is as much a mystery than the UFO subject is! There was a case from the United States, and the reader will have to excuse me as I can't recall when or where it happened, but I do remember that an 'alien' was seen suddenly materialising in the back seat of a woman's car to which it said to her, *"Do I frighten you, for if I do, I will change my shape and appearance to whatever pleases you"*. So on this issue it's really hard to understand how big or small a part that mental projections play. Is it all in the mind of the witness? Are they making things out or ordinary mundane objects? Or are images of 'Flying Saucers' and small 'grey men', being put into their minds by 'beings' from other worlds?

THE EXTRATERRESTRIAL HYPOTHESIS.

Our next hypothesis, is one in which a lot of people put a lot of faith in, that these UFOs are really alien spaceships from other worlds sent here to monitor our progress without getting to much involved the mankind. Like all the theories that I am discussing in this chapter, the E.T. theory would appear to hold the main cards and the evidence so far collated, would appear to suggest, that this theory is the more possible, although there are still many who would disagree. We know for certain, and I've mentioned it earlier, that we are only talking about a small 5% of UFO reports which we cannot be accounted for after research has been undertaken, but contained within this small 5%, are reports of objects tracked on radar, of objects which have had Military aircraft scrambled in an effort to pursue these UFOs. And of course, let us not forget that UFOs that have been fired upon by some of the air forces of planet Earth. *(Check the literature, its all there)* These type of reports are not hallucinations, are not satellites, and are not a whole range of other possibilities. For these reports are well above the normal misidentifications of mundane objects. We are talking about low level, close proximity UFO sightings. Sightings of objects which defy the normal laws of aviation, of which if we tried to achieve the quick stop start manoeuvres that these objects have been seen to do, then the G. Force exerted on the pilot, would kill him within seconds, not to mention the fact that the aircraft's structure would not bear up to the terrific changes in speed. We are dealing here with physical solid nuts and bolts objects. They have been seen to appear and disappear at will, they have even been seen to morph and change shape! Then we have the reports of UFOs that have been sighted above sensitive Military establishments, above power installations and above other areas of highly classified Defence projects.

UFO researcher Nick Redfern discusses in his book '*A Covert Agenda (The British Government's UFO Top Secrets Exposed) Simon & Shuster London 1997)*, about a breach of security at the Marconi factory in Frimley in England back in 1974. The breach was by no ordinary intruder! A security guard whilst patrolling the area, observed a blue light coming from a room. This factory worked on behalf of the British Government on classified radar related projects. Realising that there should not be anyone in that room at that hour, the guard inspected the room, and was met by a shocking sight, that of a horrible humanoid figure which was sifting through a filing cabinet. The figure upon being seen, dissolved before the terrified guard's eyes. The blue light was coming from some form of helmet on the 'entity's' head. Apparently, after the guard had explained this incident to his superiors, he was never heard of again! This is but one of the many tales of people encountering 'beings' from elsewhere. Suffice it to say the evidence pointing to the reality of E.T. visitation is strong. There are of course many wide and varied reports of strange 'beings' seen in close proximity to UFOs, and one may ask why this should be? Surely if they are from different star systems and planets, then their own atmosphere would be different from planet Earth, and as such, surely they would find it difficult to breathe in our oxygen! And yet, this does not seem to be the case. For all the different shapes and sizes of the 'beings' encountered, very rarely do you find them encountering difficulty with our own atmosphere. Why this should be, I do not know, but it is something which is clearly a puzzle and has taxed the minds of many UFOlogists the world over. Now surely after travelling from the depths of space one would think that a formal visit from a superior E.T. race would be on the cards! And yet the vast majority of UFO reports, are really only of sightings of strange objects seen in the sky. Why the shyness? Are we ourselves being observed? Are 'we' their genetic experiment? Is Planet Earth but a zoo, and we are 'their' experiment and the 'aliens' are our keepers? Of course there is the abduction phenomenon aspect, which with the A70 Incident, is the main thrust of this book. We can but surmise that the UFO abduction phenomena is an agenda which is being played out by 'beings' from elsewhere for purposes that we can but speculate. The vastness of space is immense, and we really cannot comprehend the enormity of it all, and sceptics ask, why if these truly are intelligent 'beings' from other worlds visiting planet Earth, do they come all this way, just to go back again. This is a fair point and one in which should also be addressed. Perhaps the answer to that one lies in the possibility that these far travelled 'beings' are not going back home as it were, in other words, they stay right here on planet Earth, and where better to hide yourself than in any one of the Earth's oceans! I personally believe that there is undoubtedly UFO bases here on planet Earth, and that the majority of them are under our oceans. There is numerous eye witness testimony of UFOs being seen entering and leaving the world's oceans, especially near the Canary Islands. From the book, 'Photographs Of The

Unknown' by Robert Rickard and Richard Kelly, (Granta Editions 1980), we are shown various photographs which show what appear to be UFOs leaving the sea. These photographs were taken by Antonio Llopes and show a white fiery tail heading skywards.

According to reports, this phenomenon was witnessed by many thousands of people from the Canary Islands. However, recent reports have cast doubt on the object as being a UFO, we are now being told that what really was observed and photographed, was a missile that was fired from a submarine! As we know, the vast majority of the Earth's surface is covered with water, it is therefore highly likely (if one accepts the E.T. hypothesis) that UFOs do have bases under our oceans, this would ensure that they would be able to go about their clandestine business without having to make the enormous journeys back to their home planet, unless of course, that they have developed means whereby journeys only take minutes instead of hours, days instead of weeks, months, instead of years. The possibility of 'worm holes' in space, or that perhaps these interstellar travellers have bent or warped space in order to get to destinations more quickly, is something that we just cannot quantify at this time. If we truly are dealing with a highly sophisticated race of 'beings', then who knows how far in advance of mankind their technology is, let's not forget that.

As I say, there are many reports of UFOs seen entering and leaving the seas, one of the more better instances of this, was reported by paranormal writers, Janet and Colin Bord. In the 1984 Orbis book entitled 'UFOs, Where Do They Come From', they tell of a case in which a Jorge Montoya an officer on duty on the ship Naviero as it sailed across the South Atlantic, 120 miles off the Brazilian Coast on the 30th of July 1967. Jorge saw something which shocked him to the core. The crew were all having their evening meal and Montoya was startled to see a strange cigar shaped craft gliding silently through the water at a distance of only 50 feet away. Montoya alerted his Captain where he too observed this strange vessel running alongside the ship.

Both men stood in amazement for around 15 minutes as they watched this vessel which didn't leave a wake. This strange vessel glowed with a brilliant bluish-white light and they estimated that the object's length was around 1O5 to 11O feet. Suddenly this strange object turned towards the Merchant ship glowing even more brightly as it approached nearer, it then dived beneath the ship and rapidly disappeared into the depths of the ocean. The Captain, in a later statement to the press, stated that the object was not a submarine, nor a whale, and in 2O years at sea, he had never seen anything like it. UFOlogists call these particular sightings, USO's, (Unidentified Submarine Objects). Readers might be surprised to learn that USOs are not just a recent phenomena, from the same book Janet and Colin tell of other reports from as early as 1885. In that year, the crew of the ship Innerwich, observed a huge object glowing with a brilliant red light dive into the sea throwing up columns of water. Then on the 12th of November 1887, near Cape Race Newfoundland, a Captain Moore of the British ship Siberian, watched for five minutes as a huge ball of fire rose from beneath the ocean to a height of 5O feet. It then moved towards the ship and then left the area. There have been reports of USOs from off the North American Coast, from Newport Rhode Island, to lakes in Sweden. USOs have also been seen in inland waters as well, and we also have cases of objects being seen leaving and entering lakes, rivers, harbours, and creeks. Janet and Colin tell of a story in which over 7O people who were waiting on a ferry at the Araguari River in Brazil back in November 198O, witnessed a solid object around 15 feet, rise from under the water, where it hovered above the surface of the water for around four minutes at a height estimated at 65O feet. After slowly coming close to the bank (roughly 1OO feet), the strange object headed out to sea.

Then there is the equally strange tale about the time something unusual was found on the bottom of the Spanish Mediterranean. A shiny metal cylinder 23 feet long and 1O feet in diameter, was found by a Spanish aqualung diver on the sea bed on the Mediterranean Coast back in July 197O. It was a smooth rivitless cylinder which had no openings, and it appeared very clean, as if it hadn't been in the water for that long. The next morning the diver went back to retrieve this mysterious object, but on getting to the area, the object was nowhere to be seen. Lorentz Johnson watched in amazement as a bright glowing cigar shaped object dropped two long objects into the waters of Namsen fjord during December 1959. A short while later, some UFO Investigators using sonar equipment, found an object 2O feet long by 7 feet high but it was at a depth of 3OO feet and proved very difficult for divers to reach. However, the divers did report seeing strange 'wheel tracks' on the bottom which appeared to be heading out to sea. The late Ivan T. Sanderson researcher and biologist held the opinion that beneath the world's oceans, could live a race far older than mankind, and that they possibly were descended from life that did not leave the primeval seas to develop on land, but stayed underwater to develop more. That's quite an interesting thought. Researcher John Keel was of the opinion that UFOs may have underwater bases in the regions above the Arctic circle, while other researchers Jim and Coral Lorenzen believe that UFOs are here carrying out mapping and mining operations and that they have established underwater bases in the Gulfs of San Matias and San Jorge on the Patagonian coast.

And so we should not rule out the strong possibility that UFOs do indeed have bases under the oceans. Perhaps it might be the case that we should not be looking too much to the skies, but that we should be casting our inquisitive gaze towards the seas! In all respects, the UFO phenomena has all the trappings of it being the sole result of having Extraterrestrial origins. I will be extending my thoughts on the E.T. issue in my summing up at the close of this book, for now though, let us continue on with our journey as we look at other possibilities concerning where UFOs might come from.

FROM WITHIN OR BEYOND OUR GALAXY?

The next hypothesis is that these UFOs originate from within our own Galaxy or beyond our Galaxy, this might appear a similar hypothesis as our last one, but there are a few significant differences. I have mentioned before, that planet Earth is but a tiny grain of sand on a huge cosmic beach, and many people accept the fact that it is inconceivable for there not to be life 'out there' in the vastness of space. Stars and planets are being born every minute. Our own Earth technology is surely but a babe in the woods compared to some other technology who have had thousands of years of a start on us. But would they really want to interfere with our society, and our culture? It might be too much for the people of Earth to be suddenly confronted with a massive jump of technology shown to us by visiting Extraterrestrials. We on planet Earth have progressed gradually, inventions have come slowly. But going to A to Z in one quick jump, may prove too much for us mere Earthlings. One can only take on board so much information at one time, perhaps this is why there has not been any open and direct contact with 'aliens'!

If these 'aliens' left us with knowledge and power of an immense magnitude, then knowing man, would he use it to it's correct purpose? Or would he use it for a more destructful purpose? If our bloody history is anything to go by, then that is an easy question to answer. There are billions upon billions of stars which make up just one Galaxy. It's been said that it would take man 6,000 million years travelling at the speed of light (299:783 Km per second) just to reach the limit of the observed universe. (I would like to know how they make these figures up!). There are, as we know, millions of stars in the Galaxy of which, under the right conditions, could support life, granted that life might not have evolved in the same way it has on Earth, there are many elements which come into play to dictate how a 'being' or 'life force' would look like. It's been proved that there can't be life (as we know it), on any of the planets in our own solar system. Venus is too hot, Neptune is too cold, that's not to say that microscopic life might not dwell under the surface of these and other planets, but as far as a humanoid based life form, there is no evidence to suggest that planets in our own system hold any life. Of course let us not forget that 'aliens' might have bases on the Moon! There would appear to be controversial statements made by some astronauts during the Apollo space program, that they saw numerous strange objects in space, (and on the Moon!). So again, this implies that the necessity of long space voyages are not warranted particularly as one could have either bases on Earth or bases on the Moon.

UFOS FROM OUR OWN FUTURE?

We now take a look at yet another hypothesis, however this one to some, might seem slightly ludicrous, it's certainly thought provoking, but can it hold any water? The theory is that these UFOs are from our own future on excursions into their past of which they cannot specifically interfere, and the times that they do, ie, in UFO Abductions, may be purely to continue with genetic testing or manipulation of the species. Fantastic stuff I know, but it is a theory which has been talked about from time to time in UFO circles over the years. Of course the reader might ask here,

"But if these 'beings' are from our own future, then why are so many of these reports of either hideous looking creatures, or small grey entities"?

Is this to be the shape of future man? We could speculate and state that perhaps man's genetic body shape may have been altered by some futuristic atomic warfare in which he has somehow survived a nuclear holocaust but has to endure this new and badly shaped body. Fantastic stuff, fantastic theory, but is it just that. Perhaps we may have meddled too much with genetics in the future, that we have somehow taken away our normal looking human body and somehow replaced it with what UFO witnesses describe today, as small grey creatures. A nasty thought I know, and something which doesn't bear thinking about. Time travel as it stands right now, is just a figment of the imagination. It would of course be very exciting to think that one day this might very well be possible. But where would it all lead? What if anything could it change? Would we want to change anything? And if so, how would that effect mankind? We cannot even begin to conceive the mass amount of difficulties that are involved with this theory. What we also know, is that on the odd occasion when there is some form of conversation between witnesses and 'aliens', they tell us that they are from planets either from our own solar system, or planets outside it. These statements are usually false, and there have been many 'untruths' told to humans from 'aliens' in the past. But why? Why would they want to lie to us?

Is it because of the very fact that they 'ARE' from our own future, and are putting us off the scent by giving us false information? We could of course also state an even more bizarre scenario than this. I could speculate that these 'aliens' might indeed look just like us, and are here amoungst us throughout this planet for the sole purpose of monitoring our political and social struggles for an as yet undiscovered purpose (!) I did say that some of these UFO theories were a bit on the wild side, but it would be wrong not to discuss some of these more wilder one's just because they appear preposterous.

THE PARALLEL UNIVERSE THEORY.

In the excellent UFO study book, 'The UFO Encyclopedia' written by Margaret Sachs, (Corgi Books 1981), we learn that the three dimensional space that we live in is known as the universe. This is different from the three spatial dimensions of length, width, and depth. Time is referred to as a fourth dimension. It has been speculated that there might well be numerous spatial dimensions beyond the three that we know, and that the possibility of UFOs travelling from another dimension or parallel universe might not be so fanciful. They may be coming from a dimension that vibrates at a different vibrational frequency to our own, and therefore could enter and leave our planet at will. Margaret Sachs states in her book that

The Christian Religion promotes a belief in Heaven, a non physical place where God and his Angels reside, and where the souls of people go after death. But since Heaven is a separate world beyond our physical senses, it might represent another dimension or space time continuum. She goes on to say that some Christians believe that UFOs might be God's angels manifesting themselves in a form which is acceptable to our culture. An interesting thought.

Is our Universe interpenetrating with other unseen universes? The human body may appear to be dense, as indeed are numerous objects like tables and chairs, but the units which make up our bodies are composed of tiny atoms which are as widely separated as stars in the sky. It's not within the bounds of possibility that unseen universes are indeed intertwined with our own and so therefore distances are again unnecessary. The travel would be instantaneous.

DIMENSIONS.

The dimensional theory is more or less a sister theory to the above, in so far as they both contain more or less of the same properties. If we think of a radio and that all of the signals from each radio station are transmitting, our radio is collecting each and every one, and yet they can be separated by the tuning in of a dial in which a particular frequency (station) can be heard. Quantum physics show that matter has wave like properties and that there is nothing which could prevent two or more universes from co-existing in the same place. Physicists tell us that the whole world around us is built solely from three basic building blocks called the proton, the neutron, and the electron. But it has been speculated that there are hundreds more particles, one of which is the neutrino, and it's stated that the neutrino can pass effortlessly through a block of solid lead many miles thick. These neutrino's are so insubstantial, that millions of them are passing through you right now. Of course dimensions are also a big part of the make up of the alleged spirit world in which reports of ghosts and psychic happenings occur. I do honestly believe that the dimensional theory is a sound one, not only

276

that, but I'm sure that it encompasses not only the UFO situation, but the paranormal and spirit situation as well.

Spiritualists state that we have not just one body, but several bodies which are called the etheric body, the astral body, the spirit body, to name but a few, so in a sense, each of these bodies could be made from the same matter just like a parallel universe. We may be here sleeping in bed in our normal material body, but travel out of it in our astral body. Again this all may seem highly controversial and perhaps unscientific, but I present these thoughts here for you to digest. Musical notes vibrate, animals can hear different frequencies from humans, so there is no denying, that vibrations and frequencies exist that we cannot see or hear. Another analogy that I could use to try and explain the point I am trying to make about dimensions, would be to state that we can see through a pane of glass as if there is nothing there, but when we smash the glass, we can see that it is made up of certain components of sand, limestone, and cullet (ground glass). I have stated that it's possible that the more psychic one is, the more chance they will have of seeing into these 'other dimensions'. Taking speculation further, perhaps when these UFOs descend from our skies and go through their normal colour changes, which they have been seen to do, this is possibly due to them attaining the necessary vibratory changes to enter into our own vibrational frequency! One of the most influential UFO books that I have ever read, was French man Jacques Vallee's 'Dimensions' (Souvenir Press Britain 1988). One of the most illuminating quotes that I found in this book, was when Jacques stated,

"We have come to realise that we are dealing with a genuine new phenomenon of immense scope. The UFOs are real physical objects, yet they are not necessarily Extraterrestrial spacecraft. To put it bluntly, the Extraterrestrial theory is not strange enough to explain the facts, and I will be disappointed if UFOs turn out to be nothing more than visitors from another planet".

I always remember the words that the late comedian and intrigued psychic enquirer Michael Bentine once said, he stated,

"The technologist who says these things cannot be so because my instruments do not show them to be so, invites the answer, 'then build a better instrument'. No true scientist would be guilty of such arrogance because he or she is always searching for a better understanding of ourselves and the cosmos. Only the bigoted believe that they, per se, know it all. The open minded realise that we know practically 'nothing'

There is another interesting quote that I have taken from Michael Bentine which I believe to be relevant to what is under discussion here, and that is,

"To confuse our physical brains with our minds, is just as ridiculous as saying that a computer is the same thing as the person who programmed it, or that a piano is the same thing as the person who plays it".

I think that is rather apt. To complete our brief discussion on Dimensions, I'll leave the final quote once more to Jacques Vallee. He said,

"To put it bluntly, the UFO phenomenon does not give evidence of being Extraterrestrial at all. Instead it appears to be Inter-dimensional, and to manipulate physical realities outside of our own space time continuum".

I do honestly believe, that the real and true answer to the UFO mystery, will be solved through the question of dimensions. Perhaps at this time, we don't as yet, have the proper scientific instrument to unravel the mysterious world of dimensions. Maybe sometime in the future, a young entrepreneur, will devise a machine that can 'see' into these dimensions opening up a new and as yet unexplored world. Let us now turn our attention to the psychic hypothesis and see if this can provide us with any clues as to the nature of the UFO phenomenon.

THE PSYCHIC AND THE SPIRITUAL.

I mentioned earlier, that it is my belief that the more psychic one is, the more chance they have of observing a UFO, the reason I say this, is due specifically down to the fact that I believe that the UFO phenomenon has it's roots in the dimensional world. I haven't ruled out entirely the possible fact that some of these 'alien travellers' might be from outer space, but in this moment in time, I am inclined to believe, purely through my research and what I've read, that the dimensional aspect of UFOlogy appears to be nearer the tape. Psychic individuals may see into a different spectrum of which other individuals cannot perceive, that's not to say that you 'have' to be psychic to witness a UFO, not at all, but I've lost count of the people that I have personally dealt with over the years who have been psychic and who also have had spirit manifestations in their home or paranormal occurrences happen to them. One might turn this point on it's head whereby we could look back at the events that occurred in Fatima in Portugal back in 1917 in which three girls claimed to have witnessed the Virgin Mary. Many people, (nearly 7O,OOO) stood in the pouring rain, with not all of them seeing what the three girls saw, a beautiful lady in the sky. Others saw a dancing globe of light, like a small sun which raced down from the sky and played majestically in the sky. Was this event a 'nuts and bolts' phenomena? Or was it a psychic dimensional event which 'broke through' into our own dimension for a short period of time, I think it was the latter. Of course, this was not an isolated incident, there have been many more reports of people witnessing what they claim to be the Virgin Mary. Events at Garabandal in Spain for instance, where three more youngsters (girls) witnessed the Virgin Mary. We should in no way ignore the fact that, at least to the girls involved, each who shared a visual experience of profound pleasure, this experience came through to our reality which was somehow transferred to them, in which by some strange mechanism (the psychic element) they were able to perceive a vision of profound magnitude. I mentioned above about the events at Fatima that some witnessed a globe of light, whilst

279

others some saw a brilliant pearly disc which is said to have rotated on it's own axis. This disc, as I've said, was then said to have dived towards the ground in which it then swooped upwards back into the sky leaving a trail of what UFOlogists call, *'Angels Hair'*, a fibrous substance which usually evaporates upon contact with the ground. The psychic individual is more prone to observe ghosts, and we cannot deny that there are many people throughout the world who have witnessed into this other dimension, a dimension in which contains the deceased people who once walked the Earth plane. Don't get me wrong, there are 'other' alternative explanations to account for ghostly sightings, but the fact remains, that the good reports that we have of ghosts strongly indicate that there is another dimension in which we all go to upon the death of our physical material bodies, (but that's another book!

According to the Psychic News, a Spiritualist weekly newspaper based in Stansted Essex in England, a Helen Christian had an experience when two 'aliens' materialised into her home back in 1972. In the July 26th edition of Psychic News, we are told that the two 'aliens' who materialised into her home, were like spirits of the afterlife. They appeared to be adult males, but minute size, roughly No more than four feet tall. They wore uniforms of some sort, in a style which was reminiscent to the British Army's tropical outfits, although they did have thick stockings which were tucked into their leggings. She also observed that they both had very long feet which tapered into a point into their long boots. Their arms were also long, with long tapering fingers. Their heads were long and narrow but their facial features resembled our own. Helen's initial impression of these strange characters, were that they were weary travellers who had come a long way and were unsure of a welcome. Being psychic, Helen was able to communicate with them through her guide of which her guide told her that there were many spirits from other worlds in the Galaxy. Helen listened to what her two extraordinary visitors had to say, and basically it was very similar to what the Contactees of the 1950's informed UFOlogists, ie, that planet Earth must be very careful as it is reaching a critical stage in it's development, whereby the use of atomic weapons could obliterate the Earth and make it a wasteland in which there would be very few survivors. She was told that this is what had happened to their own home planet and they wanted to inform other worlds of these hideous dangers. Of course this begs the obvious question, why Helen? Why materialise to a psychic, why not a Government leader? Of course we could say a Government leader might not have had the psychic capacity to 'see' these 'spirit aliens', and that she, (Helen) was sent on a mission to try and impart to the world about these atomic dangers. A tall order, and who is going to believe her? What Helen did understand, was that her 'visitors' were indeed spirits of aliens who had died in a terrible chemical and atomic war. Their home planet, they said, was somewhere in the region of Orion's Belt, and that some survivors of this holocaust, lived underground.

This article sparked my interest, and I wrote off to the Psychic News enclosing a short request in which I asked it's readers if anyone had, what they had felt to be, an experience not with a spirit, but with an 'alien entity'. I received a few replies, not as many as I thought I would, however one letter I received, was most informative and interesting and came from someone of whom I have traded letters with in the past, his name was Ernie Sears. Sadly Ernie is no longer with us. Ernie was a seasoned researcher who lived in Netley Abbey in Hants England, and Investigated not only UFOs, but strange phenomena in all it's capacities for over 5O years, clearly then, Ernie was someone who knew his 'stuff' and was around long enough to know what he was talking about. Ernie had seen my letter in the Psychic News, and decided to drop me a line with some information on what I was requesting. He firstly told me that he has over 4O pages of typed 'messages', from his Spiritual guide Liu Chang, (Ernie was also a psychic healer) and had seven thick notebooks filled with even more writings from Liu Chang, which, he was quick to point out, were not all of his handwriting! Some of these messages were in the handwriting from people he had once healed but who had now passed on to the 'other side'.

Ernie went on to explain that he had an 'alien source' inform him that they share 'other dimensions' and can interact with those Earth people who have died and that these meetings, were down to 'their technology' in which they could achieve these meetings, (think back to the Helen Christian meeting we read about earlier!) Ernie continued by saying, that he sometimes gets woken up at 2 in the morning to write down his spiritual messages, some of these have to do with warnings about the state of our planet and what we are doing to it. Ernie also claims that he has had a UFO abduction experience in 1995 of which he was mostly informed on health matters. This wasn't his first abduction however, and he recalls being abducted from his bed at around 11 years of age. He also recalls the time when he found himself in a pink domed 'heaven' and an 'angel' gliding towards him doing something sexual, again this experience occurred whilst he was in bed, (his spirit body was taken to this wonderful place). A few years back Ernie got involved with what's known as 'Timestream' which is a modern way of contacting spirits by way of tape recorders taping the white noise (off channel) from a radio. Apparently strange voices can be heard which are not radio broadcasts but voices from people who once lived. Conversations can be made, but sometimes one has to slow the tape speed right down in order to hear what is being said. It was during August 1995, that Ernie obtained information through this 'Timestream' process which was not a spirit, but claimed to be an 'alien'. But it was in October 1995 that he started to receive messages of which 'they' claimed were important. One message said,

"There is no stopping the flood now that the world is aware of the possibilities of other life forms, whether from the Cosmos, or what your more facetious columnists still call the 'other side'".

His 'alien' contact, went on to inform him that it knew about the amorphous being that he recently encountered as he walked into his lounge, that it had swung round and vanished. Later that same day, a friend of Ernie's who is a good dowser and what Ernie call's, 'a reluctant psychic'! telephoned him to tell him about the 'smokey looking figure' that had turned around and vanished as he had entered his kitchen! He was also informed by his 'alien' contact, that their life span is much longer than ours, purely because they do not posses negative emotions (!).

What followed next, was a major step in the development of these communications. Ernie was given a date and a location from his 'alien' contact of which he was told to turn up along with his friend, and that proof would be given to him that these messages were true and that they did indeed come from an 'alien' source. This was it, thought Ernie, at last we will be able to get concrete proof. The day duly arrived, a foggy November 1995 evening. However, as the day wore on, both men began to have a deep apprehension about what they were getting themselves in for, and Ernie's friend decided that he didn't want to be there. Ernie on the other hand, watched from his bedroom window at the allotted time of nine minutes past midnight. He stared out across the landscape and suddenly observed two bright lights which hung in the sky for a few minutes. Reaching for his binoculars, he saw that they now had joined together, after which they completely vanished! That episode over, Ernie still received messages through not only 'Timestream', but also from his spirit guide Liu Chang as well. He was told that humans should not neglect prayer, and that if he read between the lines of the Bible, he would find references to them there. He was also told that they preferred windows to walls when they abducted humans, something to do with the molecules (!) Ernie stated that he was abducted twice through his bedroom window and that the side effects that he experienced the following day from going through the window, were, very unpleasant to say the least. Another important message of which Ernie took note, was the following.

"We shake our heads in sadness and almost disbelief, emotions we once knew not as you do, and, it is our right and our decision to become involved with earthly matters, and we

are sometimes envious of your laughter, humour, music, and artistic feelings, all very Spiritual".

A most unusual if not thankful incident that Ernie recalled, was the time when he was very short of money and just needed a five pound note to keep him going through the rest of the week. As he went to his printer to print off something, he was gobsmacked to find a bright new crisp five pound note wrapped firmly around the roller. Until his death in 2009 of a heart attack, Ernie continued to receive his spirit messages and there were many strange coincidences when money suddenly came into his possession.

Welsh researcher, Randall Jones Pugh, who passed in 2003 firmly believed that UFOs had Demonic connections coming from the spiritual realms which harboured supernatural entities out to deceive and confuse mankind. This is not an uncommon theme, many other researchers from around the world, feel that the UFO phenomenon is indeed Demonic, and is manipulating the human race with stories that lead us in all different directions. American writer and author Brad Steiger was, at one point in his life, of the opinion that UFOs were evil, that they were full of hostile actions in which they abducted people, and were responsible for a whole host of other evil atrocities. The thing is, many people believe many different things. The UFO phenomenon is not a subject which has finally been put to bed, there is still so much debate about what is going on and who is doing it. The Demonic side of this is yet another piece of the jigsaw, but it's one in which I don't subscribe to. And although I accept ghosts and the spirit world, I do not believe for one minute, that Satan and his followers are flitting about the skies of our world in unearthly machines to lead us astray.

CONTINUING OUR LOOK AT WHAT COULD BE BEHIND THE UFO ABDUCTION PHENOMENON.

OK, we have looked at a few possibilities above as to what could perhaps explain the UFO and UFO Abduction enigma. That was not an exhaustive study, we'll now take a look at some more candidates. First up, is regressive hypnosis, which, as we have read, 'was' conducted on both Garry and Colin. Does it have merits? Well before we discuss the use of hypnosis as a tool to retrieve any hidden subconscious recall of a UFO abduction, one must first inform the reader about the beginnings of hypnosis. Hypnosis has been with us for a very long time, but the one man who probably (if not certainly) brought the subject out to the masses, was one Franz Anton Mesmer (23rd May 1734 - 5th March 1815) German born Mesmer, was a doctor who had, amoungst other things, a strong interest in astronomy. Anton was of the belief that there existed a 'natural energy' which could transfer between all animated and inanimate objects, he named it 'animal magnetism' but it was better know as 'mesmerism' due no doubt to Anton bringing the concept forth. However, it wasn't until 1834, that a Scottish doctor by the name of James Braid re-coined it as 'hypnotism'. All of us have no doubt seen on television the likes of Paul McKenna and others putting people under hypnosis and making them do the strangest and funniest of things. So, there is no denying that the human mind can be tricked into believing and doing the most strangest of things.

HYPNOSIS, THE PRO'S AND CON'S.

Well Known French UFOlogist Jacques Vallee is open minded as to the use of hypnosis in retrieving any possible hidden subconscious recall, but he had this to say in regards to the UFO Abduction issue,

"These events take place in a reality we simply do not understand. They have an impact on a part of the human mind we have not discovered. I believe the UFO phenomenon is one of the ways through which an alien form of intelligence of incredible complexity is communicating with us symbolically" *(Jacques Vallee.)*

In her research for her book Chosen, (Recollections of Abductions Through Hynotherapy) Yvonne R. Smith discovered that the American Medical Association and several highly respected medical schools, accepted the medical use of hypnosis. Yvonne was also surprised to learn that hypnosis was being used (on some occassions) as anesthesia on surgical procedures. The bottom line is, should we be using regressive hypnosis on people who claim UFO abductions. Well, we could argue about this all day, and I'm afraid that come what may, it would appear that the jury will always be out on this one.

THE ABDUCTION PROCEDURE

Abduction researcher Joe Nyman outlined a number of what he felt were strong characterists of the UFO abduction state.

1) That there were an anxious anticipation of something unknown. The abductee would feel that something 'familiar yet unknown' would soon occur.

2) There would be a transition of consciousness and immediate aftermath after the abduction. In other words, an altered state of consciousness would overtake the abductee rendering them docile and incapable of resistance.

3) Then we have the psycho physical imposition and interaction. Which effectively implies that the alien beings, would forcibly perform medical and scientific procedures on the abductee.

4) After the initial abduction, the beings (in some cases) would provide reassurance, with positive feelings, and a sense of purpose. The 'beings' would act more benevolently, and the experience would take a turn for positive.

5) What follows would be a transition of consciousness back to the normal waking state. The altered state of consciousness induced by the 'beings' in the second step ends.

6) There then would follow a rapid forgetfulness of most, if not all memory, of the abduction experience. Memories would gradually fade.

7) However, the end result would be what Joe calls, the 'Marker Stage'. Where missing time would be noted. Followed by bizarre and seemingly non-sensical memories of being abducted by aliens. Recurring nightmares would also be a facet of this stage.

The above is definitely a feature of the stages of a UFO abduction. There might be some differences where abductees may be shown around the craft, or shown on a screen, the future destruction of planet Earth, but in the main, the above seven steps are routinely followed by the 'captors'.

DIFFERENT DISGUISES.

Many researchers have stated that the 'beings' that we are encountering today, have always been with us, it's just that we are interpreting them differently today. We see them as visitors from space, whilst our forefathers saw them as Elves, Trolls, Pixies, and a whole range of other small and unusual type creatures. History is awash with reports of the little people, more so from Ireland. The Irish tell many tales of Leprechauns. In Peter Haining's fascinating case study book entitled, 'The Leprechaun's Kingdom' (Souvenir Press, England 1979), he informs the reader about cave fairies and the many tales of the little people which have been documented throughout Irish history. Peter explains that there are a number of cases in which the 'wee folk' have spirited away human beings, and taken them to a land which is wondrous and unusual, and that if they decide to stay they will be treated like Kings.

However, we are also told that for those people who get spirited away and do not wish to stay, they find that upon their return to their own village or town, that there is a period of missing time, that many years have elapsed, and that their family have long since died! We can see the parallels here with

287

the current day UFO abduction phenomenon, in that people get abducted and are taken to a wondrous place, the only difference is, upon their return, although there usually is a period of missing time, which is usually a couple of hours, but sometimes days, there is not the long period of time related in the past in which people have returned home to find everyone has since died. I have mentioned the writings of French Man Jacques Vallee throughout this book, and he was of the opinion that there are very strong similarities between the abduction of humans by the faerie folk and what is currently going on today. British authors Jenny Randles and Peter Hough in their book, 'The Complete Book Of UFOs' (Piatkus Books England 1994), show comparisons between the toadstools supposedly the domain of the faerie folk, to the similar shape of the present day 'Flying Saucer'. In effect, and both Jenny and Peter have the same speculations, in ancient times, those individuals would have interpreted Extraterrestrials and their 'Flying Saucers', as fairies and toadstools due to the fact that they, at this point in the history of mankind, had no concept of outer space. It's a fanciful idea, and if one thinks about it, it begins to look fairly reasonable. The small people, the kidnapping, the showing of their home location, the missing time. Some might say we have been too busy looking elsewhere, and that either these truly are Extraterrestrials, or they are small creatures who inhabit other dimensions around us, and can interpenetrate on occasions and interact with us for their own agenda.

FALSE MEMORY SYNDROME.

The idea that some people can be fooled into remembering events that have no basis in reality, is something that has been talked about by many people over the past ten years or so. Are people susceptible to this sort of thing, can people really believe in something that happened to them which has no basis in fact? Well apparently they can. The false memory syndrome can be applied to many aspects of life of which for the point of this book, we are only interested in the UFO aspect. Some researchers state that young children and the elderly and people with short attention spans, are the most likely candidates to concoct false memories. However, having said that, false memory syndrome can also apply to many other people as well, from the college graduate to the University professor. The false memory syndrome became public knowledge as an 'effect' some years back, when the Orkney Child abuse scandal broke, in which several parents were accused of abusing their children. Such was the interrogation of the children by social workers, that the kids ended up believing that their parents had indeed abused them. After a long court case, the case was eventually thrown out. The False memory Syndrome, from now on (FMS) is described as a serious form of psychopathology characterised by strongly believed pseudo-memories of childhood abuse. The term was created by (FMS) Foundation, a national organisation based in Philadelphia, Pennsylvania. As of the winter of 1995, they had over 6,OOO families nationwide who claimed that their children had falsely accused them of abuse. Flashbacks and memory retrieval can come about in a number of ways. When 1n 1987, Whitley Strieber's book "Communion" came out, which featured an illustration of one of the 'Greys on it's front cover, thousands of people across America had uncomfortable feelings and memories of which they could not explain. This also happened here in the U.K. people upon seeing this face, somehow 'knew it' and it filled them with confusion and in some cases terror.

There are a number of ways in which people may feel that they have had a 'close encounter experience' that has no basis in reality. We looked at the false memory syndrome, let us now look at yet another avenue which some people suggest could explain the UFO abduction phenomenon, and that is the subject of Electromagnetic influences on the brain, could these cause the percipient to 'believe' that he has been abducted?

PERSINGER AND BUDDEN'S THEORY.

Firstly we'll look at what Michael Persinger has to say. Persinger (Born. June 26th 1945. Died. August 14th 2018) was a psychologist whose initial work within the UFO abduction field involved geology and geophysics. Englishman Craig Roberts compiled a marvellous dissertation submitted in partial fulfilment for his Bachelor of Science Degree in Psychology at the University of Southampton of which I take the following facts. We learn that Persinger (1976) assessed 7OOO reports of unusual events spanning a 16O year period. Patterns emerged linking geophysical processes with verbal accounts of experiences within the locality of these geophysical processes.

He found that luminous phenomenon observed near or on the ground before, during, and after earthquakes (seismic activity), could quite easily be mistaken by a watchful observer, as a fanciful UFO. As a human being is a biosystem including the characteristic of being a complex structure of weak electrical and magnetic fields, Persinger (1976) theorised that the luminous phenomenon generated by seismic activity, (being electrically charged) could have a profound effect on the percipients electrical make up. For instance, if the luminous phenomenon approached the percipient, it could be labelled an attack, whereas a stable light could be conducting surveillance. Direct effects include close proximity sensations, specific brain area electrical stimulation, amnesia and exposure after effects. Close proximity sensations would include 'tingling', 'prickly sensation', coupled with piloerection and apprehension. Hippocampal and temporal lobe stimulation, could allow percipients to gain access to vivid imagery which may become indistinguishable from reality. Basically what Persinger proposed, is that luminous phenomenon produced by earth bound geological processes, not only 'mimic' UFO behaviour, but the electromagnetism released by them, effects temporal lobe structures in the percipient's brain causing them to believe they have seen an extraterrestrial craft, or in extreme cases, to have been abducted by aliens. As temporal lobe stimulation can produce vivid memories which have no object reality, the event can be easily 'mixed up' in a concoction of reality and fantasy. Of course this is all very well, and this 'theory' may well explain a number of UFO events, but I'm sure that no matter how well Persinger's theory looks, it has a long way to go before we can safely say that it explains 'all UFO events'.

ALBERT BUDDEN'S THEORY.

Another researcher who has been looking at different ways to explain the UFO phenomenon, is Englishman Albert Budden. Albert, from London, advocates that 'Electromagnetic Pollution' can solve not only the whole UFO phenomenon, but it can also solve why people experience ghosts, poltergeists, and a whole range of other weird and wonderful phenomena. Albert maintains that electromagnetic pollution, mostly from microwave transmitters and other high charge frequency transmitters, has a direct result on each and everyone of us on this planet and that this electromagnetic stress, can sometimes cause a breakdown of the body's regulatory functions, which in turn triggers visionary messages telling the individual that their health is under threat from electromagnetic fields. Albert has written three books on his theories, *'Allergies And Aliens', Discovery Times Press 1994, and 'Electric UFOs', Blandford Books 1998*, and *'UFOs, Psychic Close Encounters', Cassell/Blandford 1995.*

Albert agrees with a lot of what Michael Persinger states, but advances his theories into different areas. As stated, Albert maintains that some people who live in 'Hot Spots' which are close to radio transmission masts, power stations or which sees a lot of electromagnetic saturation, somehow become electrically hypersensitive. They may have strange dreams, perhaps of aliens and space-craft, they may begin to suffer from allergies due to the many emissions which interpenetrate their bodies. The temporal lobe area in their brain, might, when stimulated, give them a feeling of a 'presence' in the room beside them. In his thought provoking and extremely interesting and certainly different book, entitled, 'Allergies And Aliens', (Discovery Times Press 1994), Albert relates that the electrical stimulation of the hippocampal amygdaloid complex of people within 'surgical' settings, is well known to evoke specific imagery and vivid phenomenon. This includes dream like imagery, out of the body experiences, a sense of meaning, apprehension or fear, and also the experience of tingling sensations and vibrations. Some people even experience a horrible metallic taste in their mouths. All this, he states, can also occur within heavily polluted electromagnetic areas. Not only that, some people can also experience and are able to register, radio frequency transmissions acoustically as humming, buzzing, clicks, or a high pitched whine, which is all dependent on the frequency modulation, duration of signal, and pulsed modes and wave forms. It is Albert's contention therefore, that people who are subjected to prolonged exposure to sources of radio frequencies, microwave transmissions and other Electrical fields, end up exhibiting signs of unstableness, and may experience hallucinations of which could conjure up imagery of aliens and space ships not to mention ghosts and spirits. So in effect, Albert is urging caution, that we should not seek to be narrow minded and think that we are being visited by 'aliens' in their fanciful flying machines, the answer, he speculates, could be much closer to home. Again, like many of the theories we have heard so far, this one might indeed explain away *'some'* (but not all) UFO experiences. A larger study however would need to be undertaken in order to test if there is any real strength to Albert's case. Albert is not the first researcher to have speculated along these lines, but his book is certainly a masterful example of how we should not ignore any possibility just because it appears strange.

So, as stated, Albert has clearly found that electrical hypersensitivity comes through prolonged exposure to electrical field sources, (microwave transmissions etc). This can have a direct result on people experiencing a whole range of unusual phenomena, from witnessing ghosts, to seeing UFOs, to seeing alien beings to experiencing Deja Vu. Again I feel that a lot of what Persinger and Budden claim, can indeed be factual, and relevant to the UFO study, but I feel that it falls short to explain 'all' cases. There are many people who do not live in electromagnetic pollution areas, Many live out in the open or in barren wilderness, for example, who still experience UFO sightings and UFO abductions, and I do not believe for one moment that these theories could explain these cases. Then of course we have people who do indeed live next to large power sub stations or close to transmitter masts, who do 'not' have any problems, who do not witness UFOs or aliens. It is one thing to come up with a theory to explain UFO cases, but it is another to prove that theory profusely and with the utmost conviction. Nevertheless, we should not ignore the important work that Michael Persinger and Albert Budden are doing in regards to the UFO enigma and they are to be commended for their sterling and important work.

We are looking at the many ingredients that make up, (or could make up) what has come to be termed, a 'UFO Abduction'. We have to address and look down many different avenues before we can arrive at any one firm conclusion. Some people may say that there is no firm conclusion, that UFO abductions are all in the mind. People may not necessarily be making them up, but they are being misled by functions in the brain into 'believing' that what they have seen is real and has a basis in 'our world'. Just like when we see a heat haze just above the surface of a road on a hot sunny day. It may look like water, thankfully we know that this is but an illusion. But a visionary memory is one thing, how can the mind play tricks upon someone to give them scars on their bodies! Well scars too can be explained. The human mind is an incredible organ, an organ that perhaps we don't yet fully understand. We may like to think we do, but I'm sure that there are segments within the brain whose functions we can but ponder on.

They say that mankind only uses around 10% of his brain, and that those gifted psychics in our world, somehow have access to those other parts of the brain to assist them with their special powers. But can the brain really produce marks and weal's on one's body, marks which to all intents and purpose look like burns, and cuts! Believe it or not it can! Many professional hypnotists will tell you that it is entirely possible that when you place a subject under hypnosis the human mind is more receptive. I've spoken to a few hypnotists who say that they have said to someone who was under hypnosis, that they were placing a match underneath the palm of their hand, and upon doing so, the subject reacted swiftly to this suggestion by drawing their hand away. Once out of hypnosis the subject was informed that no such match was lit and placed under their palm, but when looking at their palm, they are surprised to see a red mark (similar to a burn). Another hypnotist said to me that he informed his hypnotic subject that a red hot poker was being placed on his fore-arm. All he did was touch his subject with his finger, however this brought out a cry from his subject and a red weal began to appear on his arm. These are but a few illustrations that the human mind, whilst under hypnosis, can produce marks on the body. Stigmata (the alleged marks of Christ that appear on the hands, body, and head's of people) may not be the Spiritual thing that most people believe, they may all be psychosomatic in origin.

Author Ted Harrison in his excellent book, *'Stigmata, a Medieval Mystery For A Modern Age', (Harper/Colllins 1994)* mentions the fact that, many doctors agree that emotional stress of various kinds, can produce marks on the skin. In the medical Journal 'The Lancet' of December 28th 1946, a case was described of a thirty five year old man who, while under close observation in a hospital, had produced wounds on his arms corresponding to the rope marks he had received nine years earlier when being forcibly restrained. The marks were clear indentations which also bled. His doctor concluded that there was no way to describe what he had seen other than a 'genuine psychosomatic phenomenon'. Author Ted Harrison goes on to describe many other cases from medical records of people having these marks and burns just suddenly rear up, all a product of the mind, and all having a psychosomatic origin. We have learned that not only hypnosis can produce marks and weal's on the body that previously were not there, but that these marks can suddenly appear of their own accord as well. But was this the case in our study of the A7O Incident? Both Garry and Colin came back from that Incident with marks on their bodies which previously were not there. Garry had a mark at the back of his head, whilst Colin had a strange mark at the base of his penis. Many abductees claim that when they have 'come out' of their experience, they suddenly find strange marks on their bodies, this is a very common feature of UFO abductions. But could Garry and Colin's marks have been of a psychosomatic origin? I don't think so, for these marks can still be seen to this day. Marks on UFO abductees bodies are one thing, but what about some one claiming a UFO abduction in front of people and yet those people see absolutely nothing! Well this has happened, as the following case now illustrates.

THE MAUREEN PUDDY CASE.

Before I begin to recount this fascinating case, I was just like to make this remark. *"Just because one might find that one bank note is forged, this doesn't mean to say that all bank notes are forged"*. What I am implying with this is, the following case, claimed by the witness to have been a UFO abduction, has no basis in fact, but this does not mean that 'all' UFO abductees are making these claims up. See what you make of this.

Mrs Maureen Puddy had her first UFO sighting back in July 1972, this comprised of a large UFO which hovered above her car on a road near the town of Melbourne in Australia. The object itself was the classic flying saucer shape, like two soup plates joined at the rim. Maureen also heard a low humming sound coming from the object which also exhibited a bright blue glow. Maureen was quite frightened by this object and hoped never to see it again. Sadly this was not to be the case, for on the 25th of July 1972, she encountered a similar object on the same stretch of road at almost the same location. As she tried to drive off, the engine of her car cut out and she claimed to have heard (in her head) the words, *"We mean you no harm"*.

After this event things were fine and no further UFO sightings were made, however, sometime during February 1973, Mrs Puddy received a telepathic message telling her to go back to the stretch of road where she had had her earlier UFO encounters. Mrs Puddy realised the importance of corroborating witnesses, it was one thing to witness a UFO oneself, but wouldn't it be all the better if you could get someone else there to confirm what you saw! And so Mrs Puddy decided to contact two UFO Investigators by the names of Paul Norman and Judith Magee. (Both UFO researchers had in fact been contacted by Mrs Puddy after her first UFO experience). These Investigators met up with Mrs Puddy at the site of her encounter where she informed them that on the way to this location, she saw an 'alien' who was made up out of gold foil, who 'materialised' in her car. A short while later whilst the three of them were sitting in the car, Maureen shouted out that she could see this 'alien' and continued to speak about what she was seeing and experiencing. Incredibly, Maureen claimed that she was 'kidnapped' and was now inside a UFO. But the fact of the matter was, that Maureen was still sitting in full view of both Investigators in the car! She hadn't gone anywhere! Both Investigators did state however, that she had a tranced look on her face and did not appear to know where she was.

So what can we make of that? Here was a woman who claimed to have been abducted, and yet she was sitting in full view of two UFO Investigators! Was she really taken over by some 'alien being' out of her own physical reality into some other yet undiscovered alternative reality! well I guess we'll never really know. This incident makes me recall the evidence for ghosts. There are many cases on record in which a number of people have been in a room within a haunted building and suddenly a ghost appears, yet only some of these witnesses actually see it, the rest do not! We also have on record groups of people who have been looking up into the night sky at a UFO, and only some of them see it. Why is this? Are some people more receptive to seeing strange phenomena? I think that this is a strong possibility. I think that the more psychic one is, the more chance there is of them witnessing unusual phenomenon. But that is only a personal opinion and this of course may not be the case.

In the A7O case, not only were Garry and Colin abducted, but Colin recalls seeing the car in, *("A big bright metallic room")*. The Avis family of whom we learned about earlier and who were abducted near the town of Aveley in England, also claimed that they saw their car inside the object that they found themselves in. This would certainly clear up the issue of, 'what happened to the car when both men were abducted, surely someone must have seen an abandoned car in the road'? This brings us to our next line of enquiry, the Alvin Lawson experiments. Can people who have had no real UFO experience come up with a typical UFO abduction scenario under regressive hypnosis? Alvin Lawson decided to find out.

THE ALVIN LAWSON EXPERIMENTS.

This whole series of experiments initially came about through a colleague of Alvin's, a UFO Investigator by the name of John DeHerrera. DeHerrera was puzzled when a witness of whom he had been Investigating, refused to believe that he had been abducted but once this witness was put under hypnotic regression, he came away with a startling story of UFOs and aliens. Alvin Lawson and John Deherrera, decided to pry more into this strange aspect, and with the assistance of a Dr McCall at a hospital in Anaheim in California, created 'controlled experiments'. They managed to secure the services of some students from local colleges and communities to volunteer (without pay) to be guinea pigs for an experiment to be imaginary UFO abductees. They wondered that if placed under hypnosis, these students who had no UFO abduction experience, would come out with the same wondrous recollections as those who claimed to have actually had these effects. Would this happen? They aimed to find out.

Incredibly, a number of these test students did indeed come out with amazing recollections of being taken by aliens and subjected to clinical examinations. Even more surprising, was the fact that the hypnotherapist didn't even have to give any leading questions to get this, these students came out with this direct without any prodding or suggestion! This is all very well and fine, and sceptics use the Alvin Lawson experiments to state that there is no reality to the UFO abduction phenomenon, but there is more to this than meets the eye. For there are some very important facts about this that we should not overlook, and those facts are.

(A) 'Real' UFO abductees exhibit strong emotional responses during their recounting of their experience. The volunteers of the Alvin Lawson experiments usually controlled their emotions, they were not so strong and emotional as the 'real' UFO abductees.

(B) 'Real' UFO abductees continued to have strange dreams about their experience, the volunteers of the Lawson experiments, did not.

(C) 'Real' UFO abductees experienced disturbing psychic and emotional effects long after their initial experience. The volunteers did not.

(D) Another point to bear in mind, is the fact that the volunteers in the Lawson experiments, were all keen to fabricate and colour their accounts to please the hypnotherapist. Although admittedly, all of the students used in these experiments had to sign forms to the effect that they knew next to nothing about the UFO enigma or UFO abductions. Lawson only wanted students who knew little, if anything of this enigma.

It's clear to see then, that the UFO abduction phenomena is very complex indeed. The human brain is a fascinating organ, an organ of which we know so little about. But is it an organ that is only 'making' these accounts up due to perhaps the stress of the individual? Or is it something more. We have learned that there can indeed be other 'possible' answers to account for UFO abductions, and no doubt I'm sure that there are many others. At the end of the day, no matter what, there will always be those people that no matter what type of evidence you put down to them, they won't accept. Some people just simply refuse to believe their own 'eyes'.

CHILD UFO ABDUCTIONS

It's bad enough having adult UFO abductions, but we have to bear in mind the harsh reality of children being abducted by 'beings' from elsewhere. The reports that we have from children, are just as explicit and similar to their adult counterparts. It's been said that some of these child abductees, have family members who have reported having their own UFO abduction experiences. This again leads us to consider what other UFOlogists are noting, and that is, that UFO abductions may be a generational thing. In other words, that people from the same family tree, have been abducted throughout the centuries. More so children who have family members in the Military. British researcher Jenny Randles has been quoted as saying,

"The abduction is essentially a young person's experience. Given the reproductive focus of the alleged abductions, it is not surprising that one man reported being rejected because he had undergone a vasectomy"!

CREATING A HYBRID ALIEN RACE

There are many thousands (if not millions) of claimed UFO abductions, that have happened the world over, suffice it to say that people 'do' report these things, but what are they trying to tell us? The main consensus of opinion as to what these UFO abductions really are, is the following.

That they are some form of genetic interbreeding programme by the aliens on humankind to somehow repopulate their dying race. They want to become a part of us, receive our emotions, our feelings, our fears, our loves. To do this, they need to abduct humans to experiment on, whereby ensuring that this new gene pool will be sufficient enough to create a new hybrid species!

This I admit all seems fantastic and smacks of a Star Trek episode. Of course it's incredible, of course it sounds ridiculous, but the fact of the matter is, and whether we want to believe it or not, this is what thousands of UFO abductees are telling us. Females have had their ova removed from their bodies, other females have been re-abducted and shown a hideous half human half alien child of which it's telepathically stated, (part belongs to them) This genetic interbreeding programme is something which many of us cannot comprehend, especially when we know that sperm and ova samples are stored at many world wide hospitals, why can't these intrusive 'aliens' take the samples from there, wouldn't that be a better option? One would certainly think so, but apparently not. Some researchers believe, that it is this strong show of emotion by humans whilst they are being abducted, that these alien visitors are also interested in! If they are to achieve our emotions, they want to see what fear and anger is. All abductees tell of these beings as being like robots, they have no feelings, they go about their business with no visible and outward signs of emotion. They constantly tell us that they will not harm us, that all this is being done for our own good. But the fact of the matter remains, this is downright intrusive, this is done 'without our consent' and is an affront to all that is good.

Surely highly technological beings (if that is what they are), must know that what they are doing is wrong. It's no good thinking (as some have said) that we do the same with animals. We tag cattle and sheep, we experiment on cats and dogs and perform experiments on other animals just for our own ends. This is wrong, and they must know this. Are human beings so insignificant that we don't warrant any compassion from these 'beings'. Of course the biggest and most strangest aspect of them all, is the fact that, if these 'beings' are indeed doing genetic experiments on human beings, why are they still doing them today? This has been going on now for over 50 years, surely they would by now, have enough genetic information to last them a life time! But then again, perhaps we don't fully understand their 'true' agenda, (if they have one). Maybe we are looking at the subject of UFO abductions the wrong way, ie, that we can't see the trees for the forest!

Was the event that happened to both Garry and Colin part of this genetic interbreeding programme? Why did 'they' have to take them from a moving vehicle, why couldn't they have taken them from the comfort of their own beds just like many of the other UFO abductions? I guess we'll never really know. Many researchers believe, (and it has been found to be the case) that the people that have been abducted, have actually had it happen to them before in their life's, and what they think of as a big event, was only one of many. There are a number of the world's top researchers who believe that a genetic interbreeding programme is certainly what is transpiring. Some even go so far as to say that these experiments are not only being conducted by what we call 'the Greys', but are being conducted by many other races as well. At the end of the day however, there are no real answers, and no matter 'how it looks', and whatever we may feel, we cannot say with any certainty that a genetic interbreeding programme really is the answer.

MAKES NO SENSE!

One thing that I've always pondered about when it comes to UFO abductions, is that fact that we don't appear to have clever aliens? And what I mean by that, can be shown in the following examples.

In the famous American Betty and Barney Hill UFO abduction which occurred back in 1961, the so called 'aliens' discovered that Barney's teeth were removable and when they tried to remove Betty's teeth they found that they couldn't. Surprised, one of the aliens said to Betty, *"Why do Barney's teeth come out and yours do not"?* To me, that's not very clever for a so called advanced race of superior beings! In Yvonne R. Smith's book, Chosen, (Recollections of Abductions Through Hynotherapy) *Bachstage Entertainment 2008. USA.* She discusses the case of one abductee, Laci. Laci had been scuba diving near the island of Catalina off the coast of Southern California when she had an abduction experience. Apparently whilst the aliens were touching her they suddenly got confused with the wet suit that she was wearing. They thought that it was her skin! Again I ask, 'superior all knowledgable beings'!

SO, WHAT'S GOING ON?

We have seen from above, that there a number of possible explanations to account for UFO sightings and UFO abductions, I dare say, there are those that would say there are more, from drug induced hallucinations to some medical condition etc. The answer, undoubtedly is in there somewhere. Sceptics and debunkers will also wear their coloured blinkers, whilst free thinkers, people who are prepared to look 'out of the box', will look carefully and closely at all possibilities before making a judgement. The bottom line is, dear reader, that 'something is clearly going on'. Do I have a definitive answer as to what's going on? No, I don't. But it is my own personal belief that we are dealing with other races who are entering our airspace for their clandestine operations. I don't have an answer as to why they are doing what they are doing, I can but speculate with the rest of them. It 'appears' to me, and I did say 'appears', that there is some kind of inter-breeding program being orchestrated by these 'beings'. That's as may be, but for goodness sake, when will they stop? They have been abducting people for well over 50 years (if not more) surely they have enough genetic material from us by now. Or, on the other hand, are they 'changing us'. I mentioned this earlier on in the book. If we (mankind) are their experiment, in that they seeded us here on planet Earth, then they may see us as a 'change in progress', but what, we may ask, is the outcome? Sadly all we can do at this point in time, is speculate until 'they' 'themselves' decide to come out of the closet and make their intentions know. Even if some race of extraterrestrials did seed us here on this planet, its quite incredible to think that we humans share 98% of our DNA with chimpanzees and 36% with fruit flies and 25% with rice and grapes?

In his wonderful book Aliens (Past Present Future) Watkins Media Ltd. ISBN: 978-1-78028-968-7. Ron Millar states that NASA's Kepler Space Observatory, found that 22 per cent of the stars that it has observed have planets that are potentially like our own. It can be concluded therefore, that 2 billion planets in 'our' galaxy are capable of supporting life quite an astonishing fact. Of course, SETI (The Search for Extra-terrestrial Intelligence) have invested a quarter of a billion dollars into looking for life 'out there' and as yet, other than a 'wow' signal, we have found nothing, but then again, maybe our technology is not in keeping with an alien technology and therefore for the moment, we will not make that contact!

Ron then asks about the physicality of these aliens that visit our planet, e.g., they all have two arms two legs one head all similar to humans, moreover, the 'grey aliens' can be traced right back through world mythology as their counterparts have been fairies, trolls, leprechauns, etc. Today we see aliens, yesterday we saw leprechauns. The lost time aspect of UFO abductions also has its counterpart in the similarities of people being abducted by fairies and coming back months, if not years later. Ron quite rightly states that there have been thousands of UFO abductions and yet no one has come back with a piece of their craft, or even a miniscule piece of alien technology (there might be a reason for that Ron!) Ron also asks the question about that 'first contact'! What would happen'? We are told that in a recent survey two thirds of all Americans believe that aliens exist. 80% believe that they would be far more intelligent and technologically advanced than us. But probably the biggest question of all, relates to the religions of the world, would there be any divisions between them all should an alien presence make itself known? Buddhism already accepts that life exists out there in the vastness of space, and Ron poses a very interesting question when he asks, would visiting aliens be some kind of missionaries who have travelled here to baptise us in the name of their own God? Indeed, would there be countless Messiahs from other world's that might come to planet Earth to save us from our sins? Or, if there is but one God as stated by our own Bible, would he/she come back as a saviour to mankind? How would we communicate with an alien race that is so far advanced than us? It may well be like a man trying to talk to an ant? And let's be honest, should we even be trying to communicate with an alien race? Ron quite rightly reminds us

303

on what happened when the Spanish discovered the Inca empire in the 16th century, the Incas were enslaved and had to adopt to their Christian religion, and if they didn't, they were put to death. Ron further states that another problem mankind may face, is that should an alien civilisation ever come to planet Earth, might they not inadvertently bring some type of alien diseases with them that could wipe our planet out! Or, if the shoe was on the other foot, would our own common cold destroy them as we saw in the movie 'War of the Worlds'. Ron states, and I totally agree with him, that when one is looking forward to the first contact between aliens and humans, one might be wise to stop and think, very carefully about what one is wishing for. I for one, wholeheartedly agree with that statement. For let's be honest, any visiting alien may not have our best interests at heart. But we must ask, 'what were these creatures that captured Garry and Colin really wanting with them'? We can but speculate. They were obviously taken for something, there is no denying that. But what? Author Nigel Kerner in his book, 'The Song of The Greys', Hodder And Stoughton, 338 Euston Road, London, NW1 3BH, believes that the greys are on a mission, not only to seek out sperm and ova from their unfortunate victims, but in reality they are in point of fact searching for human souls! Kerner believes that 'the greys' were manufactured rather than being born, and that they are on a mission to seek from us where our soul lies, and essentially how they can incorporate 'our' soul into their own persona of 'being'. Moreover, as they currently don't have a 'soul' of their own, they view humankind as a threat to their existence should we ever physically meet on a world wide scale, rather than their numerous intrusions that are currently ongoing. Apparently they are also aware of the survival of humans after physical material death, and that to them is the crux of their search, the soul and the continuity of life. (Albeit in a different condition) Quite an interesting concept from Nigel Kerner, and one that is shared by many UFOlogists the world over. But again, is that the answer?

There are countless thousands of UFOlogists the world over trying to uncover what is behind the UFO Enigma. Investigative journalist and sceptic Dr David Clarke, has had a life long interest in all things weird and wonderful. I've met David a few times and found him a lovely and engaging person. He certainly digs deep when it comes to trying to get some answers to explain the UFO mystery. And a few years ago, he sent me his book, 'The UFO Files'. (The Inside Story Of Real Life Sightings) Bloomsbury Publishing ISBN: 978-1-4081-6489-1 In the book, David states that the vast majority of Air Ministry, RAF and MoD Files from 1947 to 1967 were 'lost or burned' decades before the Freedom Of Information Act arrived. David quite rightly states that by allowing the destruction of these swathes of intelligence records on UFOs, the MoD (Ministry of Defence) have unintentionally provided a stick for conspiracy theorists to beat them with. I certainly would concur with that, but again, maybe that is true, in that the MoD really didn't think that there wouldn't be any significance of retaining these files and so therefore got shot of them!

David states quite clearly that today around Planet Earth, we have sophisticated early warning radar systems that can detect objects the size of a pencil in orbit around the Earth. That UFOs may not be a threat from space, but rather a threat from another country here on Earth which cannot be ruled out. The skies of the Earth are indeed being scrutinized he states, but it's by our own technology. David quite rightly states that the risk of unexpected UFOs, whatever their source, could trigger off an apocalyptic international confrontation. However, I would have to disagree with David here, because yes we have indeed amazing sophisticated systems looking into space and our radar systems may pick up a pencil sized object in space, but if we are dealing with a technology far in advance of our own, then we surely have to agree that 'they' whoever 'they' are, may be able to 'by-pass' our radar systems for them not to be seen or picked up. Their technology may be such, that it would be like showing a caveman a 50 inch flat screen television with moving pictures, would he be able to work it out and know what it was?........NO. And what we also have to bear in mind dear reader, is that for every UFO report that was sent to the MoD, just think of how many that were not! It's fair to say that in most instances when someone witnesses a UFO, they are frightened to come forward and log their sighting. So this now begs the question, how many more really great UFO sightings are 'out there in the U.K. that we will never hear from, simply because of the 'fear factor' from witnesses who don't want to come forward? I'll let you be the judge of that.

I've said it before and I'll say it again, if UFOs are indeed being piloted by visitors from outer space (and I do believe that this is the case) then they are travelling thousands of miles to planet Earth just to play 'peek a book' with mankind this massive effort is just plain ridiculous. There is an agenda, there must be. Garry and Colin were taken for something, but sadly all we can do is but speculate on what that something was. It's fair to say that I am trying to get my head around how many different races are apparently visiting planet Earth. It just seems incredible to me it really does. And it would appear that each and every one of these races don't want to show their hand and come forward to the leaders of our planet, why? They are appearing to Joe Bloggs in woods and the like, but won't appear in front of Presidents and Prime Ministers. What is their agenda? What is going on? The reports state that there are many different 'entities' being seen. Some are hairy bipedal creatures, very similar it must be said to sightings of Big Foot and Sasquatch. There are reports of the Greys of which both Garry and Colin encountered. And then we have reports of the Chupacabra, a creature mainly seen in the Americas, more often across the island of Puerto Rico. Some believe that this creature has nothing to do with UFOs, that it could have been genetically engineered by scientists and either let loose, or it got loose and has successfully breeded to ensure its survival. But that's just speculation.

But are we (mankind) ready to face another interstellar race? Let's be honest, we can't even get on with our own neighbours here on Earth, (look at North Korea, and the Middle East for instance) Would meeting another race of 'people' from another star system wreck our planet and destabilise what we Earthlings have produced and invented over the years? We have seen what the American Calvary did to the Indian Nation. That was the Indian's land for centuries, and along come the 7th Calvary and changed (dare I say wiped out) the Indian Nation and changed their way of life forever. Incredibly there are a few tribes in the jungles of South America which are being found today, and if we interact with them, will we force or pass on our technology and ways upon them? Will they soon be drinking coca cola and listening and watching our radio and television broadcasts, I'm sure you see where I am going with this.

Garry and Colin were taken into an environment that was so detached from our reality, they just couldn't comprehend what was going on. How could they, they had no yard stick in which to gauge this incredible change of environment. In a strange sort of way, it would be like an ant living next to a busy interstate highway. He would be aware that something was going on around him, he could hear and see things, but he couldn't comprehend what.

In our final chapter, I'm asking the question, should we be alarmed? Is the agenda of these 'beings' from elsewhere, something which is not beneficial to the betterment of mankind? Or, should we have no fears as to what their hidden agenda is. That come what may, whatever is going on, is totally out of our hands, and that what will be, will be. Let's speculate shall we?

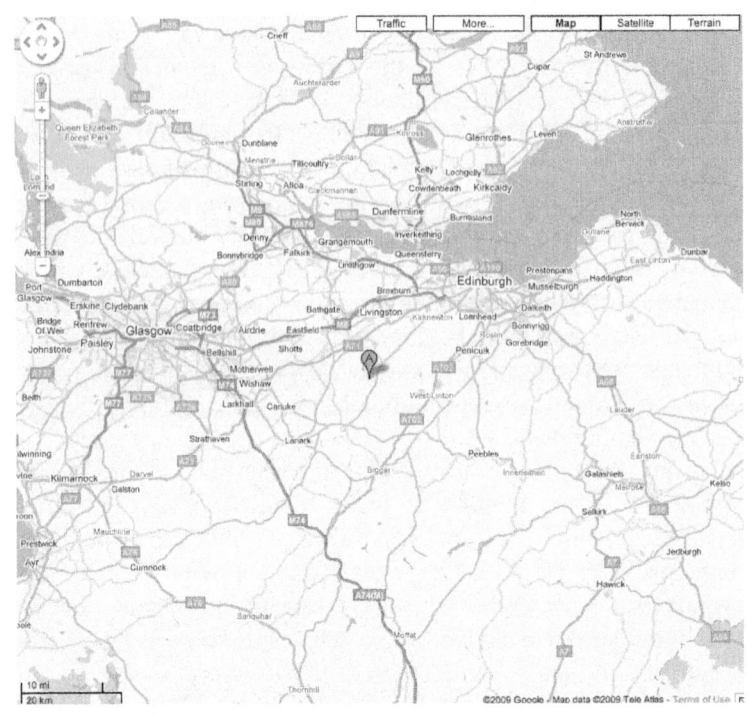

A Marks the spot where the A70 Road is.

Approaching the blind bend. (c) Google Earth

The fields opposite the abduction site. (c) Google Earth

Where the event happened.

CHAPTER FOUR

SHOULD WE BE ALARMED?

*"A die-hard UFO fan who will accept no criticism, is not so
different from the diehard sceptic who will accept no evidence"*
Ron Millar from the book 'Aliens Past Present & Future'

There are some researchers who state that some of the
World's Governments are in cahoots with these 'beings,' and if
this is the case, then this is beyond shocking. There have been
people who, after being abducted, state that they saw Military
men on board these craft, or in rooms with these 'beings'.
Again we are taking the testimony from these witnesses at face
value, but can there be any truth in it. In James Bartley's
thought provoking if not controversial article entitled, *'From
The Ashes Of Unknown MILABS (Military Abductions)* he
states that certain elements of the American Military are behind
'some' UFO abductions where people are taken to under
ground establishments for nefarious experiments. James is of
the opinion that the reptilians (a scaly race of alien beings) use,
as he puts it, 'proxies' such as the greys, Insectoids and other
E.T. 'beings' to assist in the bidding of the Military. He further
states that Milab abductees have genetic markers of non human
origin. He stated, and I quote,

" *I have spoken to a number of abductees who served in the
military and during their time in the Armed Forces, these
abductees were used in Milab and Mind Control operations. It
was as if Military Intelligence, or a deep black element thereof,
knew precisely who within the ranks were alien abductees.
Milabs who have served in the military describe being used in a
variety of Mind Control operations some of them involving
extremely high technology, very often in underground
installations. Many report being injected with hypnotic drugs
and having narco-hypnosis and memory erasure procedures
performed upon them. This is done to ensure the Milab forgets
what he has seen or heard during these experiences. Post*

hypnotic commands and programming are instilled into compartmented sections of the Milab's mind. Often times Active Duty Milabs are treated by military psychologist during, and even after, their time in the military. Abductees in all branches of the service have reported being mind controlled during their stints in the military. Many former members of the military continue to be used in Milab operations long after their military career has ended. Civilian Milabs can be found in all walks of life. Some have obvious connections to the military industrial complex whilst others have no connection whatsoever. The obvious question most Milabs ask themselves is, "how did the military find out about me?" Again, it is due to the unique genetic markers contained in the Milabs DNA. The military, being a branch of the federal government, has access to any and all medical records. Even for civilians, there is ample opportunity for the powers that be to obtain DNA samples of the general population"

Quite incredible statements, but is there any real truth in all this? Well again, some would say yes, others no. But if true, then yes, we should be alarmed. In George Bishop's article, 'Aliens? do the Governments really know'? Sent to the author, he states;

"Why would any government hesitate to tell us all they know? The obvious answer is that they don't know any more than we do! They aren't going to admit that they cannot do anything to defend us from visiting aliens are they? Another option is that they don't think we could handle the news of alien races. It would offend our religious beliefs and might cause panic a-la-the 1939 Orson Wells broadcast of War of The Worlds! Another option is that it might cause a social breakdown, as people would think that the alien races have come to save us from disease, daily toil and even perhaps from governments themselves. People would rush off to meet the aliens as some kind of 'Saviour' from Space. There would be economic collapse and the entire structure of our society would grind to a halt. One alternative would be that half the population would see the aliens as saviours and the other half

311

would see them as invaders and demand that the armed forces were sent to repel them"

"Perhaps some governments are in contact with the aliens? Why wouldn't they pass that news on? Obviously it is in their interest to keep the contact quiet. They could exchange technology from the aliens in exchange for something the aliens want from us. They could then trade the advance technology for their own advantage. What on earth could the aliens need from us? Raw materials are far more readily available in space locations than they are here. What is the only commodity that is common on the Earth, but not in space? Actually there are two. The first is water, but there is no shortage of water in space. Water is a relatively simple compound and Hydrogen and Oxygen are probably available in sufficient quantities to make manufacture a relatively simple matter, even if icy comets were not composed of water ice. The second is humanity! Are governments trading people in exchange for technology? I doubt the aliens need whole bodies, but they may well be interested in our DNA or even in blood, plasma or bits of flesh and bone. Thousands, if not millions, of people go missing every year. Where do they go? Do they create new lives elsewhere, or do they simply vanish into the unknown? Military personnel who qualify as 'of no fixed kin' could easily be enlisted into an off-world battalion and posted to some alien station where they would provide information or specimens for some alien zoological park or scientific establishment. That might sound far-fetched, but the rumour has been around for some time and is as possible as may others and more possible than some!"

"Rumours that the government has acquired advanced technology abound, and if true, will need some explanation if there is to be any kind of disclosure. It seems that these exchanges have been made for some decades. There is no doubt that governments have covered up many UFO events and incursions into our space/time. Many may have simple and obvious explanations, so why are they not disclosed immediately? Did it take years or decades to work out the

312

explanation? Do they think that by disclosing years later we won't notice the 'minor' adjustments to witness statements? If aliens are selling technology behind the scenes to our governments, wouldn't that give one government an advantage over another government? Why have they not taken advantage of that technology to overwhelm the other side? Are aliens being careful just what type of technology they trade? Making sure that they don't upset the balance of power in our world. Surely it is time for governments to realise who pays their wages? We think that the tax payers do, but obviously governments have an alternative view! The contrary view that governments do not know any more than we do, suggests that there are no such things as aliens at all! That space is filled with uninhabited and sterile planets. Whilst this is an extreme possibility, it does explain why governments haven't made any disclosures as yet, simply because there are no disclosures to be made".

"Various people have made 'whistle-blower' statements over the years, about various aspects of the aliens who inhabit our sector of space. Disclosures about government collaboration or conflicts with alien races etc. No doubt if they were in a position of trust, they had to sign a 'non-disclosure' contract. Quite stringent penalties would ensue ranging from very heavy fines to imprisonment and even death. How come the whistle blowers are still able to man the lucrative lecture circuits? Again it suggests that they may not be telling the truth, or are being paid by governments to muddy the waters. Will we ever get to hear from our governments what they know? Will there ever be full disclosure? Don't hold your breath!"

I fully accept and agree with all that George Bishop states above. Let's be honest, we've had UFO sightings a plenty, we have UFO witnesses a plenty. We've had the Disclosure Project organised by the National Press Club, where on May 9th 2001, many ex Military and Air Force personnel came forward and put their careers on the line to tell the world about their own incredible UFO encounters. These were not your ordinary Joe Bloggs, these were high standing academic people with

Military backgrounds saying they have seen craft from another world. My point is this, all this is fine and well, but where does this leave us? These stories from high standing academic Military and Naval personnel, were all just stories, some of which, admittedly, were backed up with movie and photographic film. I personally thought that this was it, here at last is testimony from serious responsible Military and Naval people that surely must be taken seriously, but sadly, after a massive media splurge of coverage, it all fell flat, it was yesterday's news, these revelations barley made a dent. There have been other disclosures since then, but again, it wasn't earth shattering. It should have been, because what was being revealed at this Disclosure Conference, was sightings of objects above Military bases, above Military Silos and nuclear bases. Surely this was a concern to someone, at least the President of the United States? But no, as I've stated, it all fell flat. One could surmise two things here.

1) The reason the Government didn't take these Military, Naval and Air Force men seriously at the Disclosure Conference, was simply because they were happy for these insane stories to come out, because it masked what was really going on, and that was highly classified black budget aircraft being test flown above certain areas. All this gave rise to false UFO reports, and boy that was a good cover story?

2) They, the Governments of the World, are in cahoots with these 'beings' from elsewhere and there is some kind of wheeling and dealing going on which you and I are not privy to.

Of course things 'did' change, and quite dramatically as well. The Unites States Government announced to the world that they could not explain what fighter jets captured on film whilst chasing UFOs. It all started when a strange fast moving radar image was caught on the radar scope aboard the USS Nuclear Aircraft Carrier Nimitz, back on November 14th 2004. The fast moving image, was initially caught on radar off the coast of Southern California. An operator onboard the USS Princeton, part of the strike group that were undertaking

314

operations in the area, had picked up this strange return. It wasn't the first time, as this object (and others) had been tracked for two weeks prior to the November 14th incursion into the area. The targets would appear at 80,000 feet, before dramatically descending at speed towards the sea, whereby abruptly stopping at 20,000 feet at which point they hovered. Commander David Fravor a fighter pilot, was despatched to intercept the object which he described as being at least forty feet long, white, and similar to a tic tac sweet.

On the Fox News web site dated December 14th 2020 came the stunning headline,

FIGHTER PILOT SAYS UFO CHASED IN 2004, COMMITTED 'ACT OF WAR'

The story told of Commander David Fravor, who was a former U.S. Navy fighter pilot on board the USS Nimitz. Fravor stated that he was dispatched to investigate these strange radar returns and described what he saw as, "Like nothing I've ever seen". He would go on to describe what he saw as incredibly fast and could turn on a dime. Thankfully Commander David Fravor was not alone in witnessing these objects, other pilots who were also tasked to investigate, also saw it. The footage which was released and de-classified by the Pentagon to the world in 2020, had a profound impact, not only on UFOlogists, but by sceptical people as well. Fravor also stated, and I quote,

"This is not like, 'we saw it and it was gone', or 'I saw lights in the sky and it's gone'. We watched this thing on a crystal clear day with four trained observers"

Fravor would also go on to say that as far as he was concerned, this strange flying object was committing an act of war by not complying with commands from the pilot. No matter how Fravor pushed his aircraft to the limit, he just couldn't get close to it.

315

In the Daily Star newspaper a U.S. Navy veteran by the name of Jason Turner, claimed that this strange object could prove a threat to National Security if it wasn't identified. Jason, a petty officer, was on board the USS Princeton when fighter jets from the nearby ship USS Nimitz, encountered this strange fast moving UFO. Jason made this statement after viewing the released footage. What really made people sit up, was when former CIA Director, John Brennan stated to the world's press that the UFO could be a different 'life form'. One of the newspapers who picked up his comments, was the English Sun. And in their 22nd of December 2020 edition, their headline read, 'WE'RE NOT ALONE' It went on to state that ex CIA Director John Brennan said that, and I quote,

"It was 'presumptuous and arrogant' for people and Governments to believe that the organisms found on earth were the only forms of life in the universe. I think some of the phenomena we're going to be seeing continues to be unexplained, and might, in fact, be some type of phenomenon that is the result of something that we don't yet understand. And that could involve some type of activity that some might say constitutes a different form of life. Life is defined in many different ways. It's a bit presumptuous and arrogant for us to believe that there's no other form of life anywhere in the entire universe".

However, Commander Fravor wasn't the only pilot to witness these strange objects. Some more fighter jets were dispatched to the area of the initial sightings from the USS Nimitz which included pilot Lieutenant Commander Chad Underwood. Underwood's jet was equipped with a state of the art infrared camera (FLIR) and it was Underwood who coined the phrase 'Tic Tac' to describe the shape of the object, which was similar in shape to a Tic Tac sweet. This was from viewing the footage from the camera, as he did not see the actual object himself in flight.

This chapter is all about asking, should we be alarmed with these UFO sightings and abductions? Well, one things for sure, if the fast moving object that was tracked on radar and out flew the Navy jets is 'not' our own technology, then it goes without saying that YES, 'we should be alarmed'. But if this extraordinary sighting was not enough, ten years later (2014) some further fast moving objects were sighted and again caught on film.

Again another set of aircraft carriers (including the USS Nimitz) were undertaking trials off the East Coast of California when more anomalous objects were sighted on radar. Fighter jets from the USS Theodore Roosevelt, were once more dispatched to intercept these fast moving objects, and again some astonishing movie footage was taken. The objects sighted were given the names, GIMBAL and GO FAST. The speed at which these objects were flying at was just astronomical and each pilot who viewed these objects could not identify them. Five years later (September 2019) this sensational news was given to the public, and what made it even more incredible, was that it was the Pentagon that released the information. In a statement to the press, a Pentagon spokeswoman stated that the videos were filmed by naval pilots, and that they were part of a larger issue of an increased number of training range incursions by unidentified aerial phenomena in recent years.

The following year, April 27th 2020, the Pentagon released the three main controversial videos to the world. Needless to say, the furore that followed was incredible, with many people having their say at what 'they' thought was behind these UFO sightings. Moreover, it was the fact that the Department of Defence stating that yes, these objects were unidentified and they couldn't explain them, which drew the most gasps from the media and general public. Was this a confession after all this time that the American Government and Department of Defence were now openly saying that yes, you guys have been right all along, we do have a UFO problem and we are now accepting it! Well not quite. Whilst the astonishing news reverberated around the world, with the incredible footage being shown on numerous T.V. shows across the globe, we were no further forward as to answering what these objects truly were. The consensus of opinion, more by sceptics than anyone else, was that these were our own objects, and due to a phenomenon known as Parallax, these objects were not going as fast as we thought we were. *"It's all to do with perceived motion"*, the sceptics said. Its a combination of perceived differences in motion which can be misconstrued due to either faster speeds or closer distances. If the observer is moving, and the object or objects are stationary, then it gives the false illusion of major differences in distance. But of course, that was but one of many alternative explanations for the Tic Tac UFOs. These ranged from human interpretive error, or a weather balloon. Wikipedia mentions that science writer Mick West, stated that the most likely explanation for at least one of these fast moving objects, was it was a slow moving bird, or even a balloon, and because the jet is moving so fast, we have the paradox of misperception of a fast moving object, which its not. West further stated that the GIMBAL video could be explained as footage of a distant plane, with the apparent rotation being the glare in the infra red camera as it was rotating. Mick West may have given his thoughts as to what these objects could be, but former chairman and member of the Senate Intelligence Committee, one Marco Rubio, went even further and stated that these objects could have been either Russian or Chinese technology!

Whatever these objects were, man made, or misinterpretations, the shock waves were felt around the world. As to these objects truly being extraterrestrial, I guess we'll never know. But again, if they were, their astonishing speeds and manoeuvrability, could prove immense problems to our own technology, and as such, we should be alarmed. There have been numerous cases where UFOs have been intercepted by other air force jets and without trace. We have strange creatures being seen across our planet, from the greys, to so called reptilian creatures and of course the Nordics, more commonly seen back in the 1950's and 60's, all of which have interacted with humans. Our main concern though, is the UFO abductions. People are being taken from either cars, bedrooms, or other buildings, and for me, and surely for you, this is a concern. The intrusion into Garry and Colin's life was unwanted, and has left them with scarred minds of an event that clearly was beyond the norm. And whilst we haven't had any alien life forms walking up to the President of the United States, or indeed the Prime Minister of the United Kingdom, that does not mean to say that we shouldn't be alarmed that one day, that presence, will make them selves know, and when it does, will we be prepared for it? Will it be earth shattering? Or will we take it in our stride and say that we knew it all along? Indeed, are we being conditioned with a slow release of information from some of the World's Governments and media platforms about an alien presence. Were the TIC TAC and GIMBLE UFOs (if they were such!) part of a plan to slowly introduce us before the 'big day'? What will eventually constitute proof of alien visitation? Will it happen in our lifetime, or your grand children's lifetime? Or will it NEVER happen? The evidence is there in abundance, and it would seem to show that we are indeed dealing with a very real phenomenon. And as the title of this chapter states, 'Should We Be Alarmed'? Well, some would say yes, others would hedge their bets. For the moment, it's like an over conscious poker player who is not yet ready to show their hand.

UFOs EXIST SAYS JAPAN OFFICIAL

This was the extraordinary headline from the BBC news department in Tokyo back in December 2007. It told of Japan's chief Government spokesman Nobutaka Machimura who stated openly and quite categorically, that in his opinion, UFOs were most definitely real. A member of the opposition had asked the Government what its policy was when it came to dealing with UFOs.

What would they do? Nobutaka stated that they would try and confirm whether they existed or not, and that there had been an 'incessant' report of sightings. He further stated that should a flying saucer be spotted in the country's airspace, a fighter jet would be scrambled to attempt visual confirmation. Japan's spokesperson Nobutaka Machimura does not stand alone when it comes to reporting to the public and media about

319

UFO sightings, many other countries the world over have also had spokespersons coming forward stating the exact same, in that they are aware of UFO reports, and would act upon them accordingly. I've said before in my lectures and other books, that I firmly believe that some of the Governments of this planet, do know what's going on. There are a lot that they are not telling us. Again I ask, should we be concerned? Or are there truly nothing at all to be worried about? I'm sure we all have our opinions on that.

ALIEN GERMS!

Other than speculating that these 'beings' who come to Earth to do their abductions and experiments are doing so to create some hybrid race, what else could be their purpose? Let us not forget, they have been with us for a very long time, and its not within the bounds of possibility that they may have inadvertently brought their own 'germs' with them! And if that is the case, then it would 'appear' that 'so far', no UFO abductee has come down with any 'alien flu', so to speak. Should we be surprised at this? That no alien bacteria has affected the individuals who they have been in contact with? Or have 'they' given us something, like some extraterrestrial antidote that ensures that we don't come down with something? We shouldn't forget what Stephen Hawking, the British theoretical physicist stated on the issue of coming into contact with an alien race. He warned us that we should avoid contact with any alien species, and that we should look as far as the Native Americans to see what happens when two cultures clash. One things for sure, these visiting aliens would surely be way in advance of mankind, and as such wouldn't take too long in controlling our planet, should that be their plan.

There was an interesting headline that was featured in the Independent Newspaper dated October 24th 2016. It stated, *'Strange Messages Coming From The Stars Are 'Probably' From Aliens, Scientists Say'*. The article was written by Andrew Griffin, and went on to say that analysis of some strange modulations which came from a tiny set of stars, would appear to indicate that it could be coming from extraterrestrial intelligence, and that these modulations, may be a way of them alerting 'us' to 'their' presence. Apparently this study found what they described as 'specific' modulations in just 234 out of the 2.5 million stars that they observed in the sky. A few of these 'modulations' appeared to be behaving strangely. A gentleman by the name of E.F. Borra was quoted as saying,

"We find that the detected signals have exactly the shape of an (extraterrestrial intelligence) signal predicted in the previous publication, and are therefore in agreement with this hypothesis," "The fact that they are only found in a very small fraction of stars within a narrow spectral range centered near the spectral type of the sun, is also in agreement with the ETI hypothesis,"

The research undertaken, appeared in the Journal Publications of the Astronomical Society of the Pacific, but they did make it clear that further work would need to be done either to confirm or deny that hypothesis. E.F. Borra further stated,

"It is too early to unequivocally attribute these purported signals to the activities of extraterrestrial civilizations. Internationally agreed upon protocols for searches for evidence of advanced life beyond Earth (SETI) require candidates to be confirmed by independent groups using their own telescopes, and for all natural explanations to be exhausted before invoking extraterrestrial agents as an explanation. "Careful work must be undertaken to determine false positive rates, to rule out natural and instrumental explanations, and most importantly, to confirm detections using two or more independent telescopes."

Breakthrough Listen, which was an initiative that was set up in 2016 to look for alien life, was supported by notable people the likes of Stephen Hawking and Mark Zuckerberg. They too stated that further work would indeed need to be done before we can say that these 'strange modulations' can be attributed to

321

aliens. The project with $100 dollars in funding, is the most comprehensive search for alien life in the cosmos and is based at Berkeley SETI Research Center in California. Needless to say, since this interesting article in the Independent newspaper, no further 'revelations' to intelligent life in the Universe has come to light (well not that they have admitted to anyway!)

THE LONG AWAITED REPORT OF UFO FILES FROM THE PENTAGON JUNE 2021

During the early months of 2021, UFOlogists the world over, were eagerly awaiting the release of the promised investigation by the Pentagon, of their enquiry into the release of the incredible footage of UFO's (or as the Pentagon called them, UAPs, Unidentified Aerial Phenomena)) that were filmed by jet pilots from the USS Nimitz and the USS Theodor Roosevelt of which I mentioned earlier. Well, that report finally came out, released by the Office of the Director of National Intelligence on June 25th 2021 and I guess that UFOlogists shouldn't have been surprised when it turned out that it was nothing but a damp squid. Some UFOlogists had high expectations of something quite considerable coming out of this long awaited report, in the sense of an acceptance by the United States Government, that yes, planet Earth has seen an intrusion into its air space by vehicles of unknown origin. This report for me, was all over the place. It says one thing, then contradicts that one thing further down the report. It was a muddle of words.

We are told that most of these objects fall into the category of airborne clutter, the likes of birds, balloons, plastic bags flying in the sky (yes really!) or natural atmospheric anomalies like ice crystals, moisture, and thermal fluctuations, and that limited data leaves most of the UAP reports unexplained. The investigation into these UAP objects fell between the years of 2004 through to November 2021. I had to laugh where at one point in the report, it states that the sensors mounted on U.S. Military platforms are only designed to fulfil specific missions, and as a result, we are told, are not suited for identifying

UAP's. Really! Overall, the report effectively stated that these UAP reports, probably lacked a single explanation, that said, the report did speculate that some of the UAPs might be Chinese or Russian or from another Governmental entity.

Interesting Points

The report did state that they found a cluster of UAP reports which were observed around U.S. training and testing grounds. We are also told that in 18 incidents described in 21 reports, observers reported unusual UAP movement patterns or flight characteristics. The report did state that some UAPs may pose a threat to flight safety and National Security, and they accept that some UAPs have been detected near Military facilities, or by aircraft which are carrying the United States Government most advanced sensor systems. My, that must be some black plastic bag flying in the wind eh! The report did state that the U.S. Government would continue its research into the UAP phenomenon, to learn as much as possible as to what is behind these reports.

Malcolm's concluding thoughts on this report.

Look folks, what has been released is effectively the same old hash. They had to bring out this report simply because of the various U.S. Senators asking the Government to come clean on those incredible images that the world saw on television, when fighter pilots dispatched from the USS Nimitz and the USS Theodore Roosevelt, captured what was referred to as the Tic Tac and Gimble UAP's whose flight characteristics defied the laws of gravity. Those images caused a right old stink in the halls and corridors of the Senate. The Pentagon and the American Government, were backed into a corner, they had to come out with something, and this report is a muddled mess of flowery words each of which, takes you down a different path of thought. I guess we shouldn't be surprised at this report.

I honestly thought that the Disclosure Press Club conference held back in 2001, would have shown the world the reality of the UFO phenomenon once and for all. Here we had high standing people from the United States Air force, the Army and Navy, all seated telling their own stories of the UFOs that they saw. These were not your street drunks, these were men of integrity, who were putting their lives on the line for America, and yet, after their testimony, it was just another day. They were seen, they were heard, and the world moved on. Nothing changed. Look folks, here's the rub, you will never ever in a million years get the United States (or Britain for that matter) to put their hands up and say, *"Yes, OK guys, you were right all along, we are dealing with an advanced technology from another world"* It isn't going happen. The only way things will change, I believe, is when our alien intruders finally show their hand, and come clean themselves. Then, and only then, will the Government back peddle, snivel, and you might, just might, get an apology.

That's it for me. I honestly, truly and firmly believe, that my Government and 'your' Government, will never come clean. They will come out with reports similar to the drivel that came out in June 2021. It's now up to 'THEM', the craft that stealthily fly in our skies to make themselves known. My research into the UFO enigma, has clearly shown to me, that 'WE ARE' dealing with a superior advanced technology whose agenda we can but speculate. Make no bones about it folks, they are real alright, and the Governments of this world know that. Those who have witnessed UFOs, or UAPs as the Pentagon would call them, know that what they have seen, was not conventional. Like me, I'm sure that they are dismayed that the powers that be, our elected officials, didn't have the guts to trust the people of Earth to accept such a fact, and to prepare mankind for a future 'main intrusion' into our air space by beings that might not have our best interests at heart.

So for me, Malcolm Robinson, I don't need a Government report to baffle me with contradictory words, I've heard it all before. I'll continue to help the man and woman in the street to get their own UFO accounts out there, and maybe one day, further down the line, we will have our interstellar friends join us for either a joyous celebration of life in the cosmos, or find out, that they don't have our best interests at heart. Whatever the outcome might be, that day will come, and its best that we all are ready for it, even although the United States Government will continue to shun the evidence.

Scientists find 29 Planets where aliens could be watching us.

Also on the 25th of June 2021, came the sensational headline above, reported by the Guardian Newspaper. Staff writer Christian Spencer stated that scientists were of the opinion that planet Earth is potentially being watched by beings out in the Cosmos, and that their planets were positioned in such a way that they could be picking up our radio and T.V. broadcasts for years. The report stated that scientists identified 1,715 star systems in which potentially another civilisation could discover planet Earth simply by observing our planet's transit. Lisa Kaltenegger, who is a professor of astronomy and director at Cornell University, said to the Guardian newspaper, and I quote;

"One way we find planets is if they block out part of the light from their host star," "We asked, 'who would we be the aliens for, if somebody else was looking?' There is this tiny sliver in the sky where other star systems have a cosmic front seat to find Earth as a transiting planet."

Of course this fact has not been lost when it comes to our own Astronomers here on Earth, for they too, have been able to detect thousands of planets in the solar system. Again this is all done by observing when other planets in our solar system pass in front of what they call, 'host stars' which in turn, blocks some of the light that comes through their telescopes. The Guardian newspaper tells us that Kaltenegger published her findings along with a J.K Faherty in the journal Nature. The paper goes on to state that the star Ross 128, is roughly around 11 light years away from planet Earth, and has a planet nearly twice the size of Earth. Both Kaltenegger and Faherty state that life on that planet is close enough to observe Earth, and could have been doing it for more than 2,000 years. Faherty was reported as saying;

"We wanted to use the closest stars," When it comes to exploring worlds, the nearest ones to us are going to be the most exciting."

I did an interview with Kay Burley from SKY News regarding this, and put forward a number of points which I'd like to share with you now. I said whilst planet Earth had indeed been putting out radio and T.V. signals into deep space since the invention of those devices, we had to be very careful on what we might get back. I spoke of it like this. Say you have a house party, and the noise of the party is coming out of your house, we have who we know we have invited inside the house, but hearing the noise coming from the house, are uninvited visitors, gatecrashers if you like. The insinuation here, is that we have to be very careful who we let into our house, planet Earth being 'our house'. If we are dealing with a highly sophisticated race of beings 'out there' in deepest space, would they have our best interest at heart? We may recall what happened when Orson Wells did a radio play based on the famous H.G. Wells novel, 'War of The Worlds' from the Mercury Theater in New York City in October 1938. That play, caused wide spread panic, as people who tuned in late, truly believed that parts of America were being invaded by Martians, indeed, its said that some people fearing that planet Earth was being run over by Martians, actually committed suicide! We might ask ourselves, would this be the case today! Things have of course moved on since then, and we'd like to think that we wouldn't be fooled with a programme of that nature. But you never know, human nature can surprise you with the most unusual of actions. I also said to SKY News that our scientists have sent probes to Mars, so could, what we see in the skies of planet Earth, be probes from an advanced Inter stellar civilisation? Pure speculation on my part of course, but worthy of consideration nonetheless. Any advanced culture 'out there' would of course, need to have the right ingredients to ensure life, and by that I mean a satellite Moon, like planet

Earth has, and also an orbiting star like our Sun. These are the conditions that would need to be met, to ensure any type of life would come into being on that planet. But then of course, what type of life would that be? And that questions takes us down many corridors and is too wide a spectrum to answer in this book.

So as this chapter says, should mankind be alarmed? By sending out our radio and T.V. signals, are we inviting visitors to this planet that we might not want? The thing is of course, whilst we may speculate about life in the cosmos, we still have to consider those that have gone through UFO Abductions, similar to both Garry and Colin, the unfortunate victims in the A70 Incident. For me, its not so much the fact that is there life in the cosmos? it's about what we are dealing with in our skies right now, and what's been interacting with the people of this planet for millennia. There is no getting away with that, there is way too much evidence to say otherwise. So, we are now nearing the end of this book. What have we learned (if anything) What was the cause of Garry and Colin's encounter on the A70? Well, I would sum it up as follows.

AND WHAT DO I, THE AUTHOR, THINK IS GOING ON?

Well I firmly believe that we are being 'visited' by 'beings' from elsewhere which are far superior to our own species. Its not an acceptance that I came to overnight. This acceptance has come after over 45 years of research into the UFO subject speaking to many hundreds of witnesses. Researching the subject of UFOs, you find that your opinions change throughout the years, you find that you bend with each new case, you think differently with each new photograph, and you take stock of all that Is possible and some that is not. The sceptics will say that there is no real concrete proof that 'aliens' have visited us, that the photographs and movie film are all suspect and can be explained away. I would say different. I would say that the veracity of the evidence that has been accumulated throughout the years from countless thousands of individuals throughout the world, speaks volumes that 'something is going on'. There is no smoke without fire. The honest testimony that has been given, could, in other circumstances, send a man to jail. But the big question is, does this testimony prove to you the reader that UFOs and UFO abductions are a reality? I've been researching UFOs for over 45 years now, which isn't really that long, and in that time my views have changed quite dramatically. I went from a sceptic to a believer. There was a time when I felt that the earthlight hypothesis was the only answer to account for the UFO phenomenon, but now I realise that it is only a *part of it.* And that's the thing with researching this subject, your views do change, you do see things in a different light. Meeting like minded people and sharing information, all helps to establish a rapport of mind in which is an education within itself. Life is the proverbial school, and there is much to learn, but to turn our back on a subject like UFOs, would really not be in keeping with man's quest to learn more, or to try and find our place in the cosmos.

The A7O UFO Incident took me off the proverbial fence, and placed me slap bang into the believers' camp, I honestly believe that those two men endured a terrible abduction experience which most certainly has altered their lives dramatically. Those men made me realise that without a shadow of a doubt, mankind is interacting with some form of 'alien presence' which is coming into our world through some dimensional window. Colin Wilson the famous paranormal researcher and sadly no longer with us, could be correct when he said that they, the 'aliens', are altering our genetic structure, that they are not taking things 'from' us, but putting things 'in' us! and that is frightening. But my conviction, as to why I believe UFO reports to be true, is also due to the fact of the many countless thousands of good sound, and reliable testimony that we have coming from Military and Civilian Radar operators. They have observed strange blips appearing on their screens to which their 'trained' eyes are not weather conditions or false returns. Let us not forget, these operators are in charge of equipment which is an extra eye for aircraft, and they wouldn't be in this job if they didn't know what they were doing. So I do accept the testimony that comes from trained radar operators. Of course, the best example of radar contact with UFOs, has got to be the RAF Bentwaters and Lakenheath Incident of 1956, and what made that case even more impressive, was the fact that this case also had the added bonus of ground based observers who all knew the various types of normal aircraft, and yet could not recognise the objects that they saw in the sky that night. All this was picked up on radar. The evidence of this case, and many others of a similar nature, clearly points to the fact that we are dealing with a phenomenon that is mysterious as it is elusive, and of which is most certainly alien to our way of thinking.

The dramatic turn of speed that these UFOs can achieve is breathtaking, and I fail to accept that any Military power on Earth at this time could match the agility and speed that these mysterious aerial machines can. We may laugh at poke fun at UFO abductees, we may laugh and poke fun at UFO witnesses. We laughed at John Logie Baird the Scottish Inventor of Television, we laughed at Marconi, the inventor of the wireless, we laughed at the Wright Brothers as they took their first flight, and there were those that laughed at the possibility that we could ever set foot upon the Moon or that a wireless or a television could work. Why does mankind laugh at things which might appear silly? Just because the tales coming from UFO abductees may sound ridiculous, that does that mean we have to ignore them? I think that there are far too many people sitting in their comfortable armchairs and making noises and blowing hot air. If only they looked, if only they would get up from their armchair and talk to the witnesses, if only they would look at this impressive data, then, they would see for themselves that the evidence is there, it's only a case of looking.

The abduction phenomenon has tremendous implications for mankind. I feel that it is as much a part of today's reality as any other major news story which is currently being aired. Does the vision of Ezekiel in the Bible constitute proof? What did he see? Was it a UFO? Those strange cave paintings in

France and Australia, do they really show ancient astronauts, or just the headgear of an ancient civilisation? No matter where you the reader lay your hat, you will always get a difference of opinion. I suppose that it's a case of what evidence you are prepared to believe, what you feel comfortable with. Like I say, for me, the evidence is strong, and the evidence for me points in the direction of Interdimensional 'beings' are making contact with us humans. Some might say, *"But what about all those different aliens"!* Yes we have small grey 'beings', and yes we have tall Nordic looking 'men', and yes we have goblin type entities and reptilian looking monstrosities, quite a mixture! But then again, here on planet Earth we have a mixture of races, from red Indians to black people. From aborigines, Chinese, Japanese, Mongolian, all who have their very own facial characteristics. If a UFO were to land in say deepest Mongolia, would they think that all humans looked like that! There are millions of people throughout the world who believe in God, but ask yourselves, how many of them have actually seen him! They believe through 'trust' whilst UFOlogists believe through 'facts'. We have to have more than belief, we have to have more than faith. To register the fact that something is occurring we need data, we need facts with evidence beyond reproach. In a sense, it's like those inspiring words by the fictional character Sherlock Holmes from the book, the Sign of the Four and they were;

"How often have I said to you, that when you have eliminated the impossible, whatever remains, however improbable, must be the truth"

The good thing to come out of UFO abductions, is support groups. Prior to support groups forming, UFO abductees had nowhere to go to with their experiences. Thankfully, these support groups which began appearing in the mid 1980s, allowed many UFO abductees to come to terms with what they experienced. The groups at this point in time, were mainly from the United States, Canada and Australia. Now we have support groups throughout the world. See the end of this book for links to UFO Abduction Support Groups.

BUT WHERE DO 'THEY' COME FROM?

The UFO phenomenon has been with us now for many years, and during this time we haven't been able to reach any clear cut conclusion as to what these strange aerial objects might be, or where they might originate from. Speculations range from the creditable, to the down right ridiculous. However, no one can dispute the sincere and honest statements that have been gathered from the UFO witnesses, and I refer mainly to Garry Wood and Colin Wright. The witnesses tell of observing objects which do not resemble any type of conventional aircraft, and in some cases, these observations have changed their whole outlook on life. How can this be? Why, if these truly are Extraterrestrial spacecraft entering the Earth's atmosphere, do they not openly contact us? Well why don't we take a wee history lesson on our place in the cosmos.

The planet Earth is a minor planet circling around an average star in a Galaxy of around 100 billion stars which occupies a pin point of space amoung untold billions of Galaxies in our Universe. The solar system, (it has been stated) is 7 billion 328 million miles in diameter, taking up a speck of space about two thirds of the way out from the centre of the Milky Way which is about 100,000 light years across. (A light year is the distance travelled at the speed of light, 186,000 miles a second). The planets have no light of their own, and only shine because they reflect the rays from our Sun. The planet Mars is a small world with a diameter only half that of Earth, while Sirius is a sun in it's own right, 26 times as luminous as our own Sun. The distance between the Earth and the Sun, is 93,000,000 miles. The nearest Galaxy to Earth is 170,000 light years away, and the nearest star is Proxima Centauri, which is 40 billion kilometres away. A few years back, some NASA equipment onboard an orbiting space probe which was only 1,000 miles above the Earth, failed to detect any life on it (!) From that height and distance, our planet looked like a beautiful blue jewel in the sky without any clear cut signs that it was inhabited, it was only when the probe got closer with it's equipment, that it started to pick up signs of life and habitation. What this implies is, even if we looked at other planets in space with today's telescopes, signs of habitable life may be hard to detect, and it would need 'perhaps', sophisticated equipment to detect such signs. It goes without saying, that many people who have an open mind, recognise the fact that 'out there' in the vastness of space, 'must reside other intelligences'. Are there really other habitable worlds 'out there', or are we just an exception, a 'one off'? Professor Brian Cox is on record as stating that there are 20 billion Earth like planets out there in the cosmos, so again, it's inconceivable that we stand alone in the vastness of space. Planet Earth is but a tiny grain of sand on a huge cosmic beach, and I've always said that we are 'not alone' in the universe, and this was why reports of UFO activity intrigued me for so long during my early years of UFO study. It obviously follows, that any extraterrestrial civilisation out there, may be well in advance to ourselves due to the fact that their planet evolved before us, then again, evolution, depending on conditions, may have stabilised, and any progression may not have advanced, however I doubt that, but it's something that we should also bring into debate.

Let us for the moment, consider how lucky we on Earth are, in the sense that, we reside on a planet which has the right conditions for life. The New York Times of April 24th 1979, pointed out to it's readers that at a distance of 93 million miles from the Sun, Earthly temperatures have supported life, but if our Earth had been slung into an orbit only 5 percent closer to the Sun, a runaway greenhouse effect would have turned our planet into something like Venus, a cloud shrouded planet with temperatures close to 900 F. If, on the other hand, we had been only one per cent farther from the Sun when the Earth came into being, runaway glaciation would have enveloped the Earth and 1.7 billion years ago our planet would have become a barren desert similar to Mars. It is somewhat incredible when we think that we have a situation here which has given us the right conditions for life, in which we have come into 'being' and in a very short space of time, (as terrestrial time spans go!) arrived at a fairly advanced level. When we consider the fact that it has been 66 years from the Wright Brothers first successful flight in 1903, to Neil Armstrong's first famous footsteps on the Moon in 1969, then it would be a fair assumption to make that these UFOs seen entering our airspace, must have attained a higher level of advancement than ourselves.

Some closed minded earth scientists try to put the UFO subject into a test tube and expect it to conform to the same laws that govern this dimension of reality, and when it does not conform, they conclude that it does not exist! This backward school yard mentality of thought is a gross insult to science. The unknown is still very much unchallenged, but more and more people are now taking a look at these subjects and asking pertinent questions. Man has not, by any means, discovered all there is to discover on this planet (and off of it), there are still, I'm sure, many wonders left for us to explore and discover. Discoveries await I'm sure, in the paranormal field as undoubtedly they do in the UFO field. Some might have you believe that the UFO phenomenon is nothing short of a 'global psychosis' which has affected all mankind and that it warrants the full attention of the world's top psychologists. Again, that narrow minded way of thinking is lost on the author, and I sometimes wonder if these scientists have really had an education! Some would say that there are more speculations on where the answer lies to the UFO mystery than there are stars in the sky, that maybe so, and we have covered a few of them earlier in this book. But there is no denying the vast amount of UFO literature worldwide to suggest the fact that 'something is going on'. Sceptics state that we (UFOlogists) cannot study the UFO phenomenon, purely because we have no UFOs to study. But I agree that the UFO phenomenon is largely a witness based phenomenon, but even so, this should not detract away from the fact that serious study should still be employed. Again, let us consider, that we only have today's scientific knowledge to go by, we cannot even begin to comprehend the enormous possibilities involved with Interstellar travel. Sceptics say that UFOs could never travel the distances involved in space, but they are basing these primary school statements, solely on our own current state of travel. I only need to remind the reader that a car can travel faster than a push bike, and any advanced Extraterrestrial civilisation may well have conquered the means of Interstellar travel, so to say that 'they' can't get here, is a preposterous statement to make.

RELIGION AND UFOs

Then of course there is the Religious aspect of UFOlogy. Many people have asked the question "If there truly is life on other worlds, did God create them as well, and if so, then was it in his own image, as we have been told is the case with ourselves"? There are many reports of hideous creatures seen in close proximity to UFOs, were they made in God's image too? Or are we dealing with an independent aspect of universal being, that there might be many Gods who made many worlds! An interesting thought. Another way around that of course, would be the genetic manipulation of 'creatures.' 'Beings' which initially were totally different to what they once were, and were genetically made different by races from other worlds to suit their own ends, and of which, have nothing to do with (in God's image). The noted author Erich Von Daniken, always stated that God was an 'astronaut', but is he responsible for other beings throughout the Universe? Is there more than one God? Is it possible that another celestial 'being' actually created mankind, and 'not' the Biblical God, that we know? Would this throw Christianity into disrepute? On the face of it, this might seem so, because this new information would contradict the Bible teachings and there might be many who would lose faith. At this point in time of course this is but pure speculation and no one knows with any certainly that there might be 'other Gods' out there, and not just our own Biblical figure. Of course these statements may seem highly controversial, but I do feel that I have to at the very least, try and provide thought to the reader, to make them think broadly on this issue. Detecting alien life forms may not be that simple. NASA have erected a series of giant radio antennas at various locations in which they hope that they will be able to detect radio signals sent out by other civilisations in outer space, as yet, there haven't been any.

Is this because Extraterrestrial civilisations might not use a radio based communication? That they might instead use an altogether different type of communication? This is highly probable, and again, let's not forget we are dealing with an entirely different culture who most certainly will be doing things differently than ourselves. Radio telescopes, no matter how big they are, might not detect alien life. I accept that even today, radio telescopes have not even touched upon a fraction of areas in space, that there are so many minute movements of the telescope which are needed to cover the vastness of the sky. We have certainly only begun our journey with radio telescopes, and there are indeed many changes that we must still do in order to test every frequency available. I suppose its like those old radios, where if you turn your radio dial to radio one, you have to turn it again to obtain radio 2. By the same token, we, on planet Earth, have been broadcasting radio signals out into space for well over 5O years now, and so any advanced technological civilisation would recognise that the strength of these signals would out weigh the normal strength of 'back ground' signals that usually come from space. It goes without saying then, that this is probably why our planet has been visited so much over the past 8O odd years. The curious aspect of enquiry from other races in 'our' civilisation, has been seen over the years, the big question is though, are these races hostile? It is a fact that usually the stronger species survives, the lion will overcome the deer. Mankind has in the past, forced his culture and presence on other less stronger cultures and totally destroyed them. And although Ancient Rome gave mankind many wondrous things, it's tyranny over less powerful peoples and cities, were seen by pillars of smoke and rivers of blood, as indeed were the journeys of the Norwegian Vikings with their murderous trips to England. Will mankind shortly fall to a superior presence? or is mankind purely an experiment by others that is systematically being looked over by the ever watchful eyes of our makers!

As I've said, mankind should not think that we know it all about this planet and our universe. It's incredible to think that it wasn't until 1847 that the Gorilla was 'scientifically classified'. The chimpanzee wasn't 'scientifically classified' until 1916. People reported these creatures as being real, whilst other people denied and laughed that they existed! So in a sense, this analogy is like the UFO phenomena, people report UFOs, whilst other people state that they do not exist! It can only be a matter of time before the knowledge of the existence of UFOs, is fully understood by mankind. History has seen many learned men laughed at by their peers as do UFOlogists today, we are laughed at for believing in such matters. Let us take a look at other people who have been laughed at throughout the centuries. Copernicus was frightened to publish his heliocentric theory about the solar system before he died for fear of punishment by the establishment, which was then the church. Galileo was almost burned at the stake due to his invention of the telescope, and that he had found craters on the moon and spots on the Sun. Newton had trouble with his gravitational theory, and was bitterly opposed by the scientific community at the time. Darwin was still fighting in the court of Tennessee as late as 1928 to prove his theory of evolution. Freud and his exploration of the human mind, met fierce resistance by the establishment of his time. Harvey was castigated for daring to state that blood circulated in the human body, and the authorities declared him wrong without even checking on living humans. Pasteur was laughed at by the medical world when he stated that small little beasties invisible to the naked eye, caused diseases. These are but some of the many people who were laughed at over the years by people who should have known better. Of course one of the biggest and best known statement, was that man would never set foot on the Moon. Now UFOlogists are laughed at for daring to suggest, that there are such things as 'Flying saucers' operating throughout the skies of our world. This, I admit, did at one time get to me as a researcher, but now I recognise that people do have the right to their opinions, and that there will come a time when they will realise that this impressive weight of UFO evidence, which is growing every day, will surely prove real, and that researchers like myself, the world over who have being doing our UFO research, will be vindicated, it's only a matter of time.

Going back to the Bible and the religious side of the UFO debate, we are told in the Bible that Jesus Christ died for our sins on a cross at Calvary, now, if there is intelligent life in outer space, firstly, did God create it? and if he did, have these planets shared similar cultural upheavals and atrocities which have prevailed here on planet Earth which ended up with the son of God, Jesus Christ, being sent to planet Earth with a view to hopefully cleansing mankind's evil ways. If other worlds have went the same way as ours, then can we expect numerous son's of God to be crucified on numerous crosses throughout the Galaxy? Or is this one son of God who we know as Jesus, now travelling the cosmos to cleanse other planets of their sins? Jesus died on the cross for planet Earth, has he re-died on other worlds for the same purpose? or have some hierarchy of Celestial beings put forward the word of Christ's demise on a planet called Earth in order to persuade, if not stop, these other Extra-terrestrial civilisations from going down the same slippery slope as planet Earth? Did God really create mankind, or are we all the result of pure chance which was brought about by the 'Big Bang theory', ie, that chemical processes in a large dense gas and dust cloud which was probably formed from the collapse of a very massive Interstellar cloud, fragmented, and went on to produce thousands of stellar and planetary systems. This in turn, owing to the heterogeneous solids, accreted to form the planets of which we know today? Were we, the human race, seeded by God, or are we just the result of 'pure chance', ie, that we evolved from a primordial soup, a mixture of chemicals and elements which helped to produce a 'species' which initially crawled across the Earth and eventually stood erect as homo sapien man? Could it not be that we might be a combination of the two, or indeed, are we the result of some Extraterrestrial experiment in which the UFOs seen flitting about the skies, are really our forefathers?

UFOlogists may insist that 'Flying Saucers' and 'UFO Abductions' are real, but this does not necessarily prove to others that these experiences are genuine. We could say that the 'aliens' technology is so far in advance to our own, that the analogy would be like trying to imagine going back in time and showing a computer to a caveman, he would have absolutely no comprehension as to what it was or how to use it. What would the school master of the 1920's have thought about the slim pocket calculator? What would the Royal Air Force of the year 1914, have thought of the Stealth Bomber? Just because things, on the surface, appear preposterous, does not mean to say that there is not something behind these claims. The analogy that I use for the cave man, may also explain why these 'beings' do not 'openly' land. They might fear that it would upset the structure of this planet both socially and in a Religious sense with this instantaneous technological knowledge. Earth, as we know, is a war like planet, and to receive advanced weapons of destruction from a superior culture, well, it goes without saying that it wouldn't be too long before we could kiss good-bye to this beautiful planet of ours. Again, another analogy of this scenario, would be like giving Stealth Bombers and twenty first century Military weaponry to General Custer at that battle of the Little Big Horn, his victory would be swift and instantaneous.

So to receive weapons of destruction from an advanced E.T. society, would surely prove to be the end for planet Earth. According to a survey done in 1993 by the British Strange Phenomena Journal the Fortean Times, the world was becoming weirder in which reports of miracles, apparitions and UFO sightings, were on the increase. According to their survey, the Philippines was said to be one of the most strangest countries on the Earth. This increase in strangeness, was not only noticed by myself, but by many other researchers as well. But could it not be the case that events of this nature are being reported more and more these days, by individuals who are not afraid anymore to come forward, and as such, we see the rise in figures? The British Teletext T.V. service conducted a poll on June the 30th 1997 in which it asked it's viewers the question,

"Do aliens exist"? And of the 2,215 votes cast, the result was that 89% voted YES, whilst 11% voted NO. A sign of the changing times perhaps. But as this chapter states, 'should we be alarmed'? It's a tough one, because as yet, other than the ongoing world wide UFO Abductions, which are in themselves traumatising to the victims, there are no clear signs that they are ready to make their presence felt anytime soon. That's not to say that we shouldn't be alarmed. We should be on our guard and wary of a potential threat from the skies. In this life, take nothing for granted, for we are living in strange times, and who knows, they could get a whole lot stranger!

EPILOGUE

For me, working 'hands on' on the A70 case along with Ron Halliday and Helen Walters, was a big eye opener, and made me question reality as I know it. It made me question Religion, ie, is our God, the God of these small Grey creatures? And if so, why did he allow these terrible and traumatic intrusions into our lives? It made me question the medical profession. Why, I thought, were not more medical people involved with this subject? It made me question the mind, for if these UFO abductions and the scars that go with them, are all in our mind, then let's look at the mind, let us delve deep into the processes of the brain and see if this is indeed a global psychosis of immense proportions that is currently reaching epidemic proportions across our globe.

The UFO abduction phenomenon is looked upon by many as being ridiculous and not having any real credence. For when one actually studies the evidence of UFO abductions, then one cannot fail to be impressed by the sincerity of the people who claim them. These people do not seek glory, they do not seek fame and fortune, they only want to get on with their lives. Garry Wood always said that he wasn't looking for this to happen in his life, this was the last thing he needed. Helen Walters who conducted the regressive hypnosis on both Garry and Colin, did it in a professional and competent manner and ensured that both men would only recount what they wanted to recount. At any signs of distress by both men, she quickly brought them out of hypnosis where they had time to reflect on what they remembered. Helen Walters, after many sessions with both men, is of the opinion that both men are telling the 'truth' and are completely sincere. She was quoted by the Scotsman newspaper of Thursday the 15th of September 1994, as saying,

"There seems little doubt that they saw an Unidentified Flying Object. The question is what. There is no doubt that

under hypnosis they appear to remember meeting aliens. The question is, are these memories or imaginings!"

For all Helen is qualified and knowledgeable about hypnosis, this for her, was something quite extraordinary, at the end of the day however, all she is prepared to say is that both men are being completely honest with her. 'They' believe that something most unusual happened to them, and they would never have come so far to find out what that 'something' was, if nothing happened to them. Helen admits that there are problems with this case, she knows 'something' happened to both men, but is not prepared to fully commit to that something as being extraterrestrial in nature. I can fully appreciate that. The hidden chambers of the mind must hold many secrets and I'm sure that there are many wonders of the mind that are still to be tapped. Hypnosis, provided many pre-hidden secrets regarding the A7O Incident, and not only Helen Walters had a look at this case. Another qualified hypnotherapist, a Dr Prem Misra from Glasgow, undertook further regressive hypnosis on Garry Wood for a BBC television documentary about this case entitled, 'Cracking Stories'.

Dr Misra has no doubt that Garry Wood genuinely believed that he had a close encounter, and explained to Garry, that he should learn self hypnosis in order to alleviate his fears. It should be noted that under the influence of Dr Misra's hypnosis, Garry recounted exactly what he recounted under the hypnosis of Helen Walters, there was no detraction from the story, no elaboration, just the plain and simply honest recollections of a man that had experienced something out of the ordinary. On Colin Wright's UFO report form that he kindly filled out for me, it asks the question, 'Did you suffer any physical effects which you consider to be attributable to the object/s seen?' Colin replied with,

"I felt very unusual, like I had been on drugs, and had the feeling of being high. I also felt I never had a care in the world".

In Garry Wood's form, again on the same question, he states,

"Felt drugged. Very high, very worried. I felt that I did not have a care in the world".

So, as we can see, both men had the same type of feelings whilst in close contact with this 'craft'. And as any student of the UFO phenomenon will tell you, this effect is quite common. The question has to be asked, 'why'? what was behind this feeling of euphoria, and why did this feeling even have to come into the equation? Science writer and author Steuart Campbell from Edinburgh, felt that the real cause of the A7O Incident, was the direct result of both men witnessing an astronomical mirage and simply became confused about the time, an explanation that didn't go down too well with both witnesses. At the end of the day both Garry and Colin are left feeling bemused by what happened to them, they go about their lives not thinking what is beyond the stars, but concern themselves with the ordinary mundane duties that each and everyone of us perform each day. Garry still believes that 'they' are still around, and that 'something' will undoubtedly happen that will convince everyone. Garry accepts that something very peculiar intruded into his life that August evening but is still unsure as to what it is all about. Both men's lives may have changed, but they are still the men they were, albeit with a different perspective on life.

After years of study, I am certain that there is ample high quality observational evidence from witnesses to indicate that there are unusual objects operating in our atmosphere. The evidence pointing to the reality of UFOs and UFO abductions is now so colossal, that it is impossible for anyone with an open mind who has studied the evidence to continue to ignore what's going on. I beg you not to be an 'armchair UFOlogist. Don't ignore this growing evidence.

I've always said, that the world in which we live in, is a far more stranger place than we ever can imagine. I do hope that you the reader, through your interest in this subject, and having bought this book, accept that both Garry Wood and Colin Wright went through a traumatic experience. You may not accept it as a UFO Abduction, but I'm sure at the very least, you will accept that these two men are not liars, that they went through an experience that they both wish they never had. Reading this book as you are, you may be a seasoned student of this puzzling enigma, or you may be getting your feet wet for the very first time. I would ask that you don't stop with this book, go out and grab as many books as you can on the UFO abduction phenomenon. Familiarise yourself with the subject. When one wants to drive a car, they have to study and learn the highway code. Well, in a round a bout way, by studying this important subject, it provides an understanding that we know so very little about ourselves and our place in the cosmos. But more importantly, it helps us understand, that we are dealing with a very real subject, something that does not appear to be letting up.

Listen dear reader, it's time to wake up and smell the coffee before we find ourselves in a predicament beyond our control. Mankind is at the bottom of a long ladder of understanding, of not just who we are, but what's 'out there'. Garry Wood and Colin Wright were subjected to a situation beyond their control on the A70. Do I have a 'cut and dried' explanation as to what happened to both Garry and Colin that night? I do not. What I will say is that I wholeheartedly believe that they are telling the truth as far as they can recall it. Did hypnosis 'muddy the waters'? Well again, some might say it did. I just hope that this one case, will stir your desire to find out more and let you understand how complex this subject can be.

UFO ABDUCTIONS ARE STILL ONGOING

Sadly what will never be in dispute, is the fact that UFO abductions are still ongoing, and it would appear that we have no control over the situation. Yes it is alarming. We as human beings have enough to worry about in our daily lives. Researchers like me have a duty to inform the public about

343

what's going on. It would be remiss of me not to. I am but a small cog in an enormous wheel of fellow researchers who are trying to get to the truth. The honest witness testimony and the incredible UFO radar visual reports, clearly show that we are dealing with a 'presence' which is very real and could pose untold dangers. To say that nothing is going on is the folly of ignorance. It's up to you, dear reader, to search for the facts and decide if UFOs and UFO abductions are fact or fiction. You owe it to yourself to find out more, and I hope that your journey will provide you with much thought and inspiration and an understanding that we most certainly, 'are not alone'. Good luck.

APPENDICES

I decided that you the reader should read some of the transcripts from some of the audio interviews that I recorded with Garry Wood and Colin Wright during the years of 1994, 1995, 1996, 1998, and 2021. Sadly, some of the audio tapes from some of the hypnotic sessions have been lost over the years in my various house moves, and I can only provide you the reader, transcripts from those sessions that we do have. Our first transcript comes from Garry's second hypnotic regression, 14th June 1994.

Intro. Helen Walters our hypnotherapist, went through her usual hypnotic regression procedure, and took Garry back to the age of five and asked him what he saw, saying that he would feel himself becoming younger and younger. She said that Garry should not invent or imagine what he is seeing, but be truthful and honest, and relate exactly what comes to his mind. Please note, that when Garry discusses what he is seeing, the reader should look to the photo section to see Garry's drawings to get a better understanding on what he is describing. This particular recording, came *'after'* hypnosis was conducted on Garry, and he was free to relate and tell us all what he remembered. I am also asking Garry questions on this session as did his friend Colin Wright.

Garry's Second Hypnotic Regression, 14th June 1994.

Abbreviations:
(GW) Garry Wood. (HW) Helen Walters. (MR) Malcolm Robinson. (CW) Colin Wright.

(GW) "I saw something horrible, then I saw something not so horrible. I felt like at one time I was moving all about. I saw a face, it's hard to describe it and I saw something coming down at the side of me. I felt scared and hopeless. I feel stupid saying it".

(HW) "Just say it, just say exactly what you are feeling, don't try to make head nor tail of it, describe what you saw".

(GW) "I thought I was going away and I wasn't coming back".

(HW) "How did you feel emotionally"?

(GW) "I know I was crying. It was like I was going somewhere. It's hard to say, it's really really difficult. I didn't know where I was, and I kept seeing like a cloud or mist. Whatever I am trying to look at, its like, its hiding. I'm trying to see it, but it won't let me see it. I saw something that way, but what I want to see, it won't let me see, I know that, but I can't see it. It's like its got a big cover over it. I'm trying to see it, but I can't see it. And I saw something coming down beside it"

(MR) "Did you see the object and…….."

(HW) "Shush" *(Author's note. Helen told me off at this point as I butted in, as I was eager to ask Garry loads of questions. But Helen said that I should let Garry tell it as he remembers it)*

(GW) "I really felt as if I wasn't coming back, and it was like I was moving. There was activity going on, I know that. Its hard to piece it together. I was looking for Colin and I said to myself, they are looking for him. Every time you were talking Helen, I was hearing this noise pulsating in my ear, and it got louder when you were talking".

(HW) "Pulsating sound, high pitched sound"?

(GW) "When you shut your eyes really hard and you hear a noise in your head, it was like that. I cannot talk, as it's hindering me talking".

(HW) "How did you feel when you were trying to talk"?

(GW) "I was wanting to talk, but I couldn't, it was that funny noise inside my ear".

(HW) "High pitched".

(GW) "No, it wasn't high pitched".

(HW) "Sharp noise, or a hollow noise"?

(GW) "No it was a pulsating noise, going wooo, woooo, wooo, wooo and it get louder when you were talking".

(HW) "Like a droning noise"?

(GW) "I was paying more attention to the noise than you".

(HW) "Do you remember crying in the craft"?

(GW) "It's hard to say."

(HW) "Are you aware of the fact that you were really crying"? *(Author's note. Garry had tears running down his face during this part of the session)*

(GW) "Yes".

(HW) "You knew that you were physically crying as well"?

(GW) "Yes. Now don't take this the wrong way. But when I looked at your face, it looked as if it was changing shape. I wanted to shut my eyes, I didn't want to look at you. It was weird".

(HW) "I did tell you, that if I took the presence of someone else, that I would do so, but it would still be under control".

(GW) "I remember seeing something like that at the beginning".

(HW) "That's what happens. Sometimes my voice becomes somebody else's

(GW) "This side of my head here, *(Author's note. Garry was pointing to the side of his head)* this ear here and that noise".

(HW) "Have you still got it"?

(GW) "Yes"

(HW) "How are you feeling right now"?

(GW) "Shaky. Really shaky, like the shivers. It's hard to explain what I saw. I don't want to tell lies. I saw something over there, I don't know what it was, but I wasn't getting to see it. And I saw something else coming down, but I wasn't getting to see. And I saw something horrible, and I am trying to look about but I'm not getting to see anything".

(HW) "That's why I said to you that it doesn't all come out in one session. That's why I said no to any time limit on it, because it would end up not doing what it was supposed to do, and do you more harm than good".

(GW) "I see a kind of physical shape and it's like its crouched. It's just too hard to make out. It's like a cloak, a big grey cloak. It's weird. I can see like a round head but it's like I'm seeing the back of a head. I don't know. I seen something coming down, I don't know how it is coming down. I know for a fact that something was facing me. And I saw something else, something not so horrible. Like, sort of in the background peeking. Something peeking at me. It wasn't startling, but it was intriguing me as to what it was".

(HW) "And did you get any feeling as to what it was"?

(GW) "I don't want to say because I'm not sure".

(HW) "Well say what you think it was".

(GW) "Whatever it was, and it may sound stupid, it was like it had zig zags on its face. It was only there, then it was away".

(HW) "You felt like this was quite good"?

(GW) "No, it was something in the background that wasn't alarming. There was something there and it wasn't alarming, and whatever it was, I wasn't meant to see. Not only were that noise, but there was something at this side of my head, and even when you were talking, that you are 30, 31, this thing was getting louder and louder, and it was a pulsing sound in my ear. And it was trying to wipe out what you were saying, I know that".

(HW) "How long did that last for, can you remember when it actually started"?

(GW) "Sometimes when you were talking it stopped, and then some of the things you were talking about, it would start again".

(HW) "Was that when you were coming forward in your age".

(GW) "Yes, when I was coming forward in my age. But I definitely felt that I wasn't coming back and that was why I was crying, I can't make head nor tail of it".

(HW) "You were definitely afraid".

(GW) "I can see two things there. Definitely two things moving. I could say 'beings' or something, but there were two things moving. And then there was this wee thing that was peeking. It had like make up on *(Author's note. Garry is referring to these coloured zig zag lines on the beings face which he likened to make up)* And when I was looking at you, it was taking form, but I wasn't wanting to look. I don't want to lie to you, I am telling you the truth of what I think, of what is in my head".

(HW) "What comes out, whether you think it is silly, it's what comes out from your head".

(GW) "With that pulsing sound, it's like you want to pop your ears. But there was something going on in that ear, definitely",

(HW) "Actually that is your conscious side, your right side is your unconscious, and your left is your conscious side. It was trying to interfere with your thoughts, it was trying to see into your subconscious".

(GW) "There was something going on anyway, I know that. I thought that I would be in my car with Colin driving along and see this thing. I couldn't find that bit". *(Author's note. Garry is of course referring to what he expected to find under hypnosis, ie, driving along the road, then seeing this object)*

(HW) "Did you just find yourself in that place that you were in, that you can't describe"?

(GW) "I know that I was looking for Colin. I said to myself, look for Colin, I didn't know if Colin was there or whatever, but I was looking for Colin".

(HW) "You were looking for him in your unconscious mind, you were reliving that situation, you were looking for him there".

(GW) "I saw things in this distance, I can't remember, hopefully I will".

Author's note. At this point we stopped for tea and coffee. And I asked Garry some more questions about that particular hypnosis session.

(GW) "I was trying to get out from what was happening. I can't make head nor tail of anything Malcolm".

(MR) "It might make sense as the days go on, things might start coming to the surface".

(GW) "I was expecting to be in the car with Colin that's what I was wanting my mind to think, that I was in the car with Colin going along the road. But that's not what was coming out! It's like I was moving, then I knew that I wasn't moving. And I saw these two things but I couldn't make out what they were, and I saw something peeking, something small. I don't want to say what it is, in case my mind is wrong. And the thing that I saw in front of me, was horrible".

(MR) "Helen, can I ask questions here"?

(HW) "I would rather that we waited till he is finished his coffee then we can chat away. As I am wanting him to finish off what he is talking about himself. Because if you are going back and forth with a lot of questions you will stop him from remembering"

(MR) "OK, no problem".

(Author's note. I went to the toilet at this point and the tape was running. Garry was talking to Colin (who was not in the room whilst Garry was being hypnotised) Some might say that with Garry speaking to Colin and relaying what came out under hypnosis to Colin, that this would surely colour the investigations. But what you have to remember is they are both friends. Friends who had travelled to Alva in a car together to meet up with Helen and I. For me to say to Garry, don't speak about what came out under hypnosis, would not have been worth it. As I'm pretty sure that Garry was keen to tell his friend. Some things are very difficult to manage. This is what Garry was saying.

(GW) "I know I'm in somewhere, and I know there are two things there, and there is one at the front and I can see. It's not a little girl, its something peeking. And I can see one of it's eyes, and I can see zig zags, make up, red and yellow under its

351

eye. It's like a child but not a child. The hypnotic regression is funny, you are sort of aware. I think I was picking up on whispering, as I could hear whispering. I know I was crying".

Author's Note: At this point Garry pretty much said to Colin what he said when he came out under hypnosis when Helen Walters was asking him questions. So I will refrain from reporting it here again. When I came back from the toilet and Garry was finished his coffee. It was agreed that I could ask more questions. I will only report what Garry said different to what's stated above.

(GW) "I didn't know what was happening to me. It's like when you know that that's it, to me anyway. And I think that's why I was crying. I know I was crying. I was wanting to really cry but I couldn't. And I was trying to stop myself crying as well, I know that".

(MR) "Did you get that strange noise on the last hypnosis session"?

(GW) "No, not that I can remember. It was pumping in my head Malcolm, in the middle of my brain, pulsing in my head. I feel like I was lying down. I want to be sure in my own mind of what I am seeing before I start saying anything to anybody. And I cannot picture things properly Malcolm. I'm just telling you what I feel. I know for definite that there are four presences at one point. Two, then something small, and something in front of me. There was a lot of activity for a short while.

(Author's note. At this point I went into the kitchen leaving Garry and Colin alone. And this is what the tape picked up.)

(GW) "I know at one point I'm frightened. I don't know what's what".

(CW) "What was going through my mind was, that I felt sorry for them".

352

(Author's note. I then came back into the room and Garry reiterated that he was really terrified)

(GW) "I hope I'm not a crackpot"

(MR) "No no don't be silly".

(GW) "It's hard to say if it was a room that I was in, it was quite wide. There was something there, one big long thing going up, and it was like blocking a door of some sort because there was a light that was there. Wherever it was that I was, it was quite open, it was quite big. Not big as in huge, but it was fairly spacious. The image I get Malcolm is funny. It might look stupid to you".

(Author's note. Garry is at this point doing a drawing of what he remembers seeing under hypnosis)

(GW) "It's like this, but it's like I am looking at the back of whatever it is. And it's like hazy or grey, I don't know. It's big, it's like a big cloak, and that's the back of its head. I cannot see it Malcolm. But that's what the two things were like, both of them. One coming down. And they didn't look like they were big. I can't make head nor tail of it Helen"

(HW) "But at least it's coming through, you are beginning to see through the picture, through the veil. And it's you, yourself that's not wanting to go right in and see that. You are pulling back. I could be a lot more formal in taking you back. But I free floated you into that. Although I went forward and back, I let you choose where you were going with it. When you didn't want to say nothing, nothing was happening to you at all, you were just lying there almost going to sleep. And you were definitely shaking and jumping in response to the months and dates. The second of August you had quite a reaction as well. With the other dates, you definitely didn't want to communicate, you just shook your head *(Author's note. This was when Helen was taking Garry back to five years of age under hypnosis. Garry didn't react or say anything to this at all)*

(GW)   "I remember there was something like clouds or something, I don't know. Then there were more clouds are they were joining together. It was like, one piece there, then one piece there, and it was all coming together".

(HW) "You did well on it though Garry. You reacted very well. At one point, I don't know if it was the noise that was bothering you or not, I thought you were going to get up and hit me. I could actually sense......."

(GW) "I could feel aggression within myself, I could feel that yes. I was raging. I knew I was feeling rage. You are twigging it off by saying it"

(HW) "It wouldn't be me that you were hitting, it would be the party that would be doing this with you".

(GW) "It feels as if I was lying down flat, and its knocking me off balance. Its not like things are walking round about, it's like I can't see any legs or anything. *(Author's note. Garry is trying to explain that as he is lying down on this flat table in this strange room, he is looking at these 'beings', but can't discern any legs on them, due no doubt, to his position on the table and that he could only move his eyes)* They were walking about. Then I saw something floating, I don't know what it was. It was like a grey, plastic which I'm looking at the back of someone's head, really round with a neck, and then it was like a big cloak cape thing. I don't know".

(HW) "It sounds as if you felt like it was a shield or armour of some kind, because you are not talking about materials you are talking about something hard, something more solid".

(GW) "It had no features whatever".

(GW) "I just feel that things are missing".

(HW) "Well we have to fill in the gaps then. We have to find out what it is. You will lose that as you go along. I think the next time that you have hypnosis, we have to take you straight in, no conversation, no nothing, just straight in. Just concentrate for me".

(GW) "See, I don't want to say anything that is not true".

(HW) "Oh I know that".

(GW) "I just want to tell you the truth".

(HW) "I know that".

(GW) "No matter how stupid it is, it's all I want to tell you".

(HW) "That's right I know that. I think that is what you are doing, but you are not allowing yourself to go where you want, because you are putting a mental block up against this. I mean, that happens quite often, it's not something unusual. It just depends on the individual".

(GW) "I know that I am here. I am just trying to be honest with you. I know that I am alright now, so when I go back, I should be alright then. I should be able to see".

(HW) "But you don't see, you don't want to see. When you went back, what did you see on any of the other dates"?.

(GW) "It's like I am seeing things blurred".

(HW) "What you are doing is trying to control the situation. You are trying to control what it is you are doing".

(GW) "But this noise, I'm not making it up, this noise keeps coming. It's like something is stuck inside my ear inside my head, and it's pumping away like wooo, wooo, wooo".

(HW) "Does it sound like a live wire"?

(GW) "It's right inside, its hard to say. There is something inside making a noise".

(HW) "Now I have reasons for asking that, that is why".

(GW) "I can feel something that takes the whole width of my ear up inside my head, and I am trying to get away from it".

(HW) "But its taking over an awful lot of you, this noise that you are getting. You are getting bogged down with this noise. You are holding onto control, you are not letting yourself go. Even when you are under the hypnosis, you are still controlling, you are holding fast onto everything. You are in control".

(GW) "I think I am doing the same with whatever is happening there".

(HW) "You can't control it in that sense, that's what's stopping you from growing and understanding what is happening on the 17th. And when you get to that date, you want to stay just holding onto that 17th".

(GW) "Uh huh".

(HW) "You don't want to go any place else or think of anything else no matter what, you always will come back".

(GW) "Yes, because when you are trying to put me somewhere else, I'm trying to get to see what's there".

(HW) "Yes, that's right. You're not moving. But that's free, its what we call 'free floating regression'. That's why you have the choice of holding on, in that particular one".

(GW) "When you were talking and trying to take me somewhere else, I was trying to stay there. There were like

362

things looking down at me all the time, loads of them looking down at me".

(HW) "As I said, the most important part, is you having to release this control, we will have to take the control from you a different way, in the sense of turning it into a control which is going to do you good, rather than an obstruction. Using it is an obstruction right now where you can use it as a guide".

(GW) "I think you feel that I am being awkward with you, but I am trying not to be. I'm trying to be straight with you".

(HW) "I don't think you are being awkward with me, as a matter of fact, what's happening tonight, shouldn't be awkward one way or another, because hypnosis you can be resistant. You were resistant because you were over trying to begin with. And you are trying too hard. You want the truth to come out, but what truth"?

(GW) "I don't know, It's hard to say. It's like, 'don't say nothing.' You know what I mean?"

(HW) "Well that is what I am saying, its resistance".

(GW) "It's like something is telling me not to say something".

(HW) "Its resistance, you are going to have to give up what its telling you not to say. Because when it comes right down to it............"

(GW) "One of them was making me laugh. It was funny, I don't know why. It was happy, it was having a laugh, and I was laughing".

(Author's note. Under hypnosis one could see from the video tape, that Garry was smiling)

(HW) "Very much so. Now when I turned aggressive with you, like as though you were being awkward, it was to try and break that away from you. It wasn't because I believed that you were being awkward. Because when you were laughing, you didn't want to change into nothing".

(GW) "I know, it seems funny now, because it seems as if they have a lot to talk about, like it was just something funny. I don't know. It was like they are something as well, just like me, and it was just funny. It's the same thing, its got a life like me, its like.....poor bugger your there and I'm here, no luck sort of thing".

(HW) *(Laughs)*

(GW) "It was funny, because it has a life like me as well. That's why I was laughing, because I was the one lying down there, and this thing is looking at me, and I know that its got the same kind of life, not like my life, but it's got a life as well. Its like I was giving, but I can take as well. You are not talking, its a weird feeling, you just know".

(HW) "Is it mental"?

(GW) "Yes but it's not like.......

(HW) "Like E.S.P.?

(GW) "It's a complete mass amount, it's not like how you would just say a sentence. Its lock stock and barrel, the whole complete shooting match"

(HW) "I can understand that".

(GW) "The way it seems to me, is like basically it has a life as well, and like us, it has its ups and down's, and it was just sort of funny. Do you understand what I mean?"

(HW) "I do understand what you mean".

(GW) "And I'm saying, I'm stuck down here and you are fannying around up there".

(HW) *(Laughs)*

(GW) "It's really weird and I am laughing, and it is laughing as well. And then, what's got to be done, has got to be done, and that's the way it is".

(Author's note. That concluded that particular audio tape).

The next transcript, comes from a taped discussion that myself and hypnotherapist Helen Walters had with Garry Wood after he had come out of hypnosis. It was recorded in September, 1994.

Hypnosis on Garry Wood, September 1994

Abbreviations:
(MR) Malcolm Robinson. (GW) Garry Wood. (HW) Helen Walters.

(MR) "You have just came out from hypnosis there Garry. Tell me what you saw on this occasion"

(GW) "I was looking about, and I saw like these really long dead things, but they were away up. I saw three of them and there was something lying on top of them. But they were really high up"

(MR) "What do you feel they were then"?

(GW) "They looked like beds".

(MR) "Were they attached to anything"?

(GW) "They were attached to something like that" *(Author's note. Garry had done a drawing of what he recalled, see photographic section)* "These poles went really really high. It

365

was like a sun bed kind of thing. The shape of it is difficult to draw".

(MR) "Apart from this bed like shape, where do you think that 'they' were"?

(GW) "They were in something. This bed thing, was quite well designed. They were really long, and there were three of them, and I could see one of the creatures, just sort of the head bit on it, as if it was lying down on it. But the first time when you hypnotised me Helen, not the first time, I mean tonight. It was like it was all red. That's what I thought was weird, that everything was all red. It was like fluid, and there were all these things like fish, they were long, and there were loads of them everywhere. And I was just watching them all moving".

(HW) "How big were they"?

(GW) "Bigger than me, and they were all moving. It just didn't make any sense".

(HW) "I mean what sounds funny to us, would not be funny to them".

(GW) "It was like I was in water or something, and it was red and I was in it. That's what made me think that it was water because they were all floating around me. I thought, am I under water, am I in a pond or something. And they were coming towards me then going away. The way they were like folding back on each other it didn't look like they were really fat, they looked very thin. But they were everywhere, and I mean everywhere. It was way bigger than this room".

(HW) "You have never came up with anything like this before".

(GW) "I saw a woman as well. The woman had dark hair. She dropped something like a clipboard, and she bent down because I was looking at her behind. I kept trying to look at her face to

see if it was changing. She was near cupboard things, like compartments"

(HW) "Where were the cupboard things"?

(GW) "She was kneeling down".

(HW) "And there were cupboard things where she was kneeling down"!

(GW) "Yes. There were loads of them, everywhere, all the way up. Like you go to the library and there all these books, all the way up. From bottom to top. I kept trying to look at her face"

(HW) "You said that she had dark eyes, I've got it all written down, and you said she was in human form".

(GW) "Oh yes, she definitely was. When you hypnotised me the first time I thought it was weird. It was like I was watching a video in fast forward, but it was in black and white. And then it was like I was moving really fast over the top of like land and seeing people".

(HW) "You can't control that part of it. You are fighting what you are seeing. You are not fighting me, you are fighting yourself. And you saw the sea".

(GW) "Yes I saw the sea".

(HW) "And you saw a barren land".

(GW) "Yes, lots of barren land. I also saw things with uniforms on. I saw a hat, like an officer's hat, and I saw people running like a sports thing".

(HW) "I'm really surprised that you saw all this. You are not an easy subject, you are definitely not an easy subject Garry".

(GW) "I thought that I would tell you what I saw, no matter how ridiculous it was".

(HW) "Yes, that's good, that's what you have to do. But as you say, you felt that you were travelling at a lot of speed".

(GW) "At first I felt like I was watching through a video screen. I'm not being funny. It was like everything that I was watching was going really fast, ultra quick, quicker than what a video can go. And then it was like I was there. It was all black and white, like world war two or something".

(HW) "Actually I was amazed that you saw as much as you did. And I've got you down as saying that you enjoyed the feeling as travelling as fast as you were travelling. And that's how you astral travel. That's how you put yourself out of your body in astral travelling. I was doing this to you, but I was doing this to you under a controlled fashion. You said you saw people looking across plains, there was lots of barren land. Some people had hats, as you said there. There were crowds and crowds of people".

(GW) "There were some people running, like a race or something. There was also loads of people standing on somewhere high, looking and pointing".

(HW) "You also said that you saw a room with a machine, and it was a white room".

(GW) "The machine was high up on a wall, I would say at least 40/50 feet".

(HW) "And the machine had bits of black in it. I'm trying to find out if this had anything to do with what you work with. You said white. I mean, what like is your room at work, is it white?"

(GW) "No. I mean, nobody could reach this machinery as to where it was. How the hell could you get to it, it was too high. It went up, really high, like up the side of a wall thing".

(HW) "And you said you saw people's faces changing, and change back again".

(GW) "When I stared at his face, I was trying to see what it was, and it just kept changing all the time, altering".

(HW) "You can't describe the people you are seeing from another angle".

(GW) "But the thing is, they were moving fast, I wasn't"

(HW) "I don't know why you are getting such a lot of experiences which coincide with the psychic experiences. I found that strange. And you are not involved in that, you are not interested in that".

(Author's note: Helen is trying to explain to Garry, that part of what he was seeing, was not necessarily part of his abduction, but could have been part of some kind of astral travelling that had infiltrated if you like, into the landscape of his hypnotic recall)

(GW) "It's not what I was looking for. I'm just telling you what I saw. I said I would do this for you".

(HW) "My first programme with you, was a relaxation programme, when I put you down in the basement, and you didn't like that too much. You just had a whole relaxed reaction through the whole thing".

(GW) "I just cannot understand it, how it is ending up like this".

(HW) "What I am doing is relaxing you".

(GW) "Am I looking in the right places"?

(HW) "Well I think that is what you will do. But right now you were so tense, and uptight in your hypnosis. It's very difficult to relax you. And because I am passing that control to you, you are going along with the relaxation. Because of my previous experience with you, I thought I would have difficulty with you. But you did it, I could see it. See people who astral travel Malcolm, what I did with Garry, that's what they do, that's how they do it. And Garry responded".

(GW) "It was like it was black and white".

(HW) "Yes, that is what it would be. The only other response you had Garry, was the car crash".

(GW) "I saw like the car tipping up, the front end. It was dark. What I saw was weird. Things were coming to me, then going away. They were everywhere. I couldn't see any eyes. They came up to me, then flicked away quick. I'm still a bit scared".

(Author's note. Garry is again referring here to these strange shapes that quickly came up to him and disappeared. They were not grey's, they were strange shapes (see photographic section)

(HW) "And you haven't been getting back up at 3:00am in the morning".

(GW) "No I haven't".

(HW) "The hypnosis is doing what it is supposed to do for you, it's helping you. The fact is, the more able you feel you can handle this and the more the hypnosis happens, the better you will get the answer and the more you will be able to cope with it. Because before you were not coping with it, it was very obvious that you were not coping with it. But now you are. You are not uptight".

(MR) "I've certainly noticed a difference in Garry".

(HW) "And Garry's attitude is different".

(GW) "It's still all weird though, honestly"

(MR) "So you thought you were in some kind of pond"!

(GW) "Everything was like red, a bright reddy colour. These things were grey black, and they would come up to me and just go away".

(HW) "Did you feel as though they had any intelligence"?

(GW) "I just wondered what the hell they were doing. Coming and going away".

(HW) "There were no bones, was it just like they could bend".

(GW) "Yes, uh huh".

(HW) "I mean fish don't bend down that way".

(GW) "These things were curling back on themselves. That's what I saw".

(HW) "And how did you feel when you saw that"?

(GW) "I just felt that it was weird".

(MR) "Did you look down and see yourself"?

(GW) "Yes I could see myself".

(MR) "And what were you wearing".

(GW) "I had on my leather jacket, I know that, and my black trousers. I wasn't touching the ground".

(MR) "Was this the type of clothes that you usually wore or…….

(GW) "It's the same type of clothes that I wear all the time. All my clothes in my wardrobe are all black. I've got 42 black tops, and I've got about nine pair of black trousers. I have got coloured clothes, but I do wear a lot of dark clothes".

(MR) "And you saw yourself in this predicament"?

(GW) "Yes, but not my face, just my body, and I was looking around me, and then I was wondering, what the hell are these things doing? but they were not threatening me. I was just wondering why they were coming to me and going away. But I didn't feel as if I was dying or anything. And what I also looked for was bubbles. But there were nothing".

(HW) "Were they a jelly like substance"?

(GW) "I don't know. It was like a fluid come gas stuff. It wasn't sticking to me or anything like that, it was just there, all around me".

(HW) "Did you feel wet or anything"?

(GW) "No, nothing. It was like I was in mid air. I couldn't see the bottom, and I couldn't see right at the side, but I saw lots of these things everywhere all around me".

(MR) "How deep or wide was this area you were in"?

(GW) "It was quite wide. It felt like it was a tube or something".

(MR) "How thick were these things that were coming towards you"?

(GW) "They were bigger than you or I".

(HW) "You are not under any threat with this".

(GW) "That machinery that I saw was weird".

(HW) "What kind of machinery was it"?

(GW) "It was all different. There was one big round thing with things coming from it. But this machinery went about fifty feet up in the air on one side. And it was all like shiny bright white plastic. Outlines like black buttons and things like that. And there was one thing which was separate from it. It had like a square thing on it with like a round dome on the top. From what I could see, these things were about fifty feet up and about forty to fifty feet across. That's really high and there were things jutting out from it, all round shapes and all different bits. It was just like one big huge enormous control panel or something. But why so big? And I saw that woman, she walked over to me and bent down. And she had dark short hair".

(HW) "Do you know of any female in your life that dresses like that, that you can compare with"?

(GW) "The only woman that I know with her hair like that, is a woman who works in at my work in our control, but her hair is not like that any more, but it had her build. She had really dark eyes, her whole eyes were dark".

(HW) "Yes, you said that her eyes were not like alien eyes, but her eyes were in human form".

(GW) "Her body was like in human form. I'm not sure about her eyes".

(HW) "You did say that her eyes weren't big".

(GW) "No no, they weren't big, they were human eyes. I didn't expect to see what I saw tonight. As I've said to you Helen, I will tell you exactly what I see, no matter how ridiculous it sounds. When I woke up, all my body was sore. It was like shaking. I felt weak, my arms and legs and joints felt weak, they still do".

(MR) "Any buzzing in your head or ears this time"?

(GW) "No".

(HW) "Any sounds".

(GW) "No. I was listening for it. Because when you were hypnotising me, I thought that those sounds were going to start".

(Author's note. As we have learned, in a previous hypnotic session, Garry was troubled by an intense buzzing sound in his head and ears)

(MR) "Visually you saw a lot there".

(GW) "That liquid stuff was funny. It felt like it was going right through me, like it was passing right through me with no problem. At first I thought that I was watching a video, that's what I don't understand. It was like a door, and I am watching seeing everything moving. I saw things happening below me. It wasn't me moving fast, it was them moving fast. Like watching a video on ultra fast forward".

(HW) "Was there anything or anyone who saw you in this thing"?

(GW) "I saw someone pointing. Somebody was high up pointing".

(HW) "How do you mean high up"?

(GW) "There was a lot of people standing up on a hill, and one of them was pointing. But this was during the day".

(HW) "If you could see what you expected to see Garry, and could manufacture what you expected to see, then you would be wasting your time and my time".

(GW) "Yes I realise that".

(HW) "And that is a good reference in the fact that this is totally out with everything. Its a good result you know. Its not a result on what we were talking about on Saturday about your drawings and what you had seen. It wasn't a result in the sense of the 17ᵗʰ of August that we expected to. But its a good result because it is totally out with what you were fighting and struggling all the time to go and do".

(MR) "It tells us that you are not elaborating in the sense that you are producing something for Helen and I to please us".

(HW) "That's right. It's a good result".

(MR) "Yes it is".

(HW) "There is so much more from this method, for allowing Garry to come out of hypnosis when he wants to, to do what he wants to. I no longer put him under on the basis that he won't waken up, or try and put him into a deep" *(Author's note. I couldn't make out what Helen said on audio tape at this point)*..........."Garry would fight it too much with my previous hypnotic method. But this method allows Garry to come in and come out with a whole lot of information which is good".

(MR) "Are you saying that this is a new hypnotic process or what Helen"?

(HW) "We do call it an infraction method. Its a different type of hypnosis from the other method I have used".

At this point the audio tape ran out. It was clear to see however, that Garry was struggling to make clear what he was seeing in this particular hypnosis session. And that's the thing, it must be neigh impossible to try and make clear and explain to someone else, something so bizarre and unusual. One thing that struck me about this hypnotic session, was that Garry never claimed to see any grey's, just weird shapes that would rush up to him and go away. He did see what he described as 'people' standing high up on a high, and also a human like female with dark hair and dark eyes. And what are we to make out of the above? Is it all mind full imagination? Is it the mind playing tricks on Garry? Was Garry so far under hypnosis, that he entered a dream state, and as such, what he was reliving, was only a dream, and not part of his UFO abduction? We can only speculate and hope that when other UFO abductees read this book, they too might have had something similar happen to them as Garry has described above. We are looking for patterns here. We are looking for similarities from abductees from across the globe, and if there is anyone reading this book who has had the same scenario unfold to them as written above, then please get in touch with the author with the address at the end of this book.

We now turn to Colin Wright, and one of his actual hypnosis sessions. The following is what Colin said under hypnosis. The following text is all together, as there were many spaces on the tape where Colin was silent, but I have grouped it all together. This transcript is from October 10th 1994.

Colin Wright Hypnosis. October 10th 1994

Abbreviations: (HW) Helen Walters. (CW) Colin Wright.

(HW) "Is there anybody afraid there"?

(CW) "I can't tell because I can't move my head, I can only see the one in front of me".

(HW) "You have no idea where you are going?"

(CW) "No".

(HW) "The cylinder is moving"!

(CW) "I don't know, I just know we are going"

(HW) "Can you feel movement"?

(CW) "I did earlier on yes".

(HW) "How do you feel at the moment"?

(CW) "Frustrated".

(HW) "Have you been given anything to eat"?

(CW) "No".

(HW) "Drink"?

(CW) "No".

(HW) "Have they approached you in any other way"?

(CW) *(Author's note. I couldn't make out on tape what Colin said here)*

(HW) "Would you like to come home"?

(CW) "Yes".

(HW) "And where's your clothes"?

(CW) "I've no idea".

(HW) "I'd like you to listen Colin, for in a few seconds time, I'm saying the word, 'present', 'present', 'present', 'present'. In a few moments time, you are back here, with me, in this room in the present. No part of you is in the past".

END OF TAPE.

The following transcript is an interview that I did with Colin Wright regarding the hypnosis that was conducted on him the previous week, (October 10th 1994) Colin speaks about being enclosed within a glass or perspex chamber. This is what he had to say.

Abbreviations: (MR) Malcolm Robinson. (CW) Colin Wright.

(MR) "Interview with Colin Wright, 17th October 1994. Now Colin, I'd like specifically to discuss with you, last week's hypnotic regression, unfortunately I couldn't attend that particular session. I'm looking at a drawing in front of me here, of you inside some sort of glass or perspex chamber. Before we go into this point, could you tell me how last week's regression went for you, how did you feel"?

(CW) "Just confused, I didn't make much sense of it at all. I couldn't seem to get out of that chamber at all. Helen was trying to move me on, but nothing worked at all. I was sort of stuck in it".

(MR) OK you found yourself inside this glass or perspex chamber. Can you go into more detail in regards to this, in regards to how you found yourself there"?

(CW) "Basically Helen took me back to that date, and I just 'appeared' in that chamber. I was kind of harnessed in. I couldn't move at all. I could move my head slightly to the right and left and I could look up, but I couldn't look down, just straight in front of me. I couldn't move at all. I had no clothes on as usual! I don't even know what I was doing there".

(MR) Looking at this drawing in front of me, you have yourself being held down and restrained by some sort of straps or whatever. Could you look at those straps and see what kind of straps that you were restrained by"?

(CW) "The way the straps were, they were over my wrists, chest and arms I couldn't see as I was restricted, I couldn't look down".

(MR) "But you don't really know what these straps were made of"?

(CW) "No I couldn't feel them, my hands were restricted so I couldn't touch them".

(MR) "Do you know how you came to be found in that particular chamber"?

(CW) "No, I've no idea at all, I was just baffled, really baffled".

(MR) "Now in this drawing that I am looking at now, you have drawn some kind of mist that was billowing around the foot of this chamber. Is that what you saw"?

CW) "Yes, that's what I saw. Some kind of mist floating around the floor, that's the only way I could describe it".

(MR) "You also in this situation, was able to view other containers, is this correct"?

(CW) "Yes, that's right, I saw loads of other people. They had no clothes on as well. I couldn't make them out properly, because the chamber I was in was sort of frosted over, so I didn't have a clear picture".

(MR) "But you say you saw other people"?

(CW) "Yes loads of other people, not just a few, loads of other people".

(MR) "In other containers"?

(CW) "In other containers yes, the very same as myself"

(MR) "Did they appear to be clothed or unclothed"?

(CW) "No, they were naked as well, male and female".

(MR) "Were there any higher concentration in males to females, or was it a combination, a mixture of both"?

(CW) "I would say the same, well maybe just slightly more males than females but there wouldn't be much in it".

(MR) Did you happen to notice if there were any particular age group at all, in regards to the people in the other containers".

(CW) "No it varied, there were all different age groups. I saw older men and younger men like myself. And it was the same with the women, there were older women and younger women".

(MR) "Were there any children"?

(CW) "No. there were no children at all".

(MR) "Do you have any further recollections about last week's hypnotic regression, or was this specifically your main recollection at this time"?

(CW) "That's all I could remember. I was asked to move on to different places but I just couldn't get out of there. For some reason I just couldn't get out of that chamber. It was frustrating".

(MR) "Colin, do you remember anything else about being in this glass or perspex chamber"?

(CW) "I remember sitting there freezing, as if I was being frozen or something like that. And then this tremendous heat came all over me and I started to sweat. Helen picked up on that point, and said that there was a warm glow about me. I got the impression that they were trying to freeze me and then they were de-frosting me again, something like that. That's the impression I got".

(MR) "Were there any smoke or mist that came into your chamber"?

(CW) "There was mist on the floor outside of the chamber, all over the room, but there was nothing inside the chamber itself, just outside. There were loads of chambers".

END OF TAPE

The following is an extract of the hypnosis session that was conducted on Garry Wood by Helen Walters on the 17th of October 1994. I should state that due to the bad hissing on the audio tape, and the fact that the audio tape was not close to Garry's mouth, plus the fact that he was speaking quite soft, a lot of what Garry said has been missed)

Garry Wood Hypnosis. 17th October 1994

Abbreviations: (HW) Helen Walters. (GW) Garry Wood.

(HW) "What can you see? Where are you just now"?

(GW) "Lying down"

(HW) "Your lying down. Where are you Garry"?

(GW) "I don't know".

(HW) "You don't know where you are? Look around. Can you feel anything? Can you see anything? Are you afraid?

(GW) "No"

(HW) "Are you still in the car"? Is Colin with you? Are you still on the road? What can you tell me about where you are Garry?

(GW) *"Unintelligible"*

(HW) "Do you know where your car is? What are you afraid of Garry"?

(GW) "A wee guy."

(HW) "There is a wee guy beside you? What's he like? Is he friendly? Is Colin still with you?

(GW) *"Unintelligible"*

(HW) "Can you speak to this wee guy"?

(GW) *"Unintelligible"*

(HW) "Could you not ask to speak to the one you met before who was friendly with you? Try. Is it light where you are?

(GW) "I can't see anything".

(HW) "What's stopping you from seeing?

(GW) "I don't know"

(HW) "Why are you lying down"?

(GW) "I don't know".

(HW) "Are you cold? Do you have a blanket over you Garry? Is the wee guy still there?

(GW) *"Unintelligible"*

(HW) "Is it someone you have met before"?

(GW) "I cannot see clear".

(HW) "Try to relax. What's frightening you?

(GW) *"Unintelligible"*

(HW) "Is he standing at your side.?

(GW) *"Unintelligible"*

(HW) "How do you know that they are there? Do you want to tell me Garry?

(GW) "I'm scared there's something up at me, *'Unintelligible'*

(HW) "Can you see who's there"?

(GW) "There are faces coming over me and....*(Unintelligible)*

(HW) "Is it big"?

(GW) "It's human"

(HW) "Human"!

(GW) "Uh huh"

(HW) "Are you scared of it"?

(GW) "Uh huh"

(HW) "How"

(GW) "Don't know".

(HW) "Did it just look at you"?

(GW) "Uh huh".

(HW) "Can you see what's happening"?

(GW) "Creepy".

(HW) "How do you mean creepy"?

(GW) *"Unintelligible."*

(HW) "Just take your time, relax. Deep breaths all the way. Remember, my voice is with you. Let your eyes focus, get accustomed to where you are. Are you clothed"?

(GW) "Don't know".

(HW) "You don't know"?

(GW) "No".

(HW) *"Unintelligible"*

(GW) "Something came at me".

(HW) "Well ask it to go away. You ask the questions. Ask it why you are here, what's the reason? What do they want of you? Do they want you to do anything? Why are you so special that they have chosen you?

(GW) "Don't know".

(HW) "Are they going to come back for you? Ask them Garry, only you can ask them".

(GW) *"Unintelligible."*

(HW) "What's disgusting you"?

(GW) *"Unintelligible."*

(HW) "Clear it away if its judging you, clear it away. Tell me Garry, what is your left eye doing?"

(GW) "Don't know."

(HW) "Does your left eye feel the same as your right eye at the moment"?

(GW) "Uh huh".

(HW) "Where you are now, is your eye open or closed?

(GW) *"Unintelligible."*

(HW) "Which one is closed"?

(GW) *"Unintelligible."*

(HW) "Do you know why your eyes are like this?

(GW) *"Unintelligible."*

(HW) "It must be uncomfortable to have one eye open like this. Has it opened on its own? What are they doing to you? Have they left you alone?

(GW) *"Unintelligible."*

(HW) "Can you not make friends with it? Does it smell bad? How do you feel about it? Is it important to you Garry?"

(GW) "Uh huh".

(HW) "It's important if you can find out, if you could meet and look into the eyes of the other being who told you their life story".

(GW) *"Unintelligible."*

(HW) "Do you have that knowledge already? That's in one of the corridors of your mind. Sift it out. Are you asking, *"Unintelligible."*

(GW) *"Unintelligible."*

(HW) "Ask harder".

(GW) "Can't see"

(HW) "See if you can just see his eyes, *"Unintelligible."* Ask him to look you in the eye".

(GW) *"Unintelligible."*

(HW) "Is it speaking to you? Is it communicating with you in any way? You are there Garry, ask it. This is what you want, this is your moment. No one else can do it".

(GW) "I can't see clear".

(HW) "Well try to hear, it's not important that you see. Listen to them. Let them whisper to your mind."

(GW) "I asked them and it was like sanctuary, or something".

(HW) "Ask them to help you understand.....*"Unintelligible."*

(GW) *"Unintelligible."*

(HW) "Do you feel violent towards them"?

(GW) "No". *"Unintelligible."* "If they are looking to me to help, what can I do?"

(HW) "Ask them how you can help. What is happening Garry"?

(GW) *"Unintelligible."*

(HW) "Ask them if its alright as to why they need you? Take a chance and ask them. How is it they want to be here? *"Unintelligible."*

(GW) *"Unintelligible."*

(HW) "Do you know? Can you see the ride home?"

(GW) "No".

(HW) *"Unintelligible."* Pool! What kind of material or clothes or whatever, is in the pool *(Author's note. It sounded like the word pool)* *"Unintelligible."* Black! Is anyone else there?

(GW) *"Unintelligible."*

(HW) "Where are you now"?

(GW) "I can't see".

(HW) *"Unintelligible."* "Are you cold where you are"?

(GW) "No".

(HW) "Are you sitting up"?

(GW) *"Unintelligible."*

(HW) "What kind of material are you lying on, what does it feel like? Is it hard?

(GW) *"Unintelligible."*

(HW) "Is it soft?

(GW) *"Unintelligible."* "There are things that are touching me…... *"Unintelligible."*

(HW) "Can you tell me what the face looks like?

(GW) *"Unintelligible."*

(HW) "Did it have big heads? *"Unintelligible."* Did it have a nose"?

(GW) *"Unintelligible."*

(HW) "Are they in a different place from you?

(GW) *"Unintelligible."*

(HW) "Who else is with you? Can you see someone else with you?"

(GW) *"Unintelligible."*

(HW) "Do you want to continue on this journey"?

(GW) *"Unintelligible."*

(HW) "Do you want them to take you home"?

(GW) "I'm not straight….I can't….I'm getting…..I'm standing up. I can see things at all different angles".

(HW) "Is you head turning on your shoulders"?

(GW) "No. I know I'm moving".

(HW) "Are you floating"

(GW) "Yes".

(HW) "Can you move in any direction"?

(GW) "No".

(HW) "Are you leaving Garry"?

(GW) "Uh huh"

(HW) "You have done well, and coped with it. We know, how hard you have tried".

(Author's note. At this point Helen clicked her fingers and asked Garry to waken. The following text is what Garry recalls under that hypnosis session)

Conversation after hypnosis.

(GW) "I know that I was in a crater. I seemed to be coming out of it. There was a big crater".

(HW) "A big crater!"

(GW) "I was coming out of a big crater. You know how you see something sloped up"?.

(HW) "Yes."

(GW) "I was asking it what you had said, and I was waiting for an answer".

(HW) "Uh huh".

(GW) "And just the one word was coming".

(HW) "Which word"?

(GW) "That word, sanctuary".

(HW) "Was it sanctuary for you? Were they giving you sanctuary or…..."

(GW) "No, I kept asking it what it was. What do you want?...what do you want? What is it, and it said sanctuary. And that is what was coming into my mind so I said it".

(HW) "I don't know what they mean. But did you get any feeling as to whether 'you' were going into a sanctuary or they were coming"?

(GW) "No, they want to be here".

(HW) "They want sanctuary here"?

(GW) "Oh yes. It was something, I don't know, it looked human but I don't know what it was. And it had nothing on. It was quite fat and it run away from me into something's arms, and this thing was cuddling it. Honestly Helen".

(HW) "I know, I know".

(GW) "I have trouble, I can't see clear. At one point I am moving about and I can't control where I am, because I am moving all around. It's like standing up here. I can see a horizontal plane, I had no control, and I was turning and moving and everything was out of perspective. One way it was over there and then it was all over there, and you are moving about and you cannot see".

(HW) "Did you feel light"?

(GW) "I was turning. It was like being in a plane where you are doing fast turns. One minute you are there, and the next minute you are facing away from it and you can't control it"

(HW) "Was it in mid air"?

(GW) "Yes".

(HW) "You were actually in mid air"!

(GW) "I was floating somewhere, I don't know where. I could see jagged rocks and things standing up. I think something wants to come here".

(HW) "What about the faces you saw"?

(GW) "They were all like looking down. There were high up".

(HW) "Do you know how many"?

(GW) "Loads".

(HW) "Do you know what they looked like"?

(GW) "Sort of. I have difficulty".

(HW) "Give me your impression".

(GW) "They want to come here I know that".

(HW) "Are they human"?

(GW) "Uh huh. Well one of them had a black suit on with a bit of a collar on it. Black suit tight".

(HW) "How different from how we look, to how they look, the one with the suit on"?

(GW) "It looked similar".

(HW) "Similar"!

(GW) "But not quite. There was something there human that was at me. It was like, she was quite fat. I think she was young, and she was small. I don't know if I did something and scared her, but she ran into the arms of this thing, and the thing was cuddling her".

(HW) "And it wasn't the same type of person"?

(GW) "I don't know. I saw like a girl's back, and she was like a wee podgy thing and she ran away from me into the arms of this thing".

(HW) "See when you looked up, and saw them above you…….."

(GW) "It was like a…..not round, it was like clouds, or something like that, they were all looking down at all different levels. And it was big".

(HW) "See when you looked at them, did you look at their face, eyes or what?"

(GW) "Yes. I was trying to".

(HW) "Can you remember what stood out most"?

(GW) "One down there, and I was asking it questions".

(HW) "What questions were you asking"?

(GW) "I was asking it what is it they want, and why do they need me"?

(HW) "And what did it say"?

(GW) "I just kept asking it what do you want, what do you want from me. I cannot help them".

(HW) "Did you ask them, why you"?

(GW) "I don't know. To me, it looks like they are looking for anyone in particular to help them".

(HW) "Did they know who you are"?

(GW) "I don't know".

(HW) "About what you do in life".

(GW) "I don't know".

(HW) "Could you see Colin at all"?

(GW) "No".

(HW) "Were you aware of Colin at all"?

(GW) "No"

(HW) "When were you aware of not being in the car"?

(GW) "I was aware of not being in the car long before you said that I wasn't in the car. I don't know if I just went ahead of you".

(HW) "But I didn't say that you weren't in the car".

(GW) "I just felt that I wasn't in the car".

(HW) "So you have travelled on! You didn't see the shimmering curtain at all"?

(GW) "No".

(HW) "There was nothing there".

(Author's note. Garry and Colin did of course see the shimmering curtain of light that descended upon their car, but consciously, and in a previous hypnotic session. But Garry didn't see it in this session)

(GW) "I can just tell you what I saw, it's the truth".

(HW) "I am just wanting to see where it cut off, and it changed to what you saw before, to see where the change came about".

(GW) "I know this, they want to come here, and I don't know what they are hiding from. They are hiding somewhere near, and they want to come here, I know that. There is no fucking doubt in my mind, I know that".

(HW) "Why did you have that off putting expression of, errghh? There was quite a lot of that. Something that gave you the creeps, that you didn't like. It was like being some place that you didn't want to touch, that there was something very very wrong with it. You were disgusted with it".

(GW) "It's not that I was disgusted, I wasn't disgusted. It's just being put through something like that, you have no choice, how are you supposed to act. I don't understand what is going on, I'm just trying to find out".

(HW) "Well, the expressions".

(GW) "Oh I know, I could feel my face. It's just these things, they are all at me. And I am trying to speak to this one here. *(Author's note. Garry pointed at one of his drawings)*

END OF TAPE

We now continue with what Garry had to say regarding this session of hypnosis. This was recorded on the other side of the tape, dated 17th of October 1994. As I transcribed this audio interview, I realised (and it's always great in hindsight), but I realised that I should have asked certain questions, and drawn more out of what Garry was saying. But Helen was the hypnotherapist, and I had already been told off not to say too much, and just to let Garry recall all what he remembered when he came out of hypnosis. If truth be told, I was a bit naive in those days, or in other words, I did what I was told by Helen. If these hypnosis sessions were done today, I would have been a bit more forceful, and just asked those questions. Hence when you read the transcript below, there are very few questions from me, but lots from Helen. That said, I am still at fault for not writing down my questions and giving them to Helen to ask. Mind you, this was the first time in Helen's life that she was having to deal with a case such as this, and as such, I guess she herself, was really wanting to know more, and therefore, she was truly in charge of all the questions. Yes hindsight is a wonderful thing!

Abbreviations: (GW) Garry Wood. (HW) Helen Walters.
(MR) Malcolm Robinson.

(GW) "I was trying to see. I am not aware if my eyes are open or not. I didn't see you, but by fuck I saw them, and wherever they are, they are close by, I know that, and they want to come here".

(HW) "How did it feel in the pool"?

(GW) "It was a pool of red, just like red light".

(HW) "How did you feel"?

(GW) "I wasn't in it, I had been in it before".

(HW) "So you were not in it this time"?

(GW) "No. I was in it in another session with you. When I was in it, it was empty".

(HW) "Is there anything else that you haven't picked up, that maybe you can remember about the whole session?

(GW) "I can remember seeing like jaggy rocks, and things standing up behind the rocks"

(HW) "Jaggy rocks! And what size were the rocks"?

(GW) "They were all different rocks, just like jaggy rocks, slate like, but round and things were standing up round about. And then I started to just lose all control of it. The way I was turning and that, and everything was going all different ways. I know that I got taken there, where ever it was. I got moved, taken somewhere. And then I'm out. It's like you are trying to get your balance but you cannot, and you are just going all round, and everything is just going all away from you. You just cannot get your balance as everything is just going round. You want to see that. Then you are looking away up the other end but you cannot see, because you are moving".

(HW) "Why have they annoyed you this time"?

(GW) "I don't think they annoyed me. I don't know how I can help them".

(HW) "You are quite aggressive this time towards them"

(GW) No I was sh*****g myself as I don't know what is going on".

(HW) "You are uptight aggressive".

(GW) "Well I've no choice with what's going on. I'm there, and I've no choice, I'm trying to ask these things, 'what the hell is going on'?

(HW) "I mean, you feel that you have no choice, no choice of what, exactly"?

(GW) "Well anything could happen to me. I know that they are not going to harm me. I know that now, I actually know that now".

(HW) "Are you secure in the fact that they are not going to harm you"?

(GW) "Oh they are not going to harm me"

(HW) "Are they strong"?

(GW) "It's not that I don't trust them, it's just, well I don't know. I kept asking them. I know I would have asked anyway, I know that. But like when you are saying certain things, its like you have no control, its happening whether you want it or not. Do you understand what I am saying. I don't know if they are hiding or trying to get away from something or what's going on, but they want to come here".

(HW) "Are you any idea on how soon or how many"?

(GW) "I don't know"

(HW) "You couldn't get any information about that, or where they are going to arrive"?

(GW) "I know one thing, and that is they are somewhere near here, and there is a load of them there. And where ever it is, they 'are' there".

(HW) "You say, near here".

(GW) "Not here. Somewhere else, but its close to us".

(HW) "So you are meaning near here, Earth! Right"?

(GW) "Yes"

(HW) "You have to remember, not a lot will come out in your logical thinking. I mean, if it was that simple, you wouldn't be sitting in that chair would you? Nobody here feels that you are cracking up".

(GW) "I know one thing, and that is I've nothing to worry about. I think they have more to worry about than me. They have a lot to worry about. They have problems".

(HW) "Can you draw the ones in the sky for me"?

(GW) "Helen, I couldn't even draw their face right. The thing that I saw when I was looking up *(Author's note. Garry is drawing at this point)* And I was looking up, and there was like

397

cloud or mist or something, I don't know, and all these things are looking down".

(HW) "Try and draw as many of them in as you can. Just let yourself relax with it. I'm not wanting a Rembrandt".

(GW) "But they are all looking around the edge of this thing whatever it is. I know that. I am really s**t scared, it's like I am disgusted".

(HW) "Yes there were different expressions when you were under".

(GW) "I'm looking up like that, and they are looking down".

(HW) "Well draw yourself at the bottom".

(GW) "How can I, that's how it is, that's them. That's me looking up there".

(Author's note. At this point, Helen was trying to get Garry's position in the drawing where his head was looking up, but Garry was insisting that he couldn't do it, that his interpretation of what he was looking at in the sky, was his best way of trying to re-create the scene)

(HW) "See how its like that, you say that they are high and they are big".

(GW) "No, its high"

(HW) "But the head's are big that you saw"

(GW) "They had an elasticated neck, I'll tell you that. Because these things can pull away to the side with their neck, their necks are elasticated like s**t. Because they can turn right round, because they gave me a fright. Because when I seen them with a straight neck, and with this thing, the neck just sort of moved right round, and moved right round again, like their neck can move a lot more than ours can".

(HW) "And is the head at the bottom of it or....."

(GW) "No, no the head is up there".

(HW) "Ah the head's up there".

(GW) "And their neck just.....wooooof, went right round like a snake. And that's what gave me the fright because I didn't expect that. The head and the neck just went right round".

(HW) "You see, you are doing well with this".

(GW) "They are different ones. I don't know how, because I can't see clear that they are different".

(HW) "They are different types, is that what you are saying?"

(GW) "I'm not sure Helen".

(HW) "They are different kinds of people or what"?

(GW) "Well I saw a human girl and she ran away from me. She had dark long hair, and she was a wee fat podgy thing. It's like she had been over eating. She had wee fat legs, and she ran over to this big one, and the big one put its arms around her. I think it was me that frightened her. You know when you get quite a lot of fat, and you get all these wee dimples in the fat".

(HW) "Uh huh".

(GW) "Like somebody has really been over doing it, it was sort of like that and she stormed away from me. And she was quite plump and heavy and went into the arms of this big thing".

(HW) "Judging by our age scale, what age was she"?

(GW) "About eight. nine, ten, like she had over indulged".

(HW) "And was the dimple effect like that on the legs as well"?

(GW) "Yes the legs were just fat, but just down the back of the legs and her backside".

(HW) "We can only go on the information that you bring forth".

(GW) "It was like quick and I got a fright, she was there, then she just ran away, and she ran into the arms of this thing over to my right, and this thing put its arms around her to comfort her".

(HW) "Do you think, because it is an ongoing situation even taking the journey on the road. Do you think you are getting closer to where you actually went"?

(GW) "I went somewhere anyway, I know that because I was moving".

(HW) "Yes I know. But what I am trying to say is, do you think you are getting closer to knowing where you are going"?

(GW) "Well I'll tell you one thing now, I'm not scared now, I've nothing to be scared about".

(HW) "Well that's good, that's another step forward. Each time you are having a step forward".

(GW) "There is no need now, for me to be scared. Not now".

(MR) "Are they desperate to get here"?

(GW) "Oh yes. They are wanting away from something. I'm not stupid, I'm not an idiot. Why are they wanting to come here? What's wrong with their own place. How can I help them? What the hell can I do"?

(HW) "Well that's very much so, and an important question to ask them, is to why is it that they know you"?

(GW) "And what about Colin"?

(HW) "Well if it was only Colin, you wouldn't have went so far with them as well. It could just be a combination of two people travelling down the road".

(GW) "I tried to see Colin, I looked about, and Colin wasn't there".

(HW) "It could be just you travelling down the road and you just happened to be the two that they picked up that night. At the right spot, at the right time. Everything was right".

(MR) "Unless they were looking for you"?

(HW) "This is what we are trying to find out. Had they chosen you, or was it a random choice, like it seems to be all over the world".

(GW) "I think that they were just picking us up. That's what I think".

(MR) "Could it be just by chance though"?

(GW) "I think that, now I do".

(HW) "At the beginning you didn't feel that way".

(GW) "I'm just trying to tell you the truth"

(HW) "Yes, that's all you can do".

(GW) "That's what I am doing Malcolm".

(HW) "That's all you can do Garry".

(MR) "Did you get any impression of how many wanted to come"?

(GW) "No idea".

(GW) "But I'll tell you one thing, they want to come here. And they are getting stopped from coming here by the Government or what. But they are getting stopped from coming here. And they are close, and they want to come here, and I am positive about that. There are a lot of them, a stack of them".

(MR) "Did you get any information of where about, about, any specific area"?

(GW) "No. The way they have done business, is not the way to do business. But then again, you look at it like that, how would you be"?.

(HW) "The subject of them coming here, you have to be so careful because of the mechanics of the situation".

(GW) "It's bad, but its good in a sense. Because then it lets people know. I think that its going to get worse, I think its going to get a lot worse".

(MR) "What, just your case, or the whole type of thing"?

(GW) "The whole type of thing. It's going to start turning up everywhere. I've no doubt in my mind now. I'm not that worried, but I want to know why do they want to come here, what are they running from?

(HW) "How can they come here, and be here at the same time? The question is never ending. Why does a country want to conquer us unless they want to remove us from it"?

(GW) "No, they need us. They don't want to remove us. No matter what, they 'need' us. We are really totally important to them they need us".

(HW) "But it is important to find out".

(GW) "They are not interested to destroy us in any manner at all. They need us. They desperately need us".

(HW) "Yes but do they need us, as us being who we are, are the questions that need to be found out"?

(Author's note. There was a change in questions at this point. Helen and Garry went back to when Garry just had the one eye open, and he was trying to look around. And then the discussion went into other aspects of what Garry saw under hypnosis)

(GW) "I don't feel that I have been talking a lot of s**t tonight Helen. I don't feel that way. I feel pretty serious about what I have been saying. Because I was trying to ask and find out. And I didn't think up that word, that word came to me".

(HW) "Sanctuary"

(GW) "That word came to me. And I don't know why I would want to bring up that word. Because if something is advanced as that. Why are they pleading like that to me".

(MR) "What about this scenery, these jagged rocks. You felt like you were in the air!"

(GW) "Yes I was floating. I'll tell you one thing, it was a big crater, a great big crater. I'm coming up the side of this crater".

(Author's note. Helen at this point was asking Garry to draw what he remembers, even if it looked ridiculous, as even the

smallest of details could prove of great interest to understanding what Garry went through)

(GW) "The rocks were funny, they were all jagged, like cuts in the rocks. And then these bloody things were standing up behind the rocks like they were hiding, but they were standing up".

(HW) "When you saw that opening, the way that you are drawing that. Did that remind you of something else that you drew"?

(GW) "At the beginning I saw rocks, a jagged rock thing, and I never ever knew what it was. It was like the Scot Monument *(Author's note. Garry is referring to the Scott Monument on Princess Street Edinburgh)* with the pointy bits on it and I couldn't understand what it was. It was like a rock, blocking a doorway".

(HW) "The good thing that you find with this is, repetition. I'm trying to look for the one common factor out of it all, but it's all changing. Although we have several common factors from what you are saying, but I am looking for your common factor. Trying to see a repetition of an area of some kind".

(GW) "I know that I was floating up a rock face, and then you started to pull me out".

(HW) "I asked if you wanted to come out, but you weren't interested in staying here".

(MR) "Were you getting led away somewhere at this point though"?

(GW) "I'll tell you one thing though, I'm not going to be scared any more. From this night on, I'm not going to be scared any more. I think I'll sleep no problem now"

(HW) "Ah, that is good, that is a big, big step forward, that means that you will be able to handle all your sessions".

(GW) "I don't think I have anything to be scared of. I know that I was pulling faces, and I was aware of my faces going like this. But when there are things moving about like that, you are scared of it, and you are not used to seeing this. How are you going to react when things are at you? If something like this is coming to you, like asking for help, how the hell can we help them? They are asking the wrong people, and that's why I think they will be back".

(HW) "But do they know that Garry? I mean its like saying why is it if there is any communication from the other side, no matter what it may be, why doesn't it come to the great intellects of the country. It always goes to a farmer or some ordinary bloke in the street or something like that. But in fact it doesn't, it can come to drunks who you wouldn't expect it to be".

(GW) "I was seeing one of them blurred. It's like its head started to move like a snake. It shot off the one way and turned round and looked round".

(HW) "See when its head was moving, did you notice as if its head was weighted"?

(GW) "No. It wasn't that big, not like huge big, but it had a pretty strong neck that could bend in the middle".

(MR) "What type of head did it have? In your earlier drawings you drew two different heads, heart shaped and round, which one was it"?.

(GW) "It looked like the rounded head to me. I couldn't see clear Malcolm, and that's the truth. I couldn't see clear, I don't know why".

(MR) "What about the eyes on their heads"?

(GW) "A couple of times I saw them. They were at the side of me, and they were looking at me, and they were black".

(MR) "Jet black!"

(GW) "It was like a shine to a couple of their eyes, like a shine. You know when you are looking and you get your reflection".

(MR) "Did you ever see any white bits, either in the center or…….."

(GW) "Well the white bits to me, looked like reflections of something. If you have a highly polished car you will get a reflection. And that's like what I saw, a reflection. If I look hard into your eyes I'll see my reflection, and that's what I saw, a reflection. They weren't that close to me though".

(HW) "When you look into that camera, do you see an eye looking back to you. Have you ever saw an eye looking back at you. Like the screen is white, you can't see the image, and then its like its covered, and you see an eye and you are looking into another eye"?

(GW) "Yes at one point. But that was the thing, it was looking at me".

(HW) "Was that while you were under hypnosis"?

(GW) "Yes"

(HW) "I'm talking about anytime you viewed consciously. So is that when you saw under hypnosis, that you saw another eye looking into you. I'm talking about one eye"?

(GW) "Yes one eye. At one time there was one eye looking at me and it was looking at me through machinery, like an angled thing".

(HW) "Was it a black or a blue eye".

(GW) "It was a black eye. There were colours under the eye, like red and yellow and green, and that was in the first session".

(HW) "And have you ever tried to look into the camera, put it on, and see an eye".

(GW) "I've never looked into a camera".

(HW) "I mean conscientiously. You have looked at the camera. I've set it up all the time *(laughs)* Just looking into the camera".

(GW) "It's the wrong shape".

(HW) "See when you look in here *(Author's note. Helen points to the camera lens)* Do you ever see an eye blanking out the screen?

(GW) "No".

(HW) "Never".

(GW) "The only time that I was worried about the camera was when I pointed it at the telly and it went on like a million miles an hour. I left it recording and it turned into the telly and it just kept going forever and I s**t myself, and I pulled it away and that's the only time".

(HW) "When I looked into the camera, the camera showed no image. *(Author's note. Helen is referring to the video camera that was pointing at Garry whilst he was under hypnosis)*

(GW) "Oh there was something here".

(HW) "Oh I know that".

(GW) "Did you not see my hand when I tried to go for it"?

(HW) "I knew that there was something here. But you were really and truly out, and relaxed, and I got up to turn on the camera and I realised that you were reacting at that moment. I said, 'my God, there is nothing there. There was absolutely nothing there".

(GW) "There was not even a reflection of your own eye!"

(HW) "I might have a reflection in my own eye, but I can't look into my own eye. I'm talking about an eye that I am looking into. It had a large pupil, a large pupil. And around it was like midnight with speckles of light. So when it happened the first time, my immediate reaction was, that must mean something, and I pulled back. And I tried again, and it was like it blanked out the whole surface. I mean if it was a reflection of even my own eye, why would it blank out the whole screen of light?"

(GW) "At that time, I thought that something was even in here. I swear on my kids life, I did feel that something was in here, I even put my hand out". *(Author's note. Garry is of course referring to Helen's room where the hypnosis was taking place, that something else was in the room with them)*

(HW) "I think so too. What we are going to have to try, is perhaps sitting concentrating, to try and bring that in. Like in a meditative state".

(GW) "Did you make any head or tail of what's been said tonight Malcolm, or do you think it's just me? It was real enough for me".

(MR) "Every time we get something new. To me it was puzzling when you saw all those faces"

(GW) "I've seen them before. And I've said that umpteen times that I have seen things looking down at me, lot's of them".

408

(MR) "Yes, that's true you have".

(GW) "That's the first time though that I've ever floated".

(MR) "What position were you when you were floating up out of the crater? Were your arms by your side, or out here like this"? *(Author's note. I extended both my arms out and horizontal from my body)*

(GW) "It was just all uncontrollable. Everything was just going away from me".

(MR) "Do you think that you might have been coming out of the hypnosis state"?

(HW) "Ah well, I must admit, that would be one of the conclusions. I thought actually when he said that, I felt that very strongly. And I'm glad, because I didn't take you out of your body".

(GW) "No, but at that time, those things were there".

(HW) "But I must admit, I felt very strongly at that period of time. I thought that you didn't have the control. And one of the things that he will have and try and learn, because it will be a similarity of weightlessness. It's like the astronauts get used to the weightlessness and they have to control that. Like when you astral travel the same way, you have learn to control your tumbling or you will fall out, and you will stay in the same spot and cannot move. Then there will be times when you soar and you are totally in control".

(GW) "Its like something is drawing me. I don't know. I can only tell you the truth of what I saw".

(HW) "Well I think this is what he has to do at night time. Because this appears to be what he is also doing at home, with your waking up state and the fact that.... *(Author's note, I couldn't make out clearly what Helen said at this point).*

(GW) "So what I am doing isn't right then, its just something that I am doing in my own mind and its nothing to do with this"?

(HW) "No, no no. Not at all. I mean, you are travelling in your mind just now Garry, right! You are reliving an experience of a time in your life. You are not in the UFO as of this moment, you are going back in time, into the UFO, and all of these states, are altered states. I've got to alter your state, and you have to cooperate in altering your state from the present to where you are".

(GW) "I should listen to you better, I just jump ahead eh".

(HW) "Well you become over eager and over try, but I know when you are doing that. I always throw in a couple of things to test you out on it, to see what would happen. I mean, I told you that you could open up your eyes if you wanted to. But this time I told you you couldn't, and I've never done that before. But you didn't jump out. And I really was surprised, I thought that how far did he allow himself to go, that he hadn't jumped out the session. Because you don't sit comfortable on your left. Your restless".

(GW) "Why did you leave me"?

(HW) "Well when I left you the first time, you jumped out of it. But you seem to feel me withdrawing away from you".

(GW) "Yes I know that".

(HW) "You feel, and you get a sense of insecurity"

(GW) "I do yes".

(HW) "I know that that's a part of the thing that happens".

410

(GW) "So what is it I am seeing then"?

(HW) "You are seeing what is happening to you. You are seeing them".

(GW) "They are definitely real".

(HW) "And what you have to remember when we are comparing other altered states to your sensations of what it is. This is not saying that this is what happened to you Garry, because we don't know that. We are trying to research into what's happening. *(Author's note. At this point Garry looked at the clock and couldn't believe what time it was. It was now 02:25am)*

(GW) "I'll tell you one thing, I've nothing to be scared of"

END OF TAPE.

My final transcript comes from January 14th 1998 where I travelled to Edinburgh to meet up with Garry Wood at his home. Part of this transcript, features Garry's eleven year old son, also called Garry, as he related about a strange light that came into his father's car. My thanks to Garry Wood for allowing me to interview his son. The following, is what I recorded with Garry that day.

Abbreviations: (MR) Malcolm Robinson. (GW) Garry Wood.

(MR) "Garry, first and foremost, were you happy that hypnosis was conducted on you. Did you feel that this was something that at the very least, you had to try to get an answer for what happened to you personally?

(GW) "When you first asked me about hypnosis, I didn't know a lot about it, so I basically looked up to find out more about it, about the technique, and how it was used. I heard a lot of good things about it, and a lot of bad things. I remember clear as day, seeing the craft, the shimmering curtain, and being in the blackness and everything, but there were parts of it, which for some reason, seemed to be missing. I seemed to have time missing that I couldn't account for. I don't know what's happened to that time. I don't know how so many minutes could go by and then run into hours. So, if somebody is offering me some form of a chance to try and retrieve memories of what might have happened, then I was fairly interested to try anything to find out what happened to me, and what happened to Colin, regardless".

(MR) "What is your conscious recall. Where does the conscious recall end on that August evening back in 1992. You saw this UFO, but where does the conscious recall end, before the hypnotic recall begins".

(GW) "What I remember up to, to make it easier, is that I remember being in the car, seeing the UFO, being underneath the craft, then a shimmering curtain of light falling over the car. Then not being in the car, being in darkness. And with not having any prior knowledge or interest in UFOs being in the darkness and not being in my car, I thought I was dead. And then I was in the car, and for some reason there was some form of time missing and I cannot account for it".

(MR) "Now Garry, did you feel, at any time that you were under pressure to go through with hypnosis on behalf of SPI. At any point did you say that, 'enough's enough'. I'm not going to please Malcolm or Helen. So were you personally under any pressure to bring forward any possible recollections through hypnosis"?

(GW) "Well we went over and over in the incident, hundreds and hundreds of times with yourself and Helen. You contacted all the other witnesses involved in the case. You offered hypnosis as a last resort. You said to me, would you be interested in possibly trying this, just to see if there was anything else. You said that it was up to myself, that there was no pressure, you can take it or leave it. And I was quite

412

interested to try it, to see what it was all about, to experience how it was. I had terrible sleep patterns, I was scared all the time. I always felt that after the hypnosis, that something was always following me. And I thought, well maybe with this hypnosis I might be able to come face to face with what it actually is".

(MR) "Have you ever been hypnotised before, maybe a stage show when you were out for an evening. Have you ever been hypnotised prior to what Helen Walters offered you"?

(GW) "I've never ever been hypnotised before. I didn't know much about it till I went through the hypnosis with Helen Walters. Its not like what a lot of people think. You go there and you are hypnotised. They contact your doctor. There is a lot involved with it. They take you in and out of trance. It's weeks and weeks of work. And how its actually worked, is by using dates. Its conducted in a very strict fashion".

(MR) "Garry, were you aware of the room and the surroundings when you were under hypnosis. Were you aware that you were perhaps in two camps. Were you aware of being in the room and being aware of being somewhere else. Or were you aware of only one situation"?

(GW) "I was aware that I was in the room at first, and then, sometimes that would drift away and I would be somewhere else, and then I would get a right fright and I would snap out of wherever I was and I would be back again. Its really strange, its difficult to understand. At some points, I honestly 110% I wasn't there in the room, I was somewhere else, it was pretty frightening".

(MR) "Garry, do you personally believe, 'Believe' what you recall under hypnosis, or, is it at the back of your mind that this could all be some kind of dream. So do you think that was real what you experienced under hypnosis"?

413

(GW) "Giving you my honest opinion I would say that perhaps 99% of what I thought was real. Things that I had never ever seen before that I couldn't tie in with any thing similar that I had seen on T.V. or anything like that. Its not like I thought it was. When Helen was doing the hypnosis, she worked purely with dates. Asking me what I was doing on that date etc".

(MR) "Garry you were in a situation where you were travelling over to Alva in Clackmannanshire and you were having meetings with Helen Walters our hypnotherapist and also with myself. Now this is a question that I have to ask, and please don't feel annoyed with me, but I have to ask it. Were you under pressure to 'please' the hypnotherapist by maybe saying and seeing things that didn't happen, just because you had travelled all the way from Edinburgh, and you had to at least, 'please' somebody. So did you please the hypnotherapist"?

(GW) "I wouldn't say that I wanted to please anybody. I was wanting to find out what had actually happened. I wasn't there to please anybody. I was there to try and tell the truth to the best of my ability. Whether that was 100% I cannot say for certain. As I say, I saw things that I have never seen before. There was too many things happening at the one time for me to think that what I was seeing was false. I was seeing other people there. I was seeing creatures doing things. I was feeling pain. No leading questions were asked in any manner or form I think. The hypnotherapy worked, purely by dates and what I was doing at certain times".

(MR) "Were you happy with the hypnotherapist. At any stage of the hypnotherapy were you annoyed by any questions"?

(GW) "Well there was no questions asked in the hypnotherapy, let me make that point clear. It was like I was acting in what was happening. I couldn't move, I felt pain. I could say that I related more to what I saw after the hypnosis sessions. Because as the hypnosis was actually working, I can't even remember half the things I said because I wasn't aware of sort of being there, as daft as that may sound. When I got really frightened I would jump out of the hypnosis session. Its not like what a lot of people think. People think that you go under and that's it. Its nothing like that. Its hours and hours of work. It's just like you have arrived for the hypnosis once its actually working then you are ready to go home. It's like time passes in an instant".

(MR) "At any point during any of the regression sessions that you came over to Alva to attend, when all these images were going through your head. Did you feel any pain? Did hypnosis induce a pain sensation, to coincide with a visual experience in your head"?

(GW) "At certain points of the hypnosis they were doing something to my stomach, and I held onto my stomach with excruciating agony. It was that sore, I think I was crying with the pain. At certain points I couldn't move. There were things that were jammed in my ear. I kept hearing noises. There was too much happening for me to think that it was just false".

(MR) "Now this is only speculation, and I am certainly not saying that it happened, but did hypnosis bring forward any lucid or prolific dreams after the hypnosis was conducted. Did you recall any dreams after coming out of hypnosis or did you just have a normal sleep pattern with normal dreams"?

(GW) "I would say that I don't dream a lot, but after the incident I was having nightmares. I would say that I was giving myself excuses not to go to sleep. I think that I was more frightened to go to sleep thinking that something might get me or something might come back. There were a couple of incidents where I ran out of bed screaming, I can't remember why. It got that bad that my wife was absolutely sick of me, it was really getting to her and it was worrying her as well".

(MR) "Garry, do you feel that hypnosis has helped you, in the sense that you have recalled images of, presumably that night, or do you feel that I wish I hadn't done that now because 'I have recalled these images' and it has made it worse. So has the hypnosis helped you to remember these things, or has it made it worse"?

(GW) "People say a lot of things that its a lot of rubbish. My own personal opinion about it, is that I am glad that I done it. I'm glad I went to the bother to see about it, because I found things out that I would never have found out. I found out. I found that whatever these 'things' were, that they weren't going to hurt me. And after the hypnosis, I actually could sleep better at night. I could actually come to terms with it better. I think that it has made a big difference in my normal life. It's put me back on the right track. So me personally, I don't care what anybody else thinks or says about it, I'm glad I done it. I think that's been the main thing that has helped me to deal with all of what's happened and I would like to thank Helen and Malcolm for it".

(MR) "Some people might say, when we talk about UFOs and they talk about evidence, that hypnosis is not the best evidence to provide Joe Public an understanding of the UFO phenomenon. Now it was used on you, and you have just said a moment ago that you were very happy with the use of it on you. So do you feel then, that the hypnosis that has been used on you, has given you, Garry Wood, the answer to what happened that night, or do you still feel, that this is 'not' the answer, that something else happened and that the answer lies elsewhere"?

(GW) "I would say that I got bits of a puzzle. I saw things happening. I couldn't construct this or put it together. The parts I do remember, the things that stick in my mind, is seeing these creatures or 'beings' whatever they are, we'll call them aliens, were saying to me, in my mind, that I've got a life like you but different. That things happen to us. They explained it to me that it was something, it wasn't what some people think an alien is, with powers etc. It was just a creature from somewhere else that had a life like me, it has its own culture and everything. If anything, it has given me a better understanding of things. As for the reason why are they here, I don't know".

416

(MR) "Garry its now January the 14th 1998, we are at the beginning of a new year. Do you feel within yourself, within your heart that these visits have finished. Do you feel that there is more to transpire, be it on a personal basis with yourself that you may encounter these beings again or on a global basis. How do you feel about that"?

(GW) "Well since the incident in 1992, I have had a couple of other incidents that have happened to me. I saw something in my room one night and I physically attacked this thing that I saw in my room. I don't know what it was. And then another time I was in my car with my kids, and the whole car illuminated white".

(MR) "Where was this Garry"?

(GW) "It was coming back from Kim's mum's at Gullane".

(MR) "What year"?

(GW) "I would say, 5 or 6 months ago, in 1997. The whole car lit up, my kids were screaming, and everything just illuminated white. And my youngest son Lee felt sick in the back of the car after it. Everything lit up a magnesium white for about 5 or 10 seconds and then went back to normal".

(MR) "Just confirm to me Garry, who was in the car".

(GW) "My son Garry who is eleven, and my son Lee, who is eight".

(MR) "What time of day did this occur Garry"?

(GW) "I would say approximately half past six at night".

(MR) "The stretch of road where this happened, was it a built up area or was it just fields on either side, what type of area was it"?

(GW) "There was fields on either side. It was along the coast road. I'm not exactly sure of the place. I know it to drive, its about five or six miles away from Gullane, quite near Longniddry".

(MR) "Did you see any source of where this light emanated from? Was it coming in a band, or was it coming in a column. How did this light enter your car, how is it possible"?

(GW) "I don't know. The light was inside the car and outside the car. And the car and everything in it, turned white. Don't ask me how, but it happened for at least 5 to 10 seconds. And it was like the light followed me as I was driving in the car at the time and I tried to stop the car".

(MR) "How did this light make you feel? Did it have any affect on your body, was it a hurtful light? How would you say"?

(GW) "It didn't affect me in any way shape or form. If anything, I think that it affected my son Lee".

(Author's note. At this point, and with Garry Wood's permission. I interviewed his young son, also called Garry regarding this white light that enveloped his father's car.)

(MR) "I'm now speaking with young Garry, Garry Wood who is eleven years of age. Garry tell me what happened in the car".

(GW Son) "We were driving along the road coming from my gran's, and suddenly this big white flash lit up the whole car, inside and outside and we all got a fright and my brother felt sick after it".

(MR) "How did the light appear to you, was it hurtful on your eyes, was it very bright, or was it just a light?"
(GW Son) "It was just a light. I only saw it inside the car and a little bit outside".

(MR) "And how did this light make you feel, were you frightened? were you alarmed? How would you say you felt when you saw this light?"

(GW Son) "Sort of scared because my little brother was sick".

(MR) "Did you see where this light came from, I mean, did you look out of the window to see a source of this light?"

(GW Son) "It came from the right hand side of us, sort of, up in the sky".

(MR) "OK, thank you for telling me this Garry".

(MR) "Garry, as you know, I did not attend all the hypnosis sessions, but on one occasion, you recalled after coming out of hypnosis that you found yourself in some sort of cave or something where you saw rocks and you saw faces in the clouds. Tell me, what was that all about?"

(GW) "I remember being taken underground somewhere. I remember being in like a huge cavern or cave. It looked like there was some kind of ship *(Craft)* over on the left hand side just floating there. I remember seeing creatures standing up behind rocks doing things. It felt to me that I was underground somewhere. And the other point that you asked me about was seeing faces in the sky. What it actually was, was when I was lying down this object was coming away from me, what I actually felt like was above me. These creatures were on another level just up from where ever it was that I was in. A craft or a room or where ever, and they were all watching like a doctor's examination or something, they were all looking interested. I saw other things".

(MR) "Were you clothed at this time, and did you have free reign of your abilities? I mean, you were in a distressing situation, did you try and lash out? Did you try and see if you could affect any disturbance on these small creatures?"

(GW) "I think at the time I had no prior interest in UFOs, I didn't know anything about them. I only recently started to learn about them after the incident to find out about the subject. I knew nothing prior to it. It was never an interest or a hobby. I was just interested in having a nice house and making money, and this has sort of changed that. Going through what has happened, I would say has had a big affect on my life and changed it".

(MR) "Garry, as you know, SPI were essentially the main research group who brought forward you and Colin's experience to the world. It's probably the best UFO abduction experience in the whole of Scotland. Do you feel upset in any manner of means that SPI have catapulted you into the public domain, because it was our society that did this, and do you not wish now, that you had never said a thing".

(GW) "Well, what happened to Colin and I was true, we experienced this. We saw it. And I've got kids like everybody else, and my concern to people is to say that there is something going on and I felt that it was my duty to try and tell people and warn them about this rather than something happen to their family. I am trying to explain that, look, this happened to me, take it or leave it. SPI done the good thing in giving me the chance to tell people. A lot of people where things happen to them, or see these kinds of things, are embarrassed to speak about it, they hide it, because of fear of ridicule. The reason why I did a lot of talks for SPI is because they did a lot for me, and I wanted to try and give something back. Plus I wanted to try and tell other people in the world that there is something going on. This is what happened to me and my friend, and it should never have happened. I want them to basically take notice of it, and that there is more to life than people think there is, and that there is something going on that should be truly looked at. All I can say, is to thank SPI for the chance that they gave me to talk on the T.V. and to try and express my feelings to people and I hope that it helps people who had an experience that I had".

(MR) "Do your family and friends see you any different now. Now that you have been on T.V. and radio. Do your friends accept what has happened to you or do you find that you are getting ridiculed by family and friends, have they shunned you or supported you".

(GW) "People that have known you all your life, know you. They know what you are like and what you are. My friends are my friends. I would say that the majority of them believe me because they 'know me', they know that I would never come out with anything like this unless it was true. My wife, it scares her, she is terrified, she doesn't like me talking about it because she knows its true. I think my kids know that something happened. I don't go onto them. I don't let them know if it was good or bad. I realise now, that there is more in the world than we think. You get the odd slagging off from some of my friends at work, but that's to be expected. If you go back five or six years ago, and if this had happened to somebody else, I would be the one slagging them, and that's the truth. As for now, I totally think differently. I know that there is something 'out there', I know that there is other things going on. I just wish that other people would take note of it".

(MR) "And finally Garry, moving back in time, well back in time, to your childhood days. I remember you telling me a story about when you were younger and you were near a school and you saw something unusual on a school roof. What happened there?"

(GW) "I was going to the Scouts that night, it was at Duddingston School and that's where the Scout meeting was being held. And one of my friends noticed something on the roof. And I looked up, and we all saw this 'thing' on the roof. Like a creature. None of us really knew what it was. To us at the time, being so young we thought it was a monster or something. I was there, Gavin was there and a number of other people, I would say that at least four or five people saw it. And then the Scout Master came running out and whatever it was, vanished".

421

(MR) "What would you say that it looked like. Was it dark when you saw it?"

(GW) "It wasn't dark, but the light was fading and it was starting to get dark, it was still half light. Whatever it was, it had a physical appearance. It looked like it had a body form to it like it had some things protruding from it and it was watching us, whatever 'it' was. And when we started screaming, we scared it off, whatever it was".

(MR) "What age were you at this point Garry"?

(GW) "I think about that time I would have been around eleven or twelve".

(MR) "And was it a humanoid form, ie, that it had a body, two arms, two legs".

(GW) "It had an odd shaped head on it. It didn't even resemble like any of the pictures that you see of aliens and that. It had two, arm like things. I couldn't see any form of hands, I could only see like two, arms or legs, or whatever and then the body and then the head and it was like, looking over the roof watching us. I would say that the roof was approximately about 10 or 15 feet up, and I would say at a distance about 10 feet across".

(MR) "Since that time, have you seen anything similar, anything like that"?

(GW) "No".

(MR) "Garry, in closing the interview, have you anything else that you would like to say about your experience. You have said quite a lot, and I must thank you for that, anything you might like to add to 'your' story"?

(GW) "Just that, some people think, that whatever these creatures are. I think people think of them as something special and they can do this and that. What people don't realise is that we are dealing with another culture. Whatever they are, they have a life, they live, I don't know how long. They may have a more advanced technology than us. I just hope that everything turns out fine, because I worry about how it ends. I mean, I've got kids, you've got kids Malcolm, will all our kids be safe when this comes to light. I hope that everything will work out fine".

(MR) "Garry Wood, I'd like to thank you very much for your time, thank you".

(GW) "Your welcome"
END OF TAPE

REFERENCES

CHAPTER ONE (The A70 UFO Incident)
Wikipedia

CHAPTER TWO (The Thoughts of Fellow UFOlogists)
None.

CHAPTER THREE (How can we explain the UFO Abduction Phenomenon?)
Perspectives on the abduction phenomenon - Wikipedia

CHAPTER FOUR (Should we be alarmed?)
Thomas E. Bullard, Ph.D. | ancientalienpedia
From the ashes of unknown: MILABS (Military Abductions) - Auricmedia - Blogman's Wonderland

FURTHER READING

The following books, whilst not an exhaustive study of UFO's, are a good place to start. Most of these books can be found on Amazon.

A Passage Through Eternity. Philip Kinsella. Paperback: 280 pages. Publisher: Independently published (2 Feb. 2018) ISBN-13: 978-1977067289

Above Top Secret. Tim Good. Publisher: William Morrow; Reprint edition (20 Sept. 1989) ISBN-13: 978-0688092023

Abducted. (The True Story of Alien Abduction in Rural England) Anne Andrew, Jean Ritchie. Paperback: 320 pages. Publisher: Headline Book Publishing; New edition (3 Jun. 1999) ISBN-13: 978-0747259138

Abducted! Lorenzen, J. and C. E. Lorenzen. Berkley, 1977.

Abducted: How People Come to Believe They Were Kidnapped by Aliens. Clancy SA (2005). Cambridge: Harvard University Press. ISBN 978-0-674-01879-2.

Alien Encounters: First Hand Accounts of UFO Abductions. David M. Jacobs. Virgin, London, 1994 ISBN: 0-86369-727-5.

Alien Contact. Jenny Randles & Paul Whetnall. Neville Spearman Ltd. 1981. ISBN: 85435-444-1

Aliens Past Present & Future. Ron Millar. Watkins Media Ltd, 11 Shepperton House, 89-93 Shepperton Road, London, N1 3DF. ISBN: 978-1-78028-968-7

Alien abductions. Rivers, Lance (2002). In Shermer, Michael (ed.). The skeptic encyclopedia of pseudoscience. ABC-CLIO. ISBN 1-57607-654-7.

Abduction: Human encounters with aliens. Mack, John E. (1995). New York: Ballantine Books. ISBN 0-345-39300-7.

Alien Abductions: Creating a Modern Phenomenon. Terry Matheson (1998).Buffalo, NY: Prometheus Books. ISBN 978-1-57392-244-9.

Communion. Whitley Stieber. Century, London, 1987 Arrow Books Ltd; ISBN:13-978-0099-534-204

Chosen: (Recollections of Abductions Through Hynotherapy) Yvonne R. Smith. Bachstage Entertainment 2008. USA.

Close Encounters: A Factual Report on UFO's. Larsen, S. J. Raintree, 1978.

Close Encounters of the Fourth Kind: Alien Abduction, UFOs, and the Conference at M.I.T. Bryan, C. D. B. (1995). New York: Knopf. ISBN 978-0-679-42975-3.

Dimensions: Jaques Vallee. Souvenir Press. 1988. ISBN: 0-285-63362-7

Electric UFOs. Albert Budden, Blandford Books, 1998. ISBN: 07-137-268-57

Humanoid Encounters. (The Others Amongst Us) 1995-1999. Albert S. Rosales. Triangulum Publishing. 2015 ISBN 13: 978-1519446275

Haunted Skies. John Hanson & Dawn Holloway. (Various volumes cataloguing UFO sightings throughout the U.K. from 1939 through to present day). E-mail them at info@hauntedskies.co.uk

Intruders. Budd Hopkins. The Incredible Visitations at Copley Woods. Sphere Books Ltd. London. 1988

McX. (Scottish X Files) Ron Halliday. B&W Publishing, Edinburgh, ISBN: 1-873631-77-4

Missing Time. Budd Hopkins. Ballentine Books New York. 1981. ISBN:978-0345-353-35-1

Onboard UFO Encounters: Preston Dennett. Blue Giant Books. ISBN: 97816-5384-2186.

One Step Beyond. (A Personal UFO Abduction Experience) Elsie Oakensen. Regency Press London. 1995. ISBN: 0-7212-0930-0

Passport to Magonia. (From Folklore to Flying Saucers) Jacques Vallee. Tandem Publishing, 1975.

Pascagoula. (The Closest Encounter, My Story) Calvin Parket. Flying Disc Press 2018. ASIN: B07HKMYJJK

Sky Crash. Jenny Randles, Brenda Butler, Dot Street. Paperback: 400 pages. Publisher: Harper Collins Publishers Ltd; New edition (22 May 1986) ISBN-13: 978-0586066782

The Walton Affair. Travis Walton. Berkley, 1978.

The Evidence for Alien Abductions. John Rimmer. Aquarian Press, Wellingborough, 1984. p.103.

The Complete Book of UFOs. (An Investigation into Alien Encounters) Peter Hough & Jenny Randles. Judy Piatkus Publishers 1994. ISBN: 0-7499-1399-1

The Andreasson Affair. Raymond E. Fowler. Bantam Books. 1979. ISBN: 0-553-13023-4

The UFO Handbook. Alan Hendry. Publisher: Doubleday; First Edition (1 Aug. 1979) ISBN-13: 978-0385143486

The UFOlogy Umbrella. (Close Encounters Are Not Enough) Jason Gleaves. Privately published. 2019 ISBN: 978-179305-5002

UFO Study. Jenny Randles. Hardcover: 208 pages. Publisher: Robert Hale Ltd; First Edition (11 May 1981) ISBN-13: 978-0709188643

UFO Abductions: (A Dangerous Game) Philip J. Klass. Prometheus Books, Buffalo New York. ISBN: 0-87975-509-1

UFO Abductions in Gulf Breeze. Ed and Frances Walters. Avon Books New York. 1994. ISBN: 0-380-77333-3

UFO Scotland. Ron Halliday, B&W Publishing Edinburgh, 1998. ISBN: 1-873631-839

UFO Case Files of Scotland (Volume 1) Malcolm Robinson Publish Nation. ISBN: 978-1-907126-02-04

UFO Case Files of Scotland (Volume 2) Malcolm Robinson Publish Nation. ISBN: 978-0-244-95154-2

UFO Abductions: Thomas Bullard. The Measure of a Mystery, Fund for UFO Research. Mount Rainier, 1987.

UFOs, Where Do They Come From? Edited by Peter Brookesmith. (The Unexplained series) Orbis Publishing Limited 1988. ISBN: 0-7481-0142-X

Walking Among Us: The Alien Plan to Control Humanity. Jacobs, David M. (Ph.D.) (2015), Disinformation Books, an imprint of Red Wheel/Weiser, LLC; The Disinformation Company Ltd., ISBN 978-1-938875-14-4.

Without Consent. Philip Mantle. Publisher: Fortune Books Ltd (2002) ASIN: B00I63L8YU

Witnessed. (The True Story of the Brooklyn Bridge Abduction) Pocket Books. 1996. ISBN: 0-7475-3341-5

U.K. UFO ADDRESSES, CONTACTS, E-MAILS.

SPI (Strange Phenomena Investigations) Malcolm Robinson. 74 Craigview, Sauchie, Alloa, Clackmannanshire, Scotland, FK10 3HF. E-mail malckyspi@yahoo.com www.facebook.com/malcolm.robinson2

SPI East Anglia. David Young. davidyoung2qn@yahoo.com

SPI Scotland. Alyson Dunlop (Glasgow) e-mail: spiscotland@gmail.com

Scottish Earth Mysteries Research. Ron Halliday. ronhalliday168@sky.com

Birmingham UFO Group. (England) Dave Hodrien. e-mail: davehodrien@bufog.com

BUFORA. Heather Dixon. e-mail: enquiries@bufora.org.uk

Contact International UFO Research. PO Box 23, Wheatley, Oxon, England OX33 1FL. Hotline: 01869 320989. Web: http://contactinternationalufo.homestead.com

Cornwall UFO Research Group. 24 Carrine Road, Truro, Cornwall, England, TR1 3XB. Phone: 01872 276381. E-mail: david.gillham@lineone.net Web: http://www.cornwall-ufo.co.uk

Exopolitics UK. e-mail - exo.pol@gmail.com Web: http://exopolitics.org.uk

LUFOIN. (The Leicestershire Unidentified Flying Object Investigation Network) e-mail: lufoin@gmail.com Web: http://lufoinregister.angelfire.com/home

Nottingham Skywatch. Phone: 07548 382 850. E-mail: nottinghamskywatch@yahoo.co.uk web: http://www.nottinghamskywatch.co.uk

Plymouth UFO Research Group. Bob Boyd, 93 Townshend Avenue, Keyham, Plymouth, England, PL2 1PB. Phone: 01752 515192. e-mail: martynhicks@yahoo.co.uk

Southend UFO Group. e-mail: doltz19@talktalk.net Web: http://www.essexufo.co.uk

Swansea UFO Network. 19 Meadowcroft Close, Waunarlwydd, Wales, SA5 4SD Swansea, United Kingdom. Phone: 07969287216. Web: http://www.sufon.co.uk

Unknown Phenomena Investigation Association. Dave Sadler. e-mail: sadler_dave@yahoo.co.uk Web: http://www.upia.co.uk

Wakefield UFO Research & Investigation Group. 62 Rutland Avenue, Wakefield, West Yorkshire. England. WF2 7JX. Phone: 07506 047649.

Welsh UFO Research Network. (WUFORN) 117 Tallis Street, Cwmparc Treorchy, Rhondda Cynon Taff, South Wales, CF42 6LY. Phone: 07411 399547 / 01443 772906. e-mail: info@wuforn.co.uk Web: http://www.wuforn.co.uk

UFO ABDUCTION HELP GROUPS

UFO Abduction Research Groups: Alien Abduction Experience and Research (AAER) at www.abduct.com

Derrel Sims UFO Abduction Research Group Support Group – Derrel Sims (alienhunter.org)

International Centre for Abduction Research (ufoabduction.com)

TO CONTACT THE AUTHOR

Research group Strange Phenomena Investigations (SPI) are always interested to hear from anyone who believe that they may have had a UFO or paranormal experience, or indeed may have a photograph or piece of film footage which may appear to show something paranormal. If so, please contact the author at the address below. (All submissions will be treated in confidence)

Malcolm Robinson
74 Craigview,
Sauchie, Alloa,
Clackmannanshire.
Scotland,
FK10 3HF

www.facebook.com/malcolm.robinson2
You can e-mail the author direct at malckyspi@yahoo.com
Facebook: www.facebook.com/malcolm.robinson2

SOME FAMOUS QUOTES

"I can assure you that, given they exist, these flying saucers are made by no power on this Earth"
Ex USA President Harry S Truman.

"The phenomenon of UFOs does exist, and it must be treated seriously"
Former Soviet Leader, Mikhail Gorbachev.

"What does all this stuff about flying saucers amount to? What can it mean? What is the truth? Let me have a report at your convenience"
Winston Churchill's memo to the Secretary of State, Air Lord Cherwell

"Is it possible for example, that contact with alien intelligences stimulates poltergeist and other psychic activity and causes witnesses to become psychically 'open' for reasons that we do not understand? It is also possible that some aliens may be thousands of years ahead of us in terms of mental development, therefore what we regard as paranormal abilities, may be second nature to them. They may be equally adept at functioning in other dimensions and manipulating space time"
Timothy Good. 'Unearthly Disclosure'

"The UFO occupants, like the elves of old, are not extraterrestrials.
They are the denizens of another reality".
Jaques Vallee Dimensions book

"Of course Flying Saucers are real, and they are interplanetary"
Former Air Chief Marshall Lord Dowding

"These UFOs are conceived and directed by intelligent beings of a very high order. They probably do not originate in our solar system, perhaps not even our galaxy!"
Dr Hermann Oberth (German father of the V1 and V2 rockets

"Flying Saucers, Unidentified Flying Objects, or whatever you call them, 'are real!"
Former Senator Barry Goldwater

"We all know that UFOs are real, the question is, where are they coming from, and why"
Captain Ed Mitchell (Sixth man to walk on the Moon)

WE'RE NOT ALONE

(A poem by Steven Taylor)

Ask one question, tell no lies
Are there nations in the skies?
Is there a life form beyond our vision
While our leaders steep in self derision?
What goes on while we grow old?
We seek an answer to stories told
We clench a fist we grind our teeth
Our world is filled with disbelief.
Is it so hard to be converted
Surely we must be alerted
Do we think our egos are too big
To be someone, something's guinea pig.
Some people have been scarred and poked
As our politicians laughed and joked
And written down in books and jotters
Are words that hurt our sons and daughters.
The non belief has gone too far
They say it's just a shooting star
A plane or maybe a meteorite
They could be wrong, they could be right.
But what if it's announced 'They're coming'
Will sceptics give in while they're running?
They've brainwashed minds conformed from youth
Too scared to bow and face the truth.
This frightening fact is arguable
Some say it's true and tangible
Must this vast cosmos seem so bare
Or is there really something out there?
From another planet or from our minds
From other galaxies with different times
For good or bad, forgotten unknown
It's time to listen - 'We're not alone'.
By Steven Taylor.

THE END

Printed in Great Britain
by Amazon

DEADLY
EVIDENCE

During her fifteen-year career as Ireland's State Pathologist, Marie Cassidy became known to the Irish public as a trusted figure whose expertise helped to solve murders and clarify unexplained deaths. In over thirty years of practice, she performed thousands of post-mortems and dealt with hundreds of murders. She has witnessed the burgeoning role of forensic science and the impact that has had on death investigation and the expectations of the general public, while embracing new technology and welcoming the input of experts in the other sciences. She retired at the end of 2018 to spend more time on the other passions in her life: her family and writing.

Marie is the author of two number-one bestselling books: her memoir *Beyond the Tape* and her debut novel *Body of Truth*.

MARIE CASSIDY

DEADLY EVIDENCE

HACHETTE
BOOKS
IRELAND

First published in Ireland in 2025 by HACHETTE BOOKS IRELAND

1

Cataloguing in Publication Data is available from the British Library.

ISBN 9781399703642

Typeset in Sabon LT Std by Bookends Publishing Services, Dublin
Printed and bound in Great Britain by Clays Ltd, Elcograf S.p.A.

Hachette Books Ireland policy is to use papers that are natural, renewable
and recyclable products and made from wood grown in sustainable forests.
The logging and manufacturing processes are expected to conform to the
environmental regulations of the country of origin.

Hachette Books Ireland
8 Castlecourt Centre
Castleknock
Dublin 15, Ireland
(email: info@hbgi.ie)

Authorised representative in the EEA

A division of Hachette UK Ltd
Carmelite House, 50 Victoria Embankment, London EC4Y 0DZ

www.hachettebooksireland.ie

'I do not wish women to have power over men,
but over themselves.'

Mary Wollstonecraft